# PRAISE FOR *LOGISTICS AN* *INNOVATION* 2ND

CW01095627

'The need for innovation in logistics was never an option and should be in the DNA of every supply chain professional. The second edition of *Logistics and Supply Chain Innovation* is an easy-to-read, substantial reference book. It is the opportunity to add new imperatives that already and will continue to disrupt the world of logistics and supply chain, such as global pandemics and the decarbonization urgency, calling for a next normal.'
**Celine Hourcade, Founder and Managing Director, Change Horizon**

'*Logistics and Supply Chain Innovation* is a classic. With the past two years highlighting the critical role that supply chain plays in our lives, John Manners-Bell and Ken Lyon have provided a timely update to their comprehensive guide to innovation in the chain. Whether it is digitalization, globalization, transformation or technological disruption, the authors provide an in-depth explanation of the current state and what the future holds for sustainable expansion to soften the pain in the chain. A must-read and must-have reference for any practising logistics and supply chain professional.'
**Raghu Ramachandran, Founder, 13 Colony Global and former Director of the Strategic Enterprise Fund, UPS**

'Given the rapid rate at which logistics systems and supply chains are evolving, both technologically and managerially, the new edition of this excellent review of innovation in the field is particularly welcome. To my knowledge, no other book is so comprehensive, up-to-date and insightful in its assessment of the major developments currently reshaping how goods are distributed.'
**Alan McKinnon, Professor of Logistics, Kuehne Logistics University and Emeritus Professor of Logistics, Heriot Watt University**

'This latest edition is a valuable read for anyone working in the supply chain. Appreciating and adopting innovation is key to business performance and to saving our planet.'
**Nick Wildgoose, CEO, Supplien Consulting and former Global Supply Chain Product Leader, Zurich Insurance**

'This latest edition demonstrates how innovation can contribute in a positive way to address disruption throughout global supply chains. It is important that the digital journey continues to develop and I warmly recommend this book to any reader who is interested in innovations within global supply chains.'
**Cecilia Strokirk, Project Manager, Seamless Transports and Logistics, RISE Research Institutes of Sweden**

'Provides the most up-to-date, essential and comprehensive "What You Need to Know" about future directions for logistics and supply chain, including practical insights on how to deal with the strategic supply chain priorities for the post-pandemic world – namely resilience, sustainability and digitalization.'
**Mark Millar, Supply Chain Thought Leader and Author,** *Global Supply Chain Ecosystems*

'In this second edition, the authors eloquently update the reader on key developments in supply chain models, technologies, digitalization, sustainability imperatives and markets. The reader is guided through the recent past towards an outlook and future directions. A timely book, which will be important for policy makers and practitioners who have become ever-more aware of the crucial importance of supply chains for today's trade and development.'
**Jan Hoffmann, Chief, Trade Logistics Branch, Division on Technology and Logistics, UNCTAD**

'There is never a dull moment in the planning and moving of material and the authors prove just that. Disruptive innovation is a story without an ending and this presentation of the broad subject matter entices readers to continue to break out, influence, and build something new'.
**Don Clark, President, DC Maritime Systems**

'Digging from the extensive knowledge and hands-on experience of its authors, this book provides a thorough analysis of technological and business model innovations in supply chains and logistics, including IoT, Big Data, artificial intelligence, blockchain and autonomous vehicles. It helps the reader understand the profound transformations that are affecting supply chains and the logistics industry, and what this could mean for the future. An excellent publication, and a lively read thanks to a wide variety of examples and case studies.'
**Anne Miroux, Faculty Fellow, Emerging Markets Institute, Cornell University and former Director, Division on Technology and Logistics, UNCTAD**

# Logistics and Supply Chain Innovation

*A practical guide to disruptive technologies and new business models*

SECOND EDITION

John Manners-Bell
Ken Lyon

KoganPage

First published in Great Britain and the United States in 2019 as *The Logistics and Supply Chain Innovation Handbook* by Kogan Page Limited
Second edition published in 2023

2nd Floor, 45 Gee Street
London
EC1V 3RS
United Kingdom
**www.koganpage.com**

8 W 38th Street, Suite 902
New York, NY 10018
USA

4737/23 Ansari Road
Daryaganj
New Delhi 110002
India

Kogan Page books are printed on paper from sustainable forests.

**ISBNs**
Hardback        978 1 3986 0750 7
Paperback       978 1 3986 0748 4
Ebook           978 1 3986 0749 1

**British Library Cataloguing-in-Publication Data**
A CIP record for this book is available from the British Library.

**Library of Congress Cataloging-in-Publication Data**
Names: Manners-Bell, John, author. | Lyon, Ken, author.
Title: Logistics and supply chain innovation : a practical guide to
   disruptive technologies and new business models / John Manners-Bell, Ken
   Lyon.
Description: Second edition. | London ; New York, NY : Kogan Page Inc,
   2022. | Includes bibliographical references and index.
Identifiers: LCCN 2022033596 (print) | LCCN 2022033597 (ebook) | ISBN
   9781398607484 (paperback) | ISBN 9781398607507 (hardback) | ISBN
   9781398607491 (ebook)
Subjects: LCSH: Business logistics–Technological innovations. | Delivery
   of goods–Management. | Electronic commerce.
Classification: LCC HD38.5 .M3638 2022 (print) | LCC HD38.5 (ebook) | DDC
   658.7–dc23/eng/20220728
LC record available at https://lccn.loc.gov/2022033596
LC ebook record available at https://lccn.loc.gov/2022033597

Typeset by Integra Software Services, Pondicherry
Print production managed by Jellyfish
Printed and bound by CPI Group (UK) Ltd, Croydon, CR0 4YY

# CONTENTS

# ABOUT THIS BOOK

Since the first edition of this book was published in 2018, the world has experienced the trauma of a global pandemic that has transformed the economy and society in which we live. The logistics and supply chain industry has played a major role in almost every aspect of the crisis, from the distribution of personal protective equipment (PPE) and vaccines, to keeping shelves replenished with groceries and other essential goods. These achievements were attained through the efficient functioning of resilient logistics systems and knowledge built up over many decades. However, just as importantly in our view, has been the impact of some of the logistics innovations, outlined in the first edition, which have allowed governments to take a far more effective policy response than would otherwise have been the case. Foremost amongst these initiatives has been the development of technologies and business models that have enabled a large proportion of the world's population to 'stay at home' and shop online. Without many of the logistics developments pioneered by companies such as Amazon (and, in Asia, Alibaba) governments would have been forced to take a different and – many would argue – less-effective approach to combating the spread of the disease. In this respect, warehousing automation, digitalization of markets, supply chain visibility and last-mile delivery – key elements of the so-called Fourth Industrial Revolution (4IR) – proved critical.

At the same time, it is clear that much more needs to be done to construct an industry fit for the 21st century. Supply chain bottlenecks, especially those in and around the West Coast ports of the United States, show that far more investment in innovations such as automation and digitalization of logistics processes is required in order to cope with future supply-and-demand volatility.

*Logistics and Supply Chain Innovation* provides a comprehensive overview of all the major new technologies and business models currently under development. From blockchain to on-demand delivery systems, it offers a straightforward and easy-to-understand assessment of these innovations and their impact on the industry as well as on society as a whole.

Topics covered include:

- the process of disruption and why the supply chain and logistics industry is so vulnerable

- sharing economy and crowdsourcing/crowd-shipping
- urban logistics
- the Internet of Things (IoT), artificial intelligence (AI) and control towers
- blockchain technologies
- autonomous vehicles
- the role of technology in mitigating the effects of climate change
- automation in the warehouse
- electric vehicles (EVs) and alternative fuels
- the phenomenon of Amazon
- the future shape of the industry

This book is intended to provide:

- insight into all the major trends transforming the supply chain and logistics industry using case studies and interviews conducted with key actors
- help for managers seeking to protect their companies from disruption and how they can ensure the sustainability of their businesses
- a guide to spotting many of the pitfalls involved in starting up or investing in a new 'disruptor'
- an understanding of how the industry will develop and how all companies in the supply chain must adapt to this new environment to survive
- a practical understanding of how disruptive technology will transform supply chain dynamics
- a vision of how supply chains will develop in the coming years and what a future logistics operation will look like
- insight into why some innovations may never be adopted and why many start-up companies fail

# ACKNOWLEDGEMENTS

The pace of transformation is accelerating and tracking these changes has become an increasingly important – and difficult – job. Therefore, we would like to acknowledge the assistance of the UK research team at Transport Intelligence in helping with the development of material for this book, in particular Nick Bailey, Michael Clover, Thomas Cullen, Violeta Keckarovska and Sarah Smith.

# Introduction

The supply chain and logistics sector is undergoing a rapid transformation as new technologies and operating models have caused a seismic shift in the global environment. Internal business pressures have been exacerbated by governmental intervention as public policy has struggled to deal with the Covid-19 pandemic and climate change.

Of course, this phenomenon has not just been limited to the supply chain and logistics sector. The Fourth Industrial Revolution (4IR), as it has been termed, is affecting almost every part of our lives, whether it's the way we move, shop, find accommodation or work.

However, as this book explains, the sector is amongst the most vulnerable to disruption. High levels of inefficiency exist due to outdated working practices, business fragmentation, low skill levels and weak technological development, to mention just a few of the challenges facing the industry.

Although supply chain and logistics companies have been responding to political and economic pressures for many decades, a range of new technologies and business models have enabled innovators to look at the industry and ask, 'Why are things done in this way?' For this reason, the market is both scary and yet exhilarating. While some companies will be looking over their shoulder at new market entrants, others will be embracing change.

The democratization of technology (through such innovations as the 'smartphone') has made developments such as 'on-demand' delivery and 'crowd-shipping' possible. It has facilitated the creation of communities of market capacity and matched these against demand in a far more efficient way than before. Uber, of course, in the personal mobility sector, is the best-known example of this, but other innovators are developing similar products with logistics applications.

The way in which technology has been democratized means that it is no longer the preserve of companies with vast internal technology departments and huge budgets. In fact, large companies must find ways to overcome the millstone of legacy systems and a sclerotic management structure.

Some of the innovations apply across the entire supply chain – take the Internet of Things (IoT), for instance. Sensors and the data they generate are as relevant at the end of life of a product as they are upstream. But some innovations apply to individual segments of the supply chain – drones, for instance, whose use may be limited to delivery to the end-user or scanning inventory in a warehouse. Crowd-shipping will apply to last-mile delivery while augmented reality is applied locally within the distribution centre.

This book will examine, explain and illustrate the key innovations that are impacting upon the industry as well as the many pitfalls awaiting the unwary start-up.

In **Part One** we describe what is meant by 'Fourth Industrial Revolution' and how it applies to the logistics and supply chain sector. We look at the concept of 'innovation' in detail and how the high levels of inefficiency in the industry have made it particularly vulnerable to disruption. As an extended case study, in Chapter 3, we look at how containerization transformed the shipping industry in the 1960s and we point to lessons that can be learnt by would-be modern-day disruptors. Bringing this book right up to date, in Chapter 4, we then examine the disruption caused by the Covid-19 pandemic.

**Part Two** includes chapters that examine innovative logistics models such as direct-to-consumer, alternative delivery solutions (such as lockers and in-car), on-demand, crowd-shipping and the changes being forced on the industry through rapid urbanization. We also look in depth at e-retailing, especially important throughout the Covid-19 pandemic, and how customer expectations have been transformed. E-retailing has also created challenges such as dealing with the huge volume of returns, the issue of trust and how to deal with the fast-growing cross-border market. Chapter 10 provides a case study of one of the world's largest e-retailers, Amazon, providing an insight into how it has come to dominate many of the world's markets. 3D printing has the potential to transform supply chains by rebalancing the trade-off between low-cost labour forces, inventory holding and transportation costs. A dedicated chapter analyses progress to date and indicates how quickly transformation of supply chains can be expected.

**Part Three** examines the key technological and operating model innovations in more detail including:

- **Internet of Things, 'Big Data' and artificial intelligence:** The IoT encompasses the use of sensors, technology and networking to allow buildings, infrastructures, devices and additional 'things' to share information without requiring human-to-human or human-to-computer interaction. It creates richer data and deeper intelligence for all parties in a supply network. The trillions of data points that are now being generated by low-cost sensors mean that humans are no longer capable of making informed decisions to increase logistics efficiency. The potential of Big Data can only be exploited by removing human involvement from the decision-making process and this is where artificial intelligence (AI) becomes critical.

- **Control towers and supply chain visibility:** Control towers, in many cases using data harvested from the IoT and employing AI, will become essential to coordinating supply chains. Opportunities exist for logistics companies to develop their roles in this capacity, monitoring, directing and driving product flows. This will enable companies to attain higher levels of supply chain visibility, which have proved so elusive for many years.

- **Blockchain:** This chapter defines and clarifies blockchain technology, what it is, how it functions and its potential for use in the logistics and supply chain management sector. It explains why the technology is widely believed to be a game changer.

- **Robotics and automation in the warehouse:** Demand- and supply-side trends, such as diminishing labour forces, Covid-19 and the rising importance of e-commerce logistics, are driving the widespread adoption of robotics and automation in the warehouse. Although increasing logistics efficiency, there are potential social repercussions due to the threat of the loss of many millions of logistics jobs.

- **Autonomous vehicles:** The advent of autonomous driving has the potential to revolutionize the global logistics industry. With technology giants such as Amazon and vehicle manufacturers such as Mercedes-Benz investing heavily in the concept, it is only a matter of time before autonomous vehicles – in some form or another – are seen on roads around the world.

**Part Four** takes a deep dive into how digitalization is transforming logistics markets through the development of new platforms. These include:

- **Digital logistics marketplaces**: Numerous new-technology platforms have entered the road freight/trucking market, promising to address the mismatch between supply and demand leading to fuller trucks for carriers and better rates for shippers. However, despite the potential economic and environmental benefits, success for many platforms has proved elusive.

- **Digitization of international freight forwarding**: Freight forwarding by its very nature involves buying and selling space from air cargo operators or shipping lines. As such they are considerably at risk from the new breed of rating and spot pricing platforms that have developed. However, the forwarding business is more robust than many people think and this chapter looks at how the sector will evolve.

- **Disruption of trade finance**: Trade finance is one of the most essential aspects of international commerce. Despite the model seemingly working well over the years (after all, it enabled globalization), the sector is on the verge of a revolution, set to become a key competitive battleground shaken up by new technologies.

Many people would argue that the most important challenge faced by the logistics and supply chain industry is that of reducing its carbon footprint. **Part Five** includes an overview of many innovative new technologies that will play a major role in abating emissions by creating operational efficiencies, designing for circularity and developing alternative fuels.

**Part Six** examines the implications of the 'Great Reset' for global supply chains. We conclude that although change is inevitable, it may not take the form envisaged by the World Economic Forum (WEF). Finally, we take the 'brave' step of predicting what the supply chain and logistics industry may look like in 2035. We review which innovations have the best chance of industry-wide adoption and how the road freight, freight forwarding, warehousing, shipping, express and air cargo sectors will develop.

Overall, we believe the supply chain and logistics sector has a bright future. Focusing on value generation, smart technologies and intellectual capital as well as using 'clean' fuels, the industry has the potential to throw off many of its negative perceptions. To reach this goal, however, there will need to be a significant disruption of established operating models and working practices. For all companies involved in the supply chain, there can be no more 'business as usual'.

# PART ONE

# The impact of innovation and disruption on the supply chain

# 1

# The Fourth Industrial Revolution and the anatomy of innovation

**This chapter will familiarize the reader with:**

- What is meant by the term 'Fourth Industrial Revolution'
- How emerging technologies are impacting supply chains
- Different types of innovation and how digital and physical technological innovations can overlap to meet business needs
- How different innovations apply at different points of the supply chain
- Descriptions of organizational innovations such as 'horizontal collaboration'
- The 'Physical Internet' and proposals to converge a range of organizational and technological innovations

## Introduction

The 'Fourth Industrial Revolution' (4IR) is the term used to describe the transformation of economies through a combination of technological, societal and business-related disruptive forces. It has led to the development of the 'sharing economy' (such as AirBnB and Uber) as well as a change in attitudes towards asset ownership.

Nowhere will the effects of 4IR have more impact than in the development of the transport, logistics and supply chain industry. However, it is far from guaranteed that the outcome for the industry will be entirely positive – much will depend on choices being made in the coming years.

The impact of 4IR on employment is a case in point. A number of the most significant innovations being considered could eliminate many millions of jobs as supply chain functions become automated by driverless vehicles, robots in the warehouse or 3D printing (WEF, 2016). Unless education and training is put in place that will equip future employees with skill sets that enable them to adapt to the changing economic environment, a large proportion of society could find itself excluded from the benefits.

In fact, the whole future of the supply chain industry has been called into doubt. 3D printing could seriously diminish volumes of components moving through upstream supply chains (especially throughout Asia) as manufacturing becomes consolidated in local plants. This would mean that the ubiquitous subcontractor/assembly model becomes redundant and the logistics services required to link production nodes are eliminated (Manners-Bell and Lyon, 2015). Instead, these will be replaced with lower-cost bulk shipments of 'printer' materials originating in large chemical plants based close to where the raw materials are extracted (e.g. in the Middle East) (see Chapter 11).

The pace of industrial change (although not the likelihood of change itself) will be impacted by the inertia created by governments and vested interests. For example, regulation often finds it difficult to keep pace with technological change and this can lead to a vacuum of governance and the lack of a legal framework. This could equally apply to the development of autonomous vehicles, employment in the 'gig' economy or drones.

Although there is always the risk of over-hyping the impact of new technologies, it seems inevitable that there will be significant changes in the very near future. Supply chain and logistics companies need to prepare for this new environment by building flexible and agile structures that allow them to respond quickly to shifting dynamics – whatever they may be.

## Themes of the Fourth Industrial Revolution

The World Economic Forum (WEF) has identified five themes related to 4IR:

1 information services
2 logistics services
3 delivery capabilities
4 circular economy and sustainability
5 shared economy

## Information services

'Digitally enabled information services will put data at the heart of logistics businesses through initiatives such as logistics control towers and analytics as a service. These will reduce operating costs while improving operational efficiency' (WEF, 2017). The WEF estimates that this presents an $810 billion opportunity for the industry as analytics can optimize routes, improve utilization and reduce maintenance. It would leverage Big Data generated by the Internet of Things, for example.

The proliferation of internet-connected devices that interact without human intervention is creating new possibilities in data gathering, predictive analytics and IT automation. For example, in conjunction with developments in autonomous vehicles, cities can share data on traffic conditions to optimize routing and create efficiencies.

Creating optimized distribution networks will have an impact on inventory holdings (lower than might have otherwise been required with less efficient transport). Centralization of inventory will remain possible, without the need for more localized holdings of stock.

The WEF also identifies data analytics as an important component of Information Services. It estimates that it would bring benefits such as:

- savings in fuel costs for road freight companies of 5 per cent
- reduction of repair costs by 30 per cent through predictive maintenance
- improve utilization of logistics by 5 per cent

The organization suggests that savings totalling $520 billion could be made by road freight companies and $30 billion and $50 billion made by air and sea freight companies respectively. Likewise, there would be savings of more than 4 billion metric tons of carbon emissions (WEF, 2017).

## Logistics services

'Digitally enabled logistics services will grow trade by creating digitally enhanced cross-border platforms' (WEF, 2017).

Businesses, particularly small and medium-sized enterprises (SMEs), have struggled with the logistical challenges related to the cross-border shipments of small parcel goods. SMEs are demanding a more simplified process and technology-powered intermediary platforms are filling that gap.

Digital logistics services, such as road freight platforms, will also help satisfy growing customer demand for faster deliveries, and promote the concept of city logistics, which will allow firms to operate efficiently in 'megacities'.

The simplification of trade processes could benefit trade platforms by $120 billion and logistics companies by $50 billion in additional profits, according to WEF (2017).

---

CASE STUDY 1.1
*eBay's Global Shipping Programme*

Businesses, particularly small businesses, have struggled with the logistical challenges related to the cross-border shipments of small parcel goods. Global e-retail platform eBay has recognized this and has developed its Global Shipping Programme to make retailers' products available to millions of buyers in more than 50 countries. The Global Shipping Programme enables fully landed costs to be displayed to international customers. It also provides businesses with the ability to ship any products bound for an international customer to a domestic shipping centre. Customs filing, international packaging and import payments are handled by an intermediary, and the item is then sent to the international buyer with complete end-to-end tracking. The Global Shipping Programme is free to join for users of eBay marketplaces.

The primary driver for the success of the Global Shipping Programme is the difficulty associated with international shipping of goods, particularly for small businesses. SMEs are demanding a more simplified process and technology-powered intermediary platforms are filling that gap. Moreover, SMEs are unlikely to have cross-border operations and therefore they need end-to-end tracking in order to monitor the status of their international shipments.

The process is also much easier than for typical international transactions because the small business is merely engaging in a domestic shipment of the good and the intermediary handles the challenges of cross-border logistics. The programme also increases transparency for the buyer by providing fully landed costs up front and providing end-to-end tracking. Finally, the programme provides business cost savings due to the aggregation of multiple outbound parcel shipments.

Key to its success has been:

- innovative software that can calculate fully landed costs upfront
- eBay's global marketplace platform with over 150 million users worldwide
- the creation of national logistics hubs where outbound international shipments can be aggregated

---

## Delivery capabilities

'New delivery options such as autonomous trucks and drones mean more efficient ways to deliver shipments' (WEF, 2017).

There can be no more disruptive technology to the global road freight industry than 'autonomous' vehicles. Whereas the headlines have mostly focused on cars, many of the world's largest manufacturers of trucks, including Daimler, and well-backed innovators such as Tesla, have already invested billions in the technology.

However, at this stage removing drivers from trucks is still a very long way off. The technology faces huge challenges, not only from labour organizations, but also safety and regulatory bodies, and even the wider population.

In summary, vehicle manufacturers believe that the benefits will be:

- reduced fuel consumption and emissions – the computer will drive the vehicle more fuel efficiently
- 'perfect' route planning
- diagnostic services, ensuring fewer breakdowns
- emergency braking will ensure fewer accidents
- less congestion
- zero accidents caused by human error

See Chapter 16 for a more detailed discussion of the subject.

Technological and regulatory barriers will constrain the development of these innovations, although over the next 10 years the WEF still believes that they will contribute $50 billion.

The WEF also includes 3D printing within this category. It effectively delivers product without the need for transportation, apart from the printer materials. For this reason, operating profits of logistics providers may fall by $1 billion by 2025 (WEF, 2017).


## Circular economy and sustainability

'A circular economy will foster a more sustainable product life cycle, helping to lessen the industry's environmental footprint by reducing carbon dioxide ($CO2$) emissions, air pollution and waste material' (WEF, 2017). The WEF estimates that digital initiatives could reduce emissions from logistics by 10 to 12 per cent by 2025.

A structural change from petrol- and diesel-powered vehicles is also under way, prompted not least by government bans on conventionally powered trucks in urban areas. Health concerns are growing over the impact of particulates as well as over carbon emissions. This will mean that operators will require fleets of alternative fuel vehicles (including electric) as well as traditional diesel, until the operational effectiveness gap between the two narrows. (See Chapter 21 for more details on alternative fuels.)

### Shared economy

'Shared warehouse and shared transport capabilities are expected to increase asset utilization in the near future' (WEF, 2017). Crowd-shipping is a major opportunity – and threat – to the industry and the WEF believes that traditional trucking companies could lose $310 billion of profits to companies using crowdsourced platforms.

Using smartphone technology, crowd-shipping apps are better able to match demand with supply (either road freight operators or individuals). In an urban context, moving parcels by bus or train could reduce congestion on roads. Drivers could use 'Uber-like' platforms to utilize spare capacity in their own cars, making money and reducing the volumes of vans on the road.

Traditional operators may benefit from higher load factors. However, the platforms could also attract more car owners to undertake parcel deliveries – actually exacerbating traffic congestion rather than improving it (see Chapter 6).

## The anatomy of innovation

'Innovation' has been a much used – and many would say overused – term in the past 20 years. Logistics companies have often been accused by their customers of lacking innovation, while they in turn have levelled accusations that manufacturers and retailers have been more focused on cost cutting than creativity. In fact, the truth is that, with a few exceptions, most logistics companies and their customers have been happy with the status quo. That is, until the latest breed of e-commerce disruptors and digital service providers have transformed consumer expectations.

There are many types of innovation. Logistics innovation itself has been defined as 'creating logistics value out of new products or services, new processes, new transaction types, new relationships or new business models' (Verweij and Cruijssen, 2006).

Cruijssen divides innovations into five separate categories, as shown in Table 1.1.

TABLE 1.1  Categorization of innovation types

| Innovation | Explanation |
| --- | --- |
| Product and service | Research and development of new products and services |
| Process | Changes in the way these products/services are performed or produced |
| Transactional | New ways of selling |
| Relationship | Development of new relationships with customers or suppliers |
| Business model | Transformation of operational model |

SOURCE  Based on Cruijssen (2006)

In many cases, these innovations are inevitably inter-related. Amazon's success, it could be argued, has been brought about by innovation in all these categories. It has developed new products; relentlessly innovated the way that these services have been delivered; implemented new ways of selling as well as initiating new relationships with customers and suppliers. This has led to the transformation not only of its business but of an entire sector.

The new technologies highlighted in this book play an important role in all these categories. It is important to note that the development of technology is not an end in itself. It is only worthwhile if it delivers demonstrable benefits to a business, either by releasing value or cutting costs. It is against this metric that the hype surrounding 3D printing, drones or blockchain must be judged.

## Digital and physical technological innovation

Figure 1.1 illustrates the relationship between business needs and technological innovation. Without a business need there is little requirement for a new technology. This may sound self-evident, but it is often very difficult for developers to truly understand if there is a market for their new application or product. There is also the risk that developers will create a new application, for instance, just because they can and not because there is a need for it. The other point to make is that some business needs may not be easily identified by the customer. For instance, the inertia of being a big corporate can militate against adopting new ways of doing things.

However, given that a need has been identified, the technological innovation to meet that need generally falls either into a 'physical' or 'digital' innovation type. As Figure 1.1 shows, physical innovations can include alternative propulsion systems, drones, 3D printing and robots. Digital innovations involve the flow of data and the enhanced decision making that this facilitates. For instance, AI, digital marketplaces and blockchain.

Of course, sometimes the physical and digital worlds overlap. Autonomous vehicles can start making decisions without human interaction as AI interprets vast streams of data provided by a combination of sensors, GPS, cameras and radar; automated warehouse technology can synchronize many hundreds of robots as they efficiently pick orders; the Internet of Things can use sensor technology to allow decisions to be made on the maintenance of vehicles or the reordering of parts. Likewise, people, smartphones and digital marketplaces combine to enable crowd-shipping.

At the nexus point of these innovations and business needs lies the Fourth Industrial Revolution and its sub-themes, for example, the 'circular economy', 'sharing economy' or 'on-demand'.

Some companies have become inextricably linked with the innovations they have been responsible for. Amazon, for instance, has transformed the retail sector and created a new model for shared fulfilment within its facilities; eBay's Global Shipping Programme seeks to do the same in cross-border e-commerce; and, of course, Uber has become synonymous with the transformation of personal mobility through its exploitation of smartphone technology and digital platforms. As Figure 1.1 indicates, *business needs* drive technological development but *technological development* facilitates business solutions.

The next schematic shows the impact that disruption and innovation are having on the various parts of the supply chain. The IoT will have a supply chain-wide impact on the movement and storage of goods from manufacturer to end-user and back again. Others, such as 'crowd-shipping', will impact on a specific leg of the delivery. Wearable technology, augmented reality glasses and 'cobots' will be found in the warehouse.

Figure 1.2 is helpful to show that some innovations are wide ranging, others very specific in their impact.

FIGURE 1.1  The relationship between technological innovation and business needs

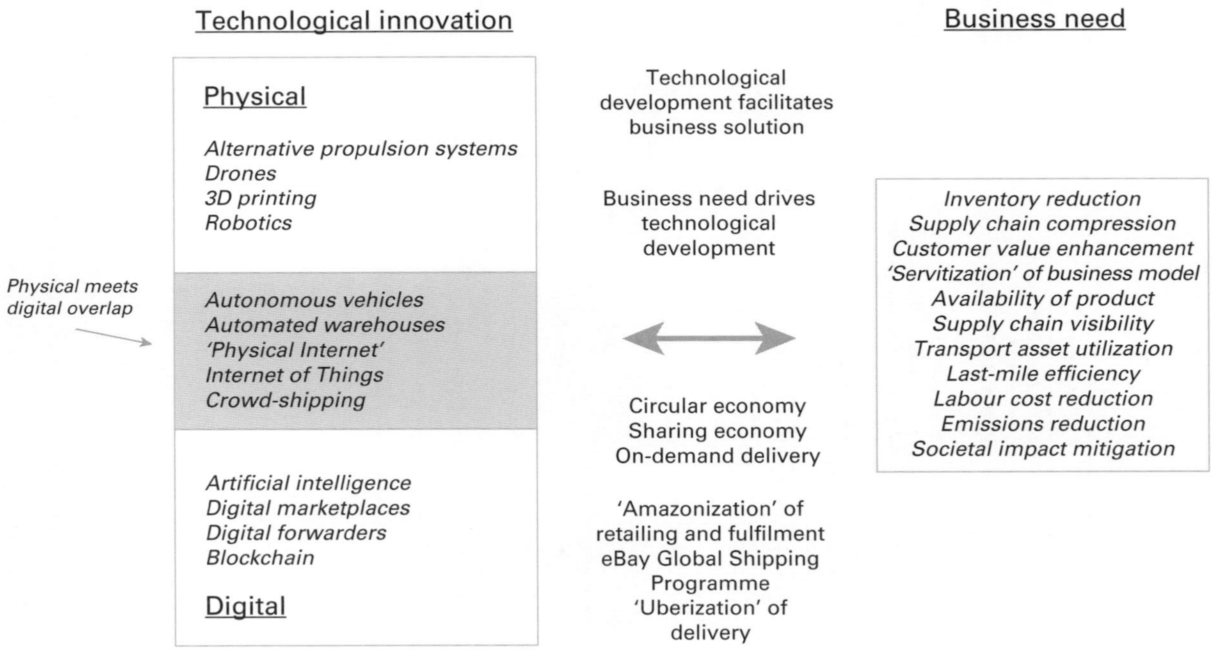

**Technological innovation**

**Physical**

Alternative propulsion systems
Drones
3D printing
Robotics

Autonomous vehicles
Automated warehouses
'Physical Internet'
Internet of Things
Crowd-shipping

Artificial intelligence
Digital marketplaces
Digital forwarders
Blockchain

**Digital**

Physical meets
digital overlap

Technological
development facilitates
business solution

Business need drives
technological
development

Circular economy
Sharing economy
On-demand delivery

'Amazonization' of
retailing and fulfilment
eBay Global Shipping
Programme
'Uberization' of
delivery

**Business need**

Inventory reduction
Supply chain compression
Customer value enhancement
'Servitization' of business model
Availability of product
Supply chain visibility
Transport asset utilization
Last-mile efficiency
Labour cost reduction
Emissions reduction
Societal impact mitigation

FIGURE 1.2  The positioning of technological innovations in the supply chain

| Upstream supply chain | Downstream distribution | | | End-of-life/spare parts |
| --- | --- | --- | --- | --- |
| Product design/Production/Sourcing | Warehousing | Transport | Last-mile delivery | |
| Internet of Things | | | | |
| Blockchain | | | | |
| Artificial intelligence | | | | |
| Payment methods (crypto-payment) | | | | |
| E-commerce | | | | |
| Cloud-based data visibility systems | | | | |
| 3D printing | Robotics and automatior | Increased vehicle utilization (telematics) | | 3D printing |
| Circular economy design | Wearable technology | Mileage reduction (route optimization) | | Circular economy design |
| Temperature-controlled packaging innovations and sensors | | | | |
| Cross-border consolidation | In-warehouse Camera-based code readers/scanning | Systematic freight dimensioning | Crowd-shipping | |
| Product miniturization | Pick by light/Pick by voice | Drive safe/ in-cab training system | Lockers and alternative delivery locations | |
| Smart packaging design | Augmented reality warehouse picking | Asset tracking | Drones | Increased returns velocity |
| | | Freight platforms | 'Uberization' of delivery systems | |
| Mass customization of design | Green warehousing | Alternative fuels | | |
| | | Autonomous vehicles | | Ease of returns |
| Near-shoring/re-shoring | Intralogistics | Predictive maintenance | Alternative addressing systems | |
| | | | Click and collect | |

# Organizational innovation

Many of the innovations occurring within the supply chain and logistics industry are organizational; that is, they relate to relationships, operational processes or business models. Although they may involve an element of technological innovation or indeed are facilitated by new technologies, they generate value predominantly through changes in the way things are done or relationships between customers and suppliers.

'Horizontal collaboration', as outlined in the study below, is one such innovation, as is the 'Physical Internet' concept. Both rely heavily on technological developments but their success will depend predominantly on a transformation in business culture and a more 'open' approach to sharing volumes, customers, assets and networks.

## Analysis: horizontal collaboration

An important organizational innovation that seeks to address inefficiencies in the warehouse and road freight transport market is 'horizontal collaboration'. The term refers to cooperative supply chain and logistics relationships between manufacturers (Horvath, 2001).

By collaborating, these partners are effectively merging their shipment volumes and distribution networks to achieve a range of efficiencies. Another term for this is 'insyncing' (as opposed to 'outsourcing') (Cruijssen, 2006).

One of the most compelling benefits of horizontal collaboration is that it has been shown to bring fast and measurable benefits and is relatively cheap – an important factor in today's market environment.

Within the warehouse, combining inventories can increase distribution centre utilization. It has been used to good effect when, for example, a supply chain re-engineering project has resulted in the reduction of stock held at centralized facilities. This then leaves an underutilized warehouse that usually has to be disposed of, incurring property and employee costs. By inviting another manufacturer to share the premises, these costs are avoided and efficiencies are increased.

On the transportation side there are also benefits. By co-loading shipments there are synergies to be gained, especially where the product is being distributed to similar retail outlets in the consumer goods sector, automotive dealerships or high-tech service parts drop-off points.

One particular project between two collaborating consumer goods manufacturing companies found that 80 per cent of delivery locations were the same. A research project for a Dutch university believed that a saving of 31 per cent in transportation costs could be achieved (Cruijsen et al, 2007a).

However, collaboration not only benefits warehousing and transportation operations. It can also enhance customer service by providing a critical mass that allows increased frequency of deliveries. Shippers do not have to weigh up the benefits of increasing the number of consignments to customers against the cost of dispatching half-empty vehicles. Co-loading with a partner ensures that vehicle break-even points are met.

The last major benefit in terms of bottom line profitability is the leverage that shippers can gain in terms of negotiating freight rates. Consolidating shipment volumes can ensure small and medium-size manufacturers can compete in the market on the same basis as larger rivals.

Horizontal collaboration can also deliver important environmental benefits:

- reducing congestion by better utilizing the vehicles deployed
- enabling modal shift by creating unit loads through consolidation of shipments
- encouraging sustainable distribution networks and partnerships
- reducing waste
- facilitating and consolidating returns

Collaboration does not work for all companies. Beyond the obvious corporate cultural barriers that may preclude working with other competitors, there is a range of pre-conditions that need to be met. In many cases collaboration will work best if the products and distribution profiles of the collaborating companies are similar.

Even if the products themselves do not need to be identical, it helps if handling characteristics, life cycles, inventory velocity and seasonality as well as environmental control and security needs are compatible. In addition, similar patterns of spatial distribution will certainly drive cost savings.

## IMPEDIMENTS TO COLLABORATION

Of course, there are reasons why collaboration can be difficult to achieve in practice. For example, it can be difficult to find suitable partners with whom to work. To aid the process, cross-industry forums have developed that foster discussions between manufacturers, consultancies and logistics providers.

However, another problem is finding a partner that can facilitate collaboration and act as an independent facilitator. The role, which can be undertaken by a third-party logistics provider or consultancy, may involve promoting the concept, identifying partners, quantifying the benefits, managing data (for confidentiality reasons as well as operational) and operations themselves.

If competing companies are collaborating there may well be anti-trust issues involved. And, in fact, this makes the role of the third party even more important to act as a 'Chinese wall', as it might be termed.

For any partnership to be long-lasting, the allocation of the cost savings as well as any costs involved in establishing the venture needs to be seen to be fair. This will involve an openness, which again may challenge many companies.

Although collaboration is considered to be a 'cheap' supply chain initiative, there may be investment needed, depending on the complexity of the relationship. For example, information and communication technology investments may be required to enable data sharing (Cruijsen et al, 2007b).

Finally, if a company sees its supply chain as a competitive advantage, then it may be best not to collaborate with a competitor. Collaboration will bring benefits, but also nullifies advantages. Therefore, while providing cost savings, it may well additionally improve a competitor's speed to market, customer service and inventory levels. In this case it may be better to collaborate with a complementary product manufacturer instead.

## The convergence of innovations: the 'Physical Internet'

Some academics believe that maximum value will accrue to the supply chain and logistics industry, as well as the wider economy, only if a completely new system can be designed to leverage the benefits of the new technologies and organizational structures (and cultures) being developed.

A discussion paper written for the International Transport Forum (Tavasszy, 2018) describes the 'Physical Internet' (PI) as 'the only comprehensive vision [in which] these innovations could converge into a single logistics system'. The concept had been developed in the United States, the brainchild of Professor Benoit Montreuil in the mid-2000s and supported in Europe by ALICE (Alliance for Logistics Innovation through Collaboration in Europe), a European-funded research organization.

The concept is certainly bold as it calls for the reimagining of the entire logistics industry on a system level. In the keynote speech at the 2017 Physical Internet conference, Professor Montreuil described PI as a 'hyperconnected global logistics system enabling seamless open asset sharing and flow consolidation through standardized encapsulation, modularization, protocols and interfaces' (Montreuil, 2017).

The basic ambition of the PI is to make logistics networks as efficient as those in the digital world. But for that to occur there needs to be root-and-branch transformation of the existing systems that have been in place, in many cases, for centuries (Montreuil, 2011). Montreuil believes that the industry will evolve from one that could be described as fragmented or atomized; to integrated; to collaborative; to finally one that is 'hyperconnected'.

### Transport and delivery

Perhaps the biggest change will be to the existing distribution structures. The proponents of the PI see private networks, hubs and transportation fleets as inherently inefficient. To achieve a step-change in efficiency, logistics companies will need to open their networks to competitors, allowing interoperability across transport assets, information technology platforms and warehousing.

Logistics hubs would become public in much the same way that ports deal with containers from a multitude of shipping lines, freight forwarders or other cargo owners. They would be cross-docked rather than stored, leading to a compression of the supply chain. Long-distance journeys would be eliminated, as each consignment would be dropped at a regional cross-dock hub and then collected promptly by another driver. Driver overnight rest periods would no longer be an issue, cutting overall transit time significantly.

By sharing logistics assets, it has been estimated that there could be up to one-third in cost savings. In addition to this, greenhouse gas emissions would be reduced by 60 per cent (Montreuil, 2017).

Although relevant on a regional basis, the need for better utilization of transport is even more pressing in an urban context as congestion levels and emissions rise. This is a key area in which it is hoped that the PI would have an impact.

### Packaging

Within the PI, all goods would be stored and moved in standardized modular containers. These, according to Montreuil, would be a cross between 'a lego block and a Russian doll' (2017). That is, smaller containers could be consolidated in larger ones efficiently with a minimum of wasted space.

These modular containers would be 'smart', reusable, recyclable and secure. As in the shipping industry, these standard containers would allow faster flows through warehouses and transport hubs as well as providing better visibility and traceability, to item level. The PI does not deal as such with freight but only the containers in which the freight is stored, in much the same way that modern ports only deal with containers.

Supporters of the concept believe that it is a development of the sharing economy, as exemplified by innovators such as Flexe (see Chapter 17). Amazon, by opening up its distribution centres to third-party retailers through its Fulfilled by Amazon programme, has already gone some way to creating a hyperconnected logistics network.

However, the key challenges that must be overcome before the PI can become a reality will be to prove to shippers and logistics companies:

- that it makes financial sense to share networks and assets
- that containerization of all products leads to more efficient use of space, not less
- the technology exists, or will exist, that facilitates the data sharing
- operationally, the processes work

In addition to this, there is the cultural barrier of giving up elements of competitive advantage. Would DHL be happy to ship UPS or FedEx packages and vice versa? This may be the biggest stumbling block to adoption. Those promoting the idea certainly do not believe the PI to be imminent, setting 2050 as the year in which they hope it will become a reality.

## Summary

The 'Fourth Industrial Revolution' as a concept brings together a range of digital, physical and organizational innovations. Significant forces for industry transformation exist within the supply chain and logistics sector due to levels of structural and operational inefficiency. Sometimes these innovations will create value at a specific point within the supply chain, such as in the warehouse, while other innovations are far more wide-reaching, such as the IoT and blockchain. The success of an innovation can be measured in different ways:

- Firstly, it may generate new business opportunities, creating new markets or customer value.
- Secondly, it may deliver operational efficiencies, cutting costs while enhancing service.
- Thirdly, it may reduce environmental impact, for example by reducing greenhouse gas emissions.

For managers to develop a compelling and comprehensive vision for their businesses in a transforming market environment, it is critical for them to understand the inter-relationship between the physical and digital world as well as the opportunity for organizational innovation. Most value will be created where these innovations converge and as such the 'Physical Internet' is the most ambitious initiative.

# References

Cruijssen, F (2006) *Horizontal Cooperation in Transport and Logistics*, University of Tilburg, Netherlands

Cruijssen, F, Braysy, O, Dullaert, W, Fleuren, H and Salomon, M (2007a) Joint route planning under varying market conditions, *International Journal of Physical Distribution & Logistics Management*, 37, pp 287–304

Cruijssen, F, Cools, M and Dullaert, W (2007b) Horizontal cooperation in logistics: opportunities and impediments, *Transportation Research Part E: Logistics and Transportation Review*, 43, pp 129–42

Horvath, L (2001) Collaboration: the key to value creation in supply chain management, *Supply Chain Management: An International Journal*, 6 (5), pp 205–7

Manners-Bell, J (2010) *How Collaboration Can Improve Your Bottom Line and Benefit the Environment*, Transport Intelligence Ltd, Bath

Manners-Bell, J and Lyon, K (2015) *The Implications of 3D Printing for the Global Logistics Industry*, Transport Intelligence, Bath

Montreuil, B (2011) Towards a Physical Internet: meeting the global logistics sustainability grand challenge, *Logistics Research*, 3 (71), https://doi.org/10.1007/s12159-011-0045-x (archived at https://perma.cc/2JYM-9ZLQ)

Montreuil, B (2017) Sustainability and competitiveness: is the Physical Internet a solution? Graz, Austria, https://www.pi.events/IPIC2017/sites/default/files/IPIC2017-Plenary%20keynote_Montreuil.pdf (archived at https://perma.cc/T4EJ-V22M)

Tavasszy, L (2018) *Innovation and Technology in Multi-Modal Supply Chains*, Delft University of Technology, Netherlands

Verweij, C and Cruijssen, F (2006) *Verbeterpotentie van Europese logistieke netwerken*, Transumo, Netherlands

WEF (2016) *The Future of Jobs*, World Economic Forum/Accenture, Geneva

WEF (2017) *Impact of the Fourth Industrial Revolution on Supply Chains*, World Economic Forum/Accenture, Geneva

# 2

# Breaking the paradigm

*The rise of the disruptors*

---

**This chapter will familiarize the reader with:**

- How innovation can lead to disruption of industries and companies
- The type of supply chain waste that innovations seek to address
- Drivers of waste and innovations in the logistics industry
- The difficulties in identifying a business need for a start-up innovator
- How disruption can release value by addressing 'waste' in a supply chain
- The key attributes of a successful innovator

---

## How to be a successful innovator: addressing supply chain inefficiency

It is exceptionally difficult to judge which of the many thousands of new start-up companies in the supply chain and logistics space will be successful or not. There are many key qualities that an innovator must exhibit. However, fundamental to success, it is essential for an innovator to tackle an industry problem that, if fixed, will release value fully or partly to the innovator.

In some cases, as will be discussed, an innovation can lead to an efficiency saving, for example, completing a task more quickly or by using fewer resources. In others, it can lead to a completely new way of doing things, disrupting existing systems and the companies that operate within them – in the term used by Braithwaite and Christopher, 'breaking the paradigm' (Braithwaite and Christopher, 2015).

This chapter examines the different types of 'innovation' and the inefficiencies that they seek to address. It will also show how difficult it is for innovators (and potential investors) to be sure that their new product or service has an accessible market due to the difficulties of measuring addressable 'waste'.

## Types of supply chain waste

One of the key goals of many innovators is to tackle supply chain inefficiency or 'waste'. In a lean supply chain context, waste is defined as anything that does not add value to the customer or, in other words, 'useless' as opposed to 'necessary' consumption or expenditure. The Japanese word 'muda' is often used to refer to this waste. Although the aim of this chapter is not to discuss the best approach to eliminating wasteful processes per se, it is always critical for innovators to understand and quantify the extent of the problem that their product, new business model, service or technology seeks to address.

These 'wastes' can be categorized into the following:

- **Overproduction**: making too much of a product or, for retailers, overstocking a product, occurs when forecasts overstate expected demand. The flow of information from customer to manufacturer is a key supply chain issue.

- **Time/inventory related**: how can the supply chain be compressed? Releasing capital tied up in inventory has long been the main goal of many manufacturers' and retailers' supply chain strategies. Reducing time-in-transit is a key issue in terms of logistics.

- **Productivity**: how can organizations become more productive? In the warehouse, this may be achieved by increasing the efficiency of the workforce by the use of technologies related to put away or picking (such as augmented reality glasses) or replacing workers with automation.

- **Imperfect market knowledge**: in terms of transportation, waste is created when shippers with cargoes are unable to access enough suppliers to make a competitive market. This may mean that they are charged more than is necessary or indeed they do not use the fastest or most appropriate transport available to them. The corollary also exists that transport providers miss the opportunity to utilize all available space on their vehicles.

- **Space mismanagement**: this could relate to sub-optimal loading of vehicles, containers or other unitized devices. Alternatively, it could relate to the poor space utilization in warehouses.

- **Inappropriate processing**: unnecessary work – such as phoning numerous shipping lines or forwarders to get a quote or the rekeying of data into trade and customs documentation. Not only is this time consuming but risks errors. Digital innovations such as cloud computing or blockchain could address this.

- **Market regulation**: a high degree of regulation exists in the transport markets, some quantitative but most qualitative. That is to say, numbers of operators are not directly restricted in the way they were, say, 50 years ago but most governments around the world impose minimum standards on the industry. This may hold back innovations (think autonomous vehicles or drones) if safety concerns are overstated. Regulations on cabotage are another example of how the European road freight sector is forced to operate sub-optimally at the expense of better-capacity utilization.

- **Transport**: the movement of goods is regarded as a 'necessary' waste. Companies, after all, have to get their goods to market. However, there are efficient and inefficient ways of managing this part of the supply chain process, some more wasteful than others. Containerization, hub-and-spoke networks and direct-to-consumer models are all attempts at balancing the cost of transport with the time taken in transit. 3D printing may eliminate some transport needs completely.

FIGURE 2.1  Process efficiency and disruption

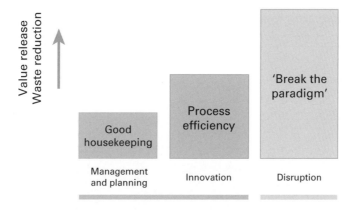

Innovation steps for waste reduction

An element of the 'wastes' identified above can be addressed by planning and efficient management. It needs no innovation. However, there are times when innovations drive efficiencies by providing new tools for managers. There are also times when innovations can lead to the complete system transformation of operating and business models, although innovating to create efficiency does not in itself necessarily lead to disruption. Figure 2.1 illustrates that while the first two steps are often closely linked, the third, 'Disruption', should be regarded as distinct.

It is often very difficult for senior management to provide the necessary internal backing to ideas that will disrupt their existing business model. For this reason, disruptors often come from outside the company or, indeed, from outside the industry. They have no vested interest in retaining the status quo.

## Addressing inefficiency

Table 2.1 examines five different logistics segments: air cargo, warehousing, road freight, freight forwarding and shipping. For each segment a number

TABLE 2.1  Drivers of waste and innovations in the logistics industry

| Sector | Waste driver | Innovation | Value release/ Waste reduction |
|---|---|---|---|
| Air cargo | • Rekeying of data<br>• Paper documentation | • Digitization<br>• Cloud computing<br>• Data standardization<br>• Blockchain | • Visibility and instant access to data<br>• Performance improvement<br>• Reduction of processing costs<br>• Reduction of waiting times |
| Warehousing | • Peaks and troughs of demand<br>• Labour shortage<br>• Errors in put away/picking<br>• Workplace accidents | • Automation<br>• Robots<br>• Augmented-reality glasses<br>• Drones | • Fewer warehouse workers<br>• Better productivity<br>• ~100% picking accuracy<br>• Fewer training costs<br>• Fewer accidents |

(continued)

TABLE 2.1  (Continued)

| Sector | Waste driver | Innovation | Value release/ Waste reduction |
|---|---|---|---|
| Road freight | • Capacity underutilization<br>• Traffic congestion<br>• Sub-optimal routing<br>• Waiting times<br>• Route and delivery bans<br>• Vehicle inefficiency<br>• Sub-optimal driver behaviour | • Digitized marketplaces<br>• Open data<br>• Dynamic routing systems<br>• Electric/hydrogen vehicles<br>• Autonomous vehicles<br>• Platooning<br>• Internet of Things sensor technology | • Fuller trucks<br>• Better productivity<br>• Fewer vehicle emissions<br>• More productive urban deliveries<br>• Lower fuel costs<br>• Effective driving retraining<br>• Lower maintenance costs and breakdowns |
| Freight forwarding | • Customs delays<br>• Quotation delays<br>• Document rekeying and errors<br>• Lack of trade finance | • Single window customs procedure<br>• Electronic tariffs<br>• Rate quotes on demand<br>• Digitization of paperwork<br>• International transport management systems<br>• Blockchain | • Faster clearance<br>• Fewer agencies to slow down transit<br>• Less corruption<br>• Better and faster rates<br>• Better visibility<br>• Better access to finance for SMEs |
| Shipping | • Overloaded/ misdeclared containers<br>• Drayage delays in port<br>• Inefficient networks<br>• Stowage management | • Digital database of tare weights<br>• 'Uberization' of drayage<br>• Algorithm-powered network design<br>• Stowage planning and container management software | • Lower risk of overloading<br>• Faster transit of containers through ports<br>• Better fuel consumption<br>• Better asset utilization |

of 'waste drivers' have been identified (there will be countless more). Against each of these an innovation has been identified that seeks to address the inefficiency and in the last column the result; either a release of value or a reduction in waste (and sometimes both).

## Quantifying 'waste'

It is one thing to identify inefficient aspects of the logistics industry, it is another to quantify the level of waste and hence assess the potential market for an innovator. The road freight/trucking sector is a good example.

In theory, it should be possible to quantify one aspect of 'waste' in road freight transportation, that is, underutilization of capacity. Many statistical bodies have published figures on this metric, not least because unnecessary road transportation is regarded as having a deleterious effect on the environment in terms of emissions. A widely quoted figure, from the European Commission, for the proportion of vehicles running empty is 26 per cent (EC, 2017). However, this only tells part of the story as it does not take into account partial loading, which arguably is more important in judging how well vehicles are being utilized. The only statistical measure relating to 'average loading' is published by the UK government, which puts it at 60 per cent (McKinnon, 2015). Consequently (at first look), it may be concluded that an operator has 40 per cent of any one of its vehicle's payload available for additional loads at any one time.

Therefore, it would seem that an innovation that was able to match trucking companies with loads more effectively would:

- reduce the number of trucks required to move the same amount of freight
- improve operators' profitability by more regularly exceeding break-even load factors
- improve overall industry efficiency
- reduce freight costs for shippers
- reduce emissions per ton moved

This logic has led to the development of numerous freight exchanges with the ambition of better matching capacity with demand. However, the reality is much more complex, a fact that explains why digital road freight marketplaces have not been as successful as might be imagined, despite providing much more visibility of loads. Figure 2.2 illustrates this.

FIGURE 2.2   Addressable waste in the road freight sector

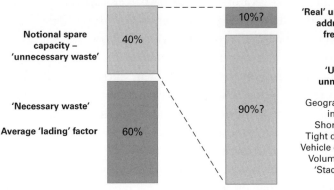

As indicated in Figure 2.2, there are a host of reasons why the truck may not be fully loaded in terms of weight. For example, in the consumer goods sector volumetric 'maxing out' is a particular issue. Low-density packages may mean that a truck is fully loaded long before the weight limit on the vehicle is reached. Consequently the 'real' addressable market that electronic road freight platforms seek to penetrate is much, much smaller. The figures used in Figure 2.2 are purely hypothetical as it is impossible to identify which waste is 'necessary' and which is not. However, they are illustrative of the problem faced by digital exchanges that are chasing a market that may not be as big as they had hoped.

## The '4Ds' of disruption

Much has been written about disruptive technologies and their impact upon societies and economies. One such book, *Bold*, by authors Diamandis and Kotler (2016), looks at the various stages of what could be called the disruptive process. Although not all of the stages apply to the disruption of business models related to physical processes such as the movement of goods, their argument still holds good in parts and is a useful framework for analysis.

The first stage of the disruptive process involves the 'digitization' of aspects of an industry sector. Although it is easier to imagine the effect that this would have, say, on a sector such as photography (the well-documented bankruptcy of Kodak, for example), digitization has also had a big impact on parts of the transport and logistics industry. The most obvious impact has been the migration of letters to email reducing the number of documents being sent through postal operators and express parcels carriers.

Relevant as this may be, it is not the most important aspect of the digital revolution in terms of the logistics industry. More transformative has been the digitization of documents carrying the 'metadata' accompanying goods throughout their storage or movement. Although once this would have involved a paper trail – a delivery note or airway bill for instance – there is no reason why this data cannot be digitized and most frequently is.

This means that data can be accessed more efficiently and used in ways that could never have been anticipated even a few years ago. This not only has implications for logistics operations but can provide far greater levels of supply chain visibility. Despite the ability of most companies to capture vast amounts of data, many are still unable to work out what to do with it all. Even if they have the capability to mine this resource effectively, most will use it as a way of making their existing operational processes more efficient. However, more excitingly, for some operators it is an opportunity to replace outmoded and inefficient business models.

This leads on to the second stage, that of 'disruption'. In the road freight industry one of the major problems has been the inefficiency of the market (as discussed above). Part of the problem is that the sector is split into silos of unitized transport capacity, i.e. private fleets of vehicles. The allocation of these resources is only as good as the access of each individual company to demand (that is, loads). Obviously, the capacity has to be of the right quality, have the right attributes (e.g. temperature controlled/bulk etc), be in the right place at the right time, and be available at the right price. However, these are largely secondary considerations. If the transport manager does not have access to the market information in the first case, these considerations are irrelevant. The inefficiency is entrenched as each company sees its ability to access loads as a key competitive advantage, a point compounded by many shippers being unwilling to share contracted assets with companies, competitors or not.

It is this environment of understandable vested interests, inefficiency and the poor utilization of data that suggests the transport industry is ripe for 'disruption'.

The development of platforms that can match supply and demand by providing a closer-to-perfect market than presently exists could deliver huge value, which presently lies latent. It remains to be seen whether this will happen by incumbents being provided with additional loads, or by a more far-reaching move, such as disintermediating the industry to allow shippers to strike deals directly with owner-drivers. It could indeed be through the consumerization of the industry: by allowing private individuals to earn additional revenues by dropping parcels on their way to work, perhaps using public transport. Whichever form it takes, given the conditions which exist, a major shift is inevitable.

The third (and for transport companies most worrying) stage of the disruptive process is demonetization. In the Kodak example, this is the stage at which consumers stopped buying its film products in favour of new digital cameras. Could something similar happen to transport companies? Could the giants of the industry – UPS, FedEx and DHL – go the same way as Kodak? It seems highly improbable as, unlike the camera industry, which went through an additional stage of 'dematerialization', products still need to be moved to market. That is, of course, unless 3D printing removes the need for transport completely.

However, there are still considerable risks for medium and large transport companies. If disruptive technology providers are able to allow shippers (the cargo owners) to access the vast pool of owner-drivers that exists in every country in the world, they would be able to benefit from vastly lower cost bases. Owner drivers do not have legacy IT systems or pensions to fund, brands to support, or massive head office overheads and so on. These attributes are all funded indirectly by customers through higher-than-needed rates. Some of the largest shippers (most notably Amazon) have already started the process of disintermediating their logistics operations by dealing directly with 'local heroes', rather than through regional or global logistics service providers. New disruptive technologies would give them even better visibility of the market and the opportunity to leverage its potential.

The final stage in Diamandis and Kotler's 'Ds' is 'democratization'. It could be argued that the logistics industry is already highly democratized as there are few barriers to market entry and exit. All that is required is a relatively small sum of money with which to buy or lease a truck. Contrast this with establishing a factory to manufacture camera film, which needed vast investment in production facilities and brand marketing. However, disruption could lower the barriers in the transport sector even further, increasing the size of the relevant supply side market from a few thousand transport entities in each national market, to millions of individuals. Using either the capacity in their own vehicles or indeed public transport, it is foreseeable that parts of the industry (especially mail and parcels) could be transformed.

So, is this the beginning of the end for the global 'mega-logistics' companies, their business model eroded by an upsurge in micro-enterprises and individuals? Probably not. Although it is highly likely that some companies will fall victim to a changing market, due to either being unwilling or unable to adapt to the new environment, others will seek to harness the new technologies and change the market to their own advantage. At the same time, not every new start-up will be successful. Many, if not most, will fall by the wayside.

Consequently, the largest players in the logistics industry should not feel threatened by every new 'disruptor'. The smartest players in the industry are often, although not always, the largest companies who have been able to invest in new technologies. They are staffed by high quality and creative IT professionals. However, at the same time, the size and inertia that many large companies exhibit mean that they are at risk from these new start-ups, regardless of how many internal innovation or research and development departments are created.

## Releasing value through disruption

Looking for sector-based inefficiencies can ignore the greater potential for releasing value by dismantling and rebuilding existing systems. Referring to the example of containerization in the shipping industry (see Chapter 3), waste existed in every aspect of the shipping supply chain. This was caused by factors such as regulation of routes and rates; lack of investment in automation; long waiting times; theft and corruption; multiple calls with small ships. Containerization was successful as a disruptor as it not so much reduced waste in existing processes as led to a strategic transformation of the entire maritime supply chain. To illustrate this point further, containerization did not result in the ports of New York and London becoming incrementally more efficient, in fact the opposite. It led to the design and development of an entirely new network of mega-ports and, further, to the globalization of the world's economy.

Innovation can spur four different types of disruption at different levels. These are:

- process
- operating model
- sector
- company

FIGURE 2.3   The innovation and disruption process in the warehouse

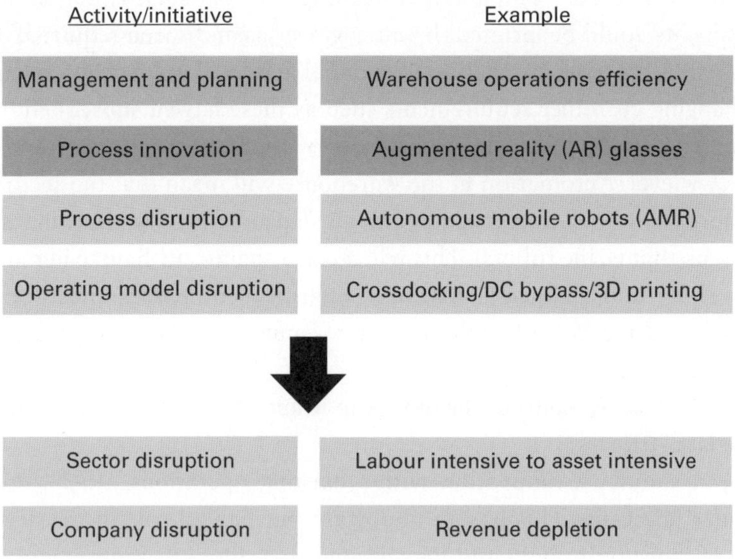

| Activity/initiative | Example |
|---|---|
| Management and planning | Warehouse operations efficiency |
| Process innovation | Augmented reality (AR) glasses |
| Process disruption | Autonomous mobile robots (AMR) |
| Operating model disruption | Crossdocking/DC bypass/3D printing |
| Sector disruption | Labour intensive to asset intensive |
| Company disruption | Revenue depletion |

The warehousing sector is a good example, as illustrated in Figure 2.3 and explained in the narrative.

Firstly, inefficiencies can be addressed by **good management and planning**. This could involve better training of workforce; flexible use of labour across multiple contracts; investment in warehouse management systems; and optimization of inventory placement.

As already discussed earlier in the chapter, **process innovation** is next, addressing inefficiencies through new technologies. Augmented reality glasses are an example of this. Not only do they guide the worker to the right picking location, saving time and increasing pick rate, but they also check what they are picking, reducing errors. This means that a process becomes more efficient, but that process is essentially unchanged.

This contrasts with an innovation such as the use of autonomous mobile robots (AMRs), such as those used by Amazon or Alibaba. These bring the pick face to the picker, resulting in **process disruption**. Where once workers would have walked miles along the aisles, they are now entirely redundant from the process.

A step further is **operating model disruption**. Examples of this are crossdocking (goods are not stored in a warehouse; the shipments are unpacked, combined with other shipments and then immediately dispatched) or distribution centre (DC) bypass, where shipments miss out the warehouse completely and are delivered directly from a port, say, to the customer's premises. Ultimately, a technology such as 3D printing could eliminate the need to store goods completely. Instead, for sectors such as service parts, components could be 'printed' by an engineer as and when required, doing away with tiers of global, national, regional and local holdings of inventory.

Changing customer requirements such as these have a subsequent effect on the logistics industry, both in terms of the *sector* dynamics and at a *company* level. Automation in the warehouse will mean that the sector will transform from one that is highly labour dependent to one that is focused on assets (that is, the robots). This will mean a significant change in management skills and financial structure. Logistics companies must prepare themselves for a considerable loss of revenue as costs in the warehouse tumble.

Table 2.2 shows some of the most important operating model disruptions of the last 70 years.

So, in summary, innovation within existing operations can be used to optimize processes. This has an important but limited role in the development of the supply chain and logistics industry. Optimization would never have brought about the systemic transformation of the shipping industry, nor the creation of the international express sector or pallet networks. These disruptive phenomena were brought about by companies and individuals willing to break the existing paradigm.

TABLE 2.2  Logistics operating model disruptions

| Logistics sector/activity | Disruptive business model |
| --- | --- |
| Breakbulk shipping | Containerization |
| Road freight | Express parcels network (hub and spoke) |
| | Pallet networks |
| Freight forwarding/air cargo | International express ('integrators') |
| Warehousing and distribution | E-commerce logistics |
| | Direct delivery/cross dock |
| | Robotics |
| Supply chain technologies | Blockchain |
| | Cloud computing |
| Express parcels | E-commerce B2C last-mile delivery |
| Freight forwarding | Digital freight platforms |

## Innovators vs disruptors: which is which?

It is useful to differentiate between process innovators and disruptors. Some companies, as has been discussed, have developed products to make the logistics process easier thereby benefiting all supply chain partners without altering industry sector structures or having a negative impact on the market incumbents. For example, tech company Freightos has created a digital freight rate platform that will significantly decrease the time it takes to get quotes. This will benefit shippers, but also freight forwarders who can integrate the product within their own offering. The proposition offers a way of addressing 'unnecessary waste' without radically altering the freight-forwarding landscape.

Flexport, in contrast, has entered the market using new technologies that have allowed it to offer a compelling proposition to global shippers and capture market share from the incumbents. It has gone head-to-head with the world's largest forwarders, which has resulted in what was referred to above as 'revenue depletion' on a company level.

Of course, Amazon has been the most successful disruptor of all. Its new way of business has had a massive impact on the retail sector; cloud computing; fulfilment and last-mile delivery. It is yet to be seen what the consequences will be for air cargo, freight forwarding and other key logistics sectors. Table 2.3 shows just a few companies categorized in this way.

## Disintermediation in the air freight-forwarding sector

A key element of disruption can be 'disintermediation'. As Braithwaite and Christopher say in their book *Business Operations Models* (2015), 'The design of disruptive business operations models is generally about disintermediating existing inefficient channels and forming new and responsive relationships with customers.' For many years, the role of the air freight forwarder has been questioned. The argument is that if travel agents can be largely eliminated from the air travel market, why shouldn't freight forwarders be bypassed by shippers working directly with air cargo carriers? In the 1990s, the airline KLM attempted to build direct relationships with shippers such as global high-tech manufacturer Philips, but was prevented from doing so by the power of its large forwarder customers – it had too much to lose if competitor airlines were not willing to change their business models too. However, times and technologies have moved on, so do forwarders have a future now?

TABLE 2.3  Example process innovators and market disruptors

| Process innovators | | Market disruptors | |
| --- | --- | --- | --- |
| Freightos | Digital freight platform | Flexport | Digital freight forwarder |
| Fleet | Digital freight platform | Amazon | E-commerce logistics |
| IContainers | Digital freight platform | Rethink Robotics | Collaborative robots |
| Cargobase | Digital freight platform | Starship Technologies | Self-driving robots |
| Elementum | Supply chain operating network | FreightHub | Digital freight forwarder |
| Atheer | Augmented reality for warehouse | Convoy | On-demand trucking service |
| Ubimax | Augmented reality for warehouse | Drive | Driverless technology |
| Project44 | API developer | Deliv | On-demand |
| SeeGrid | Forklift automation | Uber Freight | On-demand |
| E2Open | Cloud-based supply chain management | Fast Radius | 3D printing |

The answer is that they do. For the most part, the travel agent fulfilled the simple task of finding the best price for the passenger, a function that multiple platforms can perform very effectively (if the passenger doesn't want to book direct with a low-cost airline). The passengers take on responsibility for conforming with documentation requirements (passports/ID cards) and security requirements before making sure that they arrive at the right terminal at the right time and catch the right airplane.

This contrasts with the complexity of a freight movement. Finding a competitive price is just one part of the process, albeit one that will be increasingly automated. As well as identifying the best route, the forwarder will also ensure that each international shipment complies with a whole host of regulatory requirements from phytosanitary to certificate of origins; air cargo security; duty and tariff declaration obligations; letters of credit; insurance and risk as well as being responsible for all the documentation. In addition, the forwarder will arrange collection and liaise with an agent in the destination country to fulfil the final delivery.

In summary, it is likely that many processes in the movement of international goods will become more efficient. The benefits will be:

- Rates will fall as shippers are able to access more market information through new rate platforms.

- Rates will be accessible more quickly (perhaps instantly) to shippers; in seconds compared with days.

- Blockchain technology will mean fewer delays in air cargo handling operations at airports.

- This technology will also mean that smart contracts become the norm, automatically releasing payment when goods are received.

However, it seems unlikely that there will be any root-and-branch transformation of the industry, at least for a large proportion of volumes. The complexity of the process is such that there will be the requirement for a freight forwarder for many years to come. In fact, beyond this, forwarders are well placed to understand their customers' value chains and help them restructure to release value.

---

## HOW TO SPOT A SUCCESSFUL INNOVATOR

Banks, venture capitalists, private equity, hedge and investment funds spend a large proportion of their time – and of course money – trying to identify which innovative new company will succeed and which will fail.

Although this is difficult, indicators to success do exist:

1   The start-up is tackling a problem within industry (such as inefficiency), which if fixed will release value (partly, at least, to the start-up).

2   The existing market incumbents are failing to address this problem.

3   The market is large enough to support the business model.

4   There is potential for scalability of the product or solution.

5   Regulatory issues have been addressed.

6   The solution can be counter-intuitive, leverage technologies present in other sectors or bundle existing technologies in unique ways.

7   Its product is differentiated sufficiently from other start-ups.

8   The innovator has a committed and determined founder and a strong management team.

**9**   It has customers on board testing the concept (even if not paying).

**10**  It has sufficient funding – critical to provide scale to compete with incumbents and other start-ups.

**11**  The solution works in the real world (especially when involving the movement of physical goods).

**12**  It has effective PR and marketing.

TABLE 2.4  Weighted scorecard for start-up

|    | Success indicator | Score (0–10) | Weighting (adds up to 100%) | Weighted score (score x weighting %) |
|----|-------------------|--------------|------------------------------|---------------------------------------|
| 1  | Size of inefficiency or problem addressed (Large = 10) | | | |
| 2  | Strength of incumbent competition | | | |
| 3  | Addressable market size | | | |
| 4  | Scalability of solution/product | | | |
| 5  | Regulatory compliance | | | |
| 6  | Level of innovation and uniqueness | | | |
| 7  | Product differentiation | | | |
| 8  | Strength of management team | | | |
| 9  | Existing customers | | | |
| 10 | Sufficient funding | | | |
| 11 | Real-world testing | | | |
| 12 | Strength of PR and marketing team | | | |
|    | Total | | 100% | |

To some degree it is possible to quantify some of these indicators. For example, it should be possible to size the market opportunity as well as identifying which needs of customers are being addressed by incumbents and which are being ignored. In other words, a diligent investor should be able to assess the prospects of a start-up by using a quantifiable set of metrics. However, it is very easy to misinterpret data and market opportunity, as we will see below in the case study.

In addition to this, many of the points above are not quantifiable, albeit very important. For example, however good a product, the company is not guaranteed success unless it has strong and visionary management as well as excellent communications. Although every investor will look for different attributes, a weighted scorecard approach could be employed using the template shown in Table 2.4.

## Why do even 'good' start-ups fail?

Even if this systematic approach to analyse the prospect for a start-up is employed, many still fail. This is because it transpires they are either offering a solution that not enough customers want or are willing to pay for, or they misunderstand the fundamental behaviours that created the problem in the first place. This was certainly the situation in the case highlighted below.

---

CASE STUDY 2.1
*Palleter*

Palleter, established by Skype founder Märt Kelder, aimed to transform the European freight market by creating a road freight platform that it claimed would better match supply and demand.

The company was very successful in raising investment due to a compelling case:

- Management believed that its solution would address the 'inefficiency' in the European road freight industry. They relied on Eurostat figures to make this case.
- It developed what was regarded as very smart technology, linking fleet GPS telemetry providers and shippers' freight offers.
- The integration process between carrier and system was fast ('less than three minutes').
- The model would replace ad hoc communication mechanisms.
- Shipper/carrier transaction would take place on the platform.

However, in 2017 Palleter closed down and returned money to investors, a year and a half after it was established. Why? Despite the 'neat' solution addressing a major industry problem at a macro level, operational and technological problems were not addressed. Kelder provided the following reasons for the failure:

Technology:

- Companies were unwilling to spend money and time on data extraction from their existing systems.
- IT departments were focused on keeping existing systems running, not on new initiatives.
- No potential customers were willing to gamble on replacing legacy systems with new operations platforms.
- Complexity of data sharing between supply partners was underestimated.

Operations:

- Much of the vaunted spare capacity on trucks was, in reality, not accessible.
- Companies were unwilling to reroute trucks even short distances due to time constraints from existing customers.
- Platform required cooperation of existing road freight operators and a cultural shift.
- Rates quoted on the system were often higher than other traditional operators using hub-and-spoke systems.

Even though a problem had been identified, Palleter's solution only overcame some of the challenges. Its solution did not factor in its true cost to users or opposition to change at grass-roots level.

---

## Start-up value ratio – what it means for innovators

In order to understand what went wrong for Palleter in more detail it is possible to employ a variation of the value ratio as laid out by Braithwaite and Christopher (2015). This seeks to answer the question: did the solution offer compelling value for both suppliers and shippers?

$$\text{Start-up value} = \text{perceived benefits/total cost}$$

In Palleter's case:

$$\text{Perceived benefits} = \text{value of increased loads for suppliers, lower rates for shippers}$$

$$\text{Total cost} = \text{charge for using service (negligible, in Palleter's estimation)}$$

However, Palleter's mistake was to underestimate the tangible and intangible costs for suppliers (and hence shippers).

Total cost should have included:

- costs to make changes to suppliers' and shippers' technology systems as well as management time
- intangible costs such as changing operating practices (and unwillingness to adopt new operating models)
- time taken to reroute trucks

The result was:

- not enough carriers to create competitive market
- not enough shippers to provide attractive enough volumes
- higher prices on Palleter than on open market
- incumbents were actually more price competitive for less efficient transport

## Summary

There are many types of innovation, some, as we have seen, which result in process efficiencies; others that can release much greater levels of value by disrupting entire business models or the market status quo. Small start-ups do not have a monopoly on innovation – many of the large incumbents have been very successful at leveraging their resources, technological and intellectual, to continually meet the developing needs of the market and their customers. However, smaller companies can be better able to take risks and can be more agile in the development of new products and services. Often led by people from outside the industry, they can offer new perspectives and thinking. Despite this, as the demise of on-demand delivery company Shyp demonstrates, not all innovators and disruptors will be successful, however well backed. Innovating is an inherently risky business, especially when it so difficult to identify the size of the market opportunity.

# References

Braithwaite, A and Christopher, M (2015) *Business Operations Models: Becoming a disruptive competitor*, Kogan Page, London

Diamandis, P and Kotler, S (2016) *Bold: How to go big, create wealth and impact the world*, Simon and Schuster, New York

EC (2017) Road freight transport by journey characteristics, *European Commission*, http://ec.europa.eu/eurostat/statistics-explained/index.php/Road_freight_transport_by_journey_characteristics (archived at https://perma.cc/4YUL-SVCU)

McKinnon, A (2015) *Performance Measurement in Freight Transport: Its contribution to the design, implementation and monitoring of public policy*, Kuehne Logistics University, Hamburg, Germany

# 3

# Lessons from the past

*What present-day disruptors can learn*
*from the containerization of the shipping industry*

**This chapter will familiarize the reader with:**

- The high levels of inefficiency in the shipping industry that led to disruption

- The challenges faced by the pioneers of shipping containerization

- Technological, social, legislative and political barriers placed in the way of industry reform

- Opposition from market incumbents

- The economic benefits that resulted from containerization and the consequent rise of globalization

- Lessons for modern-day innovators

In terms of innovation in the supply chain and logistics industry, the introduction of the shipping container is perhaps unrivalled as regards its impact upon the industry and the global economy. The reduction in transport costs that it brought about enabled retailers and manufacturers to access low-cost products and labour forces in previously remote parts of the world, leading to a revolution in the way that supply chains operated.

The adoption of the new technology was not, as many would expect, quick and without challenge. Companies had experimented with unitizing freight for several decades, but it was not until the 1950s that containerization started to take root.

The way in which the introduction of shipping containers transformed the industry has many lessons for the disruptors of today and it is therefore useful to analyse this period of systemic change.

## The economic case for containerization

Before containerization, one of the greatest causes of delay and cost lay in the inefficient handling processes of loading and unloading ships. Typically, this could include:

- unloading of rail freight wagon/truck at the port
- handling and storage on dock
- potentially use of a 'lighter' (barge) to move freight to the dock
- the carriage of goods onto the ship (by manual labour)
- stowage on board

When the ship docked the reverse process was undertaken. Loading and unloading ships took a long time; it was labour intensive and the work was often dangerous. In addition to this, most ports had a problem both with corruption and cargo crime. This was endemic across the world.

Governments, shippers, ports, rail companies, trucking lines and shipping lines were not blind to the inefficiencies and the costs involved. Many studies have been undertaken over the years that identified the waste. However, as will be shown, the 'silo mentality' (as it would be called now) was a powerful factor against change. With the exception of shippers, the supply side of the industry benefited from many of the barriers to change that were in place. This was reinforced by resistance to reform from labour organizations fearing (rightly) that automation would reduce employment in the sector.

Shippers, it might be said, were the victims of these cosy relationships that existed across the logistics sector. However, the high levels of fragmentation in the demand side prevented any customer pressure for reform. In any case it was unclear that the containerization of shipments would produce savings. Early indications were that unitizing freight without systemic changes to the truck and rail industry, without specialized loading equipment and without the specialist container vessels on which to stow the boxes, would be more costly than the existing 'breakbulk' process. Getting every sector to buy in to the case for reform was the real challenge and even then it took many years for the economic value to be released.

In retrospect, it is clear that containerization was the first materialization of 'total supply chain management'. Before this, each logistics sector acted independently without much regard for the opportunities to connect to other modes. Each sector believed its role was to operate its assets in the most efficient way – not to create efficiency in the supply chain as a whole. The early pioneers of containerization started to change this mind set.

So why did it take so long for a new system to be developed? Looking at the barriers to the adoption of the new technologies and processes involved in containerization provides an indication to present-day would-be disruptors.

## Social and political barriers

At the time, national and local politicians were some of the most influential opponents to change in the transport industry. They had an interest in retaining the status quo, largely due to the large labour forces employed in the sector, however inefficiently.

Labour organizations (which had a large influence over the politicians) saw as their role the protection of the jobs and employment rights of their members. In many ports they also benefited from taking kickbacks from shipping lines and they had a monopoly on handling. Even politicians favourable to free markets were frightened of the power of the unions – and rightly so. In the UK a boycott of the new container terminal at Tilbury by unions led to London losing its position as one of the leading ports in the world. Instead, non-unionized Felixstowe was able to grow from a backwater to one of the world's largest terminals within a matter of years.

The resistance to the new, less labour-dependent operating model brought about by containerization has echoes in the antipathy shown to automation and robots that are starting to be deployed in warehouses. Politicians in North America, Europe and Asia are already talking about a tax on robots to slow down the onset of automation. This has echoes of the campaigns (ultimately futile) fought by labour organizations in the 1960s and 1970s to protect dockworkers' jobs and the income guarantees negotiated by many unions such as the Economic Stabilization Programme in the United States in the late 1970s.

## Legislative barriers

In the post-war era in large parts of the world, the shipping and transport markets were heavily regulated. This was no more the case than in the

United States where the Interstate Commerce Commission (ICC) controlled most aspects of the freight market. Rates were set (generally on a per commodity basis) and routes allocated to trucking companies by the ICC who saw as its role the maintenance of stability across the US transport market. Huge barriers were placed in the way of companies that wanted to innovate either with new routes or to start hauling commodities for which they had no permit. This created massive inefficiency.

The ICC was used not only by the government to maintain stability (or stymie innovation, depending on your viewpoint) but also by various parts of the industry to prevent competition. For instance, rail carriers could challenge trucking companies over the rates they were charging. Likewise, shipping lines might challenge rail carriers over the routes and services they were providing if they thought it would impact on their profitability.

The regulatory climate is less proscriptive in the present era than it was in the mid-20th century. This, however, has not stopped regulators from taking aim at disruptors such as Uber (licence revoked in London) and AirBnB (banned in various cities in Europe and Asia). As far as the logistics sector is concerned, tax authorities look to be clamping down on employment practices in the 'gig economy', which could limit the operations of many on-demand, last-mile delivery companies. With many cities also implementing 'diesel bans' to create clean air zones, the additional traffic caused by on-demand couriers could come under scrutiny. Implementation of drones has also been held back while regulators assess safety, security and privacy issues.

Regulators very unwillingly gave up their control of logistics markets when it finally became evident that even the largest incumbent players could not operate within the sclerotic systems that had been created. The signs are that there is a renewed appetite for reregulation of many parts of the industry, which may well constrain the development of new-generation innovators.

## Technological barriers

The technological challenges (albeit in the 'hardware' rather than software) involved in the development of containerization should not be underestimated. There was a long period of trial and error before successful designs of the container boxes, the ships, the trucks and the intermodal rail wagons, as well as the cranes and handling equipment capable of moving and stowing the containers, became adopted. For instance:

- The boxes had to be sturdy enough to be stacked, but not too heavy to make the tare weight uneconomic.
- There had to be a quick way to pick up and load the containers by crane.
- The system had to be standardized so that the boxes could be moved by any truck or by any rail company.
- The system used to stow the boxes on board ships had to be robust enough so that the containers would not shift during the voyage.

At the outset many companies tried different systems. For example, was it best to deploy shipboard or dock-based cranes? What was the best size for the containers, maximizing economic value of weight and volume? How many containers could be stacked on a ship without it becoming unsafe? It is easy to look back at this period and think that containerization was inevitable, but this was certainly not the thinking at the time.

Likewise, there have been many false starts for other innovations. E-commerce spawned the dot-com bubble of the early 2000s; RFID tags have been around for many decades, although it is only recently that low-cost sensor technology has taken off; excitement over delivery by drones is subsiding; how will 3D printing develop? Picking the technology that will win out today is just as difficult as it was for the pioneers of containerization 60 years ago.

## Resistance from market incumbents

The majority of the incumbent shipping lines of the time were hostile to the prospect of innovation in the form of containerization. The shipping industry had always been focused on moving ships rather than the cargo and there was what might be termed cultural indifference to improving supply chain efficiency. This was perhaps why one of the major innovators in the disruption of the sector, Malcom McLean, came from outside of the sector – trucking rather than shipping. The existing shipping lines had a vested interest in avoiding change, despite acceptance that processes were highly inefficient.

One of the reasons for this was that, from their perspective, there was little economic case for change. Although ships would spend long times in port, this was only partly problematic. Unlike today when it is important for shipping lines to maximize utilization – ships should be generating return on investment (ROI) by steaming at sea and not tied up in harbour – post-war, merchant ships were very numerous and cheap, sold off by navies after the end of the conflict. Shipping pre-containerization was not asset intensive. Stevedoring was likewise asset-light, using temporary labour rather than investing in materials-handling equipment and new technologies.

In terms of the present market incumbents there is also resistance to change, albeit for different reasons. Many large logistics companies have invested heavily in technology systems over the past 30 years and these systems are in place today. Even though there is no doubt that at some levels all companies have committed to embracing the opportunities that innovation can bring, making changes to these legacy systems is easier said than done. This has sown the seeds for disruptors such as freight forwarder Flexport to enter the market. With the benefits of working from a blank sheet of paper, the company has been able to develop systems from scratch rather than add on components to 1980s architecture. A large proportion of its employees come from outside of the freight-forwarding sector, providing an alternative perspective on many of the challenges faced.

## Unpacking the economic benefits

Although there was a good economic case for unitizing shipping volumes in the 1950s due to the reduction of handling costs and time, the benefits were certainly not clear cut. Many shippers exported or imported small consignments not large enough to fill a container (these days this is called less-than-containerloads, or LCL). Therefore, there was a large amount of consolidation to be undertaken, which, of course, involved extra handling. Whereas these days the container market is dominated by large importers, such as Walmart, filling many thousands of full containers, this was not the case in the 1950s when the market was far more fragmented. What to do with empty containers was (and still is) also a problem. Trade imbalances around the world have led to a pile up of containers in major import markets (i.e. North America and Europe) and their restitution is only possible due to the overall economic value created elsewhere in the system. This was particularly evident during the Covid-19 pandemic.

There was also the view (at least at the outset) that containerization would be unnecessary for international shipping as the time spent loading and unloading was a very small proportion of the overall travel time. When a journey might take 4–5 weeks, a few days extra in port was less critical than in a short sea-shipping operation.

However, this was a very limited view of the potential of containerization. Very quickly it was evident that shipping volumes could (and would) consolidate around a few very large terminals serving large containerships. Feeder services would move containers to these hubs from smaller ports where they would be transhipped. The huge levels of efficiency and the economies of scale that this new system created meant that rates fell significantly leading to industry transformation.

Today's innovators are trying to address inefficiencies in other transport sectors. In theory, a technological solution that better matches capacity with demand should release economic potential – and for precisely this reason many freight-forwarding, warehousing and road freight platforms have developed over the years. Unlike containerization, however, there has been no revolution. Why is this?

There are many reasons, but perhaps the most important is that although shippers can benefit from lower freight rates using such platforms, the asset-providing operators don't do so well. The 'reverse auction' nature of such platforms can lead to a race to the bottom in terms of rates. While rate reductions also occurred in the shipping industry, the leading shipping lines were able to consolidate, build bigger ships to provide lower costs, maximizing economies of scale, and call at fewer, larger, faster ports to improve asset utilization. The potential for other sectors is very much more limited in these respects. For example, delivery frequencies and just-in-time or on-demand delivery have driven the need for smaller, less-efficient commercial vehicles, not larger.

## Summary

Containerization was not a solution to a shipping problem. Rather it addressed inefficiencies within the entire supply chain. The fact that it impacted on so many parties – shippers, shipping lines, rail operators, truckers, port authorities, stevedores, labour organizations, governments, to name a few – created major barriers to its wholesale adoption. Eventually these barriers were overcome by the sheer weight of the economic case and the power of free markets.

The lesson for today's innovators is that it is not enough to design a solution that addresses the symptoms of a problem – a deep understanding of the underlying issues and the needs of all the stakeholders concerned is required. Just because something becomes technologically possible does not mean that it will be successful. Social, political, cultural and regulatory factors have to be taken into account as well as the basic economic case. There have to be benefits for all (or at least most) stakeholders, not just a few.

## References

European Commission (2017) Road freight transport by journey characteristics, http://ec.europa.eu/eurostat/statistics-explained/index.php/Road_freight_transport_by_journey_characteristics (archived at https://perma.cc/DZX8-VDFE)

Levinson, M (2016) *The Box: How the shipping container made the world smaller and the world economy bigger*, Princeton University Press, New Jersey, https://press.princeton.edu/titles/10724.html (archived at https://perma.cc/D7XY-E7A5)

# 4

# Disruption to the post-Covid-19 supply chain and logistics industry

**This chapter will familiarize the reader with:**

- The prospects that protectionism and regulation will force de-globalization of supply chains
- How the pandemic will affect inventory levels
- The implications of Covid-19 for the future of transport sectors such as air, sea and road
- What the pandemic may mean for future environmental regulations

One of the unexpected consequences of the Covid-19 pandemic has been to significantly raise the public profile of the supply chain and logistics industry. Usually largely invisible, its critical importance to societies and economies has become evident and its performance has come under intense scrutiny. On one level it has been incredibly resilient, ensuring that no one has gone hungry and providing a lifeline to people instructed to stay in their own houses. In other respects, however, its vulnerabilities – the sometimes inefficient way in which the industry is structured and operates; the fragility that has become endemic in supply chains, caused by just-in-time deliveries and low inventory; its reliance on remote low-cost labour forces; the often difficult relationship it has with government – have been laid bare and mean that change is now almost inevitable.

This chapter will address some of the many challenges faced by the industry in the coming years and explain why predicting what the sector will eventually look like is so difficult.

## De-globalization and protectionism

There have been many warnings in the past few years over the fragility of global supply chains: the Japanese tsunami, Thai floods, volcanic ash clouds, hurricanes, terrorism, earthquakes, not to mention the spread of diseases such as SARS or MERS. Some companies have already taken steps to build risk mitigation into their global supply chain strategies, developing alternative sourcing options should one of their suppliers be affected. This has also included near-shoring or reshoring to locations in Europe or North America, which are often perceived as being inherently less risky. This trend will become very much more in evidence post-crisis.

In addition to the industry response to Covid-19, there is the likelihood that governments around the world will take steps to force the relocalization of some supply chains. The lack of supply in some sectors (PPE and medical equipment, for example) has been a source of political embarrassment that governments will be keen to avoid again. This could lead to the subsidization and support of national manufacturers, especially in what are regarded as critical sectors.

FIGURE 4.1 'Coronavirus will lead to the end of globalization and the re-emergence of national/local supply chains.' Do you agree?

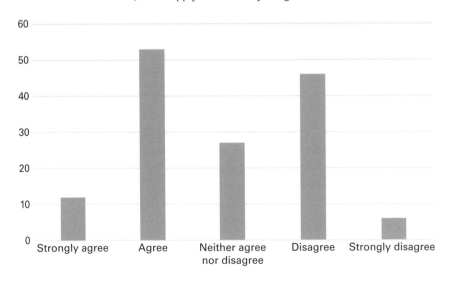

A survey by consultancy Ti Insight (undertaken in Spring 2021) indicated that a large proportion of industry executives believe that Covid-19 will indeed be a catalyst for change. As shown in Figure 4.1, 45 per cent of the 144 supply chain professionals interviewed either 'strongly agreed' or 'agreed' with the statement 'Covid-19 will lead to the end of globalization and the re-emergence of national/local supply chains.'

That such a large proportion of respondents believed that globalization could be rolled back in the coming years is highly significant. Supply chain and logistics professionals are uniquely placed to assess the benefits and disadvantages of this trend, which has influenced the global economic landscape of the past 50 years.

Protectionism and regulation of international trade is also likely to increase. The economic fallout from the pandemic as well as the political ill-will that has been created in many quarters towards China, where the disease originated, could lead to a ratcheting up of trade tensions. Protectionist sentiment in the United States will be reinforced and it is likely that progress towards a trade deal with China will be slow.

The pandemic may have other effects on supply chains:

- **Inventory levels**. Retailers will increase their holdings of safety stock throughout their supply chains, especially at locations closer to end consumers. This was a trend in any case, due to the need for retailers to compete with online platforms in terms of availability of product. Low inventory levels will no longer be seen as the primary goal of supply chain managers. This trend will place pressure on warehousing and will lead to additional smaller fulfilment centres being based in urban areas.

- **Automation**. Operators of warehouses, either in-house or outsourced, will recognize that the vulnerability of their workforces to disease is an inherent risk to their business. This will accelerate the use of technologies that make the picking process more efficient including the use of robots, augmented reality and other types of automation.

- **Labour costs**. Running counter to the trend towards greater use of automation, labour in the warehouse will become cheaper if the world slips into recession after the money from economic stimulus packages runs out. In the longer term there will also be additional labour resulting from the movement of retail workers to logistics. Employment in high-street stores has been on the decline for many years and it is highly likely that these jobs will never return following the pandemic.

- **New distribution solutions**. The pandemic led some manufacturers to implement new strategies to overcome bottlenecks in the distribution process. One option employed resulted in the bypassing of distribution centres to supply customers direct. This option could become more prevalent post-crisis.

- **Manufacturing rationalization**. Some manufacturers will use the crisis as a catalyst for change in their production strategies, accelerating existing disruptive 4IR trends, such as alternative fuels and automation. For the automotive sector, this will mean that local and regional distribution systems previously focused on major assembly plants in markets such as Germany, France, Italy, Spain, the UK and even Eastern Europe are likely to change dramatically.

## Covid-19's implications for the transport sector

### Air cargo

The exposure of the air cargo sector to the use of air passenger aircraft has long been a problem as volumes of passengers and cargo are not necessarily linked. Cargo capacity has been influenced by the numbers of people flying around the world rather than supply and demand for goods. A localized epidemic (take SARS, for example, in the early 2000s) may stop people flying to a market but may have no impact on the demand for goods from or to the country involved. However, airlines will usually make capacity decisions based on the needs of passengers (this can account for 90 per cent of their revenues) rather than cargo, resulting in high levels of rate volatility.

The pandemic may be a turning point in the industry's development. The chaos that has been wrought on the market since the ban of worldwide passenger flights may well lead to the growth of a much bigger, better-funded and more resilient all-cargo sector than presently exists. There are indications that many airlines are investing heavily in new or converted freighters that will make the sector more independent from passenger operations.

### Shipping

Whiplash effects due to demand uncertainty and capacity shortages of ships, containers, ports and trucks will all play a role in making the shipping sector unstable for some time to come. However, shipping lines are in a much better position to ride out the high levels of volatility that can be expected over the coming years. The industry has consolidated following a wave of acquisitions since the Great Recession in 2008. This has enabled it to maximize profits following the government stimulus-related surge in demand for consumer goods in 2021. In turn, this will allow shipping lines to invest heavily in alternative fuels, such as methane or liquefied natural gas (LNG), reducing the sector's previously hard-to-abate carbon emissions.

*Road freight*

Post-pandemic, digital platforms will see a benefit from an increase in volumes. Shippers will be keen to improve the efficiency of their distribution operations, not least as a result of volatility in the market of supply, demand and rates. They will also expect more visibility of their consignments, which digital platforms will be able to provide. In the last-mile sector, high volumes will be maintained (although growth moderates) as e-retailing becomes engrained in consumer shopping behaviour. Companies, such as Amazon, are encouraging new entrepreneurs to enter the market to provide and manage capacity.

## Environmental considerations

It is inevitable that, following the crisis, the demand for greater controls on traffic will increase. The data collected during the period of lockdown showed the enormous reduction in pollution – both that associated with human health (e.g. particulates and $NO_2$) and global warming ($CO_2$). It is also likely that politicians will be emboldened in their approach to regulation due to the success they had in imposing controls to prevent the spread of Covid-19. Similar measures could be taken to enforce patterns of behaviour. One of the unintended – but welcome – benefits of the lockdown for logistics operators was the lack of congestion on the roads, leading to greater productivity of vehicles and more reliability in terms of delivery times. Should traffic levels be reduced following more diesel bans these benefits will apply again.

# Summary

Predicting what the supply chain and logistics industry will look like in the coming years is exceptionally challenging. There are multiple possible outcomes due to the number and range of economic, political, societal, technological and environmental pressures, often contradictory and competing. This will create tensions that will be difficult, if not impossible, to reconcile. Below are just a few of these.

- Given what has been regarded as the failings of globalization, some governments will want to encourage, support and subsidize national supply chains. However, in many cases national manufacturing capacity does not exist and, regardless of this, subvention policy may run counter to international agreements – such as the World Trade Organization (WTO) or European Union (EU).

- Governments will want to stimulate economic activity to create employment but at the same time come under pressure to ensure that emissions levels from vehicles, ships and aircraft are reduced.

- Warehouse operators will want to increase automation (especially with the availability of loans and cheap money due to low interest rates), but conversely labour forces will become cheaper due to higher levels of unemployment and the migration of high-street retail workers to logistics facilities.

- Some industry sectors will be irrevocably changed. Take automotive, for example. The crisis will be a tipping point for many vehicle manufacturers, who may use it as an opportunity to shut down unprofitable factories and focus on the development of new electric/hybrid or other alternative energy propulsion systems. However, ironically this could mean that batteries are imported from remote markets such as China, where these technologies have already been developed. This will run counter to Western politicians' desire for more local supply chains and national industrial strategies.

What can be said with more certainty is that the trends that have taken root over the last decade will be accelerated by the crisis. However, the speed of this acceleration will depend on the extent that behaviour has become engrained amongst populations and companies and how emboldened politicians will be to impose legislation.

# PART TWO

# Transforming supply chain models

# 5

# The direct-to-consumer model and its implications for logistics

**This chapter will familiarize the reader with:**

- Why direct-to-consumer (DTC) strategies have become so important for many manufacturers

- The benefits that such strategies provide in terms of customer engagement and data

- The threat posed to those manufacturers that rely on traditional bricks-and-mortar retailers and third-party platforms

- The difficulties involved in developing an effective DTC strategy

- The implications for logistics and last-mile providers

- The importance of direct-to-patient strategies in the healthcare sector

## Why are direct-to-consumer channels important?

Even before the advent of Covid-19, many manufacturers of consumer goods were investing heavily in direct-to-consumer (DTC) strategies. Following the onset of the crisis, the distribution model was given considerable impetus as large numbers of high-street stores, the traditional route to market for many manufacturers, were forced to close due to lockdown policies. Even third-party e-commerce platforms, such as Amazon, had to limit their operations to essential items only, frustrating many manufacturers that were not able to shift their products out of Amazon's warehouses. However, those companies that already had a DTC distribution model in place managed to maintain their sales volumes throughout the crisis and many others have consequently hastened to develop similar operations.

According to retail consulting company The Good, many consumers now prefer to buy direct from brands rather than through retailers for the following reasons (MacDonald, 2021):

- Shoppers prefer brands to interact directly with them.
- Buying direct eliminates concerns over counterfeit 'knock offs'.
- Brands carry the full range of products; retailers typically don't.
- Brands stock every colour, size and style.
- Shoppers get direct access to the most accurate product information and support.
- Replacement parts are easier to find on the brand site, as are compatible accessories.
- DTC returns and service issues are often better handled.
- Shoppers often feel connection with the brand positioning of many DTC brands.

## What is 'direct-to-consumer'?

As can be seen in Figure 5.1, the traditional distribution channel is much simpler than a multichannel DTC approach. Manufacturers can concentrate their resources and skills on designing and producing goods while the retailers take responsibility for the downstream distribution, including forecasting; inventory management; storage and logistics (including reverse). Although most manufacturers will continue to retain this channel, many are establishing or augmenting their own e-retail capabilities and some even their own bricks-and-mortar outlets. This means that they will have to take on the responsibility for all these tasks in addition to making the goods themselves.

The acquisition of customer data is a critical reason for manufacturers to engage directly with end-users of their products as this allows companies to better understand buyer behaviour. Often retailers have jealously guarded such information and the lack of data sharing has been a barrier to more accurate production scheduling as well as resulting in unnecessary inventory holdings.

FIGURE 5.1 The DTC model for consumer goods manufacturers

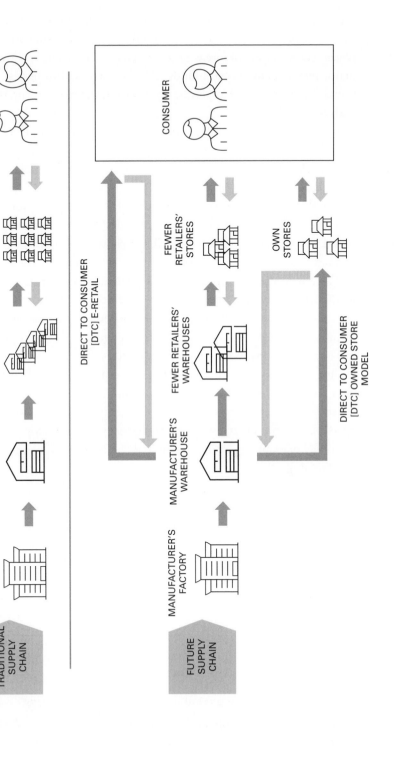

DTC also allows small and medium-sized manufacturers to reach markets that were previously off limits. In many cases they would struggle to gain placement in stores or break into the cosy relationships enjoyed between major retailers and global brands. DTC allows them to bypass these traditional channels as well as setting the terms of the relationship they develop with consumers.

Another reason why the model has appeal to manufacturers is that consumers are becoming accustomed to high levels of service. Selling via indirect channels such as wholesalers or third-party e-commerce sites means that manufacturers have little control over the customer experience. DTC means that manufacturers take control of the customer journey from the very start of the sale cycle. It also provides the opportunity to build the brand as well as create deeper relationships with end-users.

Many global manufacturers have been prompted to develop their own DTC strategies by the advent of 'pure' DTC start-ups in the 2000s (that is, manufacturers which from the very start eschewed the traditional retail approach to distribution). These include shaving companies such as Harry's, furniture maker Made.com and mattress company Casper. However, while there are still many 'pure play' manufacturers, DTC does not have to be an exclusive strategy. As already mentioned, companies like Nike are adopting it as part of an omnichannel or multichannel approach, with all the data generated by customers' online and offline activity linked. Some companies have decided that buying start-ups is the best way to develop their own DTC offering. For example, Unilever acquired Dollar Shave Club in 2016 for over a billion dollars.

## DTC challenges

Although it makes sense for many manufacturers to adopt the DTC approach, success is not guaranteed. The model involves a completely new set of skills and capabilities and often a change of culture. One of the benefits for manufacturers of using wholesalers or retailers is its simplicity; in contrast DTC involves selling to and communicating directly with a fragmented consumer base, a concept alien to many companies. Some of the issues which DTC manufacturers must resolve are:

- Establishing their own retail network and digital offering
- Building/buying supply chain technology which allows full downstream visibility

- The challenges involved in building a last-mile solution for home delivery
- Transforming a warehouse operation into one able to cope with single item picking and delivery to a fragmented customer base as well as acquiring a robust warehouse management system
- Potentially developing a new distribution facility network
- Dealing with returns and customer service

One of the problems that faces manufacturers who have traditionally sold through retailers is that building their own DTC channels can put them in direct competition with their erstwhile partners – building DTC channels may take sales away from retail or wholesale partners, which can create tension.

DTC may not be appropriate for all products. For example, shipments of soft drinks are heavy and costly to ship; other foodstuffs may be perishable and require specialized environments. Other luxury or 'indulgence' items (e.g. chocolate, cookies or nuts) or those that are required to be regularly replenished fit the model better.

An additional headwind is the consumer attitude to online shopping. Many may be unwilling to deal with multiple vendors, preferring to make all their purchases over a single platform. Personal assistants such as Amazon's Alexa or Apple's Siri have made the online buying process very simple and have meant that these tech giants increasingly 'own' the customer.

---

### EXAMPLES OF DTC STRATEGIES

#### Nike's dual channel strategy

Sports apparel manufacturer Nike found that its growth was being affected negatively by DTC start-ups and, in 2016, developed its own DTC operation under the name 'Consumer Direct Offence'. This strategy involved its own bricks-and-mortar stores as well as its own websites. It concentrated on a limited number of cities in the United States and a select number of other countries. As well as developing its own Nike stores and digital offering, curating its own range of products, it reduced the number of what it called 'undifferentiated multibrand wholesale' partners while increasing engagement with a smaller number of high-quality retail partners, including such brands as Footlocker. Part of the thinking behind the rationalization of its distribution partners was its inventory strategy. Management took the decision to reduce the number of styles in its range by 25 per cent and to therefore prioritize those partners who were most effective in achieving profits and growth. It had originally partnered with Amazon but in 2019 decided to stop selling its shoes over the platform in favour of its own DTC channels. This approach has led to DTC outpacing wholesale sales in terms of growth, although the latter is still significantly larger in scale, accounting for about two-thirds of Nike's revenues.

The strategy will have a major impact on Nike's network once rolled out globally. Worldwide, the company partners with 30,000 retailers and has 110,000 points of distribution. In North America, Nike plans to cut its retailer base to just 40 companies, allowing it to make considerable savings in terms of logistics.

The company has also invested in acquisitions of technology companies, which will provide it with the data necessary to personalize its offering. It acquired retail predictive analytics and demand-sensing company Celect in 2019, with the expectation that this would improve its ability to forecast demand and increase full-price selling.

Nespresso uses DTC to 'localize' offering

Nestlé's coffee pod business has enjoyed consistently strong growth since its launch. It sells on a DTC basis either through the internet or the many 'boutiques' it has established throughout the world. Growth of the business is core to the development of its parent company and it is expanding rapidly internationally, benefiting from what it calls 'premiumization' of coffee tastes. Every Nespresso customer is registered and therefore the company gains an enormous amount of data on usage and tastes, specific to demographics and geographies. This latter point is very important to the idea of localization – customizing products to specific local demands. As markets become more urbanized, customization to local tastes will become ever more critical.

## The implications for logistics and express companies

The implementation of a DTC model results in a transformation of logistics requirements. From unitized and stochastic flows, the new distribution demands involve high volume, single item picking and fast delivery times. During the Covid-19 crisis, there were reports that food distributors (up to that time highly dependent on restaurants) were forced to break down cases of products to individual items in order to meet the needs of a new set of consumers, confined to their homes.

The risk of getting it wrong can mean that the cost of fulfilment wipes away any benefit of disintermediating multiple downstream supply chain partners. In this respect, selecting the right warehouse management system (WMS) is essential and this will depend on each customer's specific needs. Automation of warehousing processes may well be a potential choice for some companies to create the efficiencies needed, and this is an especially relevant consideration following the Covid-19 crisis. If a shipper is employing an omnichannel approach, this could mean that its warehouse needs to be laid out in a format that supports both single item fulfilment and distribution to retail or wholesale outlets.

In terms of last-mile delivery, it is essential that the shipper is experienced in dealing and negotiating with carriers. For example:

- Dimensional weights are an important factor for the shippers of many lightweight and bulky consumer goods.
- Customers are now increasingly accustomed to have a choice of delivery options – not just 'next day' or 'economy' but timed slots. Does it offer timed updates that can be shared with the customer?
- The carrier will also be important if the shipper offers a collection service for returns from customers. What track and trace facility does it offer?
- If shipping internationally then tariffs and international trade regulations will need compliance and landed cost calculators become essential.

In short, developing a DTC operation demands that the shipper must become proficient in a whole range of non-manufacturing capabilities. If it is not able to master its logistics, then customer service, inventory holding, transportation and warehousing costs will suffer.

---

CASE STUDY 5.1
*Shopify gives SMEs the DTC option*

Shopify is one of the alternatives to using a third-party platform, such as Amazon, allowing SMEs using its software-as-a-service (SaaS) technology to set up a storefront as well as providing the entire order processing infrastructure. Shopify believes that it simplifies the whole DTC model for SMEs but also allows them to retain control of their brand and data, which could otherwise be lost if they were to use, for instance, Amazon marketplaces.

In 2019 it established its Shopify Fulfilment Network, a network of warehouses in the United States from where customers could distribute their products to consumers. The WMS is designed for single item picking, packing and dispatch – and robotic technology (River Systems) is utilized to reduce costs.

According to Shopify, 'The Shopify Fulfilment Network allows merchants to leverage different fulfilment strategies while retaining their own branding – merchants can still use their own custom packaging even while using one of the warehouses. Additionally, 99.5 per cent of orders ship the same day through the Shopify Fulfilment Network.' As yet this option is only available in the United States.

---

### Direct-to-consumer and on-demand

The DTC concept can be combined with other supply chain trends such as on-demand. Unilever's ice cream brand, Ben & Jerry's, partnered with Uber Eats and Grubhub in the United States in 2018 to deliver tubs of its product to consumers within minutes of order. Customers would order their meal and subsequently add the ice cream as an 'extra'. Speaking to the magazine *Fooddive*, Hanneke Faber, president of Unilever's foods and refreshment division, said, 'It made much more sense for us to partner with these players who already have huge traffic, know how to convert and have delivery systems in place to actually get it to you in 30 minutes.' She went on, 'Our capabilities are in brand development and product development and innovation. That's what we're good at. We're not a delivery company' (Doering, 2020).

## Direct-to-patient (DTP): disrupting pharma logistics

The success of consumer DTC and on-demand operating models has not been lost on the healthcare sector. Healthcare organizations and pharmaceutical companies are looking at the benefits that these models could provide, obviously balanced against the specific regulatory and product requirements of the industry.

There are several key reasons why DTP is being scrutinized including:

- the growing medication needs of the population
- 'bed blocking' due to inadequate home care

- overstretched hospital facilities
- shortage of doctors
- pharmacies unable to store 'delicate' therapeutic product

According to a health survey in the UK, 43 per cent of men and 50 per cent of women said that they had taken at least one prescribed medicine in the previous week, and 22 per cent of men and 24 per cent of women had taken at least three (Pharmaceutical Journal, 2017). This proportion increases with age, with more than half of participants aged 65–74, and more than 70 per cent of those aged 75 and over, having taken at least three prescribed medicines in the previous week, according to the survey. In the United States, people aged 50–64 consumed on average 27.6 prescriptions per person in 2017, more than double the number of prescriptions for adults aged 26–49 (McKesson, 2018). The increasing age profile of the demographic will mean that drug consumption will increase, especially as the most widely prescribed medications are more likely to be for conditions that worsen with age: cholesterol-lowering statins, high blood pressure drugs and prescription-only painkillers.

The ageing population also means that there are growing mobility issues. The elderly find it more difficult to access healthcare facilities, either GP surgeries, pharmacies or outpatient clinics at hospitals. In addition, many elderly patients cannot be discharged from hospital if they have no way of accessing medication at home. This leads to so-called bed-blocking, providing additional pressures on healthcare facilities.

More generally, treating patients in their own home is an important aspect of the benefits of this new model, not only freeing up some in-patient beds, but by reducing the numbers of patients coming to Accident and Emergency (A&E) or outpatient clinics. The latter can be achieved by shifting outpatient procedures to home in conjunction with nursing services. This can also help address the pressures on doctors, who are in short supply in many parts of the world. This is examined in further detail below.

## Growing need for 'cool chain'

Another challenge faced by the healthcare sector is the growth in what is called 'delicate' or 'fragile' therapeutic products, especially biopharmaceuticals that require temperature-controlled conditions in movement and storage.

Therapeutic purpose has been defined as:

- preventing, diagnosing, monitoring, alleviating, treating, curing or compensating for a disease, ailment, defect or injury

- influencing, inhibiting or modifying a physiological process
- testing the susceptibility of persons to a disease or ailment
- influencing, controlling or preventing conception
- testing for pregnancy
- investigating, replacing or modifying parts of the human anatomy (Medsafe, 2014)

Around half of newly approved medicines are of this type (Hoffmann, 2013).

These types of drugs should not be shaken and are usually stored at 2–8 degrees Celsius (frozen medications at –15 degrees or colder), although there has been progress in making these drugs more stable. Some can be held for up to three days, a change from the norm of one hour only a few years ago.

Pharmaceutical cold chain logistics is a $12.6 billion global market, according to the annual *Biopharma Cold Chain Sourcebook* by Pharmaceutical Commerce. The study shows the sector is growing at 8–9 per cent per year valued at $16.7 billion in 2020 (Pharmaceutical Commerce, 2021). The shift towards biologics and other speciality pharmaceuticals that require refrigeration is driving growth, the study says, adding that the proliferation of insulin and vaccines in Asia and developing markets is also generating higher demand.

In more developed markets, the rise of personalized medicine for the treatment of cancer patients is having an impact. According to Grand View Research, the North America dominant sector will grow at 11.8 per cent per year through to 2022, when it will reach a market size of $2.45 trillion (Grand View Research, 2021). This has major implications for healthcare companies and logistics – it is critical to ensure the right drug reaches the right patient on time and at the right temperature.

Manufacturers of these products have responsibility for the conditions in which they are stored and shipped up until the point they are delivered to the distributor, pharmacy, hospital or other clinic. After that point they can only influence these conditions indirectly by advising on the environment in which they should be handled. The responsibility passes to downstream supply chain partners, which by their very nature are far more fragmented, with many less suited to the more onerous burden of the logistics requirements.

Least of all suited to this role are local pharmacies. Although traditionally they have been able to store many types of stable drugs, it is more of a challenge to provide appropriate refrigerated facilities to hold biopharmaceuticals.

This will become an increasing problem with the growth of popularity of these medications, especially given the pressure on space in what, after all, are usually retail, high-street premises. Also, there are increased risks involved in ensuring the integrity of biopharma product. In many parts of the world consistent electricity supply cannot be guaranteed. Even short power outages would result in temperature levels in refrigerators rising, resulting in unusable drugs that will need to be discarded. Records logging the temperature in the fridge need to be kept, adding to administration costs.

Traditional retail has addressed the problem of retail space in two ways. Firstly, ensuring that products are delivered just-in-time, rather than stored in a backroom (many fashion retailers do not keep any stock on site that is not on display). Secondly, the e-commerce model has bypassed the retailer completely, more effectively keeping inventory levels low through centralization at national or regional distribution centres. It is this model that the DTP model seeks to emulate.

## ONLINE PHARMACIES WORLDWIDE

### UK

In the UK, Pharmacy2U has been established for many years as the first centralized pharmacy in the market. The company claims that it can deliver high-volume prescription orders direct to patients 'at a lower cost than the traditional high-street model'.

The company, which has been in existence since 1999 and asserts 99.98 per cent order accuracy, claims that its model is in line with the UK's NHS goals of providing more choice to patients, cutting costs and alleviating pressure of pharmacies. A new facility allows it to dispatch 1 million prescriptions per month.

However, this is just a tiny proportion of the overall market. According to the UK newspaper *The Independent*, 'the NHS in England dishes out 1 billion prescriptions a year to half of the population, 2.7 million items every single day' (Street-Porter, 2015). Most medications are dispatched using Royal Mail's 48-hour service.

In the UK, the Co-operative Group has acquired a start-up, Dimec, which also allows patients to order repeat prescriptions online, possibly combined with a click-and-collect service and e-consultations for new prescriptions.

United States

In the United States, almost inevitably, Amazon has entered the market. In June 2018, Amazon and online pharmacist PillPack merged in a deal worth reportedly $1 billion. PillPack delivers medications in pre-sorted dose packaging, coordinates refills and renewals. PillPack holds pharmacy licenses in all 50 US states and has built a proprietary set of software systems and tools called PharmacyOS. It is believed that other retailers with drugs operations – Walmart, CVS, Rite Aid and Walgreens Boots Aliance – were also bidding for the company, showing just how important this sector has become. The company uses UPS or FedEx to ship its orders, offering overnight deliveries if urgent. If the medication requires refrigeration, the company uses temperature-safe packaging and expedited shipping.

Emerging markets

Emerging markets are also following suit. US health company CVS has invested in Brazilian pharmacy Onofre to develop its digital services. The large geography of Brazil means that an online model has significant opportunity, which will be supported in this case by 49 bricks-and-mortar facilities as the distribution platform. It combines an 'on-demand' element, allowing for the delivery of prescriptions in Sao Paulo within 90 minutes (Mari, 2018).

In India, the online pharmacy business is, according to reports, worth $400 million and is doubling in size each year. The government is undergoing a consultative exercise to regulate the sector as traditional pharmacies oppose the new business model, worried about the discount policies.

## Homecare medicines services

The DTP model for prescription drugs is relatively simple (which is its strength) and with major opportunities for parcels companies. However, there is another segment of the market that involves higher-value services, that of 'homecare' services. The model, which is becoming increasingly popular with healthcare providers due to its ability to reduce pressure on hospital facilities and doctors, relies on a partnership between a homecare service provider (often outsourced) and the parcels delivery company.

Services have been classified as below (EOECPH, 2021):

## Homecare service complexity

### LOW-TECH HOMECARE SERVICE

Activities include:

- self-administration of oral therapy or medicinal products for external use only, excluding oral oncology
- products are licensed medicines or uncomplicated medical devices
- product storage conditions are 15–25 degrees Celsius and/or 2–8 degrees Celsius, suitable for storage in the patient's own fridge
- homecare team members are expected to identify and report obvious misuse of medicines and noncompliance

### MID-TECH HOMECARE SERVICE

Activities include:

- products that are unlicensed medicines
- therapy that requires significant clinical support or diagnostic testing such as blood-level monitoring as part of the homecare service, e.g. oral oncology
- patient training and competency assessment relating to self-administration
- self-administration needing basic aseptic technique and standard ancillaries, e.g. pre-filled syringes
- medications with special storage requirements
- provision of refrigeration equipment

### HIGH-TECH HOMECARE SERVICE

Activities include:

- intravenous infusion
- self-administration needing advanced aseptic technique and/or portable equipment/specialist ancillaries
- administration by a healthcare professional

### COMPLEX HOMECARE SERVICE

Activities include:

- provision of bespoke homecare solutions

- permanent or semi-permanent adaptation of the home environment required as part of the service
- permanent or semi-permanent installation of equipment in the home
- clinical responsibility delegated to a third party
- clinical trials including homecare services

Homecare services are already provided to over 200,000 patients in the UK (RPS, 2014). In the UK, the biggest provider of homecare services is Healthcare at Home (HaH), which has outsourced its logistics to Movianto, a specialist provider to the pharmaceutical sector and which uses its own vans, external couriers and Royal Mail for delivery.

In theory, very reliable services are required to pick, pack and deliver the right medication to the patient just-in-time for the healthcare professional to either administer or oversee the self-administration. Value-added services, such as ensuring product integrity is maintained, unpacking deliveries, rotating stock and removal of waste should indicate higher-margin services. However, the last-mile delivery part of the supply chain has, anecdotally, been neglected at least in the UK. Feedback on the logistics services provided in the UK in the past include:

- interface problems between logistics providers and homeservice providers
- no track and trace services
- poor proof of delivery processes (Aubrey, 2019)

This suggests that the service has been underfunded with cost-cutting measures leading to poor-quality services in what is regarded, however misguidedly, as the least important part of the operation.

In the United States, the provision of these services is often undertaken by smaller regional providers regulated by the US Department of Labour's Occupational Safety and Health Administration. However, UPS has also recognized the opportunity, saying in a communication to the market that a strategic imperative for the company is:

> Further penetration of the healthcare and life sciences logistics market, given the increasing shift towards home healthcare, where UPS's trusted residential delivery network will provide new value for healthcare companies and consumers. (Henderson, 2020)

The market in India for home care is booming, according to one report, due to a lack of hospital beds, digital adoption, increasing elderly population and the fact that homecare is 30–70 per cent cheaper than hospital care. The market is forecast to grow to $6.2 billion by 2020 at a compound annual growth rate (CAGR) of 18 per cent from 2016 (Pathak, 2018).

## Summary

The DTC model is not for every company. The supply chain and logistics complexities involved may not be suited to all manufacturers, who may prefer to continue to supply products to wholesalers and retailers or use online platforms, such as Amazon. However, many companies now see that DTC is an essential distribution channel that offers great opportunities, if executed well. It enables greater levels of customer engagement and insight into buying behaviour. It allows companies to build and control their brand values. And, of course, through disintermediation of channel partners it has the potential to increase levels of profitability.

The role of Covid-19 should not be underestimated. Many manufacturers realized early on in the crisis that alternative strategies were required to mitigate the impact of the lockdown on retailing and wholesaling channels. For some it became an absolute requirement to establish other ways to serve markets, rather than a 'potential option'. For many companies, the foundations are now in place to accelerate the growth of DTC operations.

In terms of logistics, this will mean that third-party logistics (3PLs) will need to be aware of the threats and opportunities to their businesses. There will be fewer predictable flows of unitized shipments from manufacturer warehouse to retailer distribution centre, and from distribution centre to retail outlet. Instead, more goods will bypass the retailer entirely, dispatched via parcels carriers direct to end customers using a last-mile network. Manufacturers will also continue to develop their own network of stores, which will mean more 3PLs dealing with them direct rather than through retailers.

Finally, the days of the mid-market, low-quality retailer may be coming to an end. Brands will consolidate their products on a smaller number of higher-end retailers, which will simplify supply chains as well as logistics and ensure that their brands are protected (not least from counterfeiting). 3PLs will therefore work for fewer but larger retail partners.

In terms of the impact of DTC on the healthcare sector, centralized online pharmacies now offer a cost-effective service, which – given the growing pressures being placed on bricks-and-mortar pharmacies – will grow fast over the coming years. Online pharmacies will require reliability, speed and tracking from their parcels operators. In some countries this will benefit the postal operators (such as Royal Mail in the UK); in others, express parcels carriers (such as UPS and FedEx). In emerging markets it is likely that a range of private-sector operators will be the main beneficiaries.

The delivery of medicines to patients within homecare programmes will also become extremely important. Being encouraged by healthcare providers who face pressure on budgets from increasing costs of care in hospitals, the sector will grow facilitated not least by digitization, which will allow patients to be monitored effectively remotely. However, it must be recognized that the last mile of the operation must be funded appropriately in order to maintain quality of service provision.

## References

Aubrey, P (2019) A helicopter view of homecare, Pharmacy Management National Forum, www.pharman.co.uk/imagelib/pdfs/A_Helicopter_View_of_ Homecare_-_Philip_Aubrey.pdf (archived at https://perma.cc/77Q3-M7RC)

Doering, C (2020) Consumers and manufacturers rethink DTC's promise as pandemic alters shopping habits, Fooddive, 26 May, www.fooddive.com/news/ consumers-and-manufacturers-rethink-dtcs-promise-as-pandemic-alters- shoppi/577737/ (archived at https://perma.cc/QLD2-N95Y)

EOECPH (2021) What are homecare medicines services? www.eoecph.nhs.uk/ What-are-Homecare-Medicines-Services.htm (archived at https://perma.cc/ FR5W-778A)

Grand View Research (2021) Personalized medicine market size worth $796.8 billion by 2028, May, www.grandviewresearch.com/press-release/ global-personalized-medicine-market (archived at https://perma.cc/EYD2- KNUB)

Henderson, J (2020) UPS looks to 'super hubs' and high-value markets to drive growth, Supply Chain Digital, 17 May, www.supplychaindigital.com/ technology-4/ups-looks-super-hubs-and-high-value-markets-drive-growth (archived at https://perma.cc/XE7R-FLUW)

Hoffmann, A (2013) Challenges of cold supply chain, EIPG, https://eipg.eu/ wp-content/uploads/2013/07/seminar-armin-presentation-eipg-madrid.pdf (archived at https://perma.cc/CTA5-GUDA)

MacDonald, J (2021) 16 Big manufacturer benefits of selling direct-to-consumer, the good, 28 April, https://thegood.com/insights/benefits-direct-to-consumer/ (archived at https://perma.cc/RJR6-554N)

Mari, A (2018) CVS boosts innovation investment to reinvent pharmacies in Brazil, *Forbes*, 27 September, www.forbes.com/sites/angelicamarideoliveira/2018/09/27/cvs-boosts-innovation-investment-to-reinvent-pharmacies-in-brazil/#2064b7697c6e (archived at https://perma.cc/T4NR-N8PY)

McKesson. 4 trends shaping the retail pharmacy business [blog] *McKesson*, 20 August 2018, www.mckesson.com/blog/retail-pharmacy-trends-to-watch (archived at https://perma.cc/GDJ5-97NA)

Medsafe (2014) Guideline on the regulation of therapeutic products in New Zealand, Ministry of Health, www.medsafe.govt.nz/regulatory/Guideline/GRTPNZ/overview-of-therapeutic-product-regulation.pdf (archived at https://perma.cc/QW57-UEKB)

Pathak, V (2018) How innovation is paving the way for better home healthcare, Entrepreneur India, 2 July, https://www.entrepreneur.com/article/316069 (archived at https://perma.cc/Z89K-VCHH)

Pharmaceutical Commerce (2021) *Biopharma Cold Chain Sourcebook*, 2 February, www-pharmaceuticalcommerce-com-git-summary-mjhls.vercel.app/view/sourcebook (archived at https://perma.cc/Q2JW-2DUF)

Pharmaceutical Journal (2017) NHS survey reports almost half of adults in England on prescription medicines, *Pharmaceutical Journal*, 28 December, https://pharmaceutical-journal.com/article/news/nhs-survey-reports-almost-half-of-adults-in-england-on-prescription-medicines (archived at https://perma.cc/WXU3-5SQC)

RPS (2014) Handbook for homecare services in England, Royal Pharmaceutical Society, www.rpharms.com/Portals/0/RPS%20document%20library/Open%20access/Professional%20standards/Professional%20standards%20for%20Homecare%20services/homecare-services-handbook.pdf (archived at https://perma.cc/ABU3-9E4L)

Street-Porter, J (2015) With 1 billion prescriptions written every year, it's time to wean ourselves off the drugs, *The Independent*, 15 May, www.independent.co.uk/voices/comment/with-one-billion-prescriptions-written-every-year-it-s-time-to-wean-ourselves-off-the-drugs-10254599.html (archived at https://perma.cc/5BGV-7UFP)

# 6

# Alternative downstream retail distribution models

**This chapter will familiarize the reader with:**

- The growing range of alternatives to home delivery being trialled and rolled out by e-commerce and last-mile delivery companies
- The reasoning and economics behind the trends
- The proliferation of locker networks and the various forms that they take in different parts of the world
- The investment of express parcels companies in locker solutions in the United States, Europe and Asia
- The debate over the environmental benefits of using alternative delivery solutions

## Introduction

The rapid growth in the volume of online sales has forced a rethink of the business to consumer (B2C) last-mile delivery model. Home delivery is expensive for retailers and parcels companies; sometimes inconvenient for shoppers as well as being a headache for administrators and regulators concerned about levels of traffic and pollution caused by the soaring number of delivery vans. The combination of these factors has prompted many companies involved in the e-retail sector to look for alternative delivery solutions. The situation has been complicated by the Covid-19 pandemic, with many people now working from home. However, as life returns to normal it is reasonable to expect that demand for alternative delivery locations will increase once more.

Many of these solutions involve collection points, lockers, parcels shops and even 'in-car' or 'in-house' delivery. According to a survey by UPS, 41 per cent of customers have had their orders delivered to an alternative delivery location and, amongst those who had returned an online purchase, 28 per cent had taken their returns to carrier-authorized retail stores. A quarter of customers had used a 'ship-to-store' option (i.e. click and collect). The survey also found that 63 per cent of customers in Europe, 52 per cent in the United States and 71 per cent in Asia were interested in shipping to alternative delivery locations with extended hours for a reduced fee (UPS, 2017).

The range of delivery options is also critical for consumer choice and it has been recognized that delivery location options are important in terms of preventing lost sales as well as speed and cost.

The development of alternative delivery solutions has strategic implications in the trade-off between inventory management and product availability. Many retailers are converging their online and offline operations (O2O). This combines the benefits of open-all-hours e-retail with a physical bricks-and-mortar presence, close and convenient to the customer. There are many parts to this strategy, including using stores as crowdsourcing locations. However, in terms of alternative delivery solutions, stores can be used as locations for:

- click and collect for products through a store-based picking strategy
- click and collect of products delivered from a remote distribution centre

The second option can involve either the collection of goods from a staffed counter or from an automated locker. In some parts of the world this is described as 'click and collect' and in others 'buy online pick up in-store' (BOPIS).

As is described in more detail below, in addition to leveraging stores as delivery locations, many e-retailers, express parcels companies and specialist technology companies have established locker networks. These can be located at stores, of course, but are just as likely to be located in other public spaces, such as train stations, petrol stations or car parks. They are also based in parcels shops or collection and delivery points (CDPs) and are often an extension to this parallel strategy of developing receiving and dispatching infrastructure at locations of most convenience to consumers.

FIGURE 6.1 Alternative delivery solutions taxonomy

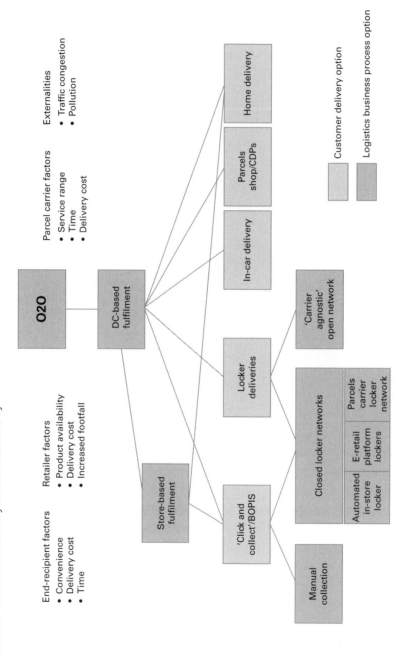

End-recipient factors
• Convenience
• Delivery cost
• Time

Retailer factors
• Product availability
• Delivery cost
• Increased footfall

Parcel carrier factors
• Service range
• Time
• Delivery cost

Externalities
• Traffic congestion
• Pollution

O2O

DC-based fulfilment

Store-based fulfilment

Home delivery

Parcels shop/CDPs

In-car delivery

Locker deliveries

'Carrier agnostic' open network

Closed locker networks

Automated in-store locker

E-retail platform lockers

Parcels carrier locker network

'Click and collect'/BOPIS

Manual collection

Customer delivery option

Logistics business process option

The last alternative delivery location dealt with in this chapter is in-car delivery. Technologies have been developed by car manufacturers that allow a boot/trunk to be opened on a one-time basis by a courier and the parcel subsequently dropped off. Similar technology is being used to allow couriers access to a garage or even direct to the home.

In terms of usage of some of these alternatives, a survey undertaken by the International Post Corporation (IPC) on cross-border e-commerce provides some insight (IPC, 2019). The most frequently used options by consumers include delivery to:

- post office: 23 per cent of respondents nominated a post office to collect their parcels from
- postal service point: 16 per cent
- express operator's parcel shop: 13 per cent
- parcel locker: 10 per cent
- e-retailer's physical store: 7 per cent

Although post offices were most widely used for the collection of cross-border parcels, they scored low in terms of convenience (just 14 per cent of respondents said that it was convenient to pick up from a post office). Most convenient (with the exception of home delivery) was said to be a 'safe place at home' such as a garage, for instance. Companies such as Amazon are presently working on making these options more secure.

Figure 6.1 shows the range of alternatives on offer to the customer. It also shows the methods and models used by various supply chain parties to fulfil these customer choices. Each of the alternatives to home delivery will be examined in more detail below.

## Alternative delivery solutions

### Click and collect/BOPIS

The concept of 'click and collect' or 'buy online pick up in-store' (BOPIS) has been around for many years and demonstrates several benefits:

- It has been successful in reducing last-mile costs (for both retailer and customer) as shipments can be consolidated to a single store rather than multiple home addresses.

- There is not the problem of coordinating when a customer will be at home to receive the goods as the store will be open to receive the goods (perhaps 24/7).

- It increases footfall, attracting end recipients to the physical bricks-and-mortar store where they are more likely to make additional purchases.

This alternative delivery solution has been adopted around the world. Below are a few examples of some of the offerings of major retailers:

- Uniqlo: with 500 shops in China, Uniqlo allows customers to nominate which store they would like to collect their orders at. They also have a deal with 7-Eleven outlets in Japan.

- IKEA: the company is developing pickup and order point (PUPs) facilities in China, which allow customers to order from its website and receive products at smaller IKEA stores that are not able to stock its full range of goods. These 'mini-IKEAs' are still substantial, selling 2,500 products in their own right.

- UK department store John Lewis was an early adopter of click and collect. It is now extending the points where online orders can be collected to Co-op stores, adding to the Waitrose and Booth's locations; 50 per cent of all online orders are collected in-store.

- Doddle is a relatively recent start-up that offers third-party click-and-collect services to retailers in the UK and selected markets in Europe, the United States and Asia. It has amongst its customers Marks & Spencer, Asos, USPS and Amazon.

- Walmart offers pick up for online grocery orders at 3,100 stores in the United States and Target has curbside pickup at over 1,250 stores.

A survey by Coresight Research stated that 46 per cent of online shoppers in the United States had collected an order in-store in the previous 12 months (Thomas, 2019). However, BOPIS is not without its issues as it requires in-store resources to operate. This not only includes additional workers to staff counters but also dedicated areas to receive and store the shipments that have been ordered and await collection. One way to reduce these costs is the use of automated in-store lockers, or automated parcel stations (APSs) as they are also known.

## In-store locker solutions/automated parcel stations (APSs)

The use of lockers in-store effectively turns an expensive business to consumer (B2C) delivery (for both shipper and recipient) into a cheaper business to business (B2B) delivery. This creates benefits for both customer and retailer:

- Customers choose the time they collect the package (time windows can be 4–7 days) and can access lockers at a convenient time.
- Customers pay less or not at all for the delivery.
- Retailers get higher levels of footfall as customers visit their premises to collect their packages.
- It reduces manual click and collect costs for the retailer by automating the process.
- It reduces retailers' in-store storage costs as lockers take up less space than other click-and-collect options.
- It eliminates last-mile delivery costs and enables retailers to utilize existing warehouse-to-store transportation.
- It reduces the potential for delays in delivery.

Before the onset of Covid-19, US retailing giant Walmart had been an enthusiastic adopter of this model. It had acquired 16-foot-high so-called 'pickup towers' deployed at 700 stores across the United States. Each tower had a robotic arm that was able to select the right parcel and deliver it, vending-machine style, to the recipient. During the pandemic, however, it changed its strategy to 'curbside collections', which meant that customers could pick up their orders outside of the store.

Another of the model's key disadvantages is the limited capacity of lockers. Presently, larger items cannot be stored within them, although some retailers are trialling larger lockers that would be able to hold shipments as large as televisions.

## E-commerce locker networks

Without a physical bricks-and-mortar presence of their own, e-commerce platforms have been at the forefront of developing locker networks. The cost of B2C last-mile operations and the problems of failed home deliveries have been the driving force behind these initiatives, combined with providing a convenient solution for their customers.

## AMAZON

Amazon has pioneered the use of lockers in many markets around the world, with 2,800 locker locations in the United States in 2019 alone. An advantage that Amazon has over many retailers, which rely on their own stores to house lockers, is the wider variety of locations where customers can pick up their parcels. For instance, Amazon has deals in place with 7-Eleven stores as well as its own Whole Stores chain. In addition, amongst many others, in the United States it has deals with Chase Bank, Stein Mart and Kohl's.

Traditional bricks-and-mortar stores are becoming keen to do deals with Amazon, as they see many benefits from the footfall it brings. Customers not only pick up parcels but can return items as well at these locations. With many traditional retailers at risk of bankruptcy, the link to Amazon is seen as a lifeline.

Amazon lockers are ubiquitous throughout Europe. In Germany, it has lockers placed in Spar stores. In France, Amazon has a partnership with Casino Group, which will see lockers placed in 1,000 supermarkets. In the UK it has lockers at Booth's, Morrison's and Co-operative stores as well as Shell petrol stations. Amazon lockers are also available at train stations, car parks, leisure centres, universities and a range of other convenient locations. It also promotes 'Apartment Lockers' to residential building owners.

Amazon's lockers also provide the ability to return packages from wherever they were delivered. If the package is not collected within three days, it is returned and the customer refunded.

## ALIBABA

Alibaba's part-owned logistics subsidiary, Cainiao, has invested in a major provider of lockers in China, Sposter (owned by Chengdu-based Santai Holdings). The investment came after a disagreement between Alibaba and parcels company SF Express, an investor in an 'open' locker network in China, Hive Box (see below), over sharing of potentially sensitive third-party tracking data.

The locker network will form part of a third strategic pillar of Alibaba's growth in addition to its data ('sky') and physical logistics operations ('ground'). Its so-called 'people' function will include lockers but also drop-off points at convenience and grocery stores. The system works by sending an automated message from the locker company to Cainiao and on to the end recipient and merchant, letting them know that the package has been dropped off.

Cainiao has also developed a smart locker, which can be installed outside people's houses or apartments. Not only can the locker be expanded to take larger parcels but it can also be temperature controlled so that it can keep food (such as pizzas, for instance) warm if the consumer is not at home. The box uses facial recognition to maintain security.

## JD.COM

In contrast with Alibaba, which has historically remained asset light and has shown a determination to work with third parties, JD.com has strategically pursued a vertical approach, launching its own smart locker system in Beijing and Shenyang in 2013. In 2018 JD.com announced that it was opening up its technology and logistics structures to other companies, providing 'retail as a service'. This includes its locker network, mirroring Amazon's 'Fulfilled by Amazon' offering.

One innovation has been its 'smart delivery stations' trialling in Chinese cities, Changsha and Hohhot. These are autonomous logistics facilities or, in effect, mobile lockers that can steer themselves to addresses within a 5-kilometre radius. Security is provided by facial recognition software and the delivery stations deploy autonomous technologies that include route planning, traffic-light recognition and obstacle avoidance. According to the company, at full capacity, the delivery stations, operating with a half–half split between robots and couriers, can deliver up to 2,000 packages per day (JD.com, 2019).

## Third-party 'carrier agnostic' platform locker networks

As well as lockers provided by retailers to automate 'click and collect' in-store and those provided by e-commerce companies to fulfil their own and merchants' orders, there is also a segment of the market developed to meet third-party requirements developed by specialized locker network companies. In some cases, express companies have invested in these companies. These lockers are provided on an open network basis.

Most of the benefits accrue from the ease of delivery for couriers and the convenience of collection for end recipients. Security is also improved as the risk of theft (from doorsteps) is removed. The locker companies can make money from charging couriers to use their network (in China, the fee is 0.2 to 0.5 yuan per delivery). However, customers can also be charged if they do not collect the package within a specified time period (Hive charges 0.5 yuan up to a maximum of 3 yuan but customers can subscribe 5 yuan per month in order to avoid these charges).

Open locker networks are not as common as it might have been thought, as a result of the high levels of capital expenditure required to establish the necessary level of density to make them economically feasible. One reason for this is the nascent state of the technologies required to make the locker model work. Many companies still see this as a competitive advantage and are unwilling to share this advantage with their competitors:

- Hive Box: Shenzhen-based Hive Box, established in 2015, and valued at $3 billion in 2021, claims to be the world's largest locker solution network. It has 170,000 locker stations in China, covering 100 cities and each containing 40–200 electronic lockers. In 2020 it acquired China Post's locker business, Zhidi, adding more lockers to its network. Parcel companies SF Express, STO Express, ZTO Express and Yunda Express, and the logistics infrastructure provider GLP, have funded the technology provider with many locker stations placed in residential blocks where couriers have had difficulty in making deliveries.

- Singapore's Locker Alliance: Locker Alliance offers an open access delivery network comprising of parcel lockers and collection points in Singapore. Courier partners include: blu, DHL, Cainiao, Singapore Post, QXpress. Blu and SingPost provide the lockers. Marketplaces and merchants include Taobao and Lazada.

In Europe, a range of options exist:

- InPost: InPost claims to have the biggest international network of parcel lockers amounting to around 15,000 in markets including Australia, the UK, Poland, France, Italy, Canada, Czech Republic, Slovakia, Russia and Hungary. Founded by Integer.pl and co-owned by PineBridge and Franklin Templeton, it has a particularly strong presence in its home market of Poland. According to the company, in the 12 months to 31 March 2021, InPost handled 440 million parcel deliveries through its networks.

## Express parcels 'captive' locker networks

Express parcels carriers provide a further category of locker provision for the delivery of parcels that are moved through their own networks.

### DHL PACKSTATION

DP DHL deploys KEBA lockers, which it calls Packstations, throughout Germany and in certain other markets including Austria and the Netherlands.

The system uses a smartcard and pin to allow customers access to a locker and requires subscription to the service. DHL has 8,000 Packstations in Germany and it intends to increase this number to 12,500 by 2023. It claims that it takes less than 10 minutes for 90 per cent of the population to access a Packstation. Most are located in central public areas such as supermarkets and train stations. They also provide other services, such as printing out parcels' stamps bought online.

### UPS ACCESS POINT

UPS started to roll out lockers at locations in the United States from 2014 onwards as an extension of its Access Point programme (see section on parcels shops below). Starting in Chicago, it expanded to 300 locations across the country. It also has a presence in Asia. In 2018 it rolled out 850 'e-lockers' in Taiwan, working in partnership with Palmbox and Chunghwa Post. UPS alerts customers to the presence of an international delivery at one of the boxes and the system allows them to pay for import duties and taxes by credit card before they collect it. A similar offering exists in Hong Kong where UPS has over 500 boxes, working with SF Stores and EF Lockers.

### FEDEX

Although FedEx launched its Ship & Get locker offering in North America in 2014, it is very limited in scale. It has locker locations in Dallas as well as in Memphis, Tennessee. Packages are held for five days before being returned to the sender. In Asia, FedEx offers its 'self-service locker' service across locations in Hong Kong in conjunction with PCCW Solutions' digital logistics platform. Customers gain access to the locker by reply to a pre-delivery notification message and indicating their preferred locker location. They then receive an SMS message containing pick-up details and a passcode. A similar service was initiated in 2020 in Singapore.

### LA POSTE

La Poste's pickup stations, supplied by KEBA, can handle 40–100 parcels a day. Expansion throughout France has been enabled by a partnership between Neopost and technology partner Packcity. Several thousand retailers offer parcel delivery through Chronopost or Colissimo to a pickup station.

### GLS

Royal Mail-owned GLS operates a locker network in Eastern Europe, specifically Hungary, Slovakia, Slovenia, Romania and, most latterly, Czech

Republic. It also has an extensive network throughout Spain. The parcel lockers open when an access code, sent to the recipient by text message, email or notification card, is entered. Cash-on-delivery dispatches can also be paid for at the terminals with credit card and, additionally, GLS will also collect parcels for dispatch.

## Parcels shop/collection and delivery points (CDPs)

As well as lockers, many e-retailers and express parcels companies have been keen to develop their own networks of parcels shops or collection and delivery points (CDPs) located in third-party stores.

## The United States

### AMAZON

After originally launching in the UK with Next and in Italy with Giunti al Punto Librerie, Fermopoint and SisalPay store, Amazon has introduced its 'Counter' service to the United States. 'Counter' is a network of staffed pickup points that gives customers the option to pick up their Amazon packages in-store at a partner location. Delivery to a Counter location is available for the tens of millions of items sold on Amazon.com and works with same-day, one-day, two-day and standard shipping, for no extra cost.

### FEDEX

FedEx offers what it calls 'in-store' shipping services through a number of outlets. These include:

- FedEx Office: 2,000+ locations offering a range of collection and delivery services plus printing, including in 100 Walmart stores
- FedEx Ship Centre: simple collect and delivery point
- Office Depot and Office Max: a partnership allows FedEx customers to ship from these outlets
- Walgreens: drop off pre-labelled packages and collection of redirected deliveries
- FedEx Authorized Ship Centre: CDPs at independently owned stores
- FedEx Drop Box: return of online orders

FedEx Office was formerly Kinko's, a network of business stores, acquired in 2004 for $2.4 billion, which was subsequently rebranded.

## UPS

In 2001 UPS acquired the North American operations of Mail Boxes Etc (MBE), rebranding as the UPS Store in 2012. Each store is locally owned and operated under a franchise system, offering a variety of packing, shipping, freight, postal, printing and business services. It has 5,000 locations across North America. MBE operates as a separate organization outside of North America.

### Europe

In Europe, express parcels carriers offer the following networks of parcel shops:

## DHL

In Europe, DHL offers e-retailers the ability to offer click-and-collect services on their websites, collecting parcels via a network of parcel shops and service points. A parcel can be redirected to a service point for collection that day, following a delivery attempt to the customer. Customers can also change their delivery destination to a service point – either before or after a delivery attempt.

## DPD PICKUP

A service offering of DPD, 'Pickup' gives the option for customers to choose their closest delivery point from which they can collect their parcel. It also allows customers to divert the shipment to a pickup point 'in flight' if they do not expect to be at home. Returns can be handled through this network too.

## UPS

In 2012, UPS acquired Kiala, based in Brussels and providing services in Belgium, Luxembourg, the Netherlands, France and Spain. Kiala software integrates a network of parcel shops providing consumers with access to products ordered online with services run by local convenience stores.

## HERMES

Hermes, part of the Otto Group, is increasing the number of its parcel shops in Germany by 30 per cent to 20,000 collection points in the medium term. To this end, nationwide partnerships are also planned with retail chains. New service offerings such as the redirection of parcels to a parcel shop will be developed.

COLLECT+

Collect+, jointly owned by parcel carrier Yodel and payment company PayPoint, has a network of parcel stores across the UK in a range of newsagents, supermarkets, filling stations and convenience stores. It works with brands such as Aldi, ao.com, Boohoo, IKEA, M&S and Sky to deliver online purchases and make returns.

## China

In China, Alibaba operates a network of 'Cainiao Terminals' while JD.com has its own 'pickup points'. Both have cultivated the 'nanostore' market (small independent retailers) in urban areas to provide them with a physical presence close to the end recipient, an essential part of the online to offline (O2O) strategy.

## In-car/in-garage/in-home delivery

Other delivery options being trialled involve access by the courier to secure locations nominated by the end recipient and facilitated by digital keys. This includes access to cars, garages and even to the shopper's home. Apps, such as 'chark', being developed by Lab1886 and Mercedes-Benz, provide couriers with a one-time-only access to a vehicle using the car's digital key. This builds on technology already in existence, which allows drivers to remotely open and close their car's boot. The app also allows customers to track who has accessed their car and when. Tested successfully in Stuttgart and Berlin, the app is due to be rolled out more widely. The app works by allowing the customer to choose a time slot, vehicle and parking address at the time they place their online order. According to the company, as soon as the delivery service is within a range of 500 metres of the indicated parking location, it is able to locate the vehicle by GPS and unlock it once.

Amazon Key In-Car Delivery is a similar app that allows customers to have packages delivered to the boots of their vehicles in the United States. Chevrolet, Buick, GMC, Cadillac and Volvo vehicles with an active connected car service plan such as OnStar or Volvo On Call are included in the programme. The service has now been expanded to include selected Ford models equipped with FordPass Connect. Amazon drivers are able to find customers' cars through GPS and leave packages inside cars. Customers receive notifications throughout the delivery process, including just before delivery takes place and a confirmation that delivery is complete and the car has been securely locked. For security purposes, Amazon authorizes the delivery driver before vehicles are unlocked only when in-car deliveries are to be made. Customers can also block car access from the Amazon Key app if they change their mind on the delivery day.

Amazon has also been behind other digital key initiatives such as Key for Garage and Key for Home. In 2017, it launched its key service for Prime members, in 37 cities in the United States. The service uses an app, smart lock and indoor security camera to enable in-home delivery when customers are out. Key for Garage uses Wi-Fi door-opening technology in conjunction with specialist door technology companies.

## Environmental and efficiency benefits

Home deliveries have been blamed for a large increase in the volume of small vans on the road with the associated disbenefits of traffic, congestion and pollution. There may be some environmental benefits to the use of alternative delivery locations, although research to quantify these benefits is still at an early stage. Research undertaken for the US Transport Research Board (TRB) using data provided by UPS showed that locker networks could be positive in terms of reducing energy usage (Moore, 2017). Initial findings concluded that:

- Parcel lockers appear to be helpful in reducing energy usage in more suburban neighbourhoods with fewer through-streets and more cul-de-sacs.
- Pairing parcel lockers with electric vehicle (EV) delivery trucks or vans will likely further reduce energy usage overall.

However, lockers in dense urban areas, where there is good connectivity between streets, may not result in a large reduction of energy usage. As another report asserted, 'The overall distance travelled by the truck as it makes deliveries is not significantly reduced by incorporating a locker' (VTO, 2019).

This contrasts with another research project undertaken in Poland that found that lockers helped to reduce the number of deliveries in an urban area, including failed deliveries and returns of goods. One courier operating in Krakow, Poland, was able to deliver 600 parcels a day travelling just 70 kilometres, compared with a baseline of 60 parcels a day and 150 kilometres (Iwan et al, 2015). $CO_2$ emissions fell from 32,500 tonnes per annum to 1,516 tonnes and fuel consumption dropped from 22,500,000 litres to 1,050,000 litres.

According to Tan Kiat How, chief executive of Singapore government's Infocomm Media Development Authority, which has set up its own initiative in the country, logistics service providers can expect to see a 50 per cent reduction in distances travelled by delivery drivers and a fivefold increase in the number of parcels that can be delivered per day (Różycki, 2019).

It should be noted that when assessing the environmental benefits of delivering packages to centralized locker locations, the trip that the recipient makes to collect the parcel also needs to be taken into account. There will obviously be more benefits if this trip is made using a mode with a low carbon footprint. If, however, the recipient makes the trip by car, environmental benefits may well be negated and even additional congestion and pollution created.

It would seem that the location of the boxes and the human geography of the operating environment (rural, semi-rural, suburban, inner city) are the critical factors in the efficiency and sustainability of alternative delivery systems.

## Summary

Customers are increasingly keen to have the option of collecting parcels securely at a time and place that is convenient for them, rather than at a time best suiting the parcels company or e-retailer. This has led to growth in the number and type of alternative delivery locations for online shoppers. This change is being driven by a confluence of factors including cost, convenience, trust and the sustainability of delivery choices.

Presently the evidence for environmental benefits is still to be confirmed. However, there is no doubt that in terms of reducing cost, alternative delivery locations will be a critical part of the last-mile delivery strategies of express parcels companies and e-retailers for many years to come.

The size of the investment opportunity in alternative delivery locations and technologies is huge. However, in terms of market development, it is still to be seen whether one single model wins out – closed or open networks of lockers; parcel shops or in-house or in-car deliveries – or whether it is economically feasible for all these options (and others) to co-exist.

# References

IPC (2019) *Cross-Border E-Commerce Shopper Survey 2018*, International Postal Corporation, Brussels

Iwan, S, Kijewska, K and Lemke, J (2015) *Analysis of Parcel Lockers' Efficiency as the Last Mile Delivery Solution: The Results of the Research in Poland*, Maritime University of Szczecin, Poland

JD.com (2019) JD delivery stations get smart ahead of CES Debut, JD.com, 6 January, https://jdcorporateblog.com/jd-delivery-stations-get-smart-ahead-of-ces-debut/ (archived at https://perma.cc/B4BP-VKFP)

Moore, A (2017) Development of a GIS-based model to examine alternative scenarios for last-mile freight delivery, Oak Ridge National Laboratory, www.ucgis.org/assets/docs/Symposia/Moore_Vehicle.pdf (archived at https://perma.cc/BR3R-UGV8)

Różycki, M (2019) Why carrier-agnostic parcel lockers are the future, Parcel and Post Technology International, 2 April, www.parcelandpostaltechnologyinternational.com/analysis/why-carrier-agnostic-parcel-lockers-are-the-future.html (archived at https://perma.cc/E7FK-V648)

Thomas, L (2019) Walmart announces next-day delivery, firing back at Amazon, CNBC, 14 May, www.cnbc.com/2019/05/13/walmart-announces-next-day-delivery-firing-back-at-amazon.html (archived at https://perma.cc/28GW-44WU)

UPS (2017) UPS pulse of the online shopper, UPS, www.ups.com/assets/resources/media/en_GB/UPS_POTOS_EU_EN_linked.pdf (archived at https://perma.cc/ZDY3-66Y2)

VTO (2019) Energy efficient mobility systems, Vehicle Technologies Office, US Department of Energy, www.energy.gov/sites/prod/files/2019/04/f62/VTO_2018_APR_EEMS_%20032919_compliant_0.pdf (archived at https://perma.cc/AXN8-CPC8)

# 7

# On-demand delivery and crowd-shipping

**This chapter will familiarize the reader with:**

- The nature of on-demand business models

- The economics of the sector

- The future of on-demand in a post-Covid-19 world

- Attempts to introduce crowd-shipping by retailers and e-commerce platforms

- Last-mile mapping innovations

## What is 'on-demand'?

The on-demand delivery sector has grown rapidly over the past few years. Developed as a way of enabling small food outlets and retailers to provide a fast home-delivery service, on-demand providers have tapped into a latent source of consumer demand across a range of sectors.

Dablanc et al (2017) provide the following definition for the on-demand concept: 'Instant delivery services provide on-demand delivery within two hours – by either private individuals, independent contractors, or employees – by connecting consignors, couriers and consignees via a digital platform.'

There are two key elements to this definition:

- On-demand has a timescale attached – in fact a very short timescale of below two hours.

- On-demand is facilitated by a digital platform that matches demand with supply, usually via a smartphone.

On-demand should not be confused with crowdsourced shipping or 'crowd-shipping', which refers to a source of transportation capacity rather than the service supplied. Crowdsourced shipping often involves private individuals using their own or public transport to fulfil a delivery. This could be a sub-section of the on-demand market but whereas on-demand is growing quickly, crowd-shipping has yet to take off. This is discussed in more detail below.

On-demand has also been used interchangeably with other terms such as 'gig economy', referring to the use of self-employed contractors working on an ad hoc basis. This also is not strictly accurate as although many platforms' business models require flexible resources to deal with the peaks and troughs of demand, some on-demand retailers are starting to employ delivery agents directly. This is partly due to regulatory issues and pressure from labour organizations, but also due to issues of control and quality.

Instacart in the United States, for example, has started hiring many of its contractors as employees, which benefits the company by allowing it to train its workers (the US tax authorities use training as one way of deciding on the status of a worker). Better-trained workers improve the customer experience, both in terms of picking goods from stores and the final delivery.

On-demand is perhaps most closely associated with the delivery of meals prepared by restaurants in a local area. However, it is certainly not confined to this sector, with some markets offering on-demand deliveries of:

- groceries
- fresh food
- alcohol
- laundry
- consumer goods

Perhaps the most important trend driving the market is the concept of 'instant gratification'. Whether meals, products bought online or fashion items bought at a shop but delivered to buyers' homes, consumers increasingly want immediate access to their purchases. Whether a good thing or not, this is an unalterable part of modern life, which suggests that on-demand will be with us for many years to come.

Moreover, it seems inevitable that the market will continue to grow. The sector received a big boost from Covid-19 lockdowns – prior to the pandemic it accounted for 9 per cent of the restaurant market in the United States but by 2025 it is expected to make up 21 per cent, according to consultancy

Apptopia (Yellowsoft, 2021). In 2021, the global market is estimated to have grown by 32 per cent (Technavio, 2021). The impact of Covid-19 on the sector will be discussed in more detail below.

## How does on-demand work?

Many on-demand platforms do not regard themselves as logistics or delivery companies. Rather they see themselves as a matching service, allowing consumers to connect with retailers or restaurants.

Some, such as Just Eat or Delivery Hero, do not provide delivery capabilities, instead solely providing the software platform over which consumers can place their orders with restaurants. These are then fulfilled by the restaurants themselves. Others, such as Deliveroo, provide the delivery networks to restaurants that otherwise would not be able to offer home delivery ('logistics-fulfilled'). Even so, the latter companies do not own assets, using the services of largely self-employed couriers.

The way these companies define themselves is important. In 2018 the European Commission decided that Uber – which regarded itself as a similar platform for personal mobility – was a 'taxi' service provider and should be regulated as such. On-demand platforms may face similar types of regulation in the future, especially if controversy continues over the treatment of subcontractors.

Another issue that has yet to be fully addressed is the issue of insurance. A normal courier company would provide a range of insurances from public liability to goods-in-transit. Responsibility is potentially unclear in the on-demand chain if the on-demand platform is variously regarded as a restaurant provider, a grocery retailer, a delivery company, or, as many would prefer, purely an online platform.

## The on-demand business model

In order to attain scale and market leadership, which are essential attributes in the on-demand market, the platforms need to build a strong marketing presence as well as being focused around price.

This is only part of the equation, however. In order to retain both customers and couriers, on-demand providers have to achieve a competitive advantage by developing best-in-class functionality involving:

- efficient dispatch of orders to couriers
- availability of good-quality couriers

- capacity planning
- integrated relationships with consignors

One critical question for companies providing on-demand delivery services is whether or not there is a large enough market to support them.

In order to make a profit, on-demand businesses need to have a high frequency of orders within an operational area, and if this frequency drops below a certain rate, the unit economics of the service are unworkable. There are two main underlying causes of this:

- the market was never large enough to support the service in the first place
- competition from rival service providers has diluted market share

So long as competing start-ups possess the funding to expand their businesses, the latter issue can be addressed by pricing incentives for both couriers and consumers in order to build effective economies of scale. However, this inevitably results in financial losses, forcing start-ups in a competitive market to make tough choices when the money begins to run out.

The economics of an on-demand service provider are reasonably straightforward. Revenue comprises:

- commission charged by the platform to the restaurant (perhaps 25–30 per cent)
- delivery fee charged to the customer (typically around €2.50/£2.50 in Europe and the UK)

Whereas the costs derive from:

- fee paid to the courier (per job or per hour)
- management, marketing and technology overhead

Therefore, revenues are driven by the value of the meal ordered, their volume and the delivery fee (if the market allows – 'free delivery' is becoming more common). Running costs depend on the utilization rate of the courier, if paid by the hour, although this is not as important if paid by the job. This explains why on-demand companies rely heavily on the 'gig economy' – the model is far harder to make work if the courier is an employee or a worker paid by the hour. Whether this is sustainable in the long run – due to lobbying by unions and governments looking to raise more money from labour taxes – is yet to be seen. Of course, couriers have a choice not to work below a certain remuneration and will find better-paying on-demand platforms. This will create a vicious cycle – the struggling company will not be able to hire sufficient couriers, leading to longer delivery times and low customer satisfaction. With reducing volumes, more couriers will leave, and so it goes on.

According to Adrien Roose, co-founder of TakeEatEasy, an on-demand platform that shut down in 2017, 'Courier utilization is one of the most important metrics in our business. Assuming couriers need to make a minimum €15 per hour not to churn, a low courier utilization (<1.5 deliveries / courier / hour) implies a negative contribution margin' (2016). Bluntly, if on-demand companies are not able to attract and retain good-quality contractors they will quickly go out of business. Pay is crucial to this, but some companies are able to provide benefits such as supplementary insurance.

As the on-demand market consolidates, so does a finite supply of financing, and it becomes harder for even some of the larger providers to find more funding when they are losing market share and money. The demise of TakeEatEasy was blamed by senior management on such a situation when even one of its own investors decided to acquire and fund a better-placed rival.

Consolidation amongst the existing companies is inevitable, through mergers and acquisitions (M&A) and bankruptcy, with a small number of companies achieving dominance in certain localities. Hong Kong, where Lalamove and GoGoX are two of the market leaders, has seen the number of competitors shrink over the past five years from approximately 300 to just a handful. Commentators believe that, for this geography at least, consumers on their own are not enough to support multiple suppliers. There needs to be a business market as well and such customers are driven by service and reliability.

These two successful on-demand companies have attracted the most investment. Lalamove has raised $2.5 billion over the past six years, with plans for an initial public offering (IPO) at some point in the future. The money has been used to build out its international HQ in Hong Kong and help it reach 363 cities across China. It is expanding throughout Asia and even entered the Brazilian market in 2019. GoGoX (formerly GoGoVan) has raised so far $376.5 million to allow it to develop operations around the world as well as in the Chinese market.

Interestingly, the market is moving so quickly that disruptors can themselves become the disrupted. Amazon, for example, in many markets can be regarded as the incumbent, and vulnerable itself to disruption by on-demand retailers. Instacart in the United States, by employing agents to pick from established bricks-and-mortar retailers, is able to provide consumers with one-hour deliveries and provide a very broad range of goods. In contrast, Amazon has a vertically integrated model, using national and regional distribution centres, perhaps similar to traditional retailers. Instacart can add an on-demand layer to existing retailers' capabilities, allowing them to participate in this sector and compete against Amazon. In response, Amazon is now reportedly thinking about launching its own on-demand grocery service for third-party retailers in the United States, following a successful rollout in the UK. The market is set to get more crowded with competitors such as Uber, DoorDash and Walmart establishing fast grocery delivery services, even by drone.

## Opportunities for parcels companies

Although on-demand is attracting huge attention from investors, the opportunities for express parcels companies to move into this fast-growing sector would seem limited. On-demand services rely on a critical mass of users and drivers, but on a localized basis. This means that there are very few synergies to be had between the national, regional or global express parcels companies and on-demand operations that work on a city-by-city basis. The likes of FedEx, UPS and DHL operate models that rely on the movement of vast volumes of parcels in order to maximize the utilization of national and international network infrastructure rather than the instant collection and delivery of an order within a limited area.

However, that has not stopped one major parcels company, GeoPost, from exploring the sector. The subsidiary of the French post office has acquired an on-demand operator, Stuart, in which it originally took a minority shareholding in 2015. As is indicated in the case study below, although there will be a certain amount of integration with GeoPost the operation will remain autonomous.

---

CASE STUDY 7.1
*GeoPost and Stuart*

Founded in 2015 by Clément Benoît and Benjamin Chemla, Stuart is a technology platform that connects retailers with a fleet of independent couriers to help businesses meet the delivery expectations of their end customers. Following acquisition of a 22 per cent share in 2015, major European parcels operator GeoPost subsequently bought the entire company in 2017.

Stuart has built algorithmic dispatch for both on-demand and scheduled jobs and integrated its application programming interface (API) with leading multinational retailers across France, the UK and Spain. With over 700 employees across technology, data, product, operations and business development, Stuart facilitates thousands of deliveries per day for more than 8,000 active customers including Carrefour, Franprix, Burger King, The Kooples, Pizza Hut and Cdiscount in over 100 cities.

At the time, Paul-Marie Chavanne, GeoPost's CEO, stated that, 'This decision logically follows our investments in Stuart over the past two years. Stuart completes our delivery service at a local level and embodies the future of express urban delivery, a rapidly expanding strategic activity for us' (O'Hear, 2017).

Stuart remains an independent brand and subsidiary in order to ensure the autonomy of its management team and its commitment to technological innovation. However, the company will be co-chaired by the management of Pickup, a start-up specializing in alternative delivery, which GeoPost acquired in 2009. Pickup's leaders will integrate Stuart within GeoPost in order to maximize synergies between the companies, including developing value-generating solutions for the group's customers.

---

As well as operational, there are several reasons why other express parcels carriers may not be keen to buy into the market. In some quarters the sector is regarded as highly toxic due to the controversy over working practices and remuneration in the 'gig economy'. Cost may also put them off. Acquiring an established player would be very expensive, with investors looking to realize highly inflated multiples. Amazon came to the rescue of a failing Deliveroo in 2020 with an investment of £575 million for less than 20 per cent of the company. Instead, as with GeoPost, it is more likely that acquirers would look at an early stage start-up (like DHL did to develop their Saloodo! road freight platform) or develop the technology internally.

Just because there are few synergies between on-demand and express parcels networks does not necessarily mean that GeoPost's acquisition of Stuart should be viewed as an isolated acquisition. As the on-demand sector becomes more mature, more opportunities for express companies to become involved in the market may well present themselves. For example, the technology that underpins the platforms may well prove useful in B2B sectors such as service parts logistics, providing a step change in the costs of fulfilling narrow delivery windows to meet service level agreements. The delivery of restaurant food may well be the start for many providers, but the future of on-demand may well be in other business sectors that still remain untouched.

In the end, the market may just become too big for the express parcels giants to ignore. However, for the time being, the risks of picking the wrong on-demand provider are probably too great – it would seem more sensible to let financial investors bear the strain of building the necessary scale, or indeed losing their stakes if they fail.

---

Start-up successes

*Shutl*

Purchased by eBay (for around $100 million). Shutl previously raised $8.69 million from UPS, La Poste and others, in seven venture capital funding rounds. eBay continues to invest in Shutl. In September 2016 it announced a revamp allowing easier access for SMEs.

*DoorDash*

The company received funding of $2.5 billion and made six acquisitions before going public in 2021 on the New York Stock Exchange with a valuation of $72 billion. Most recently it bought Finland-based Wolt for $7 billion, which gives it a presence internationally. The company had revenues of $2.9 billion in 2020 (an increase of 241 per cent over the previous year) and is estimated to have a 45 per cent market share (Edison Trends, 2020), although it is still losing money.

*Instacart*

US grocery delivery company Instacart has been valued at $39 billion, raising $265 million in 2020, which it said it would use to increase employee numbers. Plans are underway for an IPO.

*Roadie*

Describing itself as an 'on-the-way' delivery network, the company connects customers with unused capacity in passenger vehicles. It raised $62 million before being acquired by UPS in 2021. The price was not revealed.

*Delivery Hero*

Launched in 2011, German-based on-demand platform Delivery Hero went public in 2017, raising around €1 billion. It now has 43,000 employees, a turnover of €3.5 billion and is present in 50 countries worldwide. Its orders doubled in 2020 to 1.9 billion, as did its revenues.

Start-up failures

*Tok tok tok*

Originally set up as a food delivery company with $2 million in seed funding, Tok tok tok lacked the resources and cost control necessary to scale up. It sold its technology platform to Just Eat in September 2016.

*Wunwun*

Supported by various institutional and individual investors, Wunwun raised $23 million at start up. Subsequently the company closed down and was acquired by delivery service Alfred in May 2015. Fundamentally, the company had failed to scale enough to compete effectively.

*VF*

A subsidiary delivery arm of Delivery Hero, VF launched in 2015 as an outsourced delivery company for fast-food restaurants. It entered administration in April 2016 after failing to get costs under control. Its main problem was that it scaled up too quickly and found acceptable margins unattainable.

*foodpanda*

foodpanda raised $210 million in 2015 — including a $100 million injection from Goldman Sachs and a separate $110 million round. Eventually it was forced to sell its businesses in Mexico, Brazil and Indonesia and lay off employees in India and Hong Kong. It was finally acquired by Delivery Hero in 2017.

## The 'gig economy' and the status of transport workers

Many logistics companies are rightly proud of the way they treat their workforce. Despite this, the business models and employment structures that many companies in the sector operate are coming under intense scrutiny due to the impact they have on logistics workers. Many of the issues relate to the highly subcontracted nature of labour in the transport market.

### The increasing use of owner-drivers

Although the use of owner-drivers (self-employed transport workers who also provide their own vehicle) has been widespread for several decades, the demand for such workers has soared in the recent past, not least due to the spectacular growth of e-retail-related deliveries. Volatility in the market with frequent peaks and troughs has meant that the vast majority of parcels carriers have adopted an outsourced model, in effect de-risking their own operations. Subcontractors bear not only the cost of investment in transport assets but also carry business risk by being paid 'by the drop' or by the mile. The e-retail market is such that so-called 'free shipping' is a major selling point for many companies. The costs of this marketing device are pushed onto the carrier resulting in ultra-low rates of remuneration.

This has raised ethical concerns. The low barriers to market entry and a plentiful supply of people willing to take on a low-skilled job have meant that the amount paid by some carriers is barely enough to cover the cost of running a vehicle. There have been allegations that to some carriers their subcontractors are 'disposable'. They can be utilized for a period of time at an unsustainable rate, knowing that they will eventually be forced to give up due to the lack of economic viability. The carrier will then replace the owner-driver from a plentiful pool of new market entrants.

In addition to this, the status of owner-drivers provides them with fewer entitlements than those who are legally defined as employees. For example, they have none of the protection rights of employees: sick pay, maternity/ paternity leave, pensions and so on, despite fulfilling a role that could be argued is identical to that of an employee. Also, due to the likelihood in the parcels sector that the owner-driver will be providing and driving a van rather than a large goods vehicle (LGV), they do not have to comply with European drivers' hours legislation, which places a limit on the length of time for which they can drive. Consequently, work load and hours are often very long and, as discussed above, rates of pay very small.

Of course, many would argue that this state of affairs is merely derived from the healthy operation of a free market. In the developed world, many owner-drivers are migrants who have been attracted by employment opportunities and wages much higher than those in their own countries. In return, by tapping a large pool of new migrant capacity, the developed countries' economies have benefited through a lower cost base. Changing this structure would inevitably mean that supply chain costs would rise throughout industry.

### The on-demand economy – unethical or new employment model?

The development of the so-called 'on-demand' business models of delivery companies has brought the treatment of subcontractors under even more scrutiny from labour organizations and policy makers.

Start-up restaurant meal delivery company Deliveroo is facing challenges to its subcontracted labour model from both regulators and the subcontractors themselves. The company has a network of drivers and riders across many countries who collect and deliver meals from a range of food outlets that do not have their own delivery capabilities.

In the UK, in 2017 the company paid its subcontractors £7 an hour, plus £1 per delivery. However, management introduced a new pay structure that resulted in unrest amongst its drivers. The company wanted to change the remuneration to a simple £3.75 per delivery. Although this could result in higher payments during peak times, overall there was concern that the new system would result in contractors receiving less than the minimum wage across the day as a whole (Wallace, 2017).

Rival start-up UberEats faced similar dissention among its contracted workforce. The casual basis of employment for couriers means that although the opportunities to earn around £9 an hour are available, on some occasions few, if any, jobs will be allocated. However, management counters that couriers do not have set shifts, minimum hours or delivery zones that they must keep to. Many have other jobs as well.

Although some of the subcontractors may see the on-demand model as unethical, many are suited by the arrangement. After all, both Deliveroo and UberEats have attracted many thousands of couriers to sign up to their business models.

However, there have been legal challenges as to whether self-employed workers should be given access to the same rights as other employees. In a case related to the sacking of two workers by private hire company Addison Lee, the legal company of Union GMB commented, 'Employers cannot be allowed to have all the financial benefits of employees and none of the responsibilities to these people's livelihoods. The attempt to reframe normal employment as part of the gig economy is a serious threat to the financial security of thousands of hard-working people and will end up costing the tax payer huge sums while companies take all the profit' (GMB, 2017).

One of the main issues, it would appear, is that the cultural barriers to less formal employment will need to be overcome if the on-demand economy is to become mainstream. It is likely that employment status will become even more contentious in the future as labour organizations try to prevent the prevalence of more informal working structures and governments try to mitigate the loss of tax receipts.

## The future of on-demand delivery in a post-Covid-19 world

What does the lifting of lockdown policies mean for the on-demand delivery companies that have largely benefited from the regulatory impact of Covid-19 on people's lives? As people return to the office, socialize in bars and clubs and – critically – start to eat out once again, will home deliveries continue at the same level as they have been?

To make money, the on-demand delivery business relies on consumers willing to pay a premium for food or groceries to be delivered (over and above the cost and time of picking up these purchases themselves). As discussed above, they also need a high level of volume in order to leverage the necessary network benefits of their business model and repay their investment in technology as well as maintain a steady stream of work for couriers. During lockdown people were discouraged from going out, restaurants were closed and there was an increase in disposable income (due not least to lack of opportunities to socialize and savings on the daily commute), which provided a fertile economic backdrop for the on-demand sector.

At the same time as this, on-demand also relies on a large pool of delivery drivers willing to work on highly flexible terms for low remuneration. During the pandemic, many 'mobile' workers (taxi and minicab drivers, for example) migrated to the on-demand sector for employment. Worker numbers were buoyed by those made redundant or furloughed from sectors such as leisure and retail.

Finally, there needs to be a willingness from restaurants or stores to pay a fee to access on-demand platforms and a proportion of the delivery costs. Throughout the pandemic, restaurants were forbidden to host diners, meaning that home delivery was their only option if they wanted to remain operational.

The problem the on-demand sector faces is that despite soaring revenues experienced throughout the Covid-19 crisis, few companies have been able to make any profits. With conditions set to become far less benign in the coming years, it is unclear how the sector can remain sustainable – at least in developed economies.

When the economic, societal, technological, legislative and political factors combine favourably, on-demand companies can prosper (see Figure 7.1). The platform attracts customers and, as orders increase, more restaurants join.

More restaurants means more volume, which is not only good for existing drivers/riders (more revenue) but also attracts new and good quality contractors. The higher levels of service this allows, along with the greater choice of restaurants/stores, attracts more customers. All parties benefit from the value created.

However, if external factors turn negative (for example, disposable income falls) the same process works in reverse (as shown in Figure 7.1). Customers start to reduce the frequency they use the service or leave completely, meaning orders fall. Decreasing business could mean restaurants decide the fee to appear on the app/website is too high and leave the platform. Volumes decrease with the knock-on effect that drivers leave for employment elsewhere as revenues cannot support them on a full-time basis. Consequently, service levels fall and more customers leave, and so on. Without network benefits, companies quickly burn through their capital, in effect subsidizing every delivery.

Localization of services will be important to the success, or otherwise, of the business model. Deliveroo writes in its 2021 IPO prospectus, 'We are a global internet company, yet also a neighbourhood business. Deliveroo started in the London neighbourhood of Chelsea in 2013 and since then we have delivered a proven track record of global expansion through a hyperlocal lens. From the very beginning, we recognized that in order to succeed we needed to get our proposition right, neighbourhood by neighbourhood.'

However, it is extremely costly to build an operation on a location-by-location basis where volumes may not be sufficient to support the sunk costs of a national/global organization. On-demand companies talk about the use of AI to improve efficiencies of deliveries, learning about local market characteristics. However, this is where the logistics-fulfilled marketplace model will find it most difficult to compete against restaurant-fulfilled. A local outlet may already know much more about its market and issues related to delivery than an operation working on a regional or even city level. It will also have less overhead and more flexibility.

Logistics-fulfilled on-demand food delivery via apps face a challenging future. Once they stop growing and investors' money runs out, many companies will fail. If there is a downturn, consumers will rein back on discretionary purchases; investors will pull the plug on future funding and delivery companies will not be able to afford to subsidize drivers.

FIGURE 7.1 On-demand feedback loops

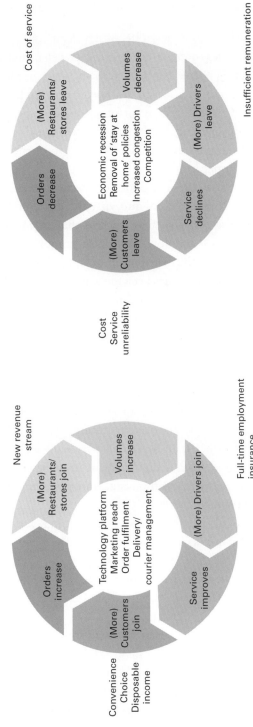

On-demand
positive feedback loop

New revenue
stream

(More)
Restaurants/
stores join

Volumes
increase

Orders
increase

Technology platform
Marketing reach
Order fulfilment
Delivery/
courier management

(More) Drivers join

Full-time employment
insurance

(More)
Customers
join

Service
improves

Convenience
Choice
Disposable
income

On-demand
negative feedback loop

Cost of service

(More)
Restaurants/
stores leave

Volumes
decrease

Orders
decrease

Economic recession
Removal of 'stay at
home' policies
Increased congestion
Competition

(More) Drivers
leave

Insufficient remuneration

(More)
Customers
leave

Service
declines

Cost
Service
unreliability

## Will crowd-shipping finally take off?

The smartphone phenomenon has effectively 'democratized' technology. These days, all companies (not just the largest), as well as individuals, have high levels of computing power available to them, which in turn has encouraged technical innovation to flourish. No longer do very large computing companies monopolize the development of software; rather, everyone has the opportunity to conceive and develop new technological solutions as well as distribute them to a mass market. This has led to disruptive, agile and continually evolving applications.

One of the benefits of these network-connected devices is that they provide the means to combine users into virtual communities. This power has been utilized by disruptors, such as Uber, to challenge regulated sectors such as personal mobility – and now also transportation.

Running in parallel with the distribution of computing power and hardware throughout the population has been the generation of massive amounts of data. This can inform decision-making opportunities that can bring significant benefits, either economic, societal or environmental.

Technological innovation, democratization and the ubiquity of low-cost sensors has combined with an important cultural shift to create the 'sharing economy'. Whereas asset ownership was once seen as highly important, a new generation is happier to forego the status that this once bestowed in return for greater levels of efficiency or service. Many see that cars will become shared assets in the foreseeable future with a focus being on 'on-demand' services rather than a way of increasing self-esteem through association with a brand. This is due partly, it must be said, to economic necessity, which puts many assets (housing, transport, etc) out of reach of many so-called 'millennials'.

Crowd-shipping is also part of this broader trend. Leading academic Professor Alan McKinnon says crowd-shipping 'effectively turns ordinary citizens into couriers, creating new informal logistics networks for the local distribution of small items ordered online' (2016). The concept involves ordinary individuals taking parcels with them on an existing journey and stopping to affect the delivery en route.

The benefit of this process is that the delivery can be made with low marginal costs both in terms of the financial and environmental implications. It also means that the person carrying out the delivery can be reimbursed for their time and effort, creating value from an essentially non-value-adding exercise. As McKinnon has also commented, 'The growth of crowd-shipping is an example of people using social networking to behave collaboratively and share services and assets for the greater good of the community' (2016).

Although the term crowd-shipping originally referred to a practice undertaken by ordinary individuals, some of the platforms that have been established, such as Zipments, are used predominantly by professional couriers. Some, such as Deliv, are focused around the delivery of goods purchased in shopping malls. Deliv (part funded by UPS in 2018 and operating in the United States), for example, says it seeks to bridge the gap between multichannel retailers and their customers. DHL was one of the first companies to trial crowd-shipping as an addition to its existing service, although there is no evidence that it has continued these operations after initial assessment of the model.

Whether or not crowd-shipping is undertaken by an individual on their way to work, for example, or by a professional courier, is an important issue. Although it may not matter to the end recipient, the shipper, or for that matter the platform, there are implications in terms of road use, congestion and environmental impact. Professional couriers may travel much longer distances to collect and deliver shipments, making dedicated journeys for each consignment. By substituting a lower-cost alternative to formal delivery networks that have been built on the consolidation of parcels in

FIGURE 7.2  Crowd-shipping: giving shippers access to enhanced supplier pool

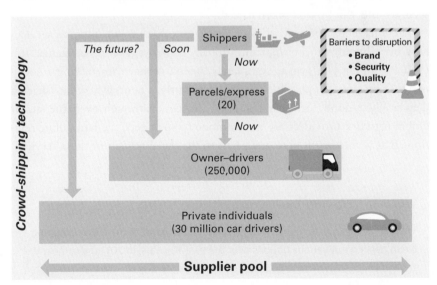

vans, the result may be higher levels of congestion and emissions. Certain popular high-density delivery locations, such as an urban area, may attract large numbers of professional couriers from outside, exacerbating already overcrowded roads.

The benefits to shippers of crowd-shipping in its purest, original form are evident from the illustrative graphic in Figure 7.2, which is based loosely around the UK market.

In the scenario, a shipper has the option of using a relatively small number of major carriers. Using new technology, a shipper now has the opportunity of bypassing these carriers to establish its own distribution solution, using local partners. This is exactly the strategy employed by one of the biggest shippers in the market, Amazon, through its subsidiary, Amazon Logistics. Using crowd-shipping technologies, a shipper would then be able to directly access a large number of owner-drivers and, beyond this, a larger number of individual drivers. In fact, this number would be of an even higher magnitude as it could include train and bus passengers, especially those who could deliver small packages very easily to an inner-city destination.

There are, however, risks involved with 'disintermediating' established carriers. Not least of these are the issues of quality and security. The major express parcels operators have been successful over the years partly due to the brands they have established and a large factor in this has been the guaranteed levels of service and trust. Although these carriers may charge their services at a premium, many shippers, especially those of high-value goods, may be willing to accept these if they know that their goods will be moved securely and will be well taken care of.

There have also been worries by regulators that crowd-shipping services may be vulnerable to misappropriation by terrorist or criminal gangs. If a crowd-shipping platform is completely 'open', perhaps resembling a social networking site, it is possible that, inadvertently, a courier may be asked to deliver illicit goods or even explosive devices. Although even the major global network providers are not immune to such acts, the bad public relations that would result may put a halt to the development of these services.

---

### WALMART TESTING CROWD-SHIPPING OPTIONS

Walmart, the giant US retailer, has been at the forefront of the crowd-shipping trend, testing out various options over the past 10 years. In 2013 the company trialled using customers to collect orders when they were in-store and deliver them to other customers on the way home. In 2017 the company examined an alternative, asking its warehouse employees to undertake the delivery of orders on the way back from work.

The model being trialled would involve the delivery of an e-commerce order to a store located closest to the customer, where the associate would collect it and deliver at the end of their day. The employee would set the parameters of their delivery capabilities, including the number of packages they could deliver as well as the size and weight limits. Walmart has stores within 10 miles of 90 per cent of the US population and over 1 million employees, which makes the concept feasible.

Three stores were involved in original trials and the company says response from staff was positive, not least as the GPS functionality of the app that Walmart provided enabled staff to find faster ways home using their smartphones.

One further advantage, which overcomes the argument that crowd-shipping could lead to more vehicle miles and emissions rather than less, is that the employee starts off at the same origin as the shipment (the store) and it is delivered en route.

In 2018, Walmart launched 'Spark Delivery' through a partnership with technology platform Bringg, targeting Nashville and New Orleans. The last-mile element is undertaken by a network of independent drivers managed by a third-party company, Delivery Drivers. In other parts of the United States, Walmart has also worked with Postmates, Uber and Deliv.

## LAST-MILE INNOVATION: ADDRESS MAPPING

Many companies are trialling new solutions by which parcels can be delivered effectively and cheaply to customers. A number of start-ups are now focusing on how to deliver to e-commerce customers in emerging markets, where formal addresses do not exist.

Markets such as China and India are attracting huge interest from e-retail companies, due to their large and growing middle classes. However, much of the Middle East and Africa also suffer from the issue of having limited, or no addresses. Large proportions of these populations live in rural areas where addresses, let alone postcodes, are few and far between. A home might have no identifier beyond a street name, or even just a part of town.

On major Asian e-commerce sites, such as Alibaba Group or Flipkart, customers who do not have formal addresses instead enter their name, town and phone number on the checkout screen. They may also include a local landmark as part of the address. Parcels are then either delivered to a convenient collection point, or the delivery drivers call the customer for specific directions as they near the 'vague' location.

Companies are now developing solutions to make deliveries to these more remote locations easier by using technologies ranging from mobile apps to bespoke global mapping systems. Surprisingly, instead of using traditional geographical coordinates, such as latitude and longitude, these companies have opted to develop their own coordinates, creating unique 'address codes' for every spot on the planet, using designations that are shorter and simpler than latitude and longitude.

Companies in this area include Fetchr and what3words. Fetchr has developed an on-demand delivery app that uses a customer's mobile phone as the postal address. The delivery company, which operates in Dubai, Bahrain, Saudi Arabia and Egypt, has raised $77 million in funding.

what3words assigns a unique series of three words to every 10 foot by 10-foot square of the earth's surface. It claims that this approach is far more accurate than a postal address and is much easier to remember than a set of coordinates. Aramex recently invested $3 million in what3words to help with its e-commerce deliveries in the Middle East, Africa and Asia. Sony, Daimler, IKEA's parent company and even Formula 1 racing driver Nico Rosberg are also investors.

In addition, Nairobi-based OkHi Ltd raised $1.78 million for its technology that creates an 'address' via a mobile app, using an amalgamation of the geographic location and a photograph of the customer's house. The company's founders say they have reduced e-commerce delivery times by as much as 50 per cent as a direct response of this technology.

## Summary

On-demand delivery and crowd-shipping are two innovations closely associated with the Fourth Industrial Revolution. Of the two, on-demand has been the most successful, with the model adopted primarily for the delivery of food. It has provided cafes and restaurants (as well as some retailers) with the ability to provide a home delivery service that previously was the preserve of only much larger competitors. However, political pressures may result in more restrictive regulation of this sector, particularly concerning the potential for large employers to exploit their workforce. As with zero-hour contracts, this will be a contentious point of debate.

In contrast, it is still to be seen whether crowd-shipping will be the game changer that many believed. In theory, the value that will be released by sharing previously underutilized transport assets should be huge. However, significant barriers will need to be overcome before the model can be more widely adopted.

# References

Dablanc, L, Morganti, E, Arvidsson, N, Woxenius, J, Browne, M and Saidi, N (2017) The rise of on-demand 'instant deliveries' in European cities, *Supply Chain Forum: An International Journal*, 18 (4), pp 203–17

Edison Trends (2020) US on-demand food delivery sales report, 19 May, https://trends.edison.tech/research/on-demand-food-delivery-sales-2020.html (archived at https://perma.cc/UXA3-CMH8)

GMB (2017) Hearing tomorrow on GMB Members unfair dismissal claim against Addison Lee, *GMB*, 24 January, www.gmblondon.org.uk/news/hearing-tomorrow-on-gmb-members-unfair-dismissal-claim-against-addison-lee (archived at https://perma.cc/32GE-JXQ5)

McKinnon, A (2016) *Crowdshipping: A communal approach to reducing urban traffic levels?* Kuehne Logistics University, Germany

O'Hear, S (2017) GeoPost acquires delivery startup Stuart, TechCrunch, https://techcrunch.com/2017/03/07/geopost-acquires-delivery-startup-stuart (archived at https://perma.cc/GB8D-Q6J9)

Roose, A (2016) From 0 to 1,000,000 to ?, Medium.com, 26 July, https://medium.com/@adrienroose/from-0-to-1-000-000-to-ecb4e2f863c7 (archived at https://perma.cc/8YCP-HB5P)

Technavio (2021) *Online On-Demand Home Services Market by Service and Geography – Forecast and Analysis 2021–25*, Technavio, London

Wallace, T (2017) Deliveroo offers workers pay per trip in bid to defuse self employment row, *Daily Telegraph*, 1 June, www.telegraph.co.uk/business/2017/05/31/deliveroo-offers-workers-pay-per-trip-in-bid-defuse-self-employment/ (archived at https://perma.cc/4YZW-VHZS)

Yellowsoft (2021) On-demand delivery in 2021: top trends and predictions, https://www.yelowsoft.com/blog/on-demand-delivery-predictions/ (archived at https://perma.cc/64PB-JBGW)

# 8

# Innovating to meet the challenge of urban distribution

**This chapter will familiarize the reader with:**

- The fast-paced growth of urban areas and the challenges this poses for supply chains and logistics companies

- The ways in which manufacturers and retailers are transforming their supply chain structures to meet the changing needs

- The importance of technology to logistics innovators

- A re-examination of the role that urban consolidation centres can play given regulators' imperative to ban diesel trucks in inner-city areas

- Imaginative ways in which existing underutilized infrastructure can be repurposed to enable smarter distribution

- The emergence of 'nano-retailing' and the opportunities this disruptive trend can have on logistics structures

## Megacity logistics – challenges of a transforming environment

The world's growing urban population presents significant logistics challenges that must be solved over the coming decades. In 2018, some 1.7 billion people lived in one of the 548 cities across the world with a population exceeding 1 million. Over the next decade or so, the number of cities of that scale will rise to 706 and home 28 per cent of all the people on earth. Megacities – those cities with more than 10 million inhabitants – require vast resources and innovative solutions to the challenges that emerge at such scale. Globally, the number of megacities is projected to rise from 33 in 2018 to 43 by 2030 (UN, 2018).

Many of the world's megacities are located in the 'global south', as is much of the population growth expected over the next decade. Of the 33 megacities in 2018, 27 were located in emerging regions, with 6 of these in China and 5 in India, including New Delhi with 26.5 million inhabitants and Mumbai, India's financial centre, with 21.4 million. Of the 10 new megacities expected by 2030, 9 are in emerging markets (UN, 2018). See Table 8.1.

While megacities create wealth, generate employment and drive human progress, the development trajectory is not always positive – urbanization is also responsible for creating climate change, inequality and exclusion.

This level of urbanization will have many implications in terms of health-care, living accommodation, consumerism and culture, as well as, of course, supply chains, logistics and transport. Each city will need to develop its own unique eco-system, which takes into account the movement of people, data, finance, energy, waste, goods and services. The efficient resolution of these challenges will be not only important for the efficient running of a city but will influence its positioning against other competing global locations.

TABLE 8.1  Fastest-growing megacities of the world

| Rank | Geography | City | Population | Growth (decade) |
|---|---|---|---|---|
| 1 | Pakistan | Karachi | 20,877,000 | 80.5% |
| 2 | China | Shenzhen | 12,506,000 | 56.1% |
| 3 | Nigeria | Lagos | 12,090,000 | 48.2% |
| 4 | China | Beijing | 18,241,000 | 47.6% |
| 5 | Thailand | Bangkok | 14,544,000 | 45.2% |
| 6 | Bangladesh | Dhaka | 14,399,000 | 45.2% |
| 7 | China | Guangzhou | 17,681,000 | 43.0% |
| 8 | China | Shanghai | 21,766,000 | 40.1% |
| 9 | India | Delhi | 22,826,000 | 39.2% |
| 10 | Indonesia | Jakarta | 26,746,000 | 25.3% |

SOURCE Demographia

A company's decision to locate in a city is not just based on internal markets but is also influenced by the robustness of the city's infrastructure and business compatibility.

Infrastructure investment may be part of the answer but it is certainly not the complete solution. In many cases, resources are constrained by space and consequently smarter ways of operating are required. This will inevitably involve better analysis of data to provide sense-and-respond decision making, not least related to traffic flows in and around the urban area.

The role of internet adoption and e-commerce in megacities will also be critical. There will be opportunities in cities where robust information and communications technology (ICT) infrastructure is in place to ensure that urban deliveries to consumers are carried out efficiently whether they are to homes, offices, lockers or other delivery points. By 2022, 1.35 billion consumers are expected to shop online in Brazil, Russia, China, India and South Africa alone – 61 per cent of the total global number (Wei, 2017). Purchasing online has the potential to create efficiencies that more traditional retailing lacks and this may eventually have an impact on city design. For example, car ownership may not become as widespread if the weekly trip to a hypermarket becomes redundant, impacting beneficially on congestion levels.

For consumer goods manufacturing companies to reach these new markets they will have to be able to supply an extremely high number of individual cities. According to Boston Consulting Group, in 2005, retailers and consumer goods manufacturers required distribution channels in 60 cities in China to reach 80 per cent of the country's population. However, in 2020, these companies had to be present in 212 cities to reach the same market (BCG, 2010). Upstream supply chains are also evolving. Megacities are creating their own economies of scale, which are increasingly being supplied by local or regional production facilities. Manufacturers, such as Unilever, have developed strategies that allow for more localized production with consumer goods customized to local tastes. For example, Unilever has invested $500 million in production and distribution facilities in Mexico (Mexico City) as well as $75 million in a factory in Colombia (Bogota).

In addition to this, intra-urban logistics challenges are complex and often evolve rapidly and with unpredictable consequences. Perhaps most significantly, no two cities are the same – indeed, nor are two neighbourhoods within a single city – demanding solutions that are not only context specific, but also flexible and adaptable to changes in demand. From high-rise commercial property in business districts to sprawling *favela* outside city limits; from high-income suburbs to poverty-stricken inner-city slums – each part of the city will need a separate logistics strategy in order to fulfil customer and end-user needs.

## Retail logistics trends in megacities

The retail sector provides many examples of trends currently emerging in megacity logistics provision. Across many of the world's emerging market megacities, retail is at various stages of an uneven process of formalization. Nanostores – small, family-owned outlets operated by fewer than five people located in a densely populated neighbourhood – are common. Estimates suggest more than 50 million nanostores globally, with the number on the rise as megacities grow. They are a valuable retail sector, too, accounting for half of the retail market in emerging economies (Blanco and Fransoo, 2013).

Many of the challenges related to distributing goods to nanostores are caused by the characteristics of emerging-market megacities. Urban population density is high and mobility is low, meaning products have to be moved to close proximity to consumers. Multiple small and independent retail locations make full-load distribution from centralized inventory holdings – common in developed markets for consumer goods – inappropriate and inoperable. This trend is discussed in more detail later in the chapter.

Last-mile networks in emerging-market megacities must also adapt to increased size and complexity as populations grow and demands shift. Evidence from China, where Alibaba and JD.com have built vast last-mile infrastructures in recent years, provides perhaps the best examples of the efficiency, flexibility and resilience required.

---

CASE STUDY 8.1
*JD's multi-tier urban logistics system*

The network of Chinese e-retailer JD.com provides evidence that multi-tier systems are emerging as a solution to urban distribution challenges. The retailer's owned fulfilment infrastructure is made up of strategically located warehouses and delivery and pickup stations. By the end of 2018, it consisted of:

- regional fulfilment centres in seven cities
- front distribution centres in 28 cities
- other additional warehouses in another 46 cities

Together, there are a total of 550 warehouses with an aggregate gross floor space of approximately 12 million square metres in 81 cities.

The network supports JD.com's '211' programme, introduced in 2010. It provides a range of same-day and next-day delivery options within China's megacities and across the country. The programme does not apply to all products or cover deliveries made through third parties or products shipped directly from third-party sellers. It does, however, offer two-hour delivery for an extra charge, provided the recipient is in a city supported by a regional distribution centre. JD also provides consumers in major cities same-day delivery of high-end luxury goods using high-speed intercity trains. The key behind the system is inventory velocity, consumer demand and delivery density – where all three are high enough, the service levels are offered, however, a lower tier of service options are in place for the remaining goods.

Retail markets in megacities are rapidly evolving and the emerging markets they call home must design, build and adapt the infrastructure that supports that growth at the same pace. The growing consumer demand for e-commerce deliveries in urban areas will result in a corresponding demand for warehouses that can serve local areas in a short timescale. This means that space needs to be made available in urban areas for distribution facilities, a requirement that is often at odds with planning policy, which tends to favour residential or office buildings.

Logistics providers must also step up to establish the networks that will support and enhance growth now and in the future. There is no doubt that pressure on retail space will increase, meaning that multiple, same-day deliveries to retailers will become more frequent, as storage facilities on site will be limited. Tiny batch quantities will become usual and product sizes will also shrink. Likewise, packaging will become minimal and recycling operations must become highly efficient.

## Will technology be the solution to urban challenges?

In many cities in the emerging world, technology, such as it exists, is highly undeveloped. Where technology is used, many small companies rely on spreadsheets rather than dedicated warehouse or transport management systems. There is also a lack of connectivity or harmonization between systems owned by forwarders, carriers and governments. One of the many issues faced in emerging market cities is the inefficiency of the commercial and regulatory processes such as the requirement to print physical documentation (permits and delivery notes, for example).

The smaller the company the lower the utilization of technology. As the market tends to be so fragmented, this is very limiting as regards to the development of the industry as a whole. The fragmentation also means that the economies of scale do not exist to buy tech or automation systems.

As regards warehousing, it is unlikely that levels of automation will increase in the short term. Capital investment in robotic systems, for example, may make commercial sense in markets where labour costs are high, but cheap labour in emerging markets means that it does not make sense for companies to replace employees with capital goods.

This is not to say that technology does not have a role to play in addressing many of the challenges faced by logistics and supply chains in megacities, in fact quite the opposite. Where cities have facilitated, encouraged and invested in technologies such as mobile communications or broadband, innovators have been allowed to develop solutions to help overcome the paucity of infrastructure and the shortcomings of the traditional logistics market.

In Bogota, Colombia, for instance, a number of on-demand platforms (such as Liftit) have been developed that connect the fragmented last-mile delivery market with retailers. Couriers that have access to smartphones can be easily integrated into online communities, allowing them to access loads, provide GPS information and provide proof of delivery. In Africa, M-Pesa, a mobile-phone-based money transfer, financing and microfinancing service has been around for over a decade. This service took advantage of the lack of financial and ICT infrastructure in the country to provide an innovative new way for customers to pay for goods.

However, not all digitalization innovations will make the market more efficient. Lower transport costs could actually stimulate freight output growth, impacting on the ability to meet emission reduction targets.

Advances in technology hold out some hope to overcome the high levels of pollution that can be found in megacities through the adoption of alternative fuels such as biofuels and electric vehicles. However, presently electric vehicles are not yet sufficiently developed to provide a practical alternative to diesel engines and it may be at least 10 years (probably longer) before electric vehicles are able to replace diesel trucks in any great quantities. There is not only the issue of the technological development required for batteries, but also (perhaps most importantly) the impact that a large-scale migration from combustion engine power to the use of grid energy would have on national power generation and distribution strategies. In many megacities, electricity grids often struggle to provide the power required for existing use without the enormous additional demand of new electric trucks and, of course, cars.

---

Best-case outlook for logistics in megacities

- Megacities invest in transport and technology infrastructure, keeping pace with population and business growth.
- Dense markets of relatively wealthy consumers attract manufacturers and retailers, resulting in a boom for logistics providers.
- Higher wages, good working conditions and good training lead to high-quality logistics services.
- Third-party logistics (3PLs) develop specialist 'city' logistics services as regulation by city planners reduces access to busy centres.
- Major out-of-town distribution centres are developed to serve ever-increasing urban areas.
- Recycling and waste management logistics is efficient, leading to minimum impact on environment.
- More people working from home encourage greater levels of e-retailing, and locker solutions become the norm for residents at work during the day.
- Alternative fuels are quickly adopted, leading to less pollution. Renewable energy networks expand to meet these needs.

Worst-case outlook for logistics in megacities

- Delivering goods into megacities becomes difficult with high levels of congestion.
- Supply chain efficiencies are affected, as inventory holdings have to be increased in order to meet service levels in inner-city areas.
- Impoverished populations and bankrupt administrations result in no investment in infrastructure.
- High degree of regulation prevents foreign investment.

- With poor levels of security, logistics companies struggle to deliver to certain regions; theft is endemic from trucks and warehouses.

- Technology networks are weak, constraining the implementation of supply chain management and execution software.

- Recycling and waste management is non-existent leading to high levels of environmental impact.

- Poor salaries and working conditions leads to societal impact and poor-quality services.

- Falling volumes make transportation utilization inefficient.


## 'Nanostores': retail supply chain challenges and opportunities in developing markets

Rather than being marginalized by modern supermarket or hypermarket formats, in the developing world traditional retailing or 'nanostores' are flourishing. This provides huge supply chain and logistics challenges to the manufacturers who want to reach this fragmented and largely urban market.

In a large part of the developing world, consumers' shopping needs are not met by e-commerce giants or indeed by superstores, but by what have been termed 'traditional' retailers or 'nanostores', usually defined as small, family-owned enterprises located in densely populated neighbourhoods. In some cases a nanostore may even consist of a handcart rather than retail premises.

It might be thought that, as in the West, 'mom-and-pop' stores would be declining. However, this is not the case. The estimated 50 million nanostores are on the increase, fuelled by the development of megacities, occurring as a result of large numbers of people migrating from rural areas in search of better prospects. It has been estimated that in many developing countries nanostores account for half of the retail market. As one consulting company stated, 'Globally, the trade channel mix is becoming more fragmented as consumers shift towards smaller store formats' (Nielsen, 2015).

Although many consumer goods companies recognize the opportunity that distributing their goods through these channels offers, dealing with a hugely fragmented and technologically undeveloped customer base has many challenges. These nanostores are not just 'small supermarkets' – they have a completely different set of needs and characteristics, as will be examined in this chapter.

## Nanostores: disrupting retail structures

Why are nanostores so important to the future supply chain and logistics strategies of the world's largest manufacturers? As mentioned above, the answer lies in the development in importance of megacities to the global economy. Serving nanostores in these megacities will become critical to the success of consumer goods manufacturers. For instance, in Bogota, Colombia, 47,000 nanostores serve 10 million consumers; in Beijing, China, 60,000 nanostores serve 20 million consumers. In China as a whole 6.8 million nanostores generate 1 trillion renminbi (RMB) a year, while in India and Sub-Saharan Africa more than 90 per cent of retail sales are generated through this format. Even in more mature parts of the developing world (such as East Asia) they account for more than 40 per cent of sales (Ge, 2017).

In terms of size, the aggregated revenues of these nanostores would make them among the largest customers for consumer packaged goods (CPG) manufacturers. However, it is not only their scale that makes them important. The fragmented nature of the market means that manufacturers can make more money from smaller customers than they can from supermarkets or hypermarkets whose scale enables them to squeeze suppliers' margins. One estimate suggests that penetrating the nanostore market could enable CPG companies to increase sales by 5–15 per cent and increase profit by 10–20 per cent (Diaz et al, 2012).

Another positive trend has been an increase in the disposable income of people living in megacities, which has brought many goods – particularly personal care products – within reach of more people. This fact has long been identified by a few of the major CPG companies, although others are still scrambling to catch up:

- Coca-Cola: 1.2 million points of sale in Mexico and serves 1.3 million nanostores in China
- Unilever: delivers ice cream to 10,000 freezers in nanostores in Mexico City
- Danone: serves 40,000 nanostores in Beijing
- Unilever: serves 1.5 million nanostores directly in India
- Grupo Bimbo (bakery): serves 7 million points of sale across Latin America

Many of the challenges related to distributing goods to nanostores are caused by the characteristics of emerging-market megacities and not least their high urban population density. While cities in Europe and North

America typically have a density of 2,000 to 5,000 people per square kilometre, the average in the developing world can be many times higher.

The low incomes of the people living in megacities means that the proportion of people owning a car is also low. This means that stores need to be in close proximity to high population centres. This has been a major inhibitor to the growth of supermarket and hypermarket models, which rely heavily on the consumer being able to transport goods from the store by car.

Megacities often have the characteristic of areas of poverty juxtaposed to areas of relative wealth. In Bogota, Colombia, for example, areas with an average pay of $100 per month and with one store per 150 population, can be located next to areas with an average pay of $1,000 per month and with one store per 250 people. This makes distribution strategies highly challenging (Blanco et al, 2013).

## What are the supply chain challenges?

If consumer goods manufacturers are to serve this fragmented customer base, they will need to adopt a very different logistics strategy to that employed in the developed world. Manufacturers in Europe and North America are used to supplying full truck loads to centralized retail distribution facilities, which in turn dispatch full truck loads to large retail premises. This is the complete opposite of the supply chain structures required to serve thousands of nanostores, and the added complexity of this has led many manufacturers to supply such markets through wholesalers. However, such an approach means that the manufacturer loses its direct relationship with retailers, and risks losing an understanding of the market and even the competition for very limited shelf space.

This direct relationship is critical to serving nanostores. In many markets, representatives are employed by manufacturers to undertake 'pre-sales' and 'on-board' van sales activities. Pre-sales involves a sales representative travelling to each store to assess needs and collect orders, which are then fulfilled at a later stage (possibly next day) by a delivery van. 'On-board' or 'van-sales' combines the pre-sales and fulfilment at the same time. Both approaches ensure shelf space for manufacturers' products but also involve promotion, order processing, restocking, after-sales support and collection of payments.

The appropriateness of each approach depends on many logistics considerations. One study, looking at the distribution of orange juice to nanostores in Casablanca, found that the pre-sales method was more effective but relied on factors such as the distance between stores, the number of stores visited, the travelling time, the collected orders and time spent in the store. Congestion was a key variable, as was the difficulty in finding a parking bay (Boulaksil, 2017).

## SIZE OF STORE

An obvious logistics challenge is the size of the nanostores. Many are no more than 15 square metres in size (perhaps a converted garage) or indeed could be a street cart. Due to the size of premises and the fact that they have very low levels of cash to buy products (buying in bulk is out of the question) they rely on very frequent deliveries. This has an impact on the drop frequencies of carriers, which resemble more a parcels distribution model than modern retail logistics in the developed world: a carrier delivering to nanostores often has more than 150 drops per day.

## CASH ECONOMIES

The majority of nanostores lack financial and communications technology (with the exception of mobile phones), which means that most transactions are either cash or credit. The reliance on cash is also due to the fact that many of these entities do not formally exist, in order to avoid tax and regulations. This creates problems in terms of the return of cash on delivery payments up the supply chain.

Informal credit facilities exist both supplied by the nanostore to regular customers who they know well (most stores have a small number of customers and so understand the risk of advancing credit) but also by suppliers to the nanostore. Although goods are often supplied on a cash on delivery basis, the proprietor may not be able to pay the supplier until the goods are actually sold and so there may be multiple trips made before the money can be collected – adding significantly to logistics costs. The movement of cash has obvious security issues, especially given the urban areas in which many of these stores are located.

## LAST-MILE DELIVERY

Although car ownership levels may be low in many cities, weak transport infrastructure and a lack of planning has meant that congestion levels are high. Streets are often narrow and/or steep, which means access for lorries is difficult.

While in developed markets deliveries of full truck loads to large stores are the most frequent type of distribution, in developing markets there may be three, four or more handoffs of products to ever smaller and less formal warehousing and transport companies. Final delivery may be made, for example, to the nanostore by a courier on a tricycle.

One of the key problems faced by delivery drivers is parking. This is caused by the limited availability of parking space as well as the problem of cars parking in dedicated loading/unloading bays. This means that unnecessary time is wasted by van drivers for each drop, causing lower productivity. It has been shown that when city administrations enforce the proper use of parking spaces, productivity increases and van emissions (caused by vehicles circling trying to find an unloading bay) decrease. In some cities new apps have been developed to show available parking bays.

## New retailer strategies in China

Both of China's e-retail giants, Alibaba and JD.com, have looked to leverage the attributes of nanostores in order to fulfil the next stage of their corporate strategy: online to offline (O2O).

Alibaba has targeted the local market through its 'Ling Shou Tong' or 'retail integrated' programme. The scheme not only provides stores with basic products, fresh and packaged foods and cigarettes as well as a makeover, but it also integrates them within Alibaba's technology platform. This provides analytics and automation that previously had only been available to modern retailers:

- When ordering via the Ling Shou Tong app, the proprietor receives suggestions based on sales of the most popular items.

- Orders are consolidated, so stores need only place one order rather than deal with multiple suppliers.

- Orders for fast-moving goods are dispatched from local warehouses on a next-day basis while slower-moving goods are dispatched on a guaranteed two-day service from regional warehouses.

The programme also provides benefits to CPG companies. The data that is generated and shared by Alibaba gives them more visibility of consumer demand and can allow them to tailor specific products for a market. For instance, the international food company Mondelez has used this within its Oreo range of snacks. The relationship allows nanostores to focus on one of their core competitive advantages – hyper-localism – by providing them with even more insight into their customers' buying behaviours.

For larger stores, there is the option to become a Tmall corner store, which provides them with higher levels of integration, product selection, a point-of-sales system, LED signage and in-store digital advertising. Alibaba and the nanostores can also use this partnership to offer other services such as mobile phone data top-ups (Alizila, 2018).

Rival retailer JD.com has followed a slightly different strategy. Alongside its 'retail-as-a-service' solution (similar to Alibaba's above) it has created a nanostore franchise network, which according to management is expanding at the colossal rate of 1,000 stores per week with a target figure of 1,000 stores per day. The plan is to open 1 million stores by 2023, owned and operated by private individuals who have the opportunity to receive a loan from the company to help with the set-up costs (Norris, 2019). As well as urban areas, the retailer is looking to push its reach into the undeveloped and underserviced rural locations. Although stocking mostly JD.com products, franchises also have the opportunity to stock items from other retailers. However, there are signs that this aggressive expansion plan has hit problems and that the rollout is well behind schedule. Part of the reason for this is that the company has struggled to convince store owners to ditch existing supplier relationships in favour of JD.com's range, especially in cities or regions where the retailer has low brand awareness.

Other innovative tools and solutions are being developed right across the developing world focused on this growing sector. These include:

- New technology platforms that have the potential to harness the combined power of thousands of nanostores. BeeQuick in Beijing creates a virtual network of nanostores that enables buyers to order consumer goods and have them delivered to their homes.
- Go Jek – an 'Uber' for motorcycles in Indonesia – works with 400,000 drivers. As well as carrying passengers on pillions, it also allows nanostores to operate a home delivery service in Jakarta.
- Colmapp in Dominican Republic. Bakery product manufacturer Grupo Bimbo equips nanostores with devices so they can take card payments using government cards.

Nanostores have grown in popularity due to their proximity to large, growing and densely packed populations within megacities. They are able to reach consumers much more effectively than formal, modern retail distribution channels and they represent a route to market that cannot be ignored by the large consumer goods manufacturers.

However, this does not mean that their future is ensured. The development of smartphone technology will allow increasingly well-off consumers (at least in relative terms) access to new platforms that will allow them even great opportunities to access a wider range of products than can be offered by nanostores.

Rather than develop large supermarket or hypermarket models in these areas, larger retailers may well be better advised to 'leapfrog' this stage of retail development and build on-demand delivery networks. After all, if consumers demand proximity, nothing is closer than access to products via the smartphone in their pocket.

## Reinventing urban consolidation centres

As already indicated, cities throughout the world, in both developed and emerging economies, are experiencing rapid increases in their populations and this trend is causing major congestion issues for the movement of freight into and around large conurbations, as well as creating unacceptably high emissions. The situation has been exacerbated by consumers' increased dependence on e-retail sales, which has led to the disaggregation of consolidated store-destined truckload deliveries into millions of individual items despatched to households on a daily basis.

Many cities have already implemented strategies to address congestion and reduce tailpipe emissions. Initiatives include:

- the introduction of congestion charges (e.g. in London)
- restrictions on access times and zones in which delivery vehicles can make deliveries
- limiting access of different vehicles to specific days, for example by numberplate (e.g. in Mexico City and Beijing)
- regular road closures (e.g. in Bogota)
- imposing car free days/zones (e.g. in Paris)

Logistics operators have been forced to absorb many of the resulting costs, both direct and indirect. However, in the near future it is likely that many authorities will ban diesel-powered vehicles from city centres completely. In fact, such bans could lead to an explosion of smaller electric vehicles, especially vans, trikes and bikes, which could increase congestion, not improve it. Electric vans and medium-weight goods trucks can only handle a fraction of the goods previously distributed by their diesel counterparts, and a greater number are required just to keep pace with current volumes. In addition to this, the demand for 'on-demand' delivery options in cities is also increasing. According to fulfilment provider Metapak, more than half (54 per cent) of respondents in its 'State of e-Commerce Delivery Report' stated that they would like this delivery option to be provided by the e-retailers that they use (Metapak, 2020).

These supply- and demand-side trends will create an imperative to develop smarter, more innovative ways of distributing goods rather than just tinkering with existing supply chain structures. Overcoming the many challenges of city logistics is a priority for logistics companies – particularly last-mile providers – as well as for retailers and e-retailers. Solutions, though, will require a detailed operational understanding of the specific problems, including the needs of the various clients, customers and communities.

One approach to addressing these issues is through the development of urban consolidation centres (UCCs). There is nothing particularly new about the concept – it has been employed over the years with varying levels of success. However, it is worthwhile re-examining the impact that introducing a UCC into an urban logistics framework will have, not least because municipal authorities remain enthusiastic about the idea as a way of addressing many of the external impacts of transport being caused by new e-retailing structures.

Benefits of using UCCs:

- costs for last-mile delivery are high
- travel speeds are low
- unloading is time-consuming
- truck capacity is underutilized
- local regulations may be restrictive

UCCs can also provide:

- temporary storage
- waste collection
- specialized value services (such as pallet splitting or placing garments on hangers)

External regulations encouraging use of UCCs include:

- road pricing

- licensing and regulation
- parking restrictions

Disadvantages are:

- cost and time element of the additional transhipment
- lack of value add from all parties' perspectives
- volumes needed to reach break-even
- lack of permanent subsidies
- carriers see UCCs as a competitor

Although there have been a number of notable success cases, including Heathrow Airport in London, Cabot Circus Shopping Centre in Bristol and Padova Cityporto in Italy, there are many examples of consolidation centres failing to deliver the benefits expected – the additional transhipment element can impact profitability or prohibit competition if, for example, retailers are forced to use a specific facility. The approach may also not necessarily meet the needs of all city-based businesses. Restaurants, which stress the use of fresh, local goods, for example, can be highly resistant to the consolidation centre model, which adds time to deliveries. Given the costs involved, it is perhaps understandable that many potential UCC solutions have achieved 'proof of concept' stage but failed to gain widespread traction.

## A smarter approach to urban distribution

One result of the complexity of city logistics has been to push the responsibility for innovation onto logistics and last-mile providers, handing them the challenge of creating a viable business operation in the face of fixed infrastructure and evolving regulatory and business-case challenges. Working in such confined spaces, these companies often find the best solutions in smarter practices that make better use of assets.

Solutions that make use of existing infrastructure provide one avenue for exploration – multistorey warehousing, for instance (discussed below) or XPO's plans at Chapelle International to transport cargo directly into Paris using rail as well as vans are examples of how underutilized infrastructure can be leveraged.

## Multi-user buildings

One potentially attractive distribution model presently being examined is the development of a network of out-of-town consolidation centres feeding centrally located 'multi-user' buildings in an inner-urban area. These buildings may comprise of a mix of logistics facilities on the ground floor and residential or office space above.

Due to the strict planning regulations in many cities and demand for space, with residential normally taking priority, networks of small logistics centres could be accommodated as part of 'multi-use' buildings. These would comprise significantly smaller footprints than traditional DCs with the warehousing element being on the ground floor (around 5,000 square feet) and residential, offices or student accommodation being on the upper floor(s). It may be appropriate to have a buffer floor between these different occupiers, which could house either a gym, a restaurant or another business.

These would be designed to serve the residents of the building itself (acting as an e-commerce collection point – adding value for any residential developers), as well as serving the residents and businesses within the immediate geographic area, and would be suitable for both e-commerce and store-based replenishment. This concept already works between retail and residential premises and the argument is strong to extend the principle to the logistics/express world.

The types of companies that would benefit from this kind of facility include:

- Retailers – wanting to maximize 'shop floor' space and have stock replenished two or three times per day.
- High-end fashion retailers – only stocking minimum goods, largely for display, and having goods purchased from their 'showrooms' and being replenished within a one- or two-hour window or delivered directly to the consumer's home/office.
- Parcel companies – developing a network of delivery and collection points, largely serving e-commerce, possibly also providing collection points and perhaps changing rooms for immediate returns should the items not be suitable.
- Those e-commerce companies providing on-demand delivery, utilizing numerous 'forward staging points' in city centres.

To justify the cost, some element of value-add, such as a repairs service or fitting room, may be required, turning the facilities from pure stock replenishment/e-commerce centres to more interactive collection points. Loading and unloading times would need to be agreed between residents and local authorities. There would be a need for dedicated off-road parking – for both staff as well as delivery vans while they are not in use.

The last-mile element will also require the provision of sufficient electric vehicle charging infrastructure as many such facilities may be within 'ultra low emissions' zones. This will involve investment by the property owner as well as energy distribution companies and rollout of smart charging software.

For 'multi-use' facilities to work, there would have to be a clause built into any planning application stating that a developer of an apartment block or office complex must allocate space on the ground floor to act as a logistics hub. This would allow local boroughs to continue with their plans to develop more residential facilities; landlords the opportunity to maximize the value of the land; and retailers, e-commerce companies and logistics operators to serve the cities more effectively.

A number of last-mile operators, as well as luxury goods retailers, are already exploring the potential of this 'multi-use' concept with one global express company believed to be developing their future European city strategy around buildings similar in design to those outlined above.

## Summary

The prospects for urban distribution are mixed. Some cities may evolve to resemble Singapore, with high levels of organization, strong investment in ICT and transport infrastructure, and models of economic success. Others may develop into cities such as Kinshasa, with relative high levels of wealth juxtaposed with endemic poverty, poor infrastructure, crime and corruption.

Inefficiency, bottlenecks and the inability of exporters to reach global markets is a considerable barrier to economic development for most. Weak infrastructure and governance are also holding back the development of the e-commerce market.

However, this characterization masks a 'grass roots' revolution that is starting to transform many urban transport and logistics markets. E-commerce demands are changing customer expectations and hence there has been a drive by logistics companies to improve their levels of service.

Disrupting the traditional express parcels market, a number of Uber-like e-platform providers are also developing. These include Loggi in Brazil, Transfast in Mexico and Tappsi Envios in Bogota, providing on-demand last-mile services. Other improvements are ongoing, such as developing comprehensive zipcode systems.

Governments have a crucial role to play in the development of the necessary transport and logistics infrastructure required to facilitate economic growth and links to global markets. This also extends to reforming domestic and international trade regulations, which encourages local, as well as foreign, investment. As regards to zero emissions zones, the regulatory environment created by municipal authorities will fundamentally influence supply chain structures. Banning diesel trucks on its own will stifle economic growth unless innovative and imaginative solutions are found to release supply chain efficiencies. This will involve creative land use policies, allowing retailers, manufacturers and logistics companies the opportunity to develop new models of distribution taking into account local market characteristics.

# References

Alizila (2018) A dose of new retail for China's convenience stores, 3 January, www.alizila.com/alibaba-gives-dose-new-retail-china-convenience-stores/ (archived at https://perma.cc/8T95-XZAQ)

BCG (2010) Winning in emerging market cities, Boston Consulting Group, New York

Blanco, E E and Fransoo, J C (2013) Reaching 50 million nanostores: retail distribution in emerging megacities, BETA publicatie: working papers, 404, Eindhoven: Technische Universiteit Eindhoven

Boulaksil, Y (2017) Serving nanostores by van-sales or pre-sales? Jan C Fransoo, 12 October, www.janfransoo.com/2017/10/12/serving-nanostores-by-van-sales-or-pre-sales/ (archived at https://perma.cc/Z4SY-7B5P)

Boulaksil, Y (2017) Distribution Strategies Toward Nanostores in Emerging Markets: The Valencia Case, Interfaces 2017, vol. 47, issue 6, 505–517

Diaz, A, Magni, M and Poh, F (2012) From oxcart to Walmart: four keys to reaching emerging-market consumers, McKinsey, 1 October, www.mckinsey.com/industries/retail/our-insights/from-oxcart-to-wal-mart-four-keys-to-reaching-emerging-market-consumers (archived at https://perma.cc/KHG3-ESMX)

Ge, J (2017) *Traditional Retail Distribution in Megacities*, Technische Universiteit Eindhoven, Netherlands

Metapak (2020) Ecommerce Delivery Benchmark Report, https://info.metapack. com/Ecommerce-Delivery-Benchmark-2020.html (archived at https://perma. cc/4ERP-LKUZ)

Nielsen (2015) The future of grocery, www.nielsen.com/wp-content/uploads/ sites/3/2019/04/nielsen-global-e-commerce-new-retail-report-april-2015.pdf (archived at https://perma.cc/JY7M-6QX2)

Norris, M (2019) Why JD is tripping up in new retail race, Technode, 11 March, www.technode.com/2019/03/11/why-jd-is-tripping-up-in-new-retail-race/ (archived at https://perma.cc/95PP-DCTA)

UN (2018) *The World's Cities in 2018*, United Nations, Geneva

Wei, H (2017) E-commerce pulls BRICS closer, China Daily, 31 August, https:// www.chinadaily.com.cn/business/2017-08/31/content_31351347.htm (archived at https://perma.cc/4249-6QJE)

# 9

# The disruptive power of e-retailing

**This chapter will familiarize the reader with:**

- The transformation of the retail sector over the past two decades and, with it, logistics and last-mile delivery operations

- The 'Amazonization' of customer expectations and the resulting compression of supply chains

- The challenges facing retailers, logistics and express parcels companies in adopting this new business model including returns, city deliveries, payments and customs procedures

- The development of the 'gig economy' and the flexibility that this has brought in matching peak and troughs of demand as well as impending government regulations

- The growth of cross-border e-retail and the challenges and opportunities that this will create

## The e-commerce phenomenon

Retailing, and the logistics and supply chain industry that supports it, has been transformed over the past two decades by the emergence of the e-commerce phenomenon. Well-known retailers, such as Woolworths, Toys 'R' Us, Sears and K-Mart, to mention just a few, have faced restructuring or even bankruptcy, unable to compete in a market that has come to be dominated by the likes of Amazon.com, Alibaba and eBay. These companies have brought a new business model to the retailing industry – stores open 24/7 via a consumer's laptop or mobile device; the ability to compare products and prices; prompt, low-cost delivery to the consumer's door, or in some cases even, to the consumer's fridge.

The changing retail environment has led to a root-and-branch restructuring of the associated logistics and transport sector. Those companies that have been agile enough to embrace the new distribution channels with a host of new services have prospered. Not least amongst these have been the parcels companies responsible for last-mile B2C deliveries. This trend has also created a welcome new revenue stream for the post offices previously struggling to come to terms with the inexorable decline of mail volumes.

The express parcels industry has undergone a major transformation over this period. At the outset, it was far from certain that many of the major express players, such as UPS, FedEx or DHL, would embrace home delivery due to the high costs involved in the number of undelivered parcels caused by 'not-at-home' end recipients. Today, B2C is an important part of the major players' thinking and revenues.

Looking to the future, delivery times are getting ever faster, with the number of same-day and one- or two-hour delivery services rising. This is having a knock-on effect on customer expectations. End recipients are also demanding greater flexibility as well as more delivery options, fitting in around their lifestyles rather than around the operational demands of parcel delivery companies. Technology is helping to bridge this gap, leading to higher levels of customer service combined with fewer failed deliveries.

Alternative delivery solutions are also being developed. Lockers, in-car, or pick up/drop off networks are growing in popularity and omnichannel retailers have placed emphasis on click-and-collect offerings, which are not only convenient for customers but prove a useful source of revenue for retailers. Many logistics providers have tailored value-added solutions for transport, fulfilment and returns. They are also playing a role in many retailers' strategies as they support the expansion of services into new international markets.

One of the greatest areas of opportunity is expected to be in the cross-border segment of the market, which is growing much faster than domestic volumes albeit from a smaller starting point. Of all markets, the Asia Pacific region is leading the way, in large part due to China, which is set to become the largest e-commerce cross-border market for both imports and exports. Rising incomes and an expanding middle class are driving China's e-commerce growth. At the same time the scope of cross-border e-commerce is also expanding. Fashion and electronics have long been cross-border top sellers, but consumers are now branching out further. Presently underserved product categories include beauty and cosmetics, pet care, food and beverage, and sporting goods.

E-commerce has the potential to link SMEs throughout the world with global markets, facilitated by the major digital e-retailing platforms. This can bring major economic benefits for those who are able to embrace the opportunity. However, as this chapter will discuss, there are many logistical challenges that will have to be overcome if the opportunities are to be spread evenly throughout the world. Failure to address these could result in the global economy becoming further split into the digital haves and have nots.

E-retailers require distribution systems that are often more complex than traditional ones. Besides the need to manage an increasing number of suppliers and varying inventory, the management of multiple delivery options, such as home delivery, in-store pickup, lockbox or elsewhere, also becomes more difficult. Convenience and prompt delivery is expected as well as flexibility. The increasing demand for such delivery services has put a strain on parcel delivery companies and has led, not least, to the greater use of self-employed drivers (the so-called 'gig-economy'). It has also created more congestion as a result of higher levels of last-mile activity as volumes of delivery vans increase, especially problematic in urban areas, adding to carbon emissions and levels of other pollutants.

## E-commerce impact on traditional retail supply chains

### Changing consumer behaviour

During the Covid-19 crisis there was an acceleration in the trend towards home shopping as people were told to 'stay at home'. It now seems that this has now become what is termed 'engrained behaviour' as new demographics of society, such as older shoppers, have adopted e-retail. There have also been other changes in consumer behaviour (see Figure 9.1) including:

- reduced seasonality in consumer sectors such as 'fast fashion'
- impulse buying, based on celebrity endorsement and blogging
- the compression of consumer electronics life cycles

FIGURE 9.1 Implications of changing consumer behaviour on logistics

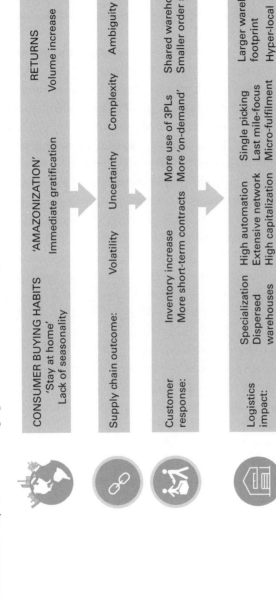

Consumers have also become conditioned to expect super-fast delivery of their orders – the so-called 'Amazonization' of consumer expectations. This is resulting in the growth of more same-day or even 'on-demand' deliveries. The adoption of e-retail has also caused the exponential growth in the volume of returns, creating its own challenges as well as opportunities for third-party logistics (3PLs) and parcels operators. Merchants who are not able to offer their customers these very high levels of return service, flexibility, visibility and refunds, will rapidly lose market share, as will be discussed later in this chapter.

What is the result of these trends? They have created an environment characterized by volatility, uncertainty, complexity and ambiguity (VUCA). Not only has this made operations challenging but it has made forecasting even more difficult. The more elements there are in a supply chain, the more 'things' and parties connected together, the worse the effect of the inventory bull whip. In this respect Covid-19 has brutally exposed the weaknesses not only of e-commerce supply chains but global supply chains as a whole.

In their response to this very challenging environment, manufacturers and retailers have consequently increased the amount of inventory that they have on hand in order to maintain production schedules. Because they are less sure about long-term demand, there is an increasing willingness to use 3PLs due to the flexibility that this provides. Along with this, contract life has become shorter; customers are more likely to use shared warehousing; and there has been a growth in 'on-demand' warehousing – although this is still very niche. There has also been the trend towards smaller orders and hence smaller shipment sizes as retailers and manufacturers ship to a much more fragmented customer base. This is having a profound effect on logistics as it requires far more specialized operations and high degrees of automation in order to deal with the increase in picking. In the short term, warehouses will have larger footprints to cater for more picking stations and crossdocking, although eventually, if and when facilities become fully automated, 'dark warehouses' will become dense cubes of materials handling equipment, exclusively dedicated to robotic pickers.

It is also likely that logistics facilities will become far more dispersed and closer to the end recipient in order to enable very short delivery times. Instead of distribution to large stores there will be a focus on last mile, and this will include 'micro-fulfilment' centres based in urban areas. These will also include a level of automation, which will mean that the whole distribution network will have to be highly capitalized.

## Impact on inventory holdings

For many decades the importance of inventory and supply chain management to the retail sector has been well understood, not least due to the often fast-moving nature of the goods sold and the thousands of different product lines involved. Retailers require a high inventory turnover to prevent stock becoming obsolete as foods perish or clothes go out of fashion when the seasons change. Even if stock is not wholly redundant, it is often sold at a reduced price, further squeezing margins. Generations of supply chain managers have been tasked with driving down inventory levels to the bare minimum while balancing the need for stock to be available to purchase by consumers.

This was difficult enough even using traditional retail distribution channels (Figure 9.2), not least due to inaccurate forecasts and the silo-mentality of retailers, wholesalers and manufacturers, which led to adversarial supply chain relationships.

However, the aggressive expansion models of the major e-retailers have transformed customer expectation and behaviour, leading to a root-and-branch transformation of the inventory strategies of the traditional retailers (Figure 9.3). To some degree, the low inventory mantra is being challenged in favour of an 'inventory availability at all costs' approach. Amazon has been a driving force behind this change of strategy. Its Amazon Prime offering, which in the United States and elsewhere offers free next-day shipping, has proved to be a game changer.

FIGURE 9.2 Traditional retail supply chains

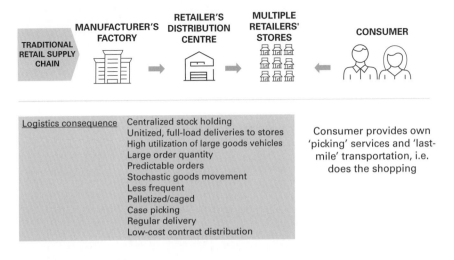

| Logistics consequence | Centralized stock holding<br>Unitized, full-load deliveries to stores<br>High utilization of large goods vehicles<br>Large order quantity<br>Predictable orders<br>Stochastic goods movement<br>Less frequent<br>Palletized/caged<br>Case picking<br>Regular delivery<br>Low-cost contract distribution | Consumer provides own 'picking' services and 'last-mile' transportation, i.e. does the shopping |

FIGURE 9.3 Supply chains following e-retail disruption

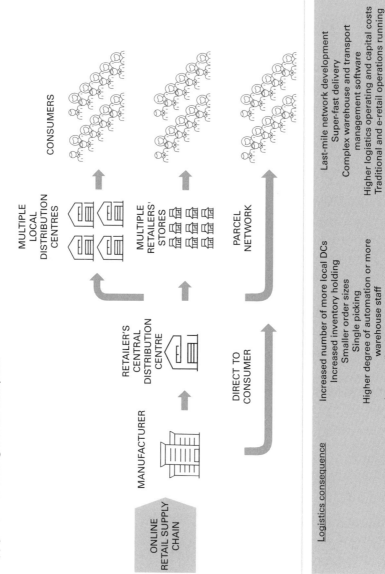

How should the retail industry respond to this need for near 'on-demand' product availability? Some, like Walmart, have used their massive resources to increase their own online presence and adopt strategies (which in Walmart's case it calls 'inventory mirroring') that seek to mitigate the impact of inevitable inventory increases by using smart algorithms and technology. For others, such as US retailer Sears, competing on cost and availability is not an option and the retailer has disappeared into inevitable bankruptcy, following a host of others.

Some retailers are leveraging their bricks-and-mortar retail networks to compete. Inditex, for example, which owns the majority of its stores, is using technology to provide complete visibility of stock both in stores and in warehouses. This means that each store can become a fulfilment centre, leading to greater inventory velocity.

Of course, there are some retailers bucking this trend, and doing so successfully. 'Hard discounters' such as Aldi have limited amount of product lines available, but their simple logistics and supply chain processes are able to provide customers with value for money, and they have carved out a niche, albeit a large one.

---

## CHANGING INVENTORY STRATEGIES IN THE UNITED STATES: AMAZON VS WALMART

### Amazon

Amazon's inventory management strategy can be characterized by the term 'inventory availability', which is repeatedly used in its annual reports, whether referring to its own e-retail operations or its US grocery operation, Whole Foods. This is not only influencing the stock levels it keeps at its own distribution centres, but its power in the market is evidenced by the fact that it is having a major impact on the strategies of its key competitors. 'Availability' is partly achieved by higher levels of inventory but it also requires that stock is located in facilities close to the customer, which has also led to increased costs related to its fulfilment network. Although inventory levels are rising, management see this as a key competitive tool that is helping the company capture market share.

Walmart

Giant US retailer Walmart reported that there had been a significant rise in inventory levels after several years on a downward trajectory. This has been driven by the adoption of its so-called 'inventory mirroring' strategy. This refers to the positioning of inventory and logistics facilities in order to compress delivery times and reduce supply chain costs. The model takes into account sales velocity, weight and product type to reduce shipping costs. Higher-velocity items are 'mirrored' at many more distribution centres than low-velocity items. Likewise heavier items are 'mirrored' at more distribution centres due to the cost involved in shipping higher-weight products over longer distances.

This strategy is coming at a cost. For years it has been accepted supply chain thinking that retailers and manufacturers must drive down inventory holdings in order to remain competitive, freeing up capital while reducing the threat of markdowns. Inventory mirroring seems to have turned this doctrine on its head. Now it seems that fulfilling the consumers' desire for immediate gratification is the most critical business requirement.

## Logistics beneficiaries of e-retailing

The e-retail revolution has had structural implications for the retail and consumer goods logistics sector. Many logistics operators that have focused on traditional contract logistics services have had to pivot their services to a model that involves far more intensive pick and packing warehouse activities, as well as investing heavily in automation. Although it might be expected that the increase in logistics costs would have benefited many market incumbents, Amazon's success in offering services to third parties has meant that it has been the main beneficiary. Likewise, Amazon and national postal operators have successfully won considerable volumes rather than express parcels carriers, although there has been plenty of new business to go around.

### E-FULFILMENT PROVIDERS
The fulfilment of orders placed online by a customer can either be undertaken by the retailer itself ('in-house') or by a third-party logistics company ('outsourced'). Many large e-retailers, such as Amazon, will undertake the

order processing, picking, packing, labelling and dispatch themselves as this provides them with a greater level of control over the process. Many smaller e-retailers opt to use 3PLs as they can benefit from their investment in technology systems and their operational know-how.

The market has become blurred in recent years as Amazon has also provided logistics services to other retailers. 'Fulfilled by Amazon', as its offering is known, allows SMEs to store their products in an Amazon distribution centre. Amazon will then take care of the whole order process and also manage the last-mile delivery. This has brought this e-retail giant into direct competition with many logistics operators, although, for the time being, many are content to enter into what has been termed 'co-opetition' – Amazon is not only a competitor but also a major customer for them as well.

The e-fulfilment market is becoming further confused as traditional last-mile delivery companies (UPS and FedEx, for example) have started to provide e-fulfilment services as well as new start-ups.

## LAST-MILE DELIVERY COMPANIES

Fulfilment is not the only online retail challenge that is changing the logistics market. In the last mile, the key drivers of change that logistics operators must respond to – quick, low-cost, high-quality delivery – is reshaping the way goods are moved through the final element of their journey.

The capacity of players in the sector to successfully respond to the rapid rise in volumes – especially during peak times – has been mixed. UPS, for example, struggled with peak volumes during the holiday seasons of 2013, while City Link, a UK operator, could not find a viable business model that allowed it to cope with high volumes at low revenue per unit.

Indeed, online retail is causing fundamental change in last-mile operations. Firstly, the express sector is shifting from a predominantly B2B operation, where parcels are delivered to a smaller number of business addresses (usually located within the boundaries of major commerce centres and with high levels of first-time-delivery success), to a predominantly B2C operation, where individual parcels are delivered to individual addresses (often in residential areas potentially located much further apart, with fewer guarantees of first-time success). The differences between the two delivery options highlight starkly different cost profiles:

1 Deliveries of individual parcels to individual customers limit the potential for the delivery of multi-parcel consignments, raising the number of stops for each driver.

2  The potentially greater spread of delivery locations increases the mileage. Greater distance between deliveries means fewer drops per day and higher cost per drop.

3  A failure to successfully deliver goods at the first attempt means the last-mile provider incurs the expense of any subsequent delivery attempt.

## Returns challenges

How retailers deal with returns is one of the most pressing issues facing the industry. Online returns can average around 25 per cent (Charlton, 2020) of sales. Up to 30 per cent of e-retail consumers will return a gift, with the most frequently returned items being jewellery, electronics, fashion and household goods (Optoro, 2017).

There is a heavy financial cost related to each return, with express company UPS estimating that it ranges from 20 per cent to 65 per cent of the total cost of goods sold, depending on the commodity involved (UPS, 2015). US-based technology provider Datex estimates that returning a 'bricks-and-mortar' shop-bought good costs the retailer on average $3 and it is usually back on the shelf by the next day. However, a return can cost an online retailer $6 and due to the complexity of the process takes at least four days before it becomes available for resale (Datex, 2017). This is probably itself an underestimation as the majority of goods never make it back into the supply chain. A consultancy, Clear Returns, estimates that, in the UK, £600 million of stock that had been bought over the Black Friday weekend at the end of November was still tied up in the return loop in mid-December (Ram, 2016).

Online retailers increasingly offer a number of product features that facilitate a smooth and efficient returns service, including:

- pre-printed returns labels and resealable packaging included in parcels
- an automated refund process with simple instructions
- simple, clear procedures
- an option to return merchandise to a physical location – either a bricks-and-mortar outlet, a post office or a location in an alternative delivery network, such as a parcelstore or locker

In many scenarios, though, the introduction of such services means that the retailer is depending on the last-mile provider to facilitate the returns process. This has an impact throughout the last-mile network, not least in terms of the volume it generates and the cost implications, which exert downward pressure on already thin margins. Last-mile providers must therefore invest in supporting returns operations. Perhaps the most notable example of this is FedEx's 2015 acquisition of reverse logistics specialist Genco Distribution Systems, for $1.4 billion. National post offices have been among the main beneficiaries, as many e-retailers require the end recipient to package the goods and return them through the postal networks, which are the lowest cost option.

## The role of the logistics provider in returns

Logistics service providers (LSPs) are important players in reverse logistics. As the returns process is often regarded as 'non-core' for many manufacturers or retailers, there is a risk that the process can be neglected or underfunded. By outsourcing to a specialist logistics company, a focus can be maintained on the main business of selling, while ensuring that customer service and inventory velocity is achieved.

It is also beneficial in terms of the balance sheet. E-retailers do not need to invest in warehouses in every market in which they operate as they can use those of the logistics provider, which can leverage its own investment over a number of customers. LSPs can also undertake inspection and refurbishment in addition to the storage and distribution of goods back into the supply chain. A further benefit is that shippers do not need to invest in expertise, as LSPs can leverage their experience in the sector equally for small, medium or large companies.

Logistics or express parcels providers can play a more strategic role in the returns process than just handling or moving the product. As they are closest to the end recipient, they are better able to make decisions on what to do with the return. This has several advantages:

- Operational decisions can be taken more quickly in the reverse logistics process.
- Products can be returned to the supply chain more quickly, repaired or disposed of.
- The returns process can be made more convenient for the end recipient.

The expertise that LSPs have developed has allowed them to offer consultancy services, mapping out returns process and suggesting ways in which cost savings can be made.

## Existing return solutions

For many e-retailers, the most crucial goal of their returns policy is to minimize the cost of transportation and delivery and this, rightly or wrongly, takes precedent over inventory velocity – that is, reintroducing the product back into the supply chain. As speed is not usually an essential factor for this operation, and neither is there a critical need for the online purchaser to have a status update, a low-cost solution is generally preferred:

- Post offices. The vast majority of returned items are channelled through pickup and drop-off points managed by postal networks.
- In-store. For bricks-and-mortar retailers that have online presence, the return of goods to any of their shops conveniently located for the customer is chosen as their lowest-cost solution.
- Parcel shops. Some carriers and independent operators offer dedicated parcel shops where goods purchased online can be returned.
- Parcel lockers. Another solution is for recipients to return their goods to parcel lockers, which are increasingly common at train stations, car parks and garage forecourts.

The returns process still involves an element of inconvenience for the online shopper as it often requires the printing of return labels (relying on the recipient owning a printer) or, in some cases, a wait at home for the collection. Post offices have the restrictions of set opening hours, and other options may involve a journey to a nearby self-service terminal to deposit the parcel.

## Future returns solutions

The use of technologies that are being developed for last-mile deliveries could, in the future, be leveraged into reverse logistics solutions.

It is envisaged that, with technological advances, drivers could be contacted on demand through apps, text, sms, social media or crowdsourcing and customers would be able to provide pre-notification alerts of parcels available for collection. It would also be possible for the customer to let the courier know when they are at home for them to collect. In a similar manner, they would be able to collect from a neighbour or from the boot of cars. As such, collection would happen in a matter of minutes, swiftly and with little inconvenience.

Visibility is also becoming more important, despite the traditionally low priority that retailers have placed upon returns. The UK's Royal Mail offers a tracked service that, according to its management, gives its customers access to tracking along key stages of the parcel journey, including confirmed delivery to returns processing centres, enabling the acceleration of returns processing and the resale of its products.

## Cross-border e-retail issues and risks

Another potential challenge has been caused by the fast growth of cross-border e-commerce. This has been a positive trend for international express providers such as DHL, FedEx and UPS, but the explosion of SMEs now trading goods internationally has created headaches for customs authorities and other regulators who have to deal with:

- increased volumes of single item shipments
- traders who are not used to the rules and documentation required to move goods internationally
- traders who have little or no understanding of tax and duties that could be payable on their consignments

Although gaining access to millions of new customers is an attractive proposition for e-commerce companies, targeting purchasers in foreign markets is not necessarily the easiest of strategies. Apart from the obvious language and currency barriers, there are a raft of additional factors that can impact a retailer's ability to successfully operate on a cross-border basis. A UPS study of European cross-border purchases (UPS, 2017) found that the top considerations when purchasing from retailers in another country included:

- payment security (75 per cent of respondents)
- clearly stating the total cost of the order including duties and fees (72 per cent)
- a clear returns policy (63 per cent)
- stating all prices in the shopper's native currency (63 per cent)
- the speed of delivery (62 per cent)

However, within Europe – an economic grouping largely governed by a set of compatible customs, taxation and trading regulations, with the vast majority of markets adopting a single currency – cross-border e-commerce is a far simpler proposition.

Trading conditions become far more complicated in regions such as Asia, where developed markets trade with emerging economies; countries have independent regulatory environments; many have different languages and currencies; and most are separated by large bodies of water. This results in a significantly different set of issues that e-commerce companies and their logistics providers must navigate.

## Payments

Fraud is a major challenge faced by e-retailers operating on a cross-border basis. E-commerce sites need to use a reputable and robust payment system that is cognizant of local customer behaviour in order to reduce possible fraudulent purchases.

Many emerging economies are 'cash societies', i.e. where bank credit or debit cards are not widely used. Consumers in these markets often rely heavily on 'cash on delivery' (COD) payments, which comes with its own set of unique issues. COD purchases, where the goods are paid for on receipt of delivery – handing cash over to the delivery driver – incur a very high return rate, especially on cross-border transactions where the transit time is far longer. Often, during the time that it takes to deliver the goods, the consumer has found a similar product locally. As there is no penalty, or need to request a refund, the purchaser simply refuses to accept the delivery. This places additional cost onto the e-commerce seller, especially as the return element often also comprises an international shipment. For those purchases that are completed, the last-mile operator will need to collect the cash payment and then transport this to a secure facility. To reduce the risk, some companies use the services of local retail outlets that offer cash collection services. The funds are then sent electronically back to the merchant.

Also, cross-border payments should be fully transparent to ensure that all transport costs, local taxes, duties and fees are included so that customers are not surprised by additional government levies when their online purchases arrive at their final destination. Understanding local taxation and ensuring that the customer pays accordingly is crucial; otherwise the purchase may be returned, incurring additional, expensive, costs.

## Cross-border returns

The cross-border returns element is also just as important as the last-mile delivery and can negatively impact the perception of a business by local customers:

- Handling international returns is expensive and difficult for retailers/ logistics providers to manage.

- Logistics solutions involve the consolidation of returned items, determining if the items can be resold or disposed and then submitting the items into the proper channel of distribution.

- Due to varying individual country laws and regulations, much of this handling is done in the country in which the returns occur.

Compared with domestic e-commerce, cross-border returns are far more expensive, and some retailers have adopted different strategies to try to reduce this expense. When UK-based e-retailer ASOS, for example, started to service US customers it did so from its UK stockholding. To reduce the returns cost ASOS subsequently directed all US returns to a US distribution centre, the intention being not just to reduce costs but also to build up inventory in the country.

## Regulations

Regulations surrounding local and overseas e-commerce sales will differ country by country and cross-border e-commerce sellers must be aware of these in order to adapt their approach in each target market.

A number of countries in Southeast Asia, and also Australia, are implementing additional taxes on online goods purchased from non-domestic sellers, and these costs will have to be either passed on to the consumer or borne by the retailer. Also, changes in tax-free import tariffs can impact growth opportunities, turning what was previously a profitable cross-border market into an unattractive proposition for overseas sellers within a very short timeframe.

## Trust

Trust is one of the biggest issues facing companies wanting to sell their products online internationally. As e-commerce sites need robust payments systems to reduce fraudulent purchases, customers must be convinced that the websites they buy from are reputable and honest – a task that is far harder to check and police internationally.

## Summary

The outlook for traditional retailers is far from clear. Inventory strategies are being driven by the large e-retailers: Amazon in the United States and Europe, and Alibaba in much of the rest of the world. In response, the largest retailers with the deepest pockets may be able to cut prices and increase product availability while investing in the technology required to mitigate inventory increases. Others will fall by the wayside, unable to meet customer expectations of immediate availability at low prices.

Although the supply chain playbook does not need to be completely rewritten just yet, many fundamental aspects of inventory management are being questioned as the retail industry undergoes a systemic transformation. What is clear is that increasing inventory on its own is still not an attractive option – this would only result in the inefficient use of hard-to-come-by capital and all the negative consequences of owning too much stock.

The retail industry continues to feel the impact of e-commerce on a daily basis. Traditional bricks-and-mortar retailers that have not embraced an 'omnichannel' approach to sales are struggling against the might of Amazon and a host of other e-retailers that offer a wide range of high-quality products, fast service and cheap prices.

However, even the e-commerce sector faces many challenges, which if not addressed will curtail the growth of the sector. Cross-border e-commerce has the potential to aid economic development in many emerging markets around the world, but only if trade processes are streamlined and regulations reformed. Other innovative solutions need to be developed to address inefficiencies in last-mile deliveries in an urban context as well as the vast number of returned goods.

## References

Charlton, G (2020) Ecommerce Returns: 2020 Stats and Trends, Salescycle, www.salecycle.com/blog/featured/ecommerce-returns-2018-stats-trends/ (archived at https://perma.cc/4FSK-Q2TA)

Datex (2017) Dirty little secrets of holiday returns (part three): 3PL reverse logistics, how 3PLs can help retailers maximize the value of returned goods, www.datexcorp.com/dirty-little-secrets-holiday-returns-part-3-3pl-reverse-logistics/ (archived at https://perma.cc/PP8J-8LUT)

Optoro (2017) Holiday shopping insights, Optoro, Washington DC

Ram, A (2016) UK retailers count the cost of returns, *Financial Times*, 27 January, www.ft.com/content/52d26de8-c0e6-11e5-846f-79b0e3d20eaf (archived at https://perma.cc/BF2M-WCLK)

UPS (2015) Rethinking online returns, comparing the return policies and processes of top online retailers to shopper preferences, www.ups.com/assets/resources/pdf/15UP31139_ReturnsExecutiveSummary_pages%20Final.pdf (archived at https://perma.cc/794C-R3ZV)

UPS (2017) UPS pulse of the online shopper, https://www.ups.com/assets/resources/media/en_GB/UPS_POTOS_EU_EN_linked.pdf (archived at https://perma.cc/8WGK-LXAN)

# 10

# Amazon – the ultimate disruptor

**This chapter will familiarize the reader with:**

- The logistics strategies employed by one of the world's largest e-retailers, Amazon

- How robotics has been employed to drive down logistics costs

- The proactive role that Amazon is playing in transforming consumer expectations and logistics operations

- The efforts being made by Amazon to reduce its increasing fulfilment and shipping costs

- The relationships that Amazon has with last-mile delivery operators and how these are likely to develop

Over the past 20 years, Amazon.com has become a giant in the e-commerce sector, developing from an online retailer of books in the 1990s to a diversified corporation spanning the delivery of software services (Amazon Web Services), consumer goods, groceries and even on-demand restaurant meals. To support sales of its own products, and those of customers using its platforms, it has developed a world leading logistics operation, providing fulfilment and last-mile services. Transforming customer service expectations, it has disrupted the entire retail industry, driving many competitors out of business by enabling almost immediate fulfilment of consumer demand. Its growth and needs have often outpaced the capabilities of the global logistics industry, forcing it to develop its own structures and solutions.

# Logistics strategy

With expenditure on fulfilment and shipping amounting to just short of one-third of its net revenues, logistics is of massive importance to the financial well-being of Amazon. However, as well as being a major cost centre, the maintenance and expansion of the company's logistics activities is vital to its ongoing business development. As such, the company has embarked on a deliberate course that attempts to reconcile the multiple goals of cutting costs, controlling customer experience and continuously differentiating its services from competitors (Banker, 2021).

---

**AMAZON'S STRATEGY**

Reduce costs

- Achieve economies of scale through ownership of a vast network of warehousing and fulfilment centres.
- Use huge volumes of shipments to create buying power in air, road and sea freight markets.

Drive revenue growth

- Leverage logistics capabilities to differentiate services from competitors.
- Transform customer expectations that other companies find difficult or impossible to meet.

Leverage platforms

- Open platforms and fulfilment centres for use by third-party retailers.
- Scale-up use of platforms at marginal cost.
- Increase logistics capacity utilization.

---

For much of the early part of its development, Amazon relied heavily on third-party transport providers, such as UPS and FedEx. Now, however, not only has it in-sourced much of its logistics needs, it is also, in some respects, acting as a competitor. For example, many small and medium-sized retailers selling over Amazon's marketplace platform use Fulfilled by Amazon (FBA) services. That is, they keep their inventory in an Amazon fulfilment centre and ship via Amazon networks. In the past, much of these volumes would have been routed via a traditional 3PL or through parcels carriers, but now they help Amazon to improve its own asset utilization, reduce costs and increase network benefits. In the future, Amazon may provide third-party transportation services for other non-FBA shippers, as discussed in more detail below. As Roy Perticucci, Amazon's European head of logistics, said 'We know we're very good at logistics. Why shouldn't we turn that into an infrastructure offer that others can use?' (Koenen et al, 2016).

Reducing costs has become an even more important imperative following a surge in volumes in 2020 due to Covid-19 'stay at home' policies (see Figure 10.1). The company reiterated in its 2021 annual report that 'We seek to mitigate costs of shipping over time in part through achieving higher sales volumes, optimizing our fulfilment network, negotiating better terms with our suppliers, and achieving better operating efficiencies.'

The increase in fulfilment costs was primarily due to:

- variable costs corresponding with increased product and service sales volume and inventory levels
- costs from expanding its fulfilment network
- Covid-19-related impact of lower productivity
- increased employee hiring and benefits
- costs to maintain safe workplaces

FIGURE 10.1   Amazon revenues, shipping and fulfilment costs

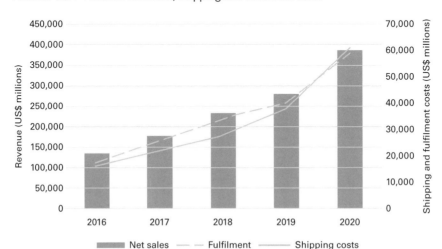

SOURCE  Amazon/author

FIGURE 10.2  Amazon logistics costs (shipping + fulfilment) as per cent net sales

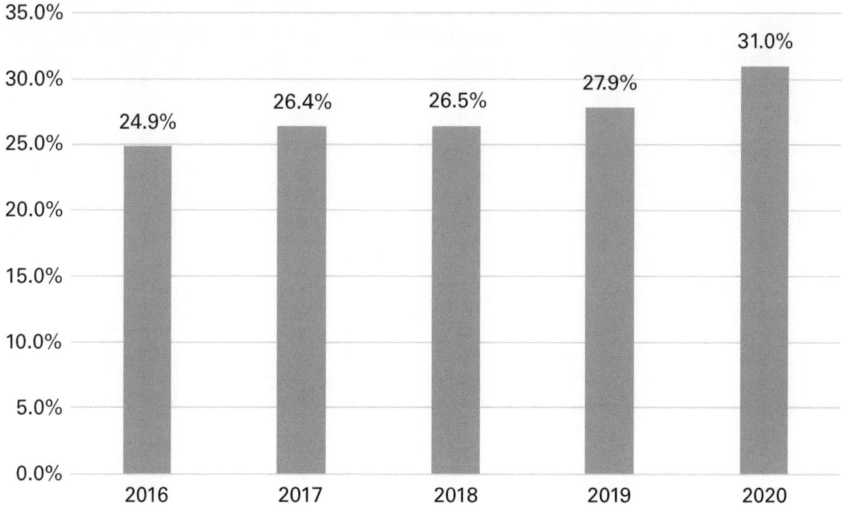

SOURCE  Amazon/author

As can be seen in Figure 10.2, overall logistics costs have risen as a proportion of the company's net revenues by just over 6 percentage points over the past five years: from 24.9 per cent to 31 per cent.

## Logistics capabilities

Amazon is at various stages of developing a compelling service offering within four core logistics competencies: fulfilment, last mile, air cargo, road freight/trucking.

### Fulfilment

Amazon's first two distribution centres – Seattle and Delaware – were opened in 1997 with many others soon following across the United States. International expansion was not far behind, with facilities established in Germany and the UK. Table 10.1 shows the number and square footage of fulfilment centres in selected markets.

TABLE 10.1  Amazon's fulfilment centres

| Country | Number | Capacity (sq. ft) |
| --- | --- | --- |
| United States | 293 | 200,387,511 |
| Canada | 14 | 8,940,442 |
| Mexico | 7 | 2,886,650 |
| Brazil | 9 | 3,995,711 |
| UK | 45 | 19,874,389 |
| Germany | 31 | 15,607,782 |
| France | 11 | 6,194,940 |
| Italy | 9 | 5,754,108 |
| Spain | 11 | 6,606,256 |
| Poland | 9 | 7,733,305 |
| Japan | 38 | 10,395,724 |
| India | 72 | 9,694,919 |
| Australia | 9 | 2,342,775 |

SOURCE  MWPVL

In Europe, Amazon's fulfilment strategy has transformed since it first entered the market. At the outset customers from anywhere in Europe were able to buy from any of the company's national websites (e.g. Amazon.co.uk) and the order would be fulfilled from that country. Over a 10-year period Amazon developed the capability to fulfil that order from any of the region's distribution centres.

Amazon fulfilment centres are characterized by the company into three main categories:

- Sortable: packages are roughly about the size 30 x 30 x 40 centimetres (i.e. they can be sorted by automated materials-handling equipment).
- Non-sortable: larger boxes that need manual put away/picking.
- Heavy-bulky: items such as washing machines, for example, which need two-man handling or specialist equipment.

While sortable accounts for up to 90 per cent of volumes, non-sortable products take up considerably more space and these facilities resemble more traditional, non-automated warehouses with movement of goods undertaken by forklift trucks.

The inbound transportation to an Amazon distribution centre of 'first party' sales (i.e. those that are sold by Amazon itself rather than a third party over its marketplace platform) is largely organized by the supplier. There have been efforts in the past (both in Europe and the United States) to take control of the inbound process (in much the same way as some grocery retailers migrated to factory gate pricing in the 2000s) but on the whole goods are delivered by the supplier against purchase orders. Relationships exist with some trusted suppliers, which allow for streamlined deliveries and receipt of goods. This can take the form of what the company calls a 'licence plate receive'. The supplier can place a number of items, consisting usually of multiple stock-keeping units (SKUs), into a 'mother' box with a master barcode. This mother box is then scanned on receipt by Amazon, saving significant time and increasing accuracy for both Amazon and supplier.

Amazon's third-party 'Fulfilled By Amazon' (FBA) offering, available to users of its marketplace, works in much the same way as its first-party model. FBA targets small to medium-size businesses and individual sellers and provides such services as pick and pack, labelling, shipping, and inventory and returns management. Instead of a purchase order, however, a customer uses a vendor portal to inform Amazon what goods are going to be sent and when they will be received. As the process is self-service, accuracy is often the biggest problem and can result in goods being refused, through mislabelling, for instance.

In 2021, the marketplace sold 3.8 billion items in the United States alone, with sales making up an estimated 62 per cent of product sold (gross merchandise value). About half of Amazon's marketplace customers use FBA to service their customers (Conley, 2021). At the outset, FBA was devised as a way of utilizing spare capacity. Now, however, it is very much driving the company's growth, not least in terms of fulfilment facilities. This has meant that Amazon also takes a much more proactive role in understanding the likely needs of its larger FBA customers, as it would do for the demand forecasting of its own first-party sales. Some warehouses in Europe and the United States are believed now to be dedicated to FBA sales.

The success of FBA, as well as the sales of its own products, has led the company to develop a sophisticated system for warehouse fulfilment, based on robotics technology acquired from Kiva Systems in 2012. By deploying robots designed to bring picking shelves to human pickers for the fulfilment of customer orders, Amazon is able to increase the velocity of inventory fulfilment within the warehouse by as much as 75 per cent, while increasing inventory capacity by as much as 50 per cent due to the lack of picking aisles. All in all, installation of the system reportedly cuts operating costs by around 20 per cent (Kim, 2016). By 2021, Amazon had installed about 350,000 robots across its fulfilment centres, an increase of 75 per cent in two years (Boyle, 2021).

Besides the development of these advanced systems to improve fulfilment operations, Amazon has also started to develop dedicated distribution services through its Seller Fulfilled Prime and Seller Flex programmes. Launched at the end of 2015, Seller Fulfilled Prime (SFP) allows Amazon marketplace sellers to ship to Amazon Prime customers from their own warehouses, rather than by routing products through Amazon fulfilment centres first. All distribution is coordinated through Amazon Logistics, a technology service layer that coordinates order and inventory management across a network of subcontracted delivery companies. It can be used for slow-moving lines that normally attract high costs if using FBA.

---

### AMAZON TO HIRE 55,000 NEW WORKERS WITH FOCUS ON ROBOTICS

In September 2021 Amazon announced plans to recruit 55,000 workers around the world, including 40,000 in the United States. As well as warehousing staff, Amazon is investing in other aspects of its business, especially robotics. As is often the case with large US tech businesses, there is significant investment in the UK, which in the case of Amazon is a mix of 'corporate' roles at administrative offices but also in 'tech hubs' in Cambridge, London, Manchester and Edinburgh. Robotics has always been important to Amazon because of its key role in warehouse operations. Amazon 'tech hubs' are in part designed to deliver greater automation not only in fulfilment centres but also in transport operations. Although its logistics capacity is vast, Amazon has traditionally been quite pragmatic in the design of its operations, with fulfilment centres still requiring substantial numbers of workers. As volumes climb ever higher at the retail business, the need for higher automation will increase.

SOURCE Logistics Briefing

---

The wide range of products that Amazon sells over its websites presents some challenges to its fulfilment operations. As all items are 'co-mingled', picking orders can be slower than a competitor that specializes in a particular product or has fewer SKUs. No two Amazon orders are the same, whereas many other e-retailers are able to better optimize warehouse picking operations due to smaller product range and sizes. In some Amazon fulfilment centres there are more than 1 million different SKUs.

### Last-mile delivery

Amazon initiated its last-mile logistics programme in 2014 following a significant number of missed deliveries by UPS and FedEx in the United States during the 2013 holiday period, as well as the need to address spiralling shipping costs. Its response was to bring last-mile management in-house under the auspices of Amazon Logistics. Key to its offering is service, reliability and speed. Amazon identified at an early stage that these attributes were more important to their customers than the brand or livery of the delivery company.

Amazon Logistics does not hire its own drivers; rather, the model consists of subcontracting last-mile delivery to a multitude of small companies (through its Delivery Service Partner scheme) and owner-operators (Amazon Flex). Amazon Logistics benefits from this arrangement as it is able to exercise greater bargaining power over these contractors than it would in negotiations with the likes of UPS or FedEx, and can therefore pay a lower rate for their services.

That is not to say that Amazon has stopped using other carriers. It takes a pragmatic view on whether to use a parcels operator, based on its own parcel volumes. If, in an urban area, for example, it has a route with 200 drops in a day (typically the maximum an urban delivery driver can manage), it will use an independent contractor. If volumes go over this 200 per day ceiling, rather than pay an additional subcontractor to deliver, say, 50 packages a day at a higher cost, it makes sense to give these volumes to a parcels network. Once volumes have been built up to 200, then delivery can be in-sourced. In rural, less-dense delivery areas Amazon is more likely to use third-party parcels carriers or postal networks, due to their inherent advantage of being able to consolidate Amazon and non-Amazon volumes on extended routes.

As indicated by the figures in Figure 10.2, costs in shipping are rising. It is likely that they will continue to rise as Amazon enhances its range of delivery options as a way of capturing more market share. Same-day delivery is an example of this. Reducing the time window in which a delivery can be made also reduces the density of the delivery network. Self-evidently, if

Amazon only offered a two- to three-day economy service, costs would be much less; however, it certainly would not have disrupted the market in the way that it has.

In order for Amazon to offer its expedited service, sophisticated last-mile transport management systems are required. Amazon uses a cloud-based app that is able to track drivers and record granular data such as when they arrive at the door of the customer, when delivery is completed and when they depart. For repeat deliveries it learns the most efficient parking spaces and the best time of day to visit, speeding up the delivery process and helping the driver to deliver more packages. This data can be shared with customers to provide them with very precise delivery windows. It also optimizes routes from a time, fuel and, of course, carbon emissions perspective.

The links between fulfilment and last mile are essential and artificial intelligence (AI) is key to Amazon's success, integrating supply chain planning and execution. As one technology expert put it, 'Because purchasing, manufacturing, warehousing, transportation and sales are traceably connected by a single platform, on-time performance reliability increases while transportation costs decrease. The time saved allows their team to remain focused on customers rather than administrative tasks' (Hollister, 2018).

Visibility throughout the fulfilment process allows accuracy in the transport management process. For example, route planning becomes 'dynamic' using up-to-the-minute data, taking into account available capacity and traffic conditions at a specific time.

## UNITED STATES

In the United States, the company has mainly focused on shifting its package delivery requirements towards the low-cost United States Postal Service and away from major parcels companies. The rise of Amazon Logistics, however, has presented another option for last-mile delivery.

In order to address the challenges it was facing in last-mile delivery, Amazon established what it calls its 'Delivery Service Partner' programme in 2018. The scheme, which helps individuals to start up parcels delivery businesses dedicated to the last-mile delivery of Amazon packages, has since been extended to other markets around the world. For a relatively small initial investment ($10,000) Amazon provides access to leasing deals on vans, insurance and mobile devices. A successful owner will manage 20–40 vans and drivers, with the possibility of achieving profits of '$75,000 to $300,000', according to the company (Montag, 2018). The benefits of the model for Amazon are that it manages a smaller number of businesses rather than managing thousands of individual subcontractors. Business owners are buying into the growth of a successful brand, although there is no doubt that they have to work exceedingly hard to make their investment of money and time worthwhile.

In addition, Amazon is also working on an even more radical solution to the last-mile problem: adopting the business model of Uber and crowd-sourcing last-mile delivery. Named Amazon Flex, this operation was initially trialled in Seattle in 2015 and has since been rolled out to multiple cities in the United States and Europe. Amazon often deploys Flex drivers to service Prime orders, as the company is able to scale-up this resource during peaks in demand.

By the end of 2021, Amazon had expanded its faster same-day delivery service to Atlanta, Baltimore, Charlotte, Chicago, Detroit, Houston, Miami, Minneapolis and Tampa – bringing the total number of cities with the service to 15.

## EUROPE

At the outset, Amazon in Europe was highly reliant on the national postal operators for its last-mile services: Royal Mail in the UK, La Poste in France and Deutsche Post/DHL in Germany. However, as volumes have grown it has developed its own capacity, not least in order to offer next-day and same-day deliveries through its Amazon Prime offering. According to one senior manager, the incumbent parcel carriers were just not able to accommodate Amazon's service needs and hence the company was forced into the position of being the main market innovator (Hemard, 2020). Trials started in the UK in around 2010 at the point when Amazon was moving about 60 million parcels a year, considered to be the threshold for initiating a national parcels operation.

Across Europe it has employed a range of strategies, often changing over time. In Germany it started its coverage by using DHL and other carriers before establishing Amazon Logistics. As well as using subcontractor partners, it has also invested in its own fleet, in 2020 ordering 40 StreetScooter Work Box electric vans to be deployed at its distribution centre in Munich. In other countries, the company has acted more directly to achieve the same aim. For example, in France, Amazon holds a stake in parcel delivery provider Colis Privé as well as using La Poste, Chronopost and DHL for door-to-door deliveries. It also has a partnership with a last-mile company, Urbit, in Paris, which delivers exclusively by foot, bike or cargo-bike.

## Air cargo

Amazon has rapidly become a major force in the air cargo sector. Following a trial period in 2015, when Amazon tested the use of contracted aircraft flown by cargo operator ATSG, it embarked upon chartered air freight operations in North America and Europe. In the former region, Amazon arranged to lease 20 aircraft on crew, maintenance and insurance (CMI) contracts with Atlas air, as well as another 20 on a five-year CMI agreement with ATSG. Moreover, the deals allowed Amazon to acquire 19.9 per cent of ATSG's stock, which it did in 2021 in a transaction worth $131 million, and 20 per cent of Atlas stock, with possible expansions.

Also in 2021, Amazon announced its purchase of 11 Boeing 767-300 aircraft, continuing to expand its transportation fleet to serve customers. The purchases include seven aircraft from Delta and four aircraft from WestJet, which will join the network in 2022.

'Our goal is to continue delivering for customers across the United States in the way that they expect from Amazon, and purchasing our own aircraft is a natural next step towards that goal', said Sarah Rhoads, vice-president of Amazon Global Air. 'Having a mix of both leased and owned aircraft in our growing fleet allows us to better manage our operations, which in turn helps us to keep pace in meeting our customer promises.'

The logic behind Amazon's move into air freight is relatively simple: by acquiring its own fleet of aircraft it will have better visibility and control over its fulfilment operations. Due to the control and improved supply chain visibility brought about by such a move, Amazon will have a much more flexible and responsive capability to redirect inventory between parts of its network.

By in-sourcing part of its air freight requirements, Amazon is strengthening its ability to serve its customers during peak times, when its logistics partners have previously struggled to cope with a surge in package volumes. Having the extra capacity on hand allows Amazon to relieve some of the pressure applied to its supply chain at such times and will supplement the services of its current partners. That being said, Amazon is a long way from being able to handle the entirety of its air freight requirements in-house and it is debatable that it will ever do so.

Nonetheless, in the long term, there exists the possibility that Amazon will sell space on its freighters to companies looking to outsource their logistics, and truly challenge the business of companies such as UPS and FedEx. It already offers fulfilment services to businesses selling through its website and, with an integrated logistics network boasting supply chain visibility and computing power superior to that of many traditional express parcels companies, Amazon could seriously disrupt the industry. It is believed that it already carries mail for the USPS in the United States (Schoolov, 2021).

In 2021, Amazon began operations at Cincinnati/Northern Kentucky International Airport following a $1.5 billion investment. The Amazon Air Hub will serve as the primary hub for Amazon Air's US cargo network. Amazon Air continues to expand globally. In 2020, it launched its first air hub at Leipzig/Halle Airport in Germany and new regional air operations at:

- Lakeland Linder International Airport
- John F Kennedy International Airport
- San Francisco International Airport
- Chicago O'Hare International Airport
- Richmond International Airport
- Austin-Bergstrom International Airport
- Luis Muñoz Marín International Airport
- Kahului Airport
- Kona International Airport
- Los Angeles International Airport
- Louis Armstrong International Airport

## Road freight/trucking

In the United States, Amazon has relatively recently built its own fleet of long haul trucks and trailers for 'trunking' between distribution centres while continuing to contract out large parts of its linehaul road transportation. The move towards asset ownership is designed to tighten the company's control over its logistics requirements to achieve a more efficient, integrated inbound logistics system in support of its sortation and fulfilment centre network. It has also created its own freight marketplace and an 'incubator' for start-ups, which encourages drivers to establish their own businesses and drive exclusively for Amazon.

Amazon's road freight operations are nascent by comparison to its position in the markets outlined above. Nonetheless, the company has taken a number of steps that will put the company in competition with external road freight companies in their own markets.

Since 2015 Amazon has purchased thousands of trailers in the United States to increase capacity for package delivery from fulfilment centres to sort centres. The significance of this move was that Amazon gained a uniform fleet of trailers optimized to interact with its existing logistics infrastructure, and therefore provided greater efficiency in the process of distributing inventory from hubs to spokes within its network. In addition, the company gained greater capability to reallocate inventory when demand shifts caused a shortage in certain parts of the network.

Furthermore in 2017, Amazon launched 'Relay', a dedicated app for truck drivers servicing its facilities. It allows truck drivers to enter information about their cargo in advance and then scan their phones to quickly check in and check out of facilities.

## Amazon's logistics infrastructure

Having launched in the United States during 1995, Amazon was quick to expand into the UK and Germany shortly after, opening its first in-country fulfilment centres in these countries during 1998 and 1999, respectively. The company opened its first Japanese fulfilment centre in 2000, and subsequently opened up in Canada during 2002. This group of countries represents much of the core of Amazon's physical logistics network and, with the exception of Japan where the e-retailer comes second to Rakuten, it is the largest e-commerce player across each of these markets.

Amazon established a physical presence in the Chinese market through the acquisition of Joyo in 2004. However, it has been unable to gain traction in the country, having been outcompeted by local players such as the dominant Alibaba. Thus far, China is the only country the company has seemingly failed to penetrate in a meaningful way, possessing only a minor market share.

Though Amazon launched a French website in 2000, the company did not establish a physical presence within the country until 2007, instead shipping from its other European facilities. The company opened up its first logistics sites in Italy and Spain during 2011 and 2012, respectively; closely following its launch of dedicated websites for each country.

The company's other European facilities, in Czech Republic (opened in 2013), Poland (2014) and Slovakia (2017), have all been established to serve other European markets; principally Germany, where Amazon has endured difficult industrial relations with its employees.

The company's most significant market entry since 2004 has been its establishment of in-country operations in India in 2013. Amazon's management views India as vital to its long-term growth, with expectations that it will eventually constitute the company's second-largest national market after the United States. Amazon has been keen to avoid the mistakes of its 'copy and paste' approach to entering China and has adapted to the idiosyncrasies of the Indian market.

Shortly after its expansion into India, Amazon also invested in physical facilities in Latin America, with fulfilment centres opened in Brazil (2014) and Mexico (2015). In Brazil, continued expansion has allowed the company to reach Amazon Prime customers in 500 cities nationwide from eight distribution centres.

The company's latest expansions have focused on the Middle East and Southeast Asia. Amazon opened up in Singapore and Australia towards the end of 2017, with its entry into the latter market expected for some time. Earlier that year, the company established itself in the Middle East, through the acquisition of Souq, the largest e-commerce player in the region. The takeover of Souq has provided the company with a well-developed logistics infrastructure in the United Arab Emirates (UAE), Saudi Arabia, Jordan and Egypt.

## Amazon's struggles with labour

Amazon's dominant position in the market is being increasingly challenged in the United States and elsewhere by a variety of different institutional organizations. In the first instance, politicians and regulators fear that it is using its hold on the market to undertake anti-competitive practices. To add to growing pressure, however, labour organizations are alleging that it is using its power to exploit workers and to reduce pay and standards across the industry.

Following the election of President Biden, the future of 'big tech', especially industry giants such as Amazon, Apple, Google and Facebook, has been in question. Their market dominance and the effect this has on competitors and customers has prompted calls by some for their break-up. One of the allegations levelled against Amazon is the behaviour of its 'Fulfilled by Amazon' (FBA) operation. It is alleged that the company has been favouring third-party marketplace customers that use its logistics services, a strategy called 'self-preferencing'.

Although third-party customers do have the ability to fulfil orders placed over the platform themselves, the argument goes that by not signing up to FBA their products lose out on placement on the site and are more at risk from penalties for late delivery. Regulators believe that rather than just a feature of healthy competition in which companies like Amazon are in their rights to promote their own products and services, their size and power acts as a form of compulsion.

This has prompted a number of bipartisan anti-trust proposals under discussion in the United States by the House Anti-trust Subcommittee, which if successful, could lead to the break-up of the company. Also, Seattle Congresswoman Pramila Jayapal has introduced legislation, the 'Ending Platform Monopolies Act', which would allow the federal government to force tech companies to sell off operations where there was an alleged 'conflict of interest'. The European Commission has also been proactive in its anti-trust fight against tech giants and could pursue similar proposals.

It should be stressed that the chances of this present anti-trust legislation being passed is remote – but it does show the general direction of movement in Washington. There has been the suggestion that rather than wait to be pushed by the federal government, Amazon might be tempted to spin off its logistics on its own terms, creating a huge independent rival to UPS and FedEx. If the company was compelled to sell off its Amazon Logistics business, Bank of America analysts believe it could be worth $230 billion.

However, Amazon is not only coming under pressure from the government but also from unions, which in its own way could also be highly disruptive to the company. The International Brotherhood of Teamsters (IBT) has announced that it will attempt to unionize the company's warehouse workers and truck drivers. Debating a resolution at its International Convention, it accused the company of 'changing the nature of work in our country' and '[exploiting] employees, contractors and employees of contractors'. The IBT is setting up a special Amazon Division to lead the campaign. Given the size of Amazon's workforce, membership would be hugely beneficial to the union should it succeed.

The campaign comes after a bitter and hard-fought vote at Amazon's Bessemer, Alabama warehouse in 2021 on whether workers should join the Retail, Wholesale and Department Store Union. In this case, the company won, although it was accused by labour organizations of using underhand tactics to persuade workers to reject the union contract.

Of course, if Amazon's workforce does become unionized there would be a huge impact not only in terms of labour cost but also flexibility. Meeting peaks and troughs in demand in a highly volatile market environment would become hugely challenging. The move may in fact accelerate the company's efforts to automate its operations, to reduce its dependence on labour.

In summary, Amazon's management will be fighting on many fronts in the coming years, as well as dealing with the operational challenges created by the boom in e-commerce. Seemingly, the future structure of the company, not least whether or not it spins off Amazon Logistics, depends on the success of its arguments and the strength of the political opposition as much as market forces.

# Sustainability

## Road freight

Transportation is a major component of Amazon's business operations and part of its plan to meet net-zero carbon by 2040. To help accelerate the market for electric vehicle (EV) technology, Amazon has invested more than $1 billion in EV manufacturer Rivian and ordered 100,000 electric delivery vans from the company. Amazon has also entered into a partnership with Mahindra Electric, another manufacturer of EVs, to deploy nearly 100 Treo Zor electric vehicles in seven Indian cities as part of Amazon India's plan to include 10,000 EVs in its delivery fleet by 2025. In Europe, it has partnered with Mercedes-Benz.

## Shipping

Amazon co-founded The Cargo Owners for Zero Emission Vessels network alongside the Aspen Institute, IKEA, Inditex, Michelin, Patagonia, Tchibo, and fellow Pledge signatories Brooks Running and Unilever. The initiative aims to transition ocean freight vessels from fossil fuels to zero-carbon fuels by 2040.

## Warehousing

Amazon has announced a total of 206 renewable energy projects globally, including 71 utility-scale wind and solar projects and 135 rooftop solar installations at facilities and stores worldwide.

Amazon's Climate Pledge Fund, a $2 billion venture capital fund to support the development of sustainable and decarbonizing technologies and services, made new investments in three companies: CMC Machinery, a technology company that designs and manufactures custom-sized boxes while eliminating the need for single-use plastic padding; Resilient Power, a builder of solid-state power stations for electric vehicles; and Infinium, a company working towards a low-carbon electrofuels solution for air transport, marine freight and heavy truck fleets. In total, the Climate Pledge Fund has invested in 11 companies.

## Amazon rides the Covid-19 wave

The logistics infrastructure built by Amazon over the past 20 years has ensured that, throughout the period of lockdown in many countries, customers were able to continue receiving a wide range of essential supplies. In fact, it is difficult to imagine how many consumers would have been able to cope without Amazon, not just through the service it provided but on account of the role it played in developing the entire e-retailing business model. Swathes of the retail sector, as well as manufacturing supply chains, have been 'Amazonized' and people in many countries were able to reap the benefits.

In order to meet demand, while other companies were laying off staff Amazon recruited 100,000 workers in the United States, hiring drivers from 'offline' retailers and platforms such as ride-hailing, personal mobility companies whose business had suffered due to 'stay-at-home' orders. The e-retailer also increased their hourly wage by $2 (or the local equivalent in other parts of the world).

Amazon was very keen to be seen to be doing the 'right thing'. In collaboration with the UK government, universities and other industry partners, Amazon used its logistics network, along with Royal Mail, to deliver test kits to critical workers and to special test sites set up around the country, free of charge. This followed other community initiatives such as the donation of medical isolation suits, protective masks, disposable gloves, and other medical supplies to healthcare professionals in badly affected cities in countries such as Italy and China. Amazon also said it would pay two weeks' salary to workers who were diagnosed with Covid-19 or who were quarantined if, for example, they were immediate co-workers of infected workers.

The company also supported companies and workers in its last-mile delivery network. The company stated at the time, 'We are establishing the Amazon Relief Fund, with a $25 million initial contribution, focused on supporting our independent delivery service partners and their drivers, Amazon Flex participants, and seasonal employees under financial distress during this challenging time' (Amazon, 2020).

However, while Amazon was praised for continuing to supply consumers throughout the Covid-19 crisis, it was accused of not taking enough precautions to protect its own warehouse workforce. Critics alleged that with the company working at full stretch, management was worried that employees would not show up to work if they believed that the virus was spreading throughout the warehouse.

The e-retailer faced problems outside of the United States too. In Italy, its main distribution centre saw absenteeism rates of 30 per cent and in France staff went on strike. Eventually the French government completely shut down its warehouses after unions alleged that it was not providing an 'essential' service. Although management asserted that it had changed its logistics, transportation, supply chain, purchasing and third-party seller processes to prioritize stocking and delivering essential items such as household staples and medical supplies, this did not convince regulators.

However, the change in priority, while being seen as critical in the Covid-19 crisis, had a direct impact on Amazon sellers that did not fall into this 'essential' category. Third-party retailers in the United States, using the 'Fulfilled by Amazon' service, were not able to sell their products and Amazon refused to accept new supplies at their warehouses. Although the company waived many of its fees, such as storage, for the duration of the crisis, being unable to sell through the platform affected many thousands of small and medium-sized retailers.

When the crisis is over, the final reckoning for Amazon will be mixed. At the height of the crisis, even Amazon struggled to cope with the demands being placed upon it. In the United States, its Amazon Prime same-day or one-day delivery service was overwhelmed. The strain on the company – due to high levels of new hires; the inability to provide services to its 'Fulfilled by Amazon' customers; the shutdown, partial or full, of its operations in certain parts of the world; as well as the risk of consumers turning to competitors to buy 'non-essential' items – affected its profitability. At the same time, however, Amazon experienced record demand, and post-crisis it may see a change in consumer buying behaviour that will benefit the company. With the likelihood of many physical retail chains shutting down for good (especially high-street stores), consumers will be increasingly driven to online alternatives, of which Amazon, in many parts of the world, is the market leader.

## Amazon's future strategy

Many people have suggested that Amazon may eventually fully enter the third-party logistics market due to its obvious expertise, geographic presence and capabilities in the sector. For some parts of Amazon's operations this could be worthwhile. For instance, as mentioned earlier in this chapter, one Amazon executive has hinted that it could look at providing transportation services to the general market, that is to customers who do not sell their products over Amazon websites. By increasing the volume of freight that it manages (both its own and third party), Amazon would increase its buying power, especially important in the ocean freight segment for instance. It would also ensure that space in its shipping containers could be fully utilized. The reasoning also holds good for last-mile operations by improving the density of delivery networks and the utilization of vans.

However, this logic does not necessarily apply to fulfilment. Illustrating this point, one former Amazon executive commented in an interview, 'I would say that Amazon will not step out and start to just do logistics [i.e. fulfilment], because that makes no sense, because it makes no sense to do that directly, if it doesn't benefit their retail business' (Hemard, 2020).

His main reasoning is that there is no standalone case for market entry into the fulfilment sector due to its low profitability – Amazon's optimization of logistics is designed to make the rest of its e-retail business more profitable as well as drive growth rates through increased service levels. Investing in additional capacity or capabilities when returns in this market are so low would not make financial sense if this involved building new fulfilment centres to serve third-party customers.

Nor would it make sense for many large manufacturers or retailers, who see Amazon as a major competitor, to use it for their third-party logistics services. This would carry a huge risk as there would be a perception that the data they shared about their operations and suppliers would be used by the retail part of Amazon to increase its own competitiveness.

## Summary

Amazon has revolutionized the global retailing sector, as many bricks-and-mortar retailers have found to their cost. Not only has it delivered a new way of shopping but it has also changed customer expectations for good. In order to facilitate these changes, it has put in place logistics systems to fit its needs rather than adapt its business models to the existing industry structures. It has been able to do this due to its sheer scale but at the same time this has become a necessity in order to suppress soaring logistics costs. As it seeks global dominance, it will surely be a major source for logistics and supply chain innovations for many years to come.

# References

Amazon (2020) Amazon's actions to help employees, communities, and customers affected by Covid-19, 26 April, https://blog.aboutamazon.co.uk/amazons-actions-to-help-employees-communities-and-customers-affected-by-covid-19 (archived at https://perma.cc/U59Z-QUQD)

Banker, S (2021) Amazon supply chain innovation continues, *Forbes*, 1 April, www.forbes.com/sites/stevebanker/2021/04/01/amazon-supply-chain-innovation-continues/?sh=4275baf577e6 (archived at https://perma.cc/84YN-FF68)

Boyle, A (2021) Amazon details how its warehouse robots are designed to help humans work safely, GeekWire, 13 June, www.geekwire.com/2021/amazon-details-warehouse-robots-designed-help-humans-work-safely/ (archived at https://perma.cc/WU43-R2ZE)

Conley, P (2021) Amazon says US marketplace sellers sold 3.8 billion products in past 12 months, DigitalCommerce360, 21 October, www.digitalcommerce360.com/article/amazon-seller-news/ (archived at https://perma.cc/V4QS-3VXU)

Hemard, P (2020) Amazon: scaling the logistics network, InPractise, 8 August, https://inpractise.com/courses/amazon-scaling-the-logistics-network/amzn-last-mile (archived at https://perma.cc/W9BW-2A53)

Hollister, B (2018) Replacing traditional TMS helps Amazon crush margins, outpacing e-tailers and manufacturers, LinkedIn, 10 May, www.linkedin.com/pulse/replacing-traditional-tms-helps-amazon-crush-margins-brad-hollister/ (archived at https://perma.cc/674N-DZJ5)

Kim, E (2016) Amazon's $775 million deal for robotics company Kiva is starting to look really smart, Insider, 15 June, http://uk.businessinsider.com/kiva-robots-save-money-for-amazon-2016-6 (archived at https://perma.cc/DN5K-93HS)

Koenen, J, Hofmann, S and Schlautmann, C (2016) Signed, sealed and also delivered, *Handelsblatt Global*, Germany

Montag, A (2018) Amazon says this business opportunity could make you up to $300K a year — here's how to get into the program, CNBC, 6 September, www.cnbc.com/2018/09/06/amazon-delivery-service-partner-program-gets-thousands-of-applications.html (archived at https://perma.cc/Q9TG-7NDG)

Schoolov, K (2021) Amazon is now shipping cargo for outside customers in its latest move to compete with FedEx and UPS, CNBC, 4 September, www.cnbc.com/2021/09/04/how-amazon-is-shipping-for-third-parties-to-compete-with-fedex-and-ups.html (archived at https://perma.cc/AD8X-ME2Y)

# 11

# 3D printing and the transformation of upstream supply chains

**This chapter will familiarize the reader with:**

- What is meant by '3D printing' and the technologies involved in additive manufacturing (AM)
- The advantages it has over traditional manufacturing techniques
- The challenges to adoption faced by the technology
- The potential for the technology to disrupt supply chains
- How the technology is being applied in industry sectors such as automotive and aerospace
- Investment by logistics companies in the technology

3D printing is a major technological innovation with significant implications for the logistics and supply chain industry. Additive manufacturing (AM), as it is otherwise known, is a key element of the Fourth Industrial Revolution. This chapter examines the development of the technology; the reality and the fantasy.

## What is 3D printing?

3D printing was originally developed as an automated method of producing prototypes. Although there are several competing technologies, most work on the basis of building up layers of material (sometimes plastic, ceramics or metal powders) using a computer-aided design. Hence, it is referred to as an 'additive' process; each layer is 'printed' until a three-dimensional product is created.

The logic for using 3D printing for prototypes is compelling. Traditional 'subtractive' manufacturing techniques (where materials are removed) can take longer to set up and are more expensive for short runs. Mechanical parts, shoes, fashion items and accessories, and other consumer goods, can all be printed for review by the designer or engineers, and revisions printed equally as easily. Whereas mass production is viable due to economies of scale, it is uneconomical for 'one-offs' and prototypes.

The end 3D printed product also has other benefits. Products can be lighter, but just as strong. There is also less wastage. In comparison, traditional subtractive manufacturing is highly inefficient in the use of materials.

For many industry sectors, the use of 3D printing is already widespread, although confined to certain specialist parts of the manufacturing process. It has many benefits over traditional reductive production techniques, these being:

- faster iteration of prototypes
- lower lead times
- elimination of tools and moulds
- reduction of component weight without compromising on strength ('light weighting')
- reduction in number of parts required
- reduction of material loss
- replacement of parts quickly and easily
- optimization of computer-aided designs
- customization of parts
- postponement of manufacturing opportunities
- reduction in supply chain risk through less outsourcing
- elimination of 'bull whip' inventory effect and safety stocks of intermediate goods

According to a report by consultancy Deloitte (2018), 3D printing will be most widely adopted in automotive 'design-rapid' prototype printing, aerospace and defence parts printing. There were an estimated 2.1 million printers in 2020, a figure that is predicted to grow to 15.3 million by 2028 (GVR, 2021).

The way in which each product is individually manufactured means that it is ideal for 'mass customization' techniques. Consumers will, in theory, be able to have a much greater say in the final format of the product they are buying, and have it manufactured to their precise specifications.

As yet, traditional manufacturing holds sway in sectors where mass production is still required but, as we will see, this is likely to change as printer technology becomes cheaper and printers get faster.

The range of materials used in the 'printers' is also developing. These now include:

- plastic
- nylon
- graphite
- ceramic
- glass-filled polyamide
- epoxy resins
- silver
- titanium
- steel
- wax
- polycarbonates

There are many types of technologies involved, perhaps the most popular being selective laser melting (SLM) and direct metal laser sintering (DMLS). These techniques both use a laser to melt metal powder particles together, building up a part layer-by-layer, but the latter can use powder composed of several materials to form an alloy.

## Challenges to adoption

Although the technology has been around for some time, progress towards adoption has been slower than first thought. No one expected the industry to be transformed overnight, but progress has been inhibited by the following factors:

- inherent inertia of big manufacturers
- complacency around the need to change

- fear of failure
- regulatory burdens
- lack of available talent
- unwillingness to take risks
- time taken to print parts
- cost per piece
- lack of standardization of raw materials
- quality assurance, reliability and liability
- risk of counterfeiting
- concerns over intellectual property

Only when these issues and worries have been addressed will the technology become more widely adopted. Many of the above are related to corporate or operational concerns. However, there is also a logistics-related challenge linked to the international movements of goods, that being the role of customs. Presently, customs authorities collect tariffs and duties on imported goods, as well as playing an important role in preventing the shipment of counterfeit or sub-standard goods. Firstly, from a tax revenue-generating perspective, if products are produced locally by 3D printer there is a strong possibility that tariffs and duties will decline in line with a drop in international shipping volumes, thus creating a shortfall for national exchequers. Will duties need to be levied on a download of a design if that design originated overseas? This seems unlikely as, in a cloud computing world, digital libraries could be located anywhere. Secondly, how will authorities react to the risk that businesses (and individuals) will be able to produce goods that may be lower than regulated standards (electrical fitments, for example, made from inadequate materials) with no traceability? At present, the low volume of parts produced by 3D printing and the oversight of the major manufacturers producing these goods has ensured that these issues have not made it onto the political agenda. The democratization of the technology will ensure that this will not remain the case for long.

## Why will 3D printing disrupt supply chains?

In a white paper on the subject (Manners-Bell and Lyon, 2015) it was asserted that 3D printing had the potential to become the biggest single disruptive phenomenon to impact global industry since assembly lines were introduced in the United States in the early 20th century.

The authors went on to say: 'New technologies that are currently being developed could revolutionize production techniques, resulting in a significant proportion of manufacturing becoming automated and removing reliance on large and costly workforces. This in turn could lead to a reversal of the trend of globalization that has characterized industry and consumption over the last few decades, itself predicated on the trade-off between transportation and labour costs.'

This assertion still holds true, although the adoption of the technology has been slower than originally thought. Many people focus on the higher cost per piece as a reason for the slow take-up, although lower prices for 3D printers and the materials they use will address this issue. Likewise, the speed of 3D printing will also increase as technology develops.

However, it is likely that these challenges will be overcome not least due to the enormous value that will be released within the supply chain. One estimate suggests that inventory and waiting comprises 92 per cent of assembly time in the automotive industry and that transport output related to these parts amounts to 45.3 billion ton-miles in the United States alone (Dohnalek, 2018). These 'hidden' costs are rarely taken into account when comparing traditional manufacturing techniques with 3D printing. Presently, in Lean Supply Chain terms, transport is seen as a 'necessary waste' – this may well change to 'unnecessary waste' in the coming years.

3D printing will mean that the intermediate goods in the supply chain will be replaced by the raw materials needed to make the printing materials. Multiple tiers of inventories held upstream and downstream will be eliminated, as will be the need to move them from location to location, often on a global basis. Instead, much simpler supply chains involving the bulk storage and movement of printer materials will develop.

An example of this is the material 'graphite'. Currently used for 3D printing in the electronics sector due to its superior conductive capabilities, the mineral is predominantly sourced from a mine in Tanzania where very pure forms can be extracted. The Australian mining company involved has partnered with a specialist 3D printing company to develop a variant 'graphene'. The relevance of this is that tiers of suppliers presently involved in traditional supply chains will be removed as mineral resource companies can supply materials direct to processing companies that supply the printer materials to be used in the production of components or final product. The implications of this to supply chains are highlighted below.

## A supply chain transformation

To illustrate the supply chain changes that could occur, it is useful to examine a number of scenarios starting with an analysis of present structures.

In the simplified supply chain shown in Figure 11.1, it can be seen that, upstream, a complex lattice work of interconnected 'tiered' suppliers exists. Although the chart just shows two tiers of suppliers, many supply chains consist of more than five tiers. They will supply each other as well as the final assembly operations undertaken by an original equipment manufacturer (OEM) or by its contract manufacturing company. This results in intensive transport requirements on an intra-regional basis, typically across Asia, supported by air cargo, shipping, road freight and freight-forwarding resources. The final products are then shipped to ports in North America or Europe, moved inland and then stored and distributed possibly to more localized warehouses before last-mile delivery to the end recipient.

FIGURE 11.1  Existing global supply chain networks

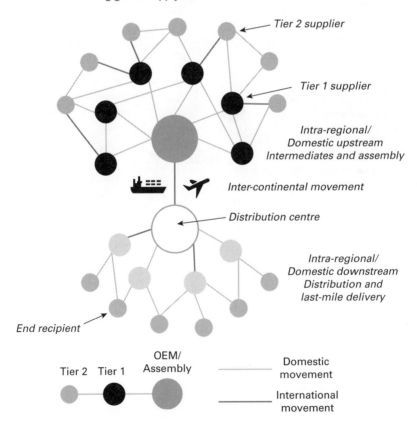

As shown in Figure 11.2, in what could be considered as Stage 1 of the evolution towards the adoption of 3D printing throughout industry, many of the existing suppliers of semi-fabricated goods become redundant as a result of the introduction of 3D printing plants. The final assembly plant also adopts this technology, doing away with the need for a proportion of its labour requirements. The goods are then shipped to ports in the developed world and stored at distribution centres in a 'vanilla' state, i.e. in a format that will allow further customization for local markets. 3D printers at the distribution centre will undertake this customization. These goods are then shipped through logistics networks to the end recipient via more

**FIGURE 11.2**  Hybrid industrial 3D supply chain networks

*Substitution of semi-fabricated goods with raw materials*

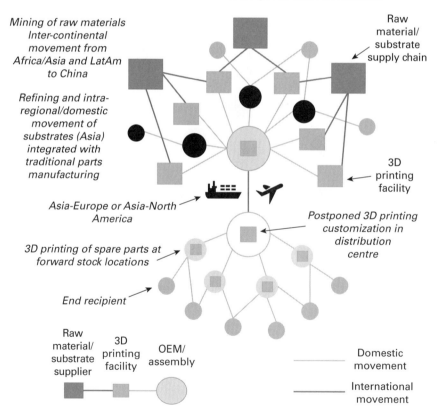

localized distribution locations. These locations also double up as 3D printer plants for spare parts, using their proximity to the customer and service engineers to meet tight service level agreements.

In the next stage, global manufacturers are able to exploit the technology to produce goods without the need for large labour forces. Hence, China and Asia lose their competitive advantage as a manufacturing location and production is 're-shored' (Figure 11.3). Raw materials are shipped direct from the regions of extraction, typically Africa, Latin America, parts of Asia and Australia to 3D printing plants in North America and Europe.

FIGURE 11.3  Re-shored 3D supply chain networks

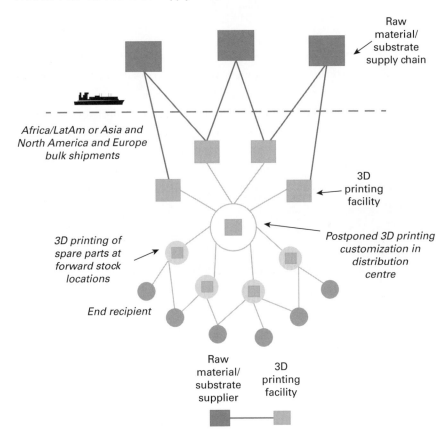

FIGURE 11.4  3D print shop model

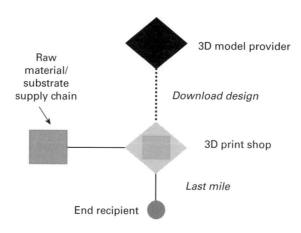

There are obviously many variations of these scenarios, but one that provides an alternative structure is highlighted in Figure 11.4.

In this example, the customer requests a 3D print shop or facility to download a design from a database (either generic or customized), which is then manufactured. The final product can then be dispatched to the end recipient or collected. The system is very simple in comparison with the previous models, which describe the impact of 3D printing on enterprise-wide structures.

## Adoption by industry sectors

### Automotive

Presently, 3D printing is used for concept modelling and prototyping as well as the printing of some production parts and low-volume replacement parts. In the future, the technique will be extended to much longer runs, creating lighter components using innovative materials and completely new designs that do not try to replicate existing parts but fully optimize the potential that 3D printers offer. This includes computer-aided honeycomb and lattice designs, which would be impossible to produce with traditional techniques but offer a combination of weight and strength.

## ENGINES

Very large 3D printers have now been developed that can be used for printing whole engine blocks. One, developed by German company Roush Industries, is aimed at companies looking to design engines rather than for large-scale production. However, management believe that soon the technology will be fast enough for production of engines to be considered feasible. Quality and size issues are no longer inhibitors. Of course, if electric vehicles replace existing internal-combustion-engine-powered vehicles, the need for printing engine blocks will become redundant.

## SPARE PARTS PRODUCTION

Many automotive manufacturers are already testing the concept of 3D printing spare parts. It has become popular for 'vintage' cars where parts are very slow moving and consequently costly to store (and source). This involves manufacturers developing digital libraries of parts, which can then be printed off on demand. 3D printers are still located at central locations so that quality can be assured, although in the future it is conceivable that printers based in garages or dealerships would be able to provide the parts, eliminating the need for transportation completely.

Manufacturers actively involved in testing the technology for parts include:

- Renault
- Audi
- Rolls-Royce
- Caterpillar
- Porsche (classic cars)
- Daimler Trucks North America (pilot project)

## TYRES

Tyre manufacturers such as Michelin are in the process of planning a new generation of tyres leveraging the potential of 3D printing to manufacture products from complex, biomimetic designs and using recycled materials. According to the company, the future tyre will be airless, recyclable, puncture-proof and strong. It will also be possible to 3D print a retread for the tyre.

### Aerospace

3D printing offers enormous potential for the production of components primarily due to their lightweight nature, essential when the weight of aircraft is so critical in the aerospace industry. The sector can claim leadership in the application, with Boeing using 3D printed parts since 2003, originally in the air defence sector. The US Department of Defence has been interested due to the potential to print parts quickly and in 'combat theatre'. Today, Boeing has 50,000 3D printed parts flying in a variety of aircraft. The company is in the process of introducing titanium parts for the 787 Dreamliner, although this will require approval by the Federal Aviation Administration (FAA), the US regulator.

The General Electric (GE) initiative is probably the most ambitious. Since 2015 it has been printing fuel nozzle injectors for its LEAP jet engine at its Auburn, Alabama facility and, by 2021, it had printed over 100,000 parts. This takes use of the technology to another level. One of the key benefits is the reduction in complexity. A GE 3D printed turboprop engine reduces the number of parts required from 855 to 12 – a fact that will have huge implications on the aerospace supply chain.

## Construction

Many of the innovations that have occurred in the construction business have been in design, engineering and operations rather than in actual building and fabrication of materials. There are good reasons why 3D printing should be embraced by the construction industry, not least the worsening labour shortage as well as the huge level of waste that is endemic in the sector.

Chinese company Winsun, which specializes in advanced building products, printed 10 complete houses in 2014 and has since printed an office building in Dubai. Since then, many other companies have entered the market, often collaborating with start-ups: for example, concrete manufacturer LafargeHolcim and XtreeE.

In terms of the construction supply chain, 3D printing would mean reductions in:

- numbers of parts
- complexity
- number of deliveries to building sites
- returns of misordered and damaged goods

However, although the technology is available, it is still very expensive and this has inhibited its adoption.

*Electronics*

Consultancy Ernst & Young believes that the electronics sector could be ripe for disruption by 3D printing, at least in the prototype stage (Ernst & Young, 2016). For example, the development and testing of printed circuit boards can take 8–40 days and is often an outsourced procedure. With minimum runs required by the outsourced suppliers, which are likely to be based in Asia, this is often a costly as well as time-consuming procedure. 3D printing allows this to occur in-house and, because no minimum run is required, is far less wasteful.

## Implications for the express and logistics industry

Ultimately 3D printing could be a major threat to express and logistics companies should traditional tiered manufacturing and spare parts networks be swept away. There is no doubt this is a possibility, although it is unlikely to happen quickly and the effects are more likely to be manifested as a head-wind to growth rather than a 'cliff edge'. More likely the technology will bring about changes to supply networks rather than their elimination.

### Scenario 1 (medium-time horizon)

3D printing becomes adopted widely for the production of parts in high-tech sectors such as automotive, aerospace, medical technology and electronics.

- The reduction of the amount of parts required in the assembly process means that supply chains become much less complex. This means that inventory storage requirements reduce at all supply chain levels.

- Manufacturing companies that were focused on the assembly of components (largely in China) invest heavily in 3D printing technology in order to capture higher levels of value-add. This means that 'Tier' suppliers in Asia lose out and intra-Asian trade in intermediate goods falls.

- Global manufacturers no longer require large labour forces and can base their facilities anywhere. This means that manufacturers with the capabilities can re-shore production.

The outcome of this last point will be difficult to assess, as although 3D printing means that in theory manufacturers will be able to base their production facilities much closer to the end market, no longer dependent on low-cost labour, the fact that generations of manufacturing know-how have been relocated to China casts considerable doubt as to whether there is the ability to redevelop sufficient manufacturing expertise in Europe or North America.

Therefore, in terms of impact on the logistics industry:

- Intra-Asian shipping and freight-forwarding volumes will be adversely affected.
- Global movements of finished goods may not be affected, with the main origin still being China. Japan would be another beneficiary.
- Domestic movements of goods in developed markets may benefit if re-shoring takes place.
- Certainly, global inventories of spare parts will be reduced as parts will be printed close to demand. It is still likely that the last-mile delivery will be undertaken by an express company (from a forward location with industrial printing capabilities).

### Scenario 2 (long-time horizon)

Less likely is the scenario that manufacturing is consumerized, that is, 3D printing allows individuals to print products in their own homes. Although this is already possible for hobbyists, it is not likely that the type of industrial 3D printing machinery needed to produce most goods will be affordable.

However, if an element of 3D printing could be introduced to households:

- The movement of goods throughout the supply chain will become redundant.
- This will be replaced by the flow of materials that are required for use in the printers.
- Raw materials from predominantly developing regions such as Africa and Latin America will be refined into printer materials. The final movement (whether domestic or international) will depend on the location of these refineries.
- Large warehouses would be required to store these printer materials.

## Investment by logistics companies

Recognizing the long-term threat of 3D printing or, more likely, looking at the short-term opportunities that it provides to add value to their operations, logistics companies are investing heavily in the technology.

### UPS

In 2016, UPS launched what it called a 3D printing manufacturing network. Working with SAP, it rolled out 3D printers to 60 UPS stores in the United States as well as a 3D printing factory in Louisville, leveraging what it saw as a need for 'manufacturing as a service'. Customers will place their orders centrally, and the part will be printed at the optimal location.

### FedEx

FedEx has followed UPS's lead and in 2018 it created 'FedEx Forward Depots', a business unit responsible, inter alia, for critical inventory and 3D printing. However, the product is still in an early stage of development.

### DB Schenker

Schenker's customers can now upload a 3D template via the online portal, eSchenker, select materials and colour, consult prices, place orders and have the end product delivered.

At present, printing includes medical devices made from stainless steel, robot gripper fingers made from plastic or customized packaging material. DB Schenker organizes the printing and delivery via its data platform. The company does not have its own printers but uses a digital business model within a partner network of start-ups as well as established companies.

## Impetus from Covid-19

The supply chain challenges created by the Covid-19 pandemic have been well documented. Manufacturers in Europe and North America have often struggled to source critical components, sometimes due to supplier shutdown but also as a result of a breakdown in air and sea logistics. It has been reported that a shortage of parts led to a surge in orders for 3D printed parts, especially for the auto and aerospace industries. Many of these were quite simple (such as bolts and hinges) rather than the sophisticated components or products in demand before the pandemic struck (Miller, 2022).

At the very least, the pandemic has highlighted the potential for the technology to play an even more important role in Western manufacturing, especially healthcare. The decentralized nature of production that it enables mitigates the impact of disruption to long lines of supply. Specifically in the fight against Covid-19, 3D printing can be deployed in the manufacture of personal protective equipment and components, medical and testing devices (e.g. airway valves and swabs), visualization/training aids and emergency dwellings such as isolation wards (Choong et al, 2020). All of these items were in short supply at the height of the crisis in 2020, not least as a result of some national governments in Asia (most importantly China) blocking their export on the grounds of securing their own national supplies. The sourcing of personal protective equipment (PPE) became a matter of strategic importance, which led some governments to turn to 3D printing as part of the solution to the crisis. In fact, in the United States, 3D printing was responsible for the production of 38 million face shield parts, 12 million nasal swabs, 2.5 million ear savers, 241,000 mask parts and 116,000 ventilator parts between February and July 2020, according to one report (AMCPR, 2021).

One of the benefits of using 3D printers was the short set-up time required. Many large-scale manufacturers that pivoted to the production of PPE took many weeks before they were able to produce at scale. 3D printing was essential to fill this hiatus, even though traditional techniques eventually took over in the long run. As the AMCPR report stated, 'Enormous latent capacity exists within the United States to quickly pivot and support a variety of emergency responses with AM [3D printing], addressing even the most unpredictable needs.' A challenge, however, was ensuring that all items conformed to stringent regulatory standards and this will be an area in which better coordination and communication will be required if a similar situation arises again.

## Summary

Although 3D printing has not yet caught on to the extent many people had expected, its implementation has been steady and its wider adoption would seem inevitable. 3D printing is being integrated within existing manufacturing processes, which will result in what could be termed 'hybrid' supply chains. Over time, increasing numbers of parts and sub-assemblies will be produced by 3D printing, either within the final assembly facility, logistics centres or in specialist plants.

This will mean that, eventually, there will be significant changes to supply chains. This may not be evident for many years, resulting perhaps in lower growth for the logistics sector rather than an overall reduction in market size. However, there is no good reason to expect the present system of globalized supply chains to remain set in stone, and technological development could well be the catalyst for transformation.

Not all changes will threaten logistics companies. As mentioned, 3D printing will provide the opportunity for more customization of parts and postponed manufacturing, which will take place as far downstream as possible. For example, at a logistics centre in a developed market.

It is clear that with so much uncertainty as to how fast and in which direction the technology will develop, all supply chain parties must remain prepared for the many opportunities and threats that 3D printing will inevitably provide.

# References

AMCPR (2021) America makes Covid-19 response assessing the role of additive manufacturing in support of the US Covid-19 response, Advanced Manufacturing Crisis Manufacturing Response, March, www.fda.gov/media/150615/download (archived at https://perma.cc/S6NA-FG8Y)

Choong, Y Y C, Tan, H W, Patel, D C et al (2020) The global rise of 3D printing during the Covid-19 pandemic, *Nature Reviews Materials*, 5, pp 637–9, https://doi.org/10.1038/s41578-020-00234-3 (archived at https://perma.cc/ZQ6R-SW3A)

Deloitte (2018) Exponential technologies in manufacturing, https://www2.deloitte.com/us/en/pages/manufacturing/articles/advanced-manufacturing-technologies-report.html (archived at https://perma.cc/4T5T-VV2V)

Dohnalek, M (2018) 3-D and the global supply chain, *Supply Chain Management Review*, 18 June, www.scmr.com/article/3_d_and_the_global_supply_chain#When:14:27:00Z (archived at https://perma.cc/D8VA-P4PC)

Ernst & Young (2016) How will 3D printing make your company the strongest link in the value chain?, New York

GVR (Grand View Research) (2021) 3D printing market size, share & trends report, www.grandviewresearch.com/industry-analysis/3d-printing-industry-analysis (archived at https://perma.cc/3JPM-XXXY)

Manners-Bell, J and Lyon, K (2015) The implications of 3D printing for the global logistics industry, Transport Intelligence, http://www.logisticsexecutive.com/wp-content/uploads/2015/01/The-Implications-of-3D-Printing-for-the-Global-Logistics-Industry.pdf (archived at https://perma.cc/4HWA-XD3Y)

Miller, J (2022) 3D printing and 'reshoring' offer limited protection to supply chains, *Financial Times*, 18 January, www.ft.com/content/deb2514d-acdf-4eb6-ad42-e60f946c1a74 (archived at https://perma.cc/2U42-XTEP)

# PART THREE

# New technology development and adoption

# 12

# The Internet of Things, Big Data and artificial intelligence

**This chapter will familiarize the reader with:**

- What is meant by the term 'Internet of Things'
- The application of the technology in supply chains and how it will impact on consumers, retailers and manufacturers
- Benefits of the new technology to the logistics industry and how it will be applied
- The role of artificial intelligence (AI) in analysing the vast levels of data being generated, in part by the Internet of Things
- AI's importance to the successful integration of the digital and physical world
- How AI will impact upon the logistics and supply chain industry
- Its role in the development of logistics innovations

## 'Internet of Things' in the supply chain

The 'Internet of Things' (IoT) is a term used to encompass the use of sensors, technology and networking to allow buildings, infrastructures, devices and additional 'things' to share information without requiring human-to-human or human-to-computer interaction. It can create richer data and deeper intelligence for all parties in a supply network.

The IoT and the technology surrounding it is expected to grow in terms of market size from \$384.7 billion in 2021 to \$2,465 billion in 2028, a compound annual growth rate of 26.4 per cent (Fortune, 2021). It is estimated that in 2021 there were 12.3 billion connected items and that by 2025 there will be more than 27 billion (IoT Analytics, 2021).

> 'The internet has changed the way we consume information and talk with each other, but now it can do more. By connecting intelligent machines to each other and ultimately to people, and by combining software and Big Data analytics, we can push the boundaries of physical and material sciences to change the way the world works.'
>
> Jeff Immelt, former CEO of GE

With the lower cost of production, sensors will become more economical for use in a range of supply chain applications. They provide visibility down to item level, a level of granularity that has thus far come at a significant cost. These visibility gains will result in substantial financial benefits, as supply chains become far better at locating and securing inventory.

## The connected consumer

Domestic automation, enabled by the IoT, includes a wide range of functions and appliances in the home, many of which are not supply chain related (controlling heating and lighting, for instance). However, other appliances can be integrated into the supply chain, such as the refrigerator. Using sensors and video cameras (monitoring the contents of the fridge), the appliance can be a portal for ordering and reordering perishable goods. Software can learn to recognize items, such as milk or tomatoes, and track buying behaviour. Eventually, smart packaging should even be able to identify when products are out of date.

The same principle applies to other household appliances. For example, washing machines and dishwashers can automatically reorder detergent, perhaps in conjunction with a virtual assistant.

Sensors can also be attached to appliances in order to perform predictive maintenance. This may enable them to perform self-diagnostics, alerting the service company to the fault and which parts are required.

According to a Worldpay report in 2018, 44 per cent of consumers used connected home devices and virtual assistants such as 'Alexa'; 46 per cent of those interviewed for the company said that they were happy for the devices to place orders automatically without human intervention (Worldpay, 2018). Other connected innovations will also change buyer behaviour – 3D bodyscanners, for example, will encourage more consumers to buy clothes at home without going to store to try them on.

Although the advent of the connected home is inevitable and to be welcomed, there is also the need to improve cyber security. Either manufacturers will need to ensure their products are harder to subvert or users will need to reinforce their domestic infrastructure. This topic is often ignored by both media and manufacturers but will become a significant issue over the next few years.

## Supply chain inventory management

### DIGITAL SHELVING

Using sensors on products to identify when stock is running low in-store (so-called 'digital shelving') will enable reordering automatically. Stock levels on the shelves as well as stockroom, distribution centres as well as other stores can be linked and viewed, theoretically, on a real-time basis. This may allow returns to be rerouted to stores where there is demand rather than being sent back to a central warehouse.

### CONTAINER AND PRODUCT TRACKING

There are many different levels of sophistication of sensors used in the tracking of containers. Some log data for download at a later point while others can use GPS technology to provide real-time tracking, alert when the door has been opened or environmental parameters exceeded (temperature, for example). Although sensors have been around for many years, integrating them within a cohesive management system and gaining visibility of the consignments within the container will be the ultimate goal. Eventually this will provide 'from floor to store and beyond' item-level tracking capabilities.

### INVENTORY OPTIMIZATION

A study by Harvard Business School found that 8 per cent of all retail items are out of stock at any given time (Corsten and Gruen, 2004). With IoT systems in place, the likelihood of stock-outs can be reduced by as much as 80 per cent according to Zebra Technologies, as the improved visibility generated by the technology allows retailers to locate and replenish their stock far more rapidly (Zebra, 2015). Automatic reordering when the weight or height of items reach a certain level would replace stochastic, rule-based methods. Item-level visibility also allows buffer stock to be reduced, delivering cost savings on both overstocking and understocking. McKinsey suggest that inventory optimization could deliver savings in inventory carrying costs of 10 per cent a year (McKinsey, 2015).

The same concept also applies in other sectors. McKinsey (2015) estimates that gains are even bigger than in the retail environment, with the potential value gain ranging from 20 to 50 per cent reduction in manufacturing/hospital inventory costs. One example is the use of sensors and cameras to monitor stock levels in supply boxes. When they have reduced to a certain point, an order to replenish the bins is made. Consequently, the IoT allows decisions to be made on real data rather than on forecasts.

INVENTORY SHRINKAGE

Furthermore, visibility at the item level allows retailers to keep much tighter control over shrinkage, which cost an estimated $46.8 billion in the United States in 2017, according to the US National Retail Federation (NRF, 2018). A notable success in this area is the French sporting goods retailer Decathlon, which reported that the deployment of sensors across its 951 stores had the impact of reducing shrinkage by 9 per cent in 2014 (Swedberg, 2015).

## Application in the logistics industry

Fleet and asset tracking is one such capability that IoT can provide, and many logistics operators have already installed new tracking technology across their fleets of vans, trucks, trailers and intermodal containers. Tracking technology can deliver continuous, real-time information regarding the location and load status of each trailer and container, often using solar or cellular power. This allows companies to pinpoint the exact location of empty containers and trailers, making the planning and dispatch process more efficient, while reducing drivers' wasted time and empty miles.

The increased level of sensor use and vehicle telematics allows logistics managers to gather data daily on mechanical performance of vehicles and behavioural patterns of drivers. This includes: vehicle speed; direction; braking; performance of engine and mechanical components. This can be used to improve driver behaviour, reducing wear on vehicle and fuel consumption (thereby reducing $CO_2$ emissions). This results in the improved maintenance of vehicles, less downtime and fewer breakdowns.

Sensors are not just being introduced to the road freight industry. Aircraft engine manufacturers have been capturing engine performance data in-flight for years. This data is constantly being transmitted to the manufacturers so that any variation from expected norms generates an alert. This information is then used to trigger specific inspections at the next point the aircraft lands, along with the appropriate recommendations for resolving the issue, such as having a replacement part available at the airport, which is then installed before the plane is allowed to continue.

This regime is well established and has resulted in enormous gains in reliability, a reduction in flight delays due to engine problems and improved engine efficiency in terms of jet fuel use. Engine manufacturers such as Rolls-Royce, GE and Pratt & Whitney now have massive amounts of data that is constantly analysed for improvements and greater insight into how the next generation of engines can be made more efficient and effective. Every flight that takes place continues to add to these data stores.

Benefits of IoT include:

- Monitoring the status of assets, parcels and people in real time
- Measuring how assets are performing (and what they will do next)
- Reducing fuel costs by optimization of fleet routes
- Automating business processes to eliminate manual interventions
- Optimizing how people, systems and assets work together, and coordinate their activities
- Applying analytics to identify wider improvement opportunities and best practices
- Monitoring inventory to reduce stock-outs

---

CASE STUDY 12.1

*Using IOT for yard management*

DHL Supply Chain and Huawei Technologies operate a Narrowband Internet of Things (NB-IoT) application at an automotive site in Liuzhou, China. Leveraging existing infrastructure and limited investments, the implemented IoT solution is designed to facilitate and streamline yard management for inbound-to-manufacturing logistics, leading to improvements in inbound processing time at the site. The operation involves 100 DHL drivers at a section comprising 30 docks.

DHL and Huawei use NB-IoT chipsets for their solution, which use common cellular telecommunications bands with the benefits of a more simple and cost-effective implementation. Vehicle detectors are embedded with these chipsets, which do not require any infrastructure investments. Within each terminal, DHL Supply Chain is now able to automatically collect clear dock availability in real time, which in return provides visibility to the dispatcher and drivers. When a truck arrives, its driver checks in via an app on his mobile, receiving a queue number and an estimated waiting time. The yard management system then automatically screens the docks for their availability, providing each driver with real-time status updates visible via the app. As soon as a dock is free, the driver is notified to proceed accordingly. This way, inbound trucks can be prioritized to the site's needs and shipments are unloaded at the most appropriate dock.

The innovation has halved the waiting time for drivers from an average of 40 minutes, significantly reducing the risks of manufacturing delays as materials arrive in time and resources are optimized appropriately.

## The future: printable electronics?

Although much attention has focused on the use of sensor technologies such as radio-frequency identification (RFID), considerable potential also exists in conventional printing systems. Inkjet systems are built for mass production, employing rollers to transfer ink onto the surface being printed, whether that be paper or plastic. If this technology could be effectively applied to the production of integrated circuits and antennae, then it could completely transform the market for sensors and unlock greater potential for the IoT.

Currently, most 'passive' sensors (the most commonly used) cost a minimum of five cents per tag, which is far too expensive for widespread use in consumer-packaged goods, for example. The reason it is difficult to produce tags at scale for a lower price is that the traditional manufacturing technique used to make integrated circuits and conductive antennae, the basic components used in passive RFID tags, is copper-etching, a process that requires several phases and wastes as much as 70 per cent of the material. While etching is considered an efficient process overall, it places a floor on the minimum cost of production.

As such, the application of inkjet printing systems to the production of microchips is something that has been talked about for some time, with silver or copper ink used as a conductor. Unfortunately, many circuits produced using the latter have suffered poor performance, while those using the former have been uneconomical.

Nonetheless, there are potential ways around this problem. Researchers have explored the use of graphene particles as a component of conductive inks in place of silver nano-particles, with promising results. A team led by Dr Tawfique Hasan of the Cambridge Graphene Centre (CGC), in collaboration with local company Novalia, has successfully developed a commercially viable system that prints at a rate exceeding 100 metres of material per minute. Moreover, the cost of the graphene ink used is around £40 per kilogram, compared to a cost of at least £1,000 per kilogram in the case of silver-based inks.

It is important to note that printable tags are still held back by a lack of economies of scale. Nonetheless, with the success of existing solutions, and with the expected cost reductions to the manufacturing process, this technology could become a lot more practical in the near future.

## Big Data and artificial intelligence (AI)

The ubiquitous nature of low-cost sensors has led to the rise of Big Data. The trillions of data points that are now being generated mean that the availability of information is no longer a problem. However, the challenge remains to be able to use such high levels of data to make informed decisions.

Control towers are a step towards utilizing this data (see Chapter 13), but on their own they are insufficient. The potential of Big Data can only be exploited by removing human involvement from the decision-making process. Humans are no longer capable of analysing the overwhelming levels of data that are being generated. This is where AI becomes critical.

Figure 12.1 shows the relationship that exists between the physical world and the digital world. Sensors in transport assets and actual products are able to communicate data about their status, location, condition and environment at every stage of the supply chain. The Big Data generated then

FIGURE 12.1  The cyber–physical relationship in supply chain

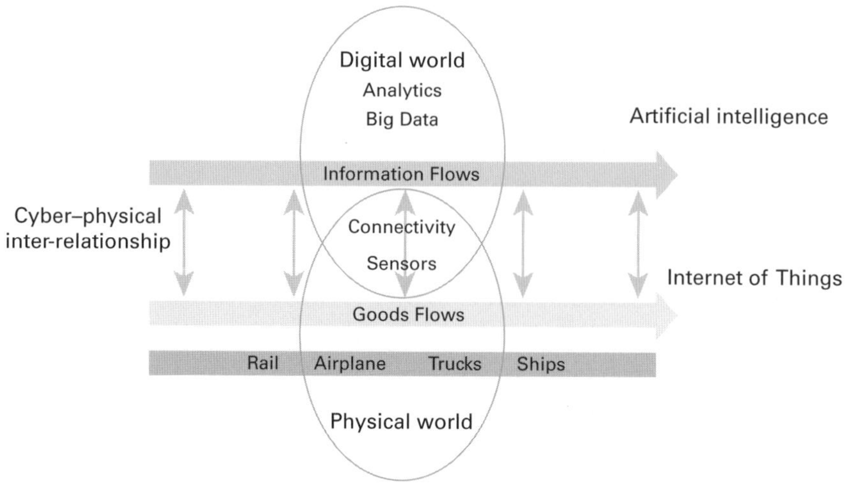

requires real-time analysis, if it is to be of any use, allowing decisions to be made that will create supply chain value. This could be:

- exception-management, resulting in rerouting or change of delivery time
- intervention, such as precautionary maintenance on a truck or ship
- deciding on the most efficient position for put-away in a warehouse

All of this occurs without human interaction, working to a set of algorithms or rules that hardwires efficiency into the supply chain.

### What is AI?

AI is a broad concept, traditionally conceived as a definition for a self-aware machine with an ability to think and act as an autonomous agent. AI within the current commercial context is now broadly accepted as a term to convey a machine capable of performing tasks that would formerly require human intelligence, such as visual perception, speech recognition, decision making and language translation. For a machine to be artificially intelligent, it may be informed by human reasoning, but it does not necessarily need to function in the same way.

A fundamental component of AI is machine learning, a term that refers to the ability of a computer to identify patterns in streams of inputs and learn by association. For example, through this process a computer can 'learn' to distinguish a dog from a cat by filtering through a data bank of thousands of categorized images, and respond to human corrections to build an association between the data.

In order to leverage the benefits of AI, it is first necessary for the computer in question to have access to vast amounts of data, which is where Big Data becomes relevant. Moreover, in understanding the analogy of Big Data as the 'fuel' for an AI 'engine', it is also important to recognize the significance of the IoT as a means of extracting useful data to be analysed. As these technologies progress and mature, they will be increasingly embedded within a mutually supportive ecosystem that operates and improves physical and virtual networks, such as supply chains.

## Supply chain and logistics applications of AI

### DELIVERY FLEXIBILITY
One area of logistics that will be increasingly influenced by AI is the operation of last-mile delivery systems. Delivery flexibility is a vital enabler for e-retailers aiming to keep up with changing consumer demands, which also vary between countries and regions. For example, customers in the UK are keen on in-store 'click and collect', while German consumers prefer to use parcel lockers, but neither preferences are static.

Overall, customers are becoming more demanding. In a 2016 survey by Metapack, 46 per cent of survey respondents said that if there were an option available that allowed them to change their delivery preferences after placing an online order, they would use it (Metapack, 2016). However, any company offering a flexible range of delivery options faces an increasingly difficult task in coordinating last-mile flows, and this is where the application of AI can dramatically improve delivery services.

Besides optimizing the distribution of shipments, AI can also submit alternatives by crunching customer data; for example, proposing that a customer pick up their consignment from a designated access point, based on geo-location data showing that it will be located on their route home as they commute from work. By analysing consumer behaviours and location data provided by mobile devices, it is likely that AI will enable companies to become increasingly capable of customizing delivery options for individual customers.

### CONNECTED CONSUMERS
The key to unlocking such advanced functionality is data. Notably, while the success of Amazon's Dash Button (released in 2015) in driving sales is

reportedly negligible, it has been an invaluable source of information on consumer behaviours.

At present, one of the main weaknesses of machine learning systems is that the data inputs they receive are restricted; Google knows what you are searching for, Facebook knows who your friends are and Apple knows what music you listen to, but none of them can combine this information to gain a more complete understanding of you as an individual.

The companies winning this race are those that have realized the potential of home-based assistants for acquiring and interpreting data. Amazon's Echo is the most prominent of these systems, which, by leveraging integrations with other smart devices, can produce helpful suggestions and enact orders. For example, by connecting to the data embedded in a user's smart fridge, such an assistant could suggest that a customer would be out of milk tomorrow morning; but if they were to submit an order they could receive a delivery in time to eat cereal for breakfast.

## AUTONOMOUS VEHICLES

Arguably the most visible manifestation of AI within the e-commerce supply chain is autonomous vehicles, chiefly in the form of drones. As the last-mile delivery of products constitutes the only visible segment of the supply chain for individual consumers, drones have captured the popular imagination and account for a sizeable proportion of the news coverage relating to AI. This notwithstanding, the development of autonomous delivery drones is significant from a commercial perspective.

## WAREHOUSE AUTOMATION

Warehouse automation is another area that has already been significantly impacted by AI. The distribution of products in an Amazon warehouse, for example, is not pre-determined by category but uses an organic shelving system where products are arranged by the company's warehouse management system, which uses algorithms to optimize placement based on picking routes.

The company's 2012 acquisition of Kiva systems allowed it to optimize fulfilment further, by deploying robots to streamline the picking process; bringing the shelves of goods to the human picker, rather than vice versa. This has speeded up picking operations and has enhanced the use of AI within the company's facilities.

This is only one model for the application of AI within a warehouse setting, however. Rather than a top-down system that controls the movements of all robots within the picking area, other companies have exploited machine learning to 'train' automated guided vehicles (AGVs) to operate in a mixed warehouse setting, alongside humans.

US start-up Seegrid has embedded this capability within several materials handling systems that learn by association. Each AGV is set up with multiple cameras, before being 'walked through' a designated warehouse route by a human operator. The company's proprietary software allows each of the vehicles to recognize a specific route based on the visual data, with each route 'memory' available to all AGVs operating within the system. The system is flexible, relies on relatively cheap hardware, and unlike Amazon's robots, does not need to read specific instructions from floor markings. Seegrid AGVs have been adopted by the USPS, and Amazon itself, among others.

## Summary

The Internet of Things has the potential to provide unparalleled levels of data related to just about every aspect of the supply chain – from consumer behaviour and needs to the location of products in the warehouse; from wear and tear on vehicle engine components to the tracking of shipments across continents. Nevertheless, generating these huge quantities of data is pointless if the data resource is not analysed in a timely fashion and the resulting intelligence not acted upon. This is where AI will play a critical role.

Fears over the unintended consequences of AI experimentation are likely to become a recurring topic of debate over the coming years in the media and for politicians. However, despite concerns, AI is set to significantly increase the efficiency of major organizations. Within supply chains, a more effective allocation of assets in response to demand peaks and troughs will reduce costs. In addition, the prospects for using AI in a creative manner will allow organizations to solve problems in different ways. For supply chains, AI applications have already allowed control towers to introduce predictive and prescriptive functions to navigate unforeseen events. As AI applications become more advanced, this will eventually create a self-correcting supply chain that is adaptable and responsive to changing circumstances. Combined with strategic analysis, this could result in an evolving system that is able to re-create itself to support different requirements.

It is also likely that AI will cause a significant upheaval in employment, as many jobs become automated. Automation has significantly reduced manufacturing employment over time, but the potential for this to also impact service jobs is a significant change.

# References

Corsten, D and Gruen, T (2004) Stock-outs cause walkouts, *Harvard Business Review*, May, hbr.org/2004/05/stock-outs-cause-walkouts (archived at https://perma.cc/Q7QN-88QU)

Fortune (2021) Internet of Things (IoT) market size, share and Covid-19 impact analysis, Fortune Business Insights, www.fortunebusinessinsights.com/industry-reports/internet-of-things-iot-market-100307 (archived at https://perma.cc/R9MH-3LYC)

IoT Analytics (2021) State of IoT 2021, 18 May, www.iot-analytics.com/number-connected-iot-devices/ (archived at https://perma.cc/8JA7-336T)

McKinsey Global Institute (2015) *The Internet of Things: Mapping the value beyond the hype*, McKinsey & Company, New York

Metapack (2016) Metapack study shines a light on the short-fall between consumers' e-commerce delivery expectations and reality, www.metapack.com/press-release/2016-consumer-research-ecommerce-delivery-expectations-vs-reality/ (archived at https://perma.cc/P99W-JTLE)

NRF (National Retail Federation) (2018) NRF/University of Florida survey says retail 'shrink' decreased to $46.8 billion in 2017, National Retail Federation, https://nrf.com/media-center/press-releases/nrfuniversity-florida-survey-says-retail-shrink-decreased-468-billion (archived at https://perma.cc/H8UY-2YPF)

Swedberg, C (2015) Decathlon sees sales rise and shrinkage drop, aided by RFID, *RFID Journal*, www.rfidjournal.com/decathlon-sees-sales-rise-and-shrinkage-drop-aided-by-rfid (archived at https://perma.cc/KJD3-SJVH)

Worldpay (2018) The connected retailer, www.worldpay.com/global/insight/articles/2017-11/internet-of-things-the-connected-retailer (archived at https://perma.cc/N28Z-MP3Y)

Zebra (2015) Item-level RFID tagging and the intelligent apparel supply chain, Zebra Technologies, www.zebra.com/content/dam/zebra_new_ia/en-us/solutions-verticals/product/RFID/GENERAL/White%20Papers/WP_Item-Level_Supply_Chain_0413.pdf (archived at https://perma.cc/CB84-V65M)

# 13

# Control towers and supply chain visibility

**This chapter will familiarize the reader with:**

- The difficulty in achieving visibility of shipments in the supply chain due to the large number of parties involved

- The trend towards building so-called 'control towers' to monitor and manage supply chain activity

- The role of 'control towers' in analysing the data generated in part by the Internet of Things (IoT)

- How control towers can direct and drive product flows through the client's supply chain effectively at the most efficient cost

- The opportunities for logistics providers to develop their roles in monitoring, directing and driving product flows

- New opportunities to build scalable solutions through cloud computing

One of the consequences of a Big Data world, created by innovations such as the IoT, is the challenge faced by supply chain managers in analysing the mass of information generated and making timely, fact-based decisions.

As has been the case for many years, running logistics operations at any scale requires the support of information systems. The difference between 'then' and 'now' is that sophisticated technology is generally available to almost anyone, at very low cost.

The application of technology in supply chain management operations has always been focused around specific areas of functionality. This usually means transportation, warehouse, inventory and order management. Complementary systems for planning and forecasting, materials and requirements planning (MRP), and obviously accounting, were also designed as separate functional programs. Support services for integration and collaboration have also been created to underpin these functional silos, helping to provide mechanisms for message exchange and file transfers both within and outside the organization. Now, however, barriers between these functional silos are being challenged and new platforms are required.

This highlights the reality that existing IT structures are not the best foundation for addressing future needs. The following section will describe what is required to support the operations of logistics service providers (LSPs) over the next few years.

## The role of the logistics service provider

As a prelude, it is perhaps appropriate to point out that the business models for funding technology acquisition and support are changing so fundamentally that many large LSPs will have to exploit new operating models. At the same time, they are managing a very complex transition away from legacy solutions and supporting contracts costing millions, much of which may never be recovered.

Information systems and services underpin all logistics operations. For decades only the biggest players have been able to invest in large, scalable solutions supporting individual operational functions. But the seismic shift resulting from the evolution of cloud services and mobile computing is challenging every aspect of the industry.

Major investments have been made in systems that manage and control the internal operations of large enterprises. These systems, usually described as enterprise resource planning (ERP) suites, codify and structure information flows through the organization. They have done an excellent job for companies that have clear, established processes that seldom change. This is assuming that they have been able to endure the costs and time required for implementation. Unfortunately, they are not proving to be well suited to the needs of nimble and agile logistics solutions providers who are subject to a constant stream of changing requirements. This is unsurprising given the origins of ERP solutions in the world of finance and accounting.

LSPs today are having to operate in a much more networked and collaborative world. It is necessary to integrate with a variety of different systems and services across the operating spectrum. At the same time, streams of data from a range of devices and sensors need to be captured and processed in support of the ever-present demand for visibility.

Many LSPs are exploring the adoption of an operations 'control tower' to monitor and manage supply chain activity on a global basis. In essence, this is really another description for the provision of complete supply chain visibility.

True supply chain visibility has been an elusive goal for many years, the closest approximation being found in the track-and-trace systems operated by the global integrators. These systems provide excellent visibility, all the time the orders and shipments remain in the custody of the integrator. However, the moment they are transferred into the domain of another operator or partner, information flows pause or disappear completely. Even now, a shipment involving movement on more than one carrier will require the manager to check multiple systems and collate the results on behalf of the client.

This has triggered a number of mergers and acquisitions between various logistics system vendors. The migration of several functional applications onto hosted platforms, accessible via the internet, has exacerbated this trend. This is commonly referred to as moving to 'the cloud', but not every application described in this way has been designed for this environment or can appropriately exploit the advantages of cloud infrastructure.

The architects of these M&A efforts are attempting to provide a single-solution platform that can support all of the operational needs of a logistics service provider. While they hope this will be a tempting solution for larger companies, it is more likely that they will be exploited by smaller LSPs or start-ups. This is probably down to political motives rather than operational logic. If the chief information officer (CIO) of a large logistics service provider has a significant budget at his or her disposal every year, he or she is unlikely to explore solutions that conflict with that construct. This is not universal, as there are some enlightened technology executives who understand that the constant demand for modifications and changes to existing systems is unlikely to reduce any time soon.

## Cloud-based services

The introduction of cloud services also heralds the new subscription-based business models that are creating huge challenges to traditional application vendors. They are having to migrate existing solutions into the cloud, invariably requiring a fundamental rewrite of the software at huge cost, while supporting existing customer service contracts. At the same time, customers are moving away from expensive licensing and support agreements in favour of more flexible, lower-cost alternatives.

It can be seen in many organizations that business units are implementing numerous low-cost applications from external cloud vendors, as they are unable to wait until the internal IT function can start servicing their requests. This has resulted in a 'Tower of Babel' inside many large companies, with numerous point solutions attempting to exchange data between themselves. This also poses a potential security and data management challenge, as much of the critical client and operational data ends up on various mobile devices operating outside of the organization.

Established LSPs, with extensive legacy investments in ERP and other internal server-based applications, are having to identify how they can migrate critical operating data onto cloud service platforms. Smaller LSPs and new market entrants can commence operations almost immediately, selecting from a variety of applications as requirements demand.

It is this realignment of cost for technology services from an in-house-focused capital expense to a more flexible subscription-based operating expense cost model that is so disruptive. It means that small LSPs can exploit these new platforms and provide solutions to customers very quickly. They can do so without having to make the massive investments that incumbent players have made and so enjoy a considerable cost advantage. Another benefit is that the inherent flexibility of new solutions means that they can implement and adapt to whatever the client needs, often within days and sometimes within hours.

The new platforms are immensely scalable, highly secure (even 'large' companies cannot match the size of the security teams available to Google, Microsoft or Amazon) and are all subject to reduced cost, while at the same time computing capacity is being increased.

## Enabling supply chain visibility

One major advantage of this new approach is the increasing availability of the technological components to enable total, global supply chain visibility. This is beguilingly simple to express, but notoriously hard to achieve. True supply chain visibility extends from procurement, through to final delivery of the finished product and sometimes beyond, if the service and support cycles are included.

This is somewhat easier to achieve if all of these activities take place within the same organization, but in today's outsourced and networked world, where many functions are shared with partners, it is extremely difficult.

The sophisticated track-and-trace systems of the global integrators probably come closest to achieving visibility. However, they only work when orders and shipments remain within the integrator's operational network. This way they can guarantee the data and status updates are captured in a timely manner and can be authenticated. They have invested billions of dollars in extensive networks, scanners and sensors, ensuring the identification and location of almost everything passing through their chain of custody. This is highly effective if the operating model and related cost is acceptable, but for many companies this is not workable. So, what should they do? Fortunately, the relentless innovation in technology over the past 10 years has made all of the necessary components needed to do this available at an affordable cost.

The most efficient logistics operators are now becoming experts in managing process flow. This is because it is very difficult to restrict efficiency improvements to just one functional discipline. In the past, improvements to a particular functional silo usually involved pushing inefficiencies and problems across into the two adjacent functional silos, which did nothing to improve the process flow across the organization (see Figure 13.1).

As the barriers between the silos have fallen away, being able to control the flow of orders and shipments relies on instant and accurate data. This is where a supply chain visibility system, of which track and trace is just one component, is essential.

The visibility platform should act as a link between various operational systems running across the supply chain. It should provide context and reference resolution between all of the various data sources. The more data sources, the greater the clarity of what is happening. Precision of available inventory status, volumes and location is essential, and with this information it is possible to derive all kinds of efficiencies (see Figure 13.2).

At the same time, accurate information about the contents of the shipment provides options to the supply chain management team. These come into play when there are inevitable delays or disruptions within the supply chain. As an order is moved through the supply chain, it changes as it is

FIGURE 13.1  Sharing information in the supply chain

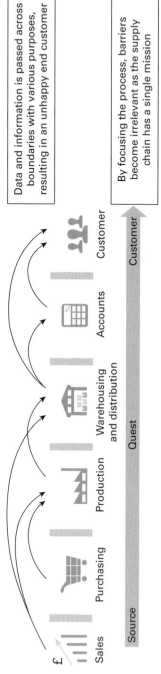

Data and information is passed across boundaries with various purposes, resulting in an unhappy end customer

By focusing the process, barriers become irrelevant as the supply chain has a single mission

FIGURE 13.2 Control tower management

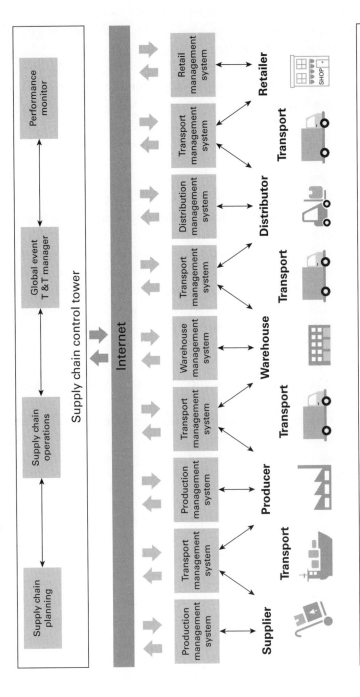

consolidated with other shipments, or is handed to other carriers. This usually results in the original references and identities being subsumed into a plethora of additional references, most of which only make sense to their parent data management systems.

It is this fact that makes it very hard to identify a specific order as it moves across the supply chain. Any unique shipment references only apply if the managing logistics service provider has identified and linked other references assigned to the order.

A great analogy for this problem is a set of Russian dolls. Each doll nests inside another doll. The viewer only sees the outermost doll but has no knowledge of how many other dolls it may contain without opening them all. A good visibility system has a flexible and robust design that is able to deal with this problem. The original order may be placed in a package, which is put in a box with other packages, added to a pallet, which in turn is put into a container or air-freight unit load device (ULD), each with its own unique reference ID. A client hoping to track the original order will expect that any visibility system they access is able to resolve this puzzle.

LSPs who have great visibility can direct and drive the product flows through the client's supply chain effectively and at the least cost. Depending on the nature of the visibility platform, new parties and data sources can be easily accommodated. The ability to extend access to the visibility platform to the edges of any supply chain is critical in being able to develop a 'single version of the truth'.

Mobile devices and RFID-enabled sensors are all capable of collaborating and cooperating with visibility platforms. As these platforms exploit emerging cloud technologies to extend their scope and scale, they become the principal operating base for all supply chain activities.

---

CASE STUDY 13.1

*Supply chain visibility for an engineering company*

A global engineering company manufacturing very high precision components was challenged to improve the availability of materials in the production process. Raw materials and semi-finished components originated from a handful of partner companies. Each partner received demand forecasts from the engineering company and these forecasts spanned a very long time horizon. As the dateline moved closer to call off and supply, the partners were expected to match their delivery schedules to the demand plan. Unfortunately, the source of the demand plan was a large ERP system that only understood the world of its owner: the engineering company.

This meant that the published demand plans carried parts references that did not match those of the suppliers, so considerable manual efforts were needed to comprehend the demand plan. More to the point, when the suppliers responded to the plan with their own schedules, there was often a reference mismatch in the other direction. As a result, the variability between demand and supply was difficult to comprehend and was addressed by the operations team consistently over-ordering to compensate.

An experiment using a visibility system was tried to see if it was possible to resolve this. The visibility solution understood the referencing conventions of all parties and contained inventory levels and status across the supply chain. It was a unique application that was accessible across the internet and not under the control of any of the involved parties. Each company had their own access and could manage their own data, and the system maintained the links between the various references and SKU data. One important point to note is that there was no master item database, as this would have been impossible to create and maintain, given the number of different parties involved.

In operation, the ERP system generated the demand plans as usual, but a copy of the plans was ingested into the visibility system and could be viewed by the partners in a form that made sense to their operational constraints. This meant that every party was looking at the same information, rather than trying to guess its interpretation.

The partner companies could then respond by putting their inventory availability and delivery schedules into the system, and again it translated the information back into a form that the ERP system was able to process. In addition, an event management capability within the visibility system was able to generate alerts if there were any deviations or unexpected problems with scheduled deliveries into the manufacturing process. These alerts automatically generated graphs that highlighted the deviations and why they were happening, and they were then automatically emailed to the logistics managers.

Although it was a pilot project, it demonstrated that considerable savings could result if the system was implemented across the entire production process. It also demonstrated the power of collaboration, provided the correct systems and visibility tools augment it.

However, the most surprising fact about this example is not the results, but that it took place some 15 years ago, using technologies that are now commonplace, but back then were deemed too experimental for full-scale deployment.

# The role of 'middleware'

Middleware – software that bridges the gap between the numerous application 'islands' that exist within large organizations – is one element in the mix of ingredients necessary to deliver a successful transition from asset-intensive operations into an information-intensive enterprise. Middleware platforms manage the flows of data between various applications so that data and information flows match those of the operational process flows.

Middleware has been around since the 1990s but now, thanks to advances in technology, many more components of systems exist as services provided by a combination of cloud and specialist application vendors. Because they exist as services, they can be accessed through standard interfaces, simplifying many aspects of integration. But linking together many of these components is pointless if the processes they support and the data they require is inaccurate and lacks meaning.

In the same way that the previous iteration of middleware technologies was used to link various systems within organizations, today's middleware solutions are called on to do the same thing between organizations. But while the intent may be similar, the challenges are more complex. This is due to the huge variety of different data sources and the need to understand the context of that data. As more companies have outsourced their systems infrastructure and applications to the cloud, standardized application programming interfaces (APIs) should make the exchange of data easier.

The rapid transfer of data across the network is a necessity as it enables real-time decision making because any unexpected events should show up faster. However, a 'controlling mind' is often augmented by machine learning algorithms providing decision support to the supply chain managers. This is why the precision and context of any data is not just desirable, but a necessity. The role of a middleware component is vital in this context, as it must enforce conformance to the requirements designed into the operational systems.

## Middleware integration providers

There are a number of vendors providing 'middleware' integration solutions and services. These include Mulesoft, Snaplogic, Boomi and others. IBM and Tibco also continue to provide solutions in this area. Some of these solutions have excellent user interfaces that enable operators to build connections between different systems and services using 'drag and drop' techniques in hours, rather than days.

As the size of a logistics network grows, the ability to quickly incorporate the systems and services of the new entrants will be critical. Making these connections in a manner that also adapts to frequent change, along with maintaining the context of any data, will also be essential.

By focusing on the management of data and information rather than owning physical assets, logistics operators will be able to identify where there are opportunities for greater margins. This approach is also likely to be the most consistent way to maintain those margins, as it allows for a degree of agility when circumstances change.

The conundrum is that the best way to establish this kind of organization requires systems expertise and operational experience, attributes that often reside with large, established and asset-intensive organizations – the very structures this approach will challenge. Well-capitalized start-ups may have the systems expertise and financial resources to compete, but they need to accumulate the expertise and then learn how to operate at scale, in a very complex 'real-world' industrial landscape. This is not dissimilar to the growing competition between Amazon Logistics (Excellent IT and scale) and Walmart, UPS, FedEx, etc (massive scale, very large asset base and deep operational expertise).

---

CASE STUDIES 13.2
*Real-world integration benefits of using middleware*

Mulesoft and Airbus

Data held in multiple systems across operations. Needed reusable APIs to share data between internal systems, employees, suppliers and external stakeholders. Airbus established separate organization to exploit Mulesoft solutions to unlock value from data held in legacy SAP ERP, SAP S4/Hana and other data sources. It created a platform so that mobiles and other devices could leverage the data and information faster and in innovative ways. Projects were accelerated from 4–6 months to a few weeks. Now Airbus has a consistent environment to build new solutions and quickly integrate new partners.

Mulesoft and Unilever

Operations landscape comprising in excess of 1,000 applications, 10,000 interfaces and multiple global operations. Needed a mechanism to create reusable services that could unify multiple systems and data sources into a common operating environment. By using the off-the-shelf tools provided by the vendor, Unilever was able to swiftly achieve goals, and new deployments now take days and weeks instead of months and (in some cases) years.

### Snaplogic and Aramark

Operational data spread across multiple silos in different business units, difficult or impossible to access in a timely manner. Aramark used Snaplogic middleware tools to create a single source of the truth that now supports the deployment of new applications through a consistent service platform that also leverages data from legacy systems.

### Boomi and Eddie Stobart

Needed to integrate multiple data sources, B2B/EDI (electronic data interchange) implementations and various applications from customers and partners. Business was constantly demanding new APIs, improved customer order workflows, better warehouse system integrations and connections to industry agencies such as port operators and others. Using Boomi tools, integration times at Eddie Stobart have been reduced by 50 per cent and customers can be onboarded much faster and at lower cost.

## Supply chain visibility platforms

A relatively recent addition to the market is the emergence of supply chain visibility platforms (Figure 13.3) such as Fourkites, Project 44 and Sixfold.

Real-time tracking is a major element of the latest visibility platforms. Firstly, the systems pull information about the shipment and the carrier from the shipper's transport management system (TMS). This data allows the truck, trailer and GPS identifier to be pulled from the carrier's dispatch system. The telematics device is subsequently 'pinged' by the visibility platform at regular intervals (every 15 minutes, for instance). Some systems also allow proof of delivery to be undertaken via an app that updates the platform immediately.

Collecting the data is just the starting point. Algorithms using the data from GPS, electronic logging device (ELD) and telematics networks, combine with predictive weather, traffic and routing information to generate accurate arrival time predictions.

FIGURE 13.3 Supply chain visibility universe

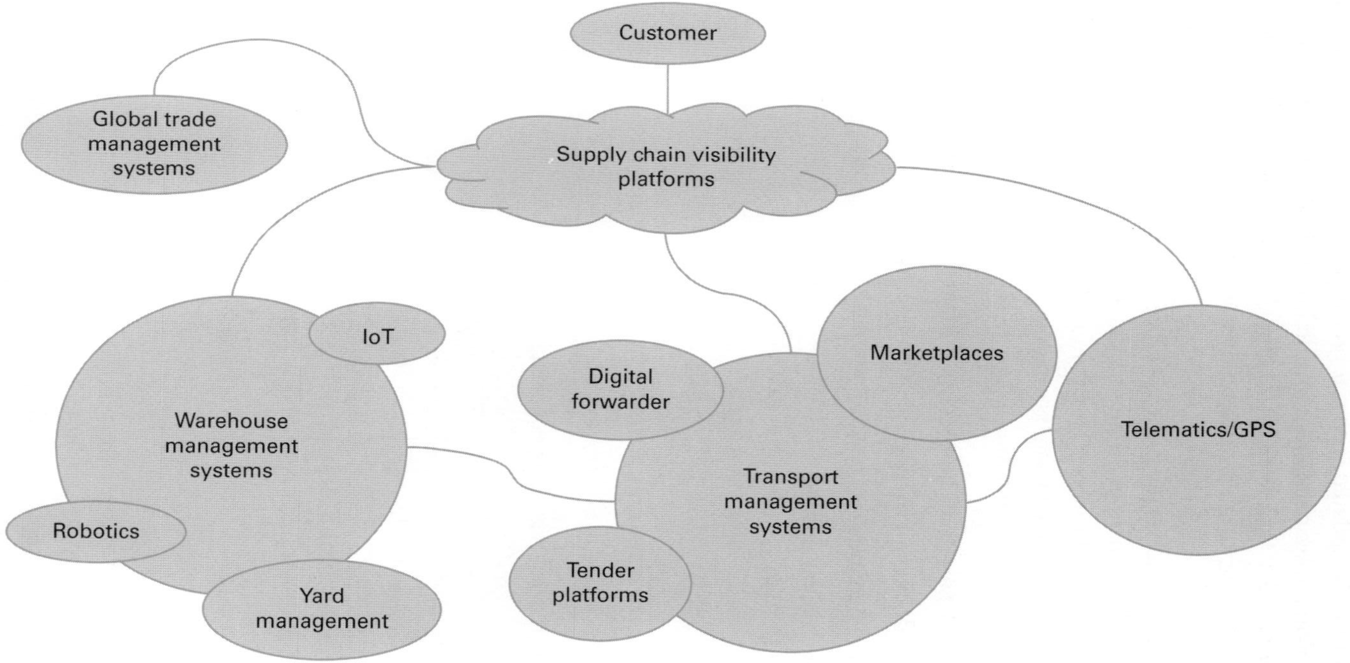

A 'digital twin' is created representing the physical end-to-end supply chain and is continuously updated with information from the underlying systems. The digital twin allows companies to collaborate instantly, balancing supply and demand in real time without manual intervention. Push notifications can also be sent out to alert stakeholders when milestones are missed, for example.

One of the critical issues for a visibility platform is the ability to make sense of information held in different formats and then make this data available in a standardized format. This requires the automation of the complex task of consolidating, cleansing, normalizing and enriching all data.

Other functionalities include:

- automated, transparent and secure onboarding process for suppliers
- settlement document management and invoicing
- customer e-signature
- mobile document upload
- delivery site ratings

## The future: increasing shipper choice and systems convergence

FIGURE 13.4  The new digital environment

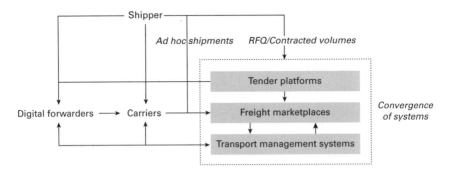

Figure 13.4 illustrates the increased level of choice that is available to shippers in this new digital environment. For larger volumes, they can now use 'one-stop-shop' systems providers, which integrate tender platforms, marketplaces and transport management systems. An example of this 'convergence' of systems is Alpega Group. According to the company,

through its acquired TenderEasy unit, users are able to search and analyse its 50,000+ carrier databases (present on Teleroute, WTransNet and 123Cargo marketplaces) and issue requests for quotation and optimize and analyse the results. Along with its Transwide TMS the company claims that it is now able to support the complete procurement life cycle from pre-tender data analysis and supplier management to automated carrier allocation and freight audit.

For ad hoc shipments shippers can also access some marketplaces direct, whether their own ('closed' and curated) or 'open'. There is also the option of engaging directly with digital forwarders (usually for ad hoc shipments), who also have access to similar systems, or directly with carriers.

With so many options now available to shippers looking to go down the digital route, what considerations must they take into account? For a start, 'quality' is seen as an important distinction between digital forwarders and some freight marketplaces. An argument employed by the former is that trust is essential to the process and that a forwarder is critical to ensuring the successful completion of the transaction.

In other words, 'relationship' is essential to the offering of the forwarder both in terms of customers and carriers. Customers develop trust with companies and individuals who hold responsibility should anything go wrong. Relationships are important for carriers too. They will trust a forwarder and build long-term partnerships to ensure consistent volumes at sustainable prices in return for a commitment to quality.

Although load-matching marketplaces may check the credentials of the carriers using their platforms ('curated'), ultimately the risk is borne by the shipper who may or may not have had any prior contact with the carrier.

Whether digital forwarder or marketplace, in order to be successful, these businesses need to maintain both an effective service and a large supply of capacity (carriers). However, as competition commoditizes the basic load-matching service they provide, shippers risk receiving low-quality service and carriers risk attaining low rates – it can become a race to the bottom based on price.

'Network effects', or demand-side economies of scale, are critical to success in these platforms. These occur when a service becomes more valuable to its users as more people adopt it, creating barriers to entry for rivals, and barriers to exit for users. Eventually, this can allow a single firm to dominate the market.

The successful digital players will integrate a range of technologies (including mobile) for their customers, not just a technological layer. Moreover, they will establish a strategic lock-in with both carriers and shippers by effectively serving the needs of both parties.

## Summary

Although supply chain visibility has been talked about for many decades, it is still difficult to achieve. This is not due to a lack of data, which is being generated in enormous quantities by various applications, not least the IoT. Rather it is the quality of this data that is the key issue as well as the capabilities to interpret and act upon it. Control towers are an important innovation in this respect. Eventually, powered by AI, supply chain and logistics management, decisions will be made seamlessly to deliver customer service, while minimizing inventory. They will also provide logistics service providers with an important new product and lead to their reinvention as valued supply chain coordinators.

# 14

# Blockchain in supply chains

*Game changer or hype?*

**This chapter will familiarize the reader with:**

- What is meant by the term 'blockchain'

- The stages of the technology's development

- The benefits that 'blockchain' will deliver to all supply chain parties

- Supply chain and logistics segments in which blockchain will be applied

- Case studies of how the technology is already being utilized

- Its role in facilitating smart contracts and what this means for industry

- Problems facing the adoption of the technology

## What is blockchain?

This chapter seeks to explain and clarify blockchain technology – what it is, how it functions and its potential for use in the logistics and supply chain management sector. As can be seen from a 2018 market survey by consultancy Transport Intelligence (Figure 14.1), more than half respondents believed the technology to be a 'game changer' (Ti, 2018).

The blockchain is a permanent digital record (or ledger) of transactions that is stored across a distributed or decentralized network of computers. The 'blocks' that are chained together are cryptographically sealed records of transactions. The blockchain itself is not split across multiple computers but copied to every computer and they all agree it is identical by consensus.

FIGURE 14.1  The importance of blockchain to the logistics industry

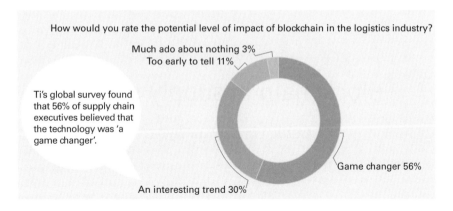

At the moment, each computer stores the entire blockchain and this represents a limitation of the technology. However, a lot of research has been done to develop solutions where computers do not store the entire blockchain, but they are challenged randomly to judge if a transaction is correct or not.

Although there is one clear master record, in a 'public' blockchain the computers involved are not owned or controlled by any single party or organization. The network of computers supporting the blockchain confirm, verify and record the transactions independently, providing trust through consensus (Figure 14.2). This is an alternative approach to the explicit trust that is provided by a third party sitting between all of the participants, for example, banks or market exchanges. This guarantees that transactions cannot be modified once confirmed in the blockchain unless every computer (node), or a majority of them in the network, all agree to do so at the same time. If the blockchain network involved comprises a random number of machines outside the control of any single party, it becomes impossible to subvert. The implication of this is that public blockchains are likely to be most trusted and implicitly more secure.

In contrast, 'private' blockchains require participants to be registered and conform to rules established by the owner of the blockchain. However, this poses the question of why a private blockchain would be preferred as opposed to a solution built around a centralized database. This is perhaps similar to the situation when the internet became generally available to all. Many companies used the technologies supporting the internet to build their

FIGURE 14.2  How do blockchains work?

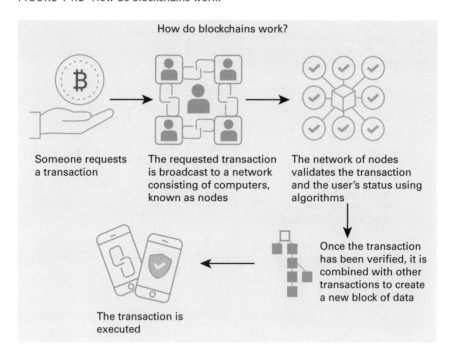

own private intranets. After creating these 'walled gardens' (often for perfectly valid reasons) they soon realized that the open (public) internet provided much more capability. These walled gardens soon opened up and, these days, companies only maintain their private intranets where industry legislation requires – banks, for example.

There are now a number of very large organizations coming together to collaborate around blockchain developments across industries. The Linux foundation's Hyperledger Fabric, Corda from R3 and Coco from Microsoft are all examples of these, with Amazon's AWS about to enter the market as well.

Despite the emergence of platforms such as those mentioned above, no comprehensive supply chain standards are currently in place for blockchain solutions or providers. This means there are no definitive solutions to questions relating to consensus on blocks and which encryption technology to use. A solid interoperability standard is very likely to emerge as the technology advances. An absence of such standards would add complexities, hindering supply chain applications due to confusing information exchanges.

## BLOCKCHAIN'S TIMELINE: FOUR STAGES OF BLOCKCHAIN EVOLUTION

FIGURE 14.3  Four stages of the evolution of blockchain

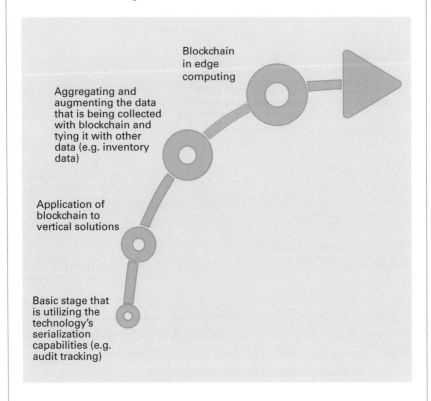

1  Basic stage, or entry-point blockchain, utilizing the technology's serialization capabilities. The life science industry is one of the most prominent use cases in which the technology is being used for audit tracking.

2  Application of blockchain to vertical solutions. One example would be the finance supply chain where the technology is being used to create new products and services that take out cost and remove friction.

3  Aggregating and augmenting the data that is being collected with blockchain and tying it with other data (e.g. inventory data) to drive better decision making.

4  Blockchain in edge computing, which refers to the trend of reverting from the 'cloud-based' centralized solutions to 'computing on the edge', where businesses can create a massive amount of processing capability. The current cloud computing models are not designed to be able to handle the volume and velocity of data that the IoT generates. This development requires a new kind of infrastructure.

Many companies are still gathering information about blockchain and its implications. There is also an acute shortage of real technical expertise, but this is changing rapidly due to the explosion in interest and pilot projects across the globe. Blockchain technology is still evolving, particularly the number of transactions that can be processed per second. This is a function of block size, storage and bandwidth limits. These should improve over time.

## Potential areas of use in logistics and supply chain

Blockchain has applications in many parts of the logistics and supply chain sector. Not least of these is in cost saving. Current industry estimates indicate that 10 per cent of all freight invoices contain inaccurate data, including duplication, wrong freight mode charges and incorrect fees (Tanner, 2018). This leads to disputes as well as many other inefficiencies in the logistics industry. One of the major advantages of the blockchain is that it can power leaner, more automated and error-free processes.

It will also have important implications for international trade. 'Smart contracts' are applications that are stored and executed on a blockchain depending on their embedded rules. These are agreements, or contracts, which have embedded business rules that can exist and operate independently of any centralized control. Once a contract is stored on a blockchain it becomes immutable and cannot be changed, embedding any flaws that might be exploited by hackers.

Other examples of applications in the sector are:

- asset tracking
- total visibility across and down into multiple tiers of the supply chain
- accountability
- process conformance
- improved collaboration across the supply chain

## Examples of blockchain in the supply chain

### IBM: asset tracking

IBM recognized an opportunity to improve its asset management system through the use of blockchain technology. A blockchain would capture all transactions and record changes that occur as the assets move from manufacturing to deployment, including those actions that occur outside of IBM's systems. Capturing this information in the blockchain would give IBM and its supply chain partners a 'single source of truth' with regard to core asset information. This way, no matter what happened to an asset as it moved through the supply chain, all stakeholders and systems would know its status.

### Visibility: OriginTrail and Provenance

OriginTrail protocol enables exchange of different data sets between multi-organization supply chains. Input and sharing data is based on a common set of data standards that allow multiple organizations (companies involved in production, distribution or retail of goods) to exchange data.

Provenance provides transparency between manufacturers, sellers and buyers. The Provenance platform allows buyers to gain a transparent insight into the people, places and processes that have contributed to the creation of a particular product. Data verification allows for proven business and supply chain claims. This gives consumers trust in the company from which they are buying. Batches or even individual items are given digital passports, enabling buyers to follow a digitally verified journey from start to finish.

### Improved collaboration across the supply chain

A leading logistics provider has built a platform that allows it to offer extended payments terms to its customer base. This is an area where the provider has seen an increased demand from customers and has worked with a blockchain provider to build the platform to obtain cheaper funding from insurers and banks for the extended payments terms. The use of the blockchain element offers more simplified administration procedure for the banks and insurers as well as a better audit trail and validation, which removes costs and ultimately allows them to offer cheaper funding rates to the logistics provider. At the moment, this solution is focused on receivables, but the company is hoping they can expand this relationship and broaden it out to include other types of data and customer information that would also be of value for banks and insurers and offer more security about the way they are lending.

## DO YOU NEED A BLOCKCHAIN?

- DO NOT consider blockchain solutions as replacements for existing solutions that are built around a central database and that continue to work well and do not share data outside the organization.

- DO NOT consider blockchain as a solution component if you need to control/validate access from a known group of users that seldom change.

- DO NOT consider blockchain for data storage. Blockchain is a very inefficient database so if you need to solve a storage problem blockchain is not the suitable solution.

- DO consider blockchain if you need to capture and/or share data from a variable number of suppliers, partners, customers. This is especially true if many of them do not know each other, are competitors and need to use a verified, immutable and accurate single version of the truth, e.g. operating in an industry that requires detailed traceability across extended supply chains.

- DO consider blockchain if you are thinking about establishing, reviewing or replacing an IT strategy for your organization.

## Assuring supply chain integrity

Supply chains are constantly evolving and changing in response to the massive shifts in manufacturing and fulfilment. As e-commerce growth has accelerated and extended into numerous sectors, conventional supply chain structures are struggling to adapt. More significantly, the information systems supporting them cannot cope. Data remains in silos in a digital environment and there is no real incentive to share it.

This results in disconnects in the information flows and missing pieces of data. In concert with this, huge volumes of data generated by mobile devices and sensors attached to inventory and assets as they move through the chain are ignored. This is because many of the operational systems underpinning the core supply chain operations were never designed to operate in an interconnected world where data was constantly being generated from every direction. This kind of fragmentation makes it difficult to attain whole supply chain visibility.

In many sectors, supply chains are becoming faster, more fragmented and often controlled by companies with whom the supply chain owner has no direct relationship. They are perhaps depending on the suppliers to the suppliers that may be many tiers down the chain. However, their performance has a direct impact on the efficiency of the chain. Blockchain is one way in which these participants can be held accountable for their actions both during and after the fact. This is because irrefutable transparency can be established if the information flow across the supply chain is recorded on a blockchain.

In China, food chain transparency is considered a national priority and there have been several pilot projects testing the appropriateness of such solutions. Many of these have moved into production processes. Consumers can access this information trail at any time by scanning product bar codes in the supermarket or local store and the information trail is revealed – literally a record of what took place on the journey 'from farm to fork'.

---

CASE STUDY 14.1
*The food supply chain*

Food supply chains are increasingly complex and dynamic, relying on a large number of suppliers, so transparency is essential to guarantee food quality and provenance to all consumers of food products. This is, however, not an easy task. In fact, it has become almost impossible for food producers and retailers to guarantee the provenance of their products. Indeed, according to the Lockton Food and Beverage 2017 Report, 32 per cent of supply chain food executives stated they cannot vouch for the authenticity of ingredients they put into end products (Lockton, 2017). Given these problems, it comes as no surprise that several blockchain initiatives have already been established in the sector:

- IBM and Walmart launched blockchain food safety alliance in China with JD.com. Ten food suppliers and retailers – Dole, Driscoll's, Golden State Foods, Kroger, McCormick and Company, McLane Company, Nestlé, Tyson Foods, Unilever and Walmart – signalled their intention to collaborate.

- Provenance – tracks the origin and authenticity of products from origin to sale using the blockchain platforms of Etherium and Bitcoin. Currently working on fresh food trials with various retailers.

- OriginTrail developed the first middleware protocol based on blockchain that is purpose-built for data exchange between organizations along the supply chain. The company started collaborating with scientific laboratories focused on verifying the integrity of food supply chains by analysing samples from batches of food using modern analytical and scientific technologies.

This access to the data generated at each stage in the supply chain process can reduce costs and provide a very rapid response to any problems that occur. Precise identification characterizes the value of transparency that blockchain can bring. This capability is usually only available through advanced track-and-trace systems, although these systems often only operate within the operational envelope of logistics services providers. They are frequently challenged when custody of shipments or inventory is passed across to another supply chain partner, who may only be transferring shipment IDs rather than a whole suite of additional information that provides vital context.

An appropriate blockchain-based solution can reveal all of the relevant information captured at every stage across the chain, irrespective of the parties involved and the myriad of different systems each participant may be using. Indeed, it can be 'the single version of the truth' that supply chain managers have been seeking for decades.

Of course, there is the fundamental question of trust at the heart of any information-sharing exercise. This is particularly contentious where competitors contribute to the same supply chains or procure inventory from the same suppliers. Decentralized networks act as a neutral platform that incentivizes data exchanges while using cryptography to keep data both secure and accessible only by the parties authorized to do so.

## Developing trust

Trust is the glue that binds together commercial relationships. Across all manner of supply chains trust is enforced and assumed by a series of contracts and legislative convention. These trusted relationships and arrangements have been established over long periods of time and have been successful in providing a mechanism for compensation and dispute resolution. However, due to the fragmented nature of many of today's supply chains, and the velocity at which they operate, a new kind of trust model would be helpful.

Existing trust models are almost always constructed around a third party acting as the reference point. For example, a bank guaranteeing the transfer of funds between parties or foreign exchange markets using brokers to manage the transaction flows between buyer and seller. In these cases, the third party is required to validate and confirm the transactions. This has generally worked very well, but they also have drawbacks in terms of efficiencies and sometimes cost.

Blockchain protocols remove the requirement for a single third party to sit between all of the participants in a transaction chain. Therefore, in a commercial environment where there are numerous participants who need to establish relationships and transfer funds, often for the first time in a very compressed timeframe, blockchain can provide a trust mechanism to do this.

It does this through a consensus model that distributes trust across a network, using mathematics and cryptography to enforce the trusted environment guaranteed by the consensus of all of the participants. In effect, it is replacing the single intermediary/arbitrator that usually validates any transactions with a series of consensus rules. In short, the network provides the consensus.

One of the other factors of this model is that the identity of the party contributing data and information onto the blockchain is recorded. Thus, it is impossible to assert that, 'it wasn't me who did this' when assigning responsibility.

The blockchain trust model in many respects is the biggest innovation with this technology, as it is redefining what trust means and how it can work at scale across digital services. In interviews conducted for a study for Ti (2018), there was a consensus from all of the interviewees that blockchain will be able to resolve trust fears along the supply chain. According to IBM, 'the absence of a single controlling organization will encourage more participation and disputes will be minimized as the truth is distributed across the network' (Ti, 2018).

There are some good examples of pilots in the shipping industry (see above) exploring how blockchain-based platforms can reduce the number of documents and paper-based exchanges that take place. By streamlining many of the processes, there are efficiency gains and cost reductions that can be realized.

While the use of the technology can help reduce the number of paper-based exchanges along the supply chain, it is unlikely that the blockchain will make these processes completely disappear. While these manual processes are likely to persist, organizations might also be motivated to digitize their processes in order to monetize their data.

## Blockchains and false data

The various parties that participate in the blockchain need to record their transactions. For instance, as soon as a carrier delivers a shipment to the warehouse, details about the shipment are recorded on the blockchain. Upon receiving the shipment at the warehouse, the warehouse recipient should record the same information. Neither of these parties can see what the other party has reported – it is the computers that verify that the information they have provided is identical. This is, in fact, one of the key aspects where blockchain can transform the supply chain – it allows supply chain stakeholders to identify any issues that may arise in the chain as everyone can see what is happening at all times. Overall, the more nodes, the harder it is to put false information onto the blockchain.

Moreover, the more automated the processes are, the more difficult it is to tamper with the data. By digitizing the supply chain processes, the relevant information is captured directly from sensors (e.g. sensors placed on trucks, temperature sensors, etc) and entered onto the blockchain. If a process involves lots of systems generating or sharing data, and that data originates from an established system, it is likely to be viable and trustworthy:

> False data usually occurs when plain text is used as the data point. While plain text is necessary, it should be used to augment data generated by a machine. The GS1 barcodes are generally found on most consumer products and there you have a very established data set that can be trusted if used as the basis for correctly identifying products. So, if you accidentally describe a tin of beans as a can of hairspray in a text field and the barcode says beans, it is pretty clear what should be trusted.
>
> Mark Parsons, former DHL senior executive and supply chain innovator
> (Ti, 2018)

The more data that is captured from these kinds of systems, the better, as it should result in very accurate information. The 'farm to fork' food supply chain is an example (the concept involves the regulation of every stage of the supply chain and in the United States is administered by the Food and Drug Administration (FDA) through legislation). Within that platform there are so many checks involved, and automated systems measuring the processes, that any attempts to insert false data would be very difficult. Similar rigour should spread to other supply chains as automation is increased across manufacturing and order processes.

## Blockchain and smart contracts

One of the other aspects of blockchain technology is its ability to be used to define so-called 'smart contracts'. These are agreements, or contracts, which have embedded business rules that can exist and operate independently of any centralized control. They can act as the system of record confirming ownership, operational life cycle and any related stores of value.

The principle behind them is that they are essentially 'self-executing' in that they are defined similarly to a computer application (or app). This means they are stored on the system and execute according to the various rules that are embedded within them. Because they are stored on a blockchain, it is very difficult (if not impossible) to tamper or subvert the transactions related to the contract.

One example of their use might be the registration of an asset identified by a smart contract. Depending on how the contract is defined, the contract will record how the asset is used, who rents it, and it can also deduct and store small amounts of value from each transaction. This provides the means to cover costs of repair or provide a return for the ultimate owners of the asset. Due to the decentralized nature of the smart contract, it is not 'owned' by any one party; its related information only exists on the blockchain.

In this regard and as an example, blockchain-based smart contracts might control fleets of autonomous delivery vehicles that are available for use in urban areas by anyone. They could be rented, operated and funded independently of any company, available on demand as a general resource. This approach echoes the rise of cloud computing environments that provide a general platform that can be rented and used as required.

## Blockchain problems

While blockchain can certainly add value, every technology has its limitations, and such is the case with blockchain at the moment.

## Latency and scalability

All blockchain solutions have scalability problems and limited transactional input. Latency refers to the time it takes for transactions to be confirmed on the blockchain (i.e. the creation of the blocks of data and their subsequent confirmation and verification in the blockchain). Unlike conventional transaction-processing systems used for credit cards and banking, adding records to a blockchain is more analogous to an airline reservation and other booking systems that commit orders to a database, which may take several seconds. What is highly likely is that the speed of these systems will improve as technology advances.

## Cost and energy usage

The processing power required to verify blockchains is huge. This is a significant cost and explains why many of the large server farms that process these transactions do so in areas where energy is cheap and ambient air temperatures are as cool as possible, e.g. Iceland, Scandinavia, northern Canada, Siberia, etc.

## Lack of regulation

As with all emerging technologies, legislation is still very much a grey area in relation to blockchain. Some legal frameworks are emerging (e.g. Slovenia is seen as a pioneer in this area recording contracts subject to EU laws) but it will be some time before the situation is clear.

This implies that dispute resolution will be an issue for the foreseeable future. This is not a reason to do nothing, but it is a reason to proceed with caution before any significant investments are made. As a reference point, exactly the same situation applies to autonomous/driverless vehicles and drone operations. Projects are still happening, but their legislative boundaries are constantly evolving.

## Data quality

Ensuring data quality (i.e. the ability to capture the data as close to the source as possible and ensuring its accuracy) is a big challenge. Organizations and supply chain managers will need to undertake more audits of data quality, which is essential for many of the merging systems and technologies to work effectively. If random quality checks can be carried out on data across the supply chain at regular intervals, it should be possible to avoid the issue of false data corrupting trust in the information.

### Lack of knowledge

As with all nascent technologies, related knowledge is confined to the early adopters. This situation will improve as the number of pilot projects continue to grow. Fortunately, the developer communities are far more collaborative these days and many of the key developments are 'open sourced' and shared across the community. This is very similar to the way the internet protocols and the world wide web spread across the globe rather than being under the control of a proprietary corporate regime. Of course, how organizations seek to exploit the technology for their own benefit may remain confidential, but the underlying technology will be publicly available.

According to a major logistics provider, in addition to the lack of knowledge, cultural awareness is another key determinant of blockchain adoption:

> When we can clearly articulate to our customers what the value proposition of blockchain is then the adoption is going much faster. So, ultimately, when companies will be able to quantify the value of the technology they will come onboard much faster. Time is another factor. Businesses are working on a number of initiatives to drive value in and deal with new technologies. Blockchain is just one of the initiatives on the portfolio, so the wider acceptance and implementation of the technology will take a little time, just like IoT is taking a little time. (Ti, 2018)

Due to the points raised previously, it would be wise to proceed with caution and avoid making any significant 'bets' on the technology until pilot projects have validated any assumptions. As more trials take place using this technology, confidence will grow and lessons will be learnt.

## The outlook for blockchain

As blockchain and other technologies are adopted by organizations across the supply chain industry, their capabilities to streamline and accelerate information flows are hard to ignore. The general acceptance of a neutral third-party technology platform that is available to anyone, recording inventory, order and shipment transactions, will be the point of transformation.

Any platform such as this, that is not controlled by a single commercial entity and provides blockchain-based transaction records that are immune to tampering, may very well lead to the restructuring of the industry.

Moving forward, while the use cases of blockchain along the supply chain will be plentiful, the most promising application of the technology would be the food and perishable and the pharmaceutical sectors. Overall, the most valuable use cases of blockchain are likely to be in sectors that are prone to risks of counterfeiting.

## Summary

The blockchain is a permanent digital record (or ledger) of transactions that is stored across a distributed or decentralized network of computers. This guarantees that transactions cannot be modified once confirmed in the blockchain unless every computer (node), or a majority of them in the network, all agree to do so at the same time.

Blockchain is not a silver bullet for any and all problems found with supply chain technology, but it does have great potential to resolve some practical problems that have been around for years, e.g. supply chain visibility.

Blockchain provides:

- total transparency
- immutability and transactional integrity across the supply chain
- scalability – reliable and verifiable inclusivity from almost any number of participants in any location
- the potential to dramatically reduce cost of operations

There has been an increasing interest in the technology and various claims have been made regarding its potential for transforming businesses and their trading partnerships.

In many cases, it may make no sense to implement blockchain technology, for example applications built around a centralized database and accessed by specific users. But where many companies need to share data between themselves, their suppliers, partners, customers and competitors, the most obvious being supply chain visibility, blockchain is an exciting option.

It should also be kept in mind that blockchain technology is still evolving and has a number of challenges ahead of it, not least performance. But this is the same for all technologies that emerge. The successful ones improve, adapt and evolve so long as they provide utility and value.

## References

ITPRO (2018) DHL trials blockchain in pharma supply chain to cut out counterfeit drugs, 13 March, www.itpro.co.uk/Blockchain/30748/dhl-trials-Blockchain-in-pharma-supply-chain-to-cut-out-counterfeit-drugs (archived at https://perma.cc/Z5UB-DXVP)

Lockton (2017) Lockton food and beverage 2017 report, https://lockbox.lockton.com/m/5984aca4db35921d/original/01253-foodbeveragereport-brochure_final.pdf (archived at https://perma.cc/XAQ5-3XRK)

Tanner, M (2018) Why China will drive blockchain and 4 related myths, *Forbes*, www.forbes.com/sites/tannermark/2018/08/01/blockchain-china-misunderstandings/ (archived at https://perma.cc/X2NJ-QQH8)

Ti (2018) Why is blockchain a game changer for supply chain management?, www.ti-insight.com/product/why-is-Blockchain-a-game-changer-for-supply-chain-management/ (archived at https://perma.cc/SH7R-D3MA)

# 15

# The disruptive potential of robots and automation in the warehouse

**This chapter will familiarize the reader with:**

- The changing demand-side trends that have led to the increased need for automation in the warehouse
- The type of robots being employed within the warehouse environment
- The use of robots by companies such as Amazon and Ocado
- How 'gamification' will increase employee productivity
- Threats to logistics service providers from automation
- How the use of robots in production processes may influence future supply chain structures

## The rise of the robots

Automation in the warehouse through the use of robots is gathering pace. Although robotic systems have been around for some time, a number of demand- and supply-side trends are driving their widespread adoption.

Not least of these is the e-commerce phenomenon that has led to many retailers adopting omnichannel and multichannel marketing and distribution strategies, transforming the characterization of supply chain volumes from unitized and quite predictable, to single item and volatile. According to a report by consultancy ABI research, more than 50,000 warehouses will include robotics by 2025, up from 4,000 in 2018 (Melton, 2019).

At the same time, many new entrants have emerged, challenging bricks-and-mortar incumbents through the ability to develop new distribution centres custom-built for the demands of e-retail customers. A further driver is the increasing cost of labour and its shortage. Automation is being seen as a way of increasing efficiencies in the warehouse, reducing the need for human workers and at the same time providing more flexibility to fulfil peaks and troughs of demand using modular systems.

Apart from the labour cost element, automation also means lower real-estate costs as a human-free environment allows greater density of storage, i.e. operating with narrower aisles (or in some cases, no aisles at all). What is more, robot technology is becoming more robust and the cost per robot is falling, bringing them into the reach of smaller customers. Robotics-as-a-service solutions are being developed by some suppliers, which work on a 'pay-per-pick' basis, therefore taking away the large capital outlay formerly required.

However, automating such a labour-intensive sector as warehousing will have repercussions. These may well be at a macro level, affecting governments and policy makers due to the impact on employment. It will also be felt among logistics service providers (LSPs) whose revenues are largely made up by managing or providing labour forces.

## Types of robots

Although there have been many developments in the automation sector as a whole (which includes a range of materials-handling equipment such as conveyors and forklift trucks), robots are likely to have a transformative effect. There are several types of these already in use:

### MATERIAL TRANSPORT ROBOTS

- Autonomous mobile robots (AMRs) – robots that move materials around the warehouse environment. They work alongside humans and forklift trucks using a pre-programmed warehouse map. They use sensors such as lasers and cameras to interact with their environment. Costs on average $30,000 per unit upwards.

- Automated guided vehicles (AGVs) – another type of material transport robot, but this time restricted to certain routes using wires, magnetic strips or sensors. Good for repetitive movements for high volume and consistent demand, but inflexible and unable to navigate obstacles.

While AGVs have been around longer, it is likely that AMRs will become the future of material transport robots due to their higher levels of flexibility, the fact that they can operate without special infrastructure being built for them and their lower overall cost.

A hybrid system involves self-driving carts leading workers around the warehouse and telling them where to replenish stocks or when to pick an item to place in the carrier. One of the benefits of this system is the lack of investment needed in the warehouse itself and the lower cost of the robots.

### COLLABORATIVE ROBOTS

Collaborative robots, or 'cobots' as they are known for short, are designed to help human workers in their tasks, usually deployed where a good deal of repetition is involved. It can be 'trained' by the worker to undertake a task and thereafter needs no further intervention (apart from maintenance). A distinction between 'collaborative robots' and 'industrial robots' is that while the former can be retrained, the latter is less flexible and set up for one role only, unless reprogrammed (a more complex process). Cobots are often used for packaging functions such as wrapping, sealing and boxing, or 'pick and place'.

### AUTOMATED PICKING

Robotic picking relies on the development of arms that are capable of grasping and manipulation. The ultimate aim for many companies is to eliminate human pickers completely. Two-armed robots, developed by Hitachi, use cameras to identify multiple items at the same time, which allows it to work more quickly than existing alternatives.

## Robotics in logistics

Although most robots fall into one of these categories, the way they are used can differ significantly. Amazon uses robots to bring the picking face to the human pickers, rather than have staff walk up the aisles to the right picking location. Amazon now employs 350,000 robots at its fulfilment centres worldwide (see Chapter 10).

This automation has allowed Amazon to offer industry-leading service levels at a much lower cost than is the case with a wholly human solution. It is estimated that robots have resulted in a 40 per cent fulfilment cost reduction; warehouses can now store up to 50 per cent more inventory and an item can be retrieved in 15 minutes compared to 60–75 minutes for a manual worker (Roser, 2019). In the United States, this has allowed Amazon to push back two-day delivery cut-off times from 3pm to midnight, achieving an impressive extension for this service option.

The solution still requires human participation; not only pickers, but the workers needed to unload trucks, unpack the boxes and place items in racks. These racks are then taken by robots to locations in a caged, 'non-human' area, awaiting collection by another robot.

Amazon has adopted one particular strategy, but there are many other manufacturers. The best known of these are Rethink Robotics, Locus and Fetch from the United States and Singapore-based GreyOrange, which is heavily focused on the Indian market. Alibaba uses a system that looks similar to Amazon's in that it uses robots to lift stacks of boxes, which it then moves to the picker.

British company Ocado has been pioneering robotics for groceries for many years. The grocery e-retail sector faces different challenges to the relatively low number of items needed to be picked per shipment in the Amazon model. Ocado's management claims that its system, where robots swarm over a specifically designed (human-free) matrix, can pick 50 items for an order in a matter of minutes.

Logistics companies, such as DHL, have invested heavily in trialling different solutions, including the widespread use of cobots. For example, it has deployed Rethink Robotics's Sawyer cobots in packing contracts in the UK.

## Warehouse design and demand

The use of robots can make the layout of a warehouse more efficient as aisle space can be narrower. The increased inventory density means that more products can be stored under one roof.

However, this is not as easy as it sounds. A report by real-estate company CBRE (2018) says that in the United States the average age of a warehouse is 34 years, with many having low ceilings and uneven floors, conditions that are either sub-optimal for automated warehouse design or prevent the use of material transport robots of any type.

This means that new warehousing is in great demand with 1 billion square feet of warehousing being developed in the last 10 years alone in the United States. However, CBRE estimates that this is just 11 per cent of the total warehousing inventory and the lack of appropriate building has seen development land prices soar by up to a quarter since 2016.

## People versus robots

The number of people employed in the warehouse environment is still growing but their role is already changing. Many of the most highly repetitive jobs are the best suited to be automated. This means that human roles can become more value adding with the benefit that they become more personally fulfilling. For example, human workers, whose role was once to stack containers, a physical and tiring but necessary function, now oversee robots who have taken over this function.

According to one US-based logistics company that has successfully trialled material transport robots, 'For the 4,500 deliveries that the robots have traversed our warehouse floor in the past six months, that's 1,000 kilometres our workers haven't had to spend time transporting items. By allocating mundane transportation tasks away from our employees to the robots, we are freeing up our people for higher-value work.' Management says that return on investment (ROI) was within 'a few months' (RK Logistics, 2017).

For the time being it would seem that human jobs are safe in the warehouse. The economic value that is being created by greater levels of efficiency has, so far, led to the need for more workers not fewer. In fact, jobs could be set to become less monotonous and physical, which labour organizations should welcome.

However, there are two clouds on the horizon. Firstly, due to the fact that Amazon and other e-commerce companies have created efficiencies in the warehouse that allow them to out-compete many bricks-and-mortar retailers, the employees that they take on may be at the cost of employment in traditional retailing as well as their distribution systems. What this means is that there is a migration of jobs to the likes of Amazon rather than an overall job generation. The logic (although this will be difficult to prove without more data) is that there must be a net loss in employment as many of the jobs that would have been created have been taken by automation.

Secondly, robots are getting cheaper, which will mean that eventually all segments of industry will be able to use them. At the same time as this, employing humans is getting more expensive due to increasing costs and regulation that is involved with each employee hire. Consequently robots, which don't require breaks, health insurance or holidays and can work around the clock at peak times, to mention just a few benefits, will be very attractive to many companies. How governments can deal with the social fallout from this and the loss of tax revenue is another problem. Indeed, this is something that Amazon may have to address sooner rather than later. Given that it has received tax breaks from many US states eager to attract the e-retailer for the jobs it promised to create, administrators may want their money back if the investment results in 'jobless' warehouses.

To understand the economics of robots and, consequently, how likely they are to replace humans, it is necessary to identify their cost. This is not easy as the price of a robot depends on:

- their complexity
- their payload-carrying ability and reach
- the tools they use
- the sophistication of the software required to run them
- the 'teaching' interface

Popular collaborative robot models cost approximately $30,000 although this can easily rise to $100,000 with customization. Although this might sound expensive, anecdotally one cobot can replace two human workers on a line and so the payback is fast and the economic case is obvious. ROI can be achieved in six months to a year.

## Turning workers into robots?

An alternative to investment in new materials-handling equipment is to increase the productivity of workers, within the regulatory parameters laid down by authorities. Warehouse operatives are essentially a physical extension of warehouse management systems (WMSs) albeit with human inefficiencies and weaknesses such as:

- speed to picking face
- picking inaccuracy
- need for breaks
- health and safety concerns
- illness, e.g. Covid-19
- limited working hours

Some of the efficiency challenges can be overcome by 'assistive' technologies without replacing the human worker with a robot. Many of these systems have been around for years including:

- virtual/augmented reality goggles or glasses

- pick by voice or light
- positive RF scanning

The WMS will also plan the most efficient route for the picker, which may involve picking by individual order or, where more appropriate, picking by batch (Manners-Bell, 2016).

However, a new technique is being used to improve efficiency and accuracy of warehouse workers: 'gamification'. As companies continue to exploit technology to improve information flows and productivity, they are challenged to keep tasks 'interesting' – especially those tasks that would generally be classed as repetitive, or boring, but that may also require a high degree of precision and consistency. Gamification is the description of using game techniques and elements to enable workers to achieve goals and complete tasks, while ensuring the worker enjoys the exercise. This can often include rewards for completing tasks within specific timeframes or against other teams doing similar tasks.

Amazon has been using these techniques in some of its warehousing and distribution centres as pilots for a more large-scale rollout. Alongside regular salaries, staff can also win digital rewards that can be exchanged in some cases for goods and services from the company. Some employees have praised the effort as a welcome distraction across a lengthy shift. Also, the program (FC Games) is entirely optional for employees. It is well known that Amazon is one of the largest users of robots across its fulfilment and distribution landscape, as it continues with a relentless obsession with improving productivity and reducing operational costs. Therefore it is trying to ensure that while it still employs huge numbers of people (while automating many repetitive and boring tasks), the human workforce remains engaged.

Using technology to enhance the working experience and 'entertain' the workforce is a natural evolution of the general move towards digitization. Companies will choose if, when and how they engage with this development. If done correctly, it should be possible to do so with the encouragement of the workforce and generate real benefits for the organization.

## What will be the future role of the LSP?

Increasing automation in the warehouse will change the role of the outsourced contract logistics provider. If there are no longer large labour forces to manage in the distribution centre, then what function will it perform?

It could be that the logistics provider becomes an additional source of capital for its customer, providing the robotics equipment, as DHL does with cobots for co-packing services. But it may well be that the customer actually has better access to cheap capital itself and may want to benefit from the tax breaks that are available in many markets for capital investment.

As mentioned above, Robotics-as-a-Service is now being offered by some robot manufacturers, which would also remove the LSP from the equation. This involves the integration of robots into the web and cloud computing environment. Data captured by the robot, such as number and location of items picked or remaining inventory levels, can be shared and retrieved as required. Data on the robot's performance itself can also be shared and fed into planned maintenance programmes.

That contract logistics is very much a labour management operation can be seen by example figures based on actual profit and loss figures of a $15 million European distribution centre dedicated contract (not including transportation). Of the operating costs necessary to generate this revenue, payroll and benefits of the staff amounted to $6.4 million. Depreciation of equipment was just $200,000 and occupancy costs were $1.2 million. In fact, looking at a wide variety of other logistics contracts, the proportion of staff costs to revenue for this contract was at the lower end of the spectrum: depending on the services being provided, direct labour costs can amount to two-thirds of revenues.

From a financial point of view, in the coming years the payroll and benefits profit and loss line looks likely to diminish, while depreciation of assets (such as robots) increases.

It should be noted that this example is for a dedicated outsourced contract. The situation regarding the impact of automation is more complicated for shared-user contracts. While many, if not all, of the costs in a dedicated open book contract can be passed on to the customer, in a shared-user environment, the logistics provider is likely to bear more of the risks. It may be that it makes sense for an LSP to invest in robots in order to increase productivity across a variety of operations in a single distribution centre, especially where labour is in short supply and expensive. Therefore, they will bear the financial risk if volumes are lower than forecast, although the corollary is that they have a better upside.

However, whatever relationship the LSP has with its customers, the efficiencies gained in the warehouse will inevitably have a short-term impact on revenues for the sector as a whole. One US bank, Janney Capital Markets, has suggested that retailer fulfilment costs in the United States will fall by one-third (Bhaiya, 2017). Logistics companies may still benefit in terms of margins, but to do so they will have to change their operating models substantially to focus on their value add.

## Robots in the supply chain

Logistics companies will also be affected by the increasing use of robots and automation in production processes. These could have as much an impact on logistics companies' businesses as the tactical use of robots in warehouses, not least due to the shift in global trade patterns that could result. If robots remove the need to locate production in low-cost labour markets, one of the key drivers for globalization will have been eliminated.

The economic use of robots in production lines is generally a trade-off between the time it takes a skilled human to train them, against the consistent, reliable output that results from the machine. In the past the dexterity of a low-skilled but cheap human has usually outperformed the robot. As manufacturing has evolved, robots have become cheaper and more dexterous, while at the same time people have become more expensive. Consequently, more robots are being seen in production facilities, especially those of high-tech manufacturers. As collaborative manufacturing networks emerge, intelligent devices and machines will be harnessed to support faster and more agile production runs.

---

FASHION SUPPLY CHAINS SET FOR DISRUPTION

The apparel sector currently embraces many innovations discussed in this book to compete in the e-commerce space. Nike, for instance, is one manufacturer who is using 3D printing to customize sport shoes for specific individuals. Adidas is also innovating in this area along with other major sports apparel brands. But it is not only technologies such as 3D printing that are being used: robots, advanced smartphone apps and high-definition optics are all being exploited by the fashion business.

One major Chinese contract manufacturer has built a plant in the United States with multiple production lines manned by 'Sewbots'. These are robots that can manufacture clothing, in this case T-shirts for the German company Adidas, incredibly fast. The 'bots' can cut and sew a new shirt every 22 seconds from very soft and flexible fabric. This was something that was impossible to conceive a few years ago. The designs can also be changed very swiftly according to market demand.

Amazon is thought to have major plans in this area. The company is exploring customized clothes that can be manufactured to order using the techniques mentioned above. By using the high-definition cameras and a related app on a smartphone, customers will be able to take precise images and measurements of themselves. This will provide very detailed sizing information. Any garments the customer selects from the online stores are then cut, sewed and finished for rapid delivery by the closest facility.

The implications for logistics companies are clear. This kind of innovation, if successful, would have a major impact on the flows of garments from Asia to Europe and North America, negatively affecting shipping lines and air cargo operators as well as freight forwarders. However, key beneficiaries will be the express and last-mile delivery companies and, should manufacturing take place in distribution facilities close to the end recipient, contract logistics providers.

## Summary

Automation, and robotics in particular, will transform the warehouse environment in the coming years. Although the sector is a long way from becoming 'jobless' there is no doubt that, as robots become cheaper and more ubiquitous, the role of the warehouse worker will change. It remains to be seen whether the economic value created by robotics will generate a net gain in jobs, but with many retail jobs being lost to more commoditized warehouse functions, which are then at risk from automation, it seems inevitable that labour requirements will diminish. The quality of work for those left, however, will improve.

Although the role of LSPs will remain significant for years to come, the services they will be asked to provide will change. There will be more focus on the value they can bring to the overall supply chain as labour becomes less important. This will impact on gross revenues as well as change the character of LSPs' profit and loss accounts and balance sheets. More importantly it will also change the relationship they have with their customers.

# References

Bhaiya, A (2017) Is robotic automation the future of e-commerce warehouses? *Huffington Post*, 14 November, www.huffingtonpost.com/amit-bhaiya/ is-robotic-automation-the_b_12909658.html (archived at https://perma.cc/ CVV5-UESF)

CBRE (2018) Most US warehouses are inadequate for e-commerce distribution, despite recent construction push, www.cbre.com/press-releases/cbre-most-us-warehouses-are-inadequate-for-ecommerce-distribution-despite-recent-construction-push (archived at https://perma.cc/ZG44-9833)

Manners-Bell, J (2016) *Introduction to Global Logistics*, Kogan Page, London

Melton, J (2019) The number of robotic warehouses is expected to grow more than 1200% by 2025, Digital Commerce 360, 2 April, www.digitalcommerce360.com/ 2019/04/02/number-robotic-warehouse-will-grow/ (archived at https://perma.cc/ N96V-NCEG)

RK Logistics (2017) RK Logistics increases productivity with robots, 30 March, www.rklogisticsgroup.com/robotics/rk-logistics-increases-productivity-with-robots/ (archived at https://perma.cc/BMG2-5X8X)

Roser, C (2019) The inner workings of Amazon fulfilment centres – part 1, AllAboutLean.com, 22 October, www.allaboutlean.com/amazon-fulfillment-1/ (archived at https://perma.cc/NT9G-JQUD)

# 16

# Autonomous vehicles
# and delivery robots

**This chapter will familiarize the reader with:**

- The reasons behind the development of autonomous vehicles

- The barriers to their adoption

- The levels of vehicle autonomy

- What is meant by 'platooning' and its benefits

- The prospects for the future of 'drones'

- The development of autonomous ships and their prospects

- 'Delivery robots' and their potential role in last-mile delivery

## Introduction

With technology giants such as Google and Uber and vehicle manufacturers investing heavily in 'autonomous vehicles', it is only a matter of time before they are seen on roads around the world. In fact, many 'assistive' technologies (such as help with parking) are already being used. Vehicles now have the capability to interact not only with other vehicles around them, but also with highway infrastructure.

While the headlines have mostly focused on cars, automotive manufacturers – both incumbent and start-up – have invested billions in developing autonomous trucks. Significant progress has already been made. For example, a Mercedes-Benz prototype truck has driven autonomously on an autobahn in Germany, successfully navigating a junction in real-life driving conditions.

It is also increasingly possible to 'harvest' a huge amount of data from vehicles, both cars and trucks, which if analysed in a proper and timely way will result in efficiencies, mostly related to the avoidance of congestion. This data can be generated either by traffic authorities (such as municipalities or highway agencies), by private companies that provide information to users on speed of traffic or, more recently, mobile applications that allow individuals to log incidents as they observe them. The latter can theoretically mobilize thousands of drivers who act as monitors of traffic situations in areas that no other organization could reach.

## The forces behind autonomous trucks

### Increase in efficiency

One of the foremost reasons for the investment in this technology is the potential increase in transport efficiency that could be achieved. With congestion forecast to rise substantially in the near future, there is a need to break the link between economic growth and vehicle movements. German authorities predict that truck transport volume will increase by 39 per cent by 2030 unless steps are taken (Newbold, 2016). Construction of new roads is unpopular from an environmental perspective, and many countries in Europe just do not have the money available to make the sort of investment required. Major trunk road networks in Western Europe have barely grown in the past decade. Therefore, it becomes essential to utilize existing road capacity more efficiently – and new technologies can aid in this goal.

### Cost savings

In many countries, it is estimated that around 45 per cent of total cost for road freight operators is related to the driver (Ti, 2021). Eventually removing the driver (although no one is suggesting this is likely for many years) would obviously then have an enormous impact on road freight costs, profits and margins.

Another issue is the looming driver shortage crisis. Many people are increasingly unwilling to commit to a career as a driver, given the hours away from home, the relative low pay and the conditions. This will eventually translate into higher costs for road operators and their customers. By taking away much of the stress from driving by leaving most of the important decisions to a computer, working conditions will become more attractive. There may also be the opportunity for the role to become more value adding as the driver will have the time and connectivity to undertake an enhanced role, perhaps in transport management activities.

In summary, vehicle manufacturers believe that the efficiencies the technology will deliver will come in the form of:

- Reduced fuel consumption – the computer will drive the vehicle more fuel efficiently.
- Reduced emissions – for the same reason.
- 100 per cent connectivity and location services, which allow for 'perfect' route planning.
- Diagnostic services that ensure correct maintenance and fewer breakdowns.
- Emergency braking will ensure fewer accidents, gaps between vehicles will be adhered to.
- Routes can be replanned around known areas of congestion.
- Accidents caused by human error (through tiredness, for example) will be considerably reduced.
- Communications can be shared with customers to provide visibility of delivery times, changing in line with the traffic situation.

## Barriers to autonomous driving

The United States is leading the way in the development of autonomous vehicles, although other jurisdictions have not been slow to catch on. However, at this early stage of development, removing drivers from trucks is still a very long way off and will face huge challenges, not only from labour organizations, but also safety and regulatory bodies and even the wider population. A cursory look at the railway industry throws up some of the barriers faced. Although the technology has existed for many years for driverless trains on rapid transits, very few are in service. In theory, the highly controlled environment of a railway should lend itself ideally to such technologies. Given the congestion that exists on many rail networks and the expense of building new infrastructure, it would seem obvious that autonomous driving should have been adopted several years ago. At the very least, plans should be in place to implement these technologies. However, this is not the case, and this perhaps hints at the problems such initiatives in the road freight sector will face.

It is for this reason that vehicle manufacturers such as Mercedes-Benz (Daimler) are being very careful with the language they use, unwilling as they are to upset vested interests. For the foreseeable future the technology they are developing will assist the driver rather than take over the driving. A comparison perhaps would be with airline pilots who use an autopilot once they have taken off, and only return controls to manual when they are about to land. This is despite the fact that at many airports some newer airliners are quite capable of landing themselves.

Other barriers relate to:

- data security
- insurance liability
- driving and resting times

## Technology progress

Vehicle autonomy will not advance to its greatest extent overnight, but rather, through a series of incremental improvements, manufacturers will introduce a range of enhancements that eventually combine to provide high levels of autonomy. The Society of Automotive Engineers categorizes these levels, as set out in Table 16.1.

Level 3 and above are described as autonomous. Lower levels are already being adopted by truck manufacturers – for example, autonomous emer-

TABLE 16.1  Levels of autonomy

| Level | Type | Example |
|---|---|---|
| 0 | No driving automation | - |
| 1 | Driver assistance | Adaptive cruise control or lane centring |
| 2 | Partial driving automation | Adaptive cruise control and lane centring |
| 3 | Automated driving (conditional) | Automated driving at low speeds |
| 4 | Automated driving (high) | Automated driving within city centre |
| 5 | Automated driving (full) | Automated driving everywhere |

SOURCE  Society of Automotive Engineers

gency braking systems (AEBs) that have been a mandatory feature for new heavy goods vehicles (HGVs) deployed in Europe since November 2015.

At present, the most advanced autonomous driving system commercially available is Tesla's Autopilot feature, which is classified as Level 2 autonomous by the National Highway Transportation Safety Administration (NHTSA). First made available in October 2014, Autopilot provides drivers with forward collision warning, automatic emergency braking, adaptive cruise control and automatic steering. Together, these features allow the system to match the vehicle's speed to traffic conditions, stay within a lane, change lanes, transition between motorways, exit the motorway and self-park.

Human supervision is still required in order to operate these features, as there are instances where manual control is necessary. This was highlighted in May 2016, when a Tesla Model S driver died after his vehicle collided with an articulated truck. The Autopilot system had been operational at the point of impact, and it later emerged that the car had failed to differentiate the trailer of the truck from the sky as it approached.

The legality of Autopilot varies by country, though it is likely that most will update their legislation to permit it, along with similar systems provided by other manufacturers. For example, German lawmakers updated their rules to permit certain types of vehicle autonomy in May 2017 with a view to normalizing the use of such systems. The UK introduced the Automated and Electric Vehicles Act in 2020 and is set to allow automated lane-keeping systems (ALKS) in 2022, which will enable drivers to take their hands off the steering wheel at speeds of up to 37mph on motorways.

Level 3 autonomous driving, whereby vehicles can operate without driver intervention in certain situations (such as ALKS), is technically feasible for the majority of car manufacturers exploring the technology. HGV manufacturers possess the same technology, but due to the dangers of operating such large and heavy vehicles, Level 3 road trials have been largely restricted.

## Platooning

Classified as a Level 2 automation technology, a platoon is classified as a group of two or more vehicles driving in concert as part of a convoy. When linked together by machine to machine (M2M) communication technologies, a local network can be formed between the vehicles, allowing them to act in concert. Thus, when the first vehicle brakes, each of the other vehicles in the platoon also brakes at the same time, with no delay.

As a result of this technology, vehicles in a platoon can drive much closer to one another than would be safe based on human reaction times, consequently benefiting from significant reductions in drag. According to ERTICO, this leads to a reduction in fuel consumption; ranging from 1 to 8 per cent for the lead vehicle, and 7 to 16 per cent from trailing vehicles (Winder, 2016). In practice, each driver retains independent control over their vehicle, and can disengage from the platoon where necessary, such as on approaches to motorway ramps and other points where traffic merges.

Following the Amsterdam Declaration on 14 April 2016, the European Union established a roadmap for the steps necessary for the development of self-driving technology within its jurisdiction. The declaration focused on the implementation of multibrand platooning in Europe before 2025, and consists of a set of trials for manufacturers, adaptation of the regulatory framework governing vehicle autonomy, and the development of incentives to encourage the uptake of the technology.

As part of this plan, several semi-automated platoons of trucks drove across Europe in 2016, arriving in Rotterdam from Sweden, Denmark, Germany, Belgium and the Netherlands as part of a challenge coordinated by DAF, Daimler, Iveco, MAN, Scania and Volvo. The report on the trial, by the Dutch Ministry of Infrastructure and the Environment, found that truck drivers regarded merging traffic and on/off ramps as the most challenging elements of platooning in practice. Issues here centred on the policy of decoupling on the approach to motorway ramps, with one instance suggesting that maintaining the integrity of a small platoon may prove safer in practice than if two or three trucks decoupled (MIE, 2016).

Steady progress has been made since the early days of the technology and trials have generally provided positive results in terms of the benefits, the resilience and functionality of the technology itself, safety, and also driver acceptance. This has encouraged several states in the United States to allow platooning and it is expected that platooning will be allowed in many countries in Europe by 2024 (Bishop, 2020).

In summary, vehicle platooning is a technology that is likely to become adopted within commercial road freight operations. The business case is solid, and the technology is approaching the stage where it is safe enough to become accepted by regulators. Issues on both aspects still need to be worked out, but the prospects for adoption are substantial.

## Prospects for full autonomy

Although significant progress has been made, the likelihood of full (Level 5) autonomy – or 'driverless trucks' – is still some way off. Current programming techniques employed in AI are unable to provide a computer with the ability to infer potential actions in an unfamiliar situation. Hence, without access to any data relating to a similar situation, none of today's autonomous systems are able to determine how to respond to extremely low probability events.

Moreover, conceiving of such events in order to simulate an AI response is challenging in itself. As such, the physical safety of autonomous vehicles is incredibly difficult to determine because it is essentially impossible to test exhaustively.

Some companies, such as the Swedish start-up Einride, have proposed remote operation as a partial solution to this problem. The company aims to produce vehicles capable of fully autonomous driving on motorways where environmental conditions are easier to control, while human operators will handle the vehicles within, and on approach to, urban areas.

Unfortunately, this solution presents manufacturers with a different set of problems. With an increasing reliance on connectivity over distance, the physical threat of cyberattacks increases significantly. In 2015, hackers exploited a 'zero-day' vulnerability (a system vulnerability unknown to the vendor), which allowed them to take full control of a Jeep Cherokee by connecting to its entertainment system over the internet. While the attackers in this instance were demonstrating the vulnerability in order to assist Fiat Chrysler with security, their success highlights a substantial problem for all manufacturers.

Although security vulnerabilities are not a problem specific to autonomous systems, the increasing reliance of these vehicles on external connectivity, as with platooning operations for instance, means that they are worryingly susceptible to intrusions.

It should be noted that the above is merely an appraisal of autonomous vehicles as they exist today. The rapid development of AI research and development over the past five years, enabled in part by the commoditization of advanced hardware developed for gaming, conveys incredible potential.

## Other autonomous vehicles

Although the development of autonomous trucks has, by far, the largest potential to disrupt transport systems, opportunities exist for other modes, not least, of course, unmanned aerial vehicles (UAVs) or, as they are popularly known, 'drones'. However, technology is also being developed for guiding crewless ships and, of course, autopilots have been in use in aircraft for many decades.

## Unmanned aerial vehicles (UAVs) or 'drones'

In terms of attracting media attention, drones have been hugely successful. In reality, though, they will never be able to replace the utility of trucks and vans, which deliver many millions of parcels across the world each day. Drones, which can only carry one parcel at a time, simply cannot compete in terms of speed and efficiency, at least in the mainstream market.

Challenges that still need to be overcome include:

- **Range and payload**: the maximum payload for most drones being developed is around 3 kilograms, although Chinese retailer JD.com's drone can carry up to 15 kilograms. Largely as a result of the payload issue, however, the drone systems have a short battery life. This is a potentially significant hurdle to commercial operations for obvious reasons, most notably delivery range. Of the delivery drones currently being trialled by Amazon, DPD (produced by Atechsys), Flirtey and Matternet (all of which are powered by lithium-ion batteries), none have a top range of more than 20 miles. JD.com is trialling a drone with a range of up to 31 miles.

- **Safety and regulatory**: battery life and the associated scenarios accompanying a loss of power are other major issues. The implications of a power loss mid-flight over a crowded public area, for instance, are severe. There has also been much concern about drones flying into other users' airspace such as an airport or military zone.

- **Security**: the security of the drones, and the products they are carrying, is another concern undergoing rigorous testing. Companies such as Matternet, which is partnering with Swiss Post on its drone programme, advocate the use of a network of secure landing pads to protect (and recharge) the vehicles. Nonetheless, physical security is not the only issue under scrutiny here. The potential to jam radio signals or hack into drones is a real and significant threat.

- **Noise and privacy**: if drones were to become widely used for delivery of parcels, the air would become congested. This would create considerable noise pollution as well as visual intrusion.

- **Delivery practicalities**: there is also the problem of how drones would practically deliver to many residential or office locations if there were no landing areas.

- **Technology**: overcoming some of the technological challenges has been too much for at least one of the innovators. One report suggested that Amazon's drone project was 'collapsing inwards' and 'dysfunctional', leading to job losses (Kersley, 2021). Problems were allegedly caused by the company's desire to land the drone at the delivery location rather than drop the parcel from a height. This advanced requirement led to the need for 3D mapping and machine learning, which not only pushed up budgets and increased timescales but led to the drone becoming much heavier, resulting in more regulatory hurdles to clear.

## SUITABILITY FOR NICHE SECTORS

A preoccupation with e-commerce deliveries (precipitated originally by Amazon's marketing) has diverted attention away from a role that drones can play much more effectively. Leveraging their ability to move quickly over terrain that may have little or no transport infrastructure, drones are already proving to be well-suited to the transport of urgent shipments in remote locations. Examples of successful trials include:

- DHL drones delivering medications from the German mainland to the North Sea island of Juist.

- Zipline's drone-based transportation of medical supplies throughout Rwanda.

- Matternet's operational network serving hospitals throughout Switzerland, transporting blood and pathology samples between hospital facilities on-demand.

What makes each of these business models viable is the absence of transport infrastructure. The mountainous terrain of Switzerland constitutes one of the few areas in Western Europe where the delivery of medical samples cannot be executed rapidly through conventional channels, while the underdeveloped road network in Rwanda is more representative of its region.

While conditions in parts of Europe and Africa appear amenable to the niche use of drone delivery systems in support of medical operations, the vast geography of China makes the application of drone technology appropriate for e-commerce packages. Both SF Express and JD.com are deploying drones in order to fulfil e-commerce deliveries throughout rural areas in

China. The former has been running limited drone delivery operations in Beijing, Sichuan, Shaanxi and Jiangsu and sees the technology as a competitive advantage over e-commerce rival Alibaba.

Speaking to CNBC, JD.com's CEO, Richard Liu, said the cost of serving rural areas 'will drop down at least 70 per cent' (Choudhury and Yoon, 2017) with the use of drones as opposed to cars or vans. JD runs a more vertically integrated business than rival Alibaba, in which it owns and operates its own logistics infrastructure to serve customers. By being able to serve rural customers more rapidly than its rival, the company may be able to expand its market share.

The conclusions to be taken from recent activity are clear: drones used for logistics in Europe and North America are likely to provide deliveries in niche, time-critical areas where no other suitable options exist. In China, India and other emerging markets, however, it may be that drone delivery will serve as a leapfrogging technology, allowing the expanding e-commerce industry to overcome substantial infrastructure deficits to reach consumers.

## Delivery robots

An alternative to drones is self-driving robots. These navigate along paths rather than fly and as a result lack many of the problems associated with UAVs. The delivery robots travel at walking pace on pavements and in pedestrian zones, navigate autonomously to their destination and avoid obstacles and danger points automatically. They have a load capacity of up to 10 kilograms and can transport goods over a distance of around 6 kilometres.

Since 2016, Swiss Post has been conducting tests with self-driving delivery robots, provided by Starship Technologies, to assess their suitability for goods delivery over the last mile. In specific terms, Swiss Post envisages using this solution for special items that need to be delivered flexibly, quickly and inexpensively in a local neighbourhood. Some of the applications include same-day and same-hour delivery, grocery deliveries or even home deliveries of medical products.

Just Eat is also trialling these robots in the UK, Germany and Switzerland. The trial also includes Hermes, Metro Group and London food start-up Pronto.co.uk. As part of the European programme, dozens of robots will be deployed in five cities to run test deliveries and introduce the devices to the public. The robots have been developed for delivering packages, groceries and food to consumers in up to a three-mile radius.

As with drones, it is too early to judge whether this delivery system will be a success or not. Many barriers to adoption exist, not least issues such as return on capital compared with employing a courier; security considerations; practical issues such as obstructions; and, critically, how the consignment is delivered from robot to house.

### Autonomous ships

Many in the shipping industry believe that autonomous ships will eventually totally replace the crewed alternative. There are good commercial arguments for this belief:

- lower labour costs due to the removal of crew
- lower fuel costs due to the removal of accommodation (perhaps 6 per cent lower)
- lower construction costs and more room for paying freight
- lower insurance for accidents involving humans

However, the cost situation is not completely positive. As there would be no crew on hand to carry out repair and maintenance, there will need to be considerable redundancy built in to the ship's design, which will push up construction costs. Although some insurance costs may go down, the crew's existing role in mitigating accidents at sea involving other ships or port infrastructure has yet to be fully assessed.

Given that a ship's life may extend to 25 years, there is also a considerable disincentive to take a risk on complete redesigns should they prove to be uneconomic. This has meant that smaller investments in short sea shipping are occurring first as shipping lines test the market with the new technologies.

An example of this involves two Norwegian companies that are developing what they claim would be the first fully electric and autonomous container ship. The task is being undertaken by Yara International ASA, an agricultural and chemicals company, and Kongsberg, a high-tech systems manufacturer for the merchant marine, defence, aerospace and offshore oil and gas sectors.

Their project, the Yara Birkeland, cost $25 million, undertaking its maiden voyage in late 2021. It was planned that it would transport fertilizer 37 miles in Norwegian waters from Yara's production port in Larvik to Brevik. The ship has a capacity of around 100–150 20-foot equivalent units (TEUs) and runs on a 3.5–4MWh set of batteries. In its original stages, the operation will be manned but by 2023 it will be fully autonomous, if trials go to plan.

The initial cost is high as it incorporates the costs of GPS, lidar, infra-red and high-resolution cameras needed to operate this new type of vessel. However, its operating costs are likely to be dramatically lower than a normal container ship. Reports suggest annual operating costs could fall by up to 90 per cent, with no fuel costs or seafarers to pay for (Paris, 2017).

There are a variety of other developments within the sector too:

- Kongsberg is involved in a separate undertaking with UK-based Automated Ships Ltd and French offshore services company Bourbon Offshore, in which they are developing an autonomous prototype vessel for servicing the offshore energy, hydrographic and scientific and offshore fish-farming industries.

- Rolls-Royce Holdings initiated a project called the Advanced Autonomous Waterborne Applications (AAWA) initiative (now Safer Vessel with Autonomous Navigation), which coordinates the private sector and universities to develop new solutions in the area.

- One Baltic operator involved in this project, Finferries, is utilizing a variety of sensors and thermal cameras, alongside its manned operations in its Stella Ferry. These are said to be improving safety, by increasing awareness of the environment and making it easier for crews to navigate.

'Autonomous shipping is the future of the maritime industry. As disruptive as the smartphone, the smart ship will revolutionize the landscape of ship design and operations.'

Mikael Mäkinen, President, Marine, Rolls-Royce

The success of such projects thus far has shown the strength of the concept. Petter Ostbo, Yara's head of production, told the *Wall Street Journal* that the company hopes to invest in larger autonomous ships for even longer routes and 'maybe even move our fertilizer from Holland all the way to Brazil' when international regulations for crewless vessels are set (Paris, 2017).

The International Maritime Organization (IMO) has also announced that it would launch a study into amending laws to permit the use of unmanned vessels. However, it is likely to be some time before any full regulations are set. As with autonomous cars, regulation will delay the deployment of fully autonomous ships. However, the technology involved has already a part to play in aiding maritime transport by cutting fuel costs, increasing safety and helping navigation. In the short term, these developments will complement manned operations on vessels, though in the long term they may replace them altogether.

## Summary

The acceptance of autonomous vehicles will likely increase steadily over time, as various levels of autonomy are adopted – for example, the platooning of vehicles on motorway systems, and low-speed movements of robotics systems such as Starship Technologies' delivery robot. The automation of transportation systems will reduce labour costs significantly and, along with the rise of on-demand services, will likely promote asset-sharing. Drone-based deliveries in areas where infrastructure is weak and populations dispersed will connect previously uneconomical delivery areas to mainstream services.

However, whether road, air or sea, it will be many years before autonomous vehicles become the norm. Regulatory barriers, security and safety concerns, not to mention commercial realities, will prove sizable delays to the adoption of the new technologies, which for the time being will assist human drivers and crew rather than replace them.

## References

Bishop, R (2020) US states are allowing automated follower truck platooning while the swedes may lead in Europe, *Forbes*, 2 May, www.forbes.com/sites/richardbishop1/2020/05/02/us-states-are-allowing-automated-follower-truck-platooning-while-the-swedes-may-lead-in-europe/?sh=fffde8fd7e8d (archived at https://perma.cc/C6BR-CYJG)

Choudhury, S and Yoon, E (2017) JD.com chief Richard Liu sees drone delivery as the way to reach China's rural consumers, CNBC, www.cnbc.com/2017/06/18/jd-com-ceo-richard-liu-talks-drones-automation-and-logistics.html (archived at https://perma.cc/MHZ2-MQYC)

Kersley, A (2021) The slow collapse of Amazon's drone delivery dream, *Wired*, 3 August, www.wired.co.uk/article/amazon-drone-delivery-prime-air (archived at https://perma.cc/Q6EX-6U6H)

Lammert, M, Duran, A (National Renewable Energy Laboratory), Diez, J, Burton, K (Intertek) and Nicholson, A (2014) Effect of platooning on fuel consumption of Class 8 vehicles over a range of speeds, following distances, and mass, *SAE International Journal of Commercial Vehicles*, 7 (2), doi:10.4271/2014-01-2438

MIE (2016) *European Truck Platooning Challenge 2016*, Ministry of Infrastructure and the Environment, Netherlands

Newbold, R (2016) Five driving forces behind driverless trucks, *Inbound Logistics*, January, http://www.inboundlogistics.com/cms/article/five-driving-forces-behind-driverless-trucks/ (archived at https://perma.cc/4R7Z-4KMM)

Paris, C (2017) Norway takes lead in race to build autonomous cargo ships, *Wall Street Journal*, 22 July, www.wsj.com/articles/norway-takes-lead-in-race-to-build-autonomous-cargo-ships-1500721202 (archived at https://perma.cc/53HF-WTGP)

Ti (2021) *European Road Freight Transport 2021*, Ti Insight, UK

Winder, A (2016) 'ITS4CV' – ITS for commercial vehicles, ERTICO, Brussels, 9 September, http://erticonetwork.com/wp-content/uploads/2016/09/ITS4CV-Report-final-2016-09-09.pdf (archived at https://perma.cc/8VWX-LKYJ)

# PART FOUR

# Digitalization of logistics markets

# 17

# Digital road freight and warehousing platforms

> **This chapter will familiarize the reader with:**
>
> - How levels of inefficiency in the road freight market have led to the development of new digital marketplaces
> - The different types of road freight platforms
> - The importance of scale to platforms and charging mechanisms
> - Leading freight marketplace start-ups in Europe, North America and Asia
> - How 'shared economy' business models can benefit the warehouse sector
> - The benefits and disadvantages of 'on-demand' warehousing
> - Two leading digital warehouse platforms

## Digital road freight platforms

As has been outlined in Chapter 2, disruption can occur in a sector where the incumbent players are failing to develop solutions to address industry inefficiency. In the road freight sector 'inefficiency' can be measured in terms of underutilized capacity, i.e. empty or part-loaded running, although the industry also faces many other challenges including:

- levels of fragmentation
- lack of collaboration between carriers

- commoditization of products
- lack of insight into prices and capacity
- often low-quality services
- lack of investment in technology
- manual processes
- paper documentation
- lack of real-time tracking

In Europe and Asia, the problems are exacerbated by the numerous individual country markets that exist with a diverse range of regulations, cultures and languages to overcome. This is even the case on an intra-country basis in markets such as India and China, where efforts to integrate local, city and regional markets are ongoing.

Numerous new technology platforms have entered the road freight/trucking market, each promising to address many of the problems outlined above. However, their fundamental aim is to better match supply with demand, leading to fuller trucks for carriers and better rates for shippers. The merit of this premise and an analysis of the sector as a whole is discussed in more detail below.

## Types of digital freight marketplaces

The taxonomy of the sector can be outlined as follows:

1 'E-forwarders', 'digital' or 'virtual forwarders' actively intermediate the process and take on execution and pricing risk. These can be categorized as:

   a. 'captives' (subsidiaries of major road freight companies)

   b. 'non-captives' or independents

2 'Load boards' or 'marketplaces' provide an exchange between shippers and carriers but do not take responsibility for the successful execution of the transaction. Some focus on 'shipper to carrier' relationships, helping locate available capacity in the market, for instance on specific routes. Others help carriers collaborate among themselves ('carrier to carrier'). Many of these exchanges have been around for decades and are now developing additional services such as 'digital warehousing'.

3  Tender platforms: these provide for longer-term relationships between carrier and shipper. In addition, they are able to provide value-added solutions, such as helping to balance the volumes on carriers' networks.

4  Data connectors/aggregators: these provide standardized connections between many market participants for purposes of pricing, freight allocation, visibility and/or payments.

5  Traditional freight forwarders are also targeting this market in the customer portal/quoting engine area.

'Quality' is seen as an important distinction between e-forwarders and freight exchanges. An argument employed by the former is that trust is essential to the process and that a forwarder is critical to ensuring the successful completion of the transaction. In other words, 'relationship' is essential to the offering of the forwarder both in terms of customers and carriers. Customers develop trust with companies and individuals, which take responsibility should anything go wrong. Relationships are important for carriers too. They will trust a forwarder and build long-term partnerships to ensure consistent volumes at sustainable prices in return for a commitment to quality.

Although load-matching platforms may check the credentials of the carriers using their platforms ('curated'), ultimately the risk is borne by the shipper, who may or may not have had any prior contact with the carrier.

As can be seen from the cross-section of e-forwarders and freight exchanges highlighted above, there are many options available for both shippers and carriers. The categorization above differentiates the players in terms of their varying business models. However, many platforms also differentiate themselves by:

- **Geography**: as discussed in more detail below, Germany is the biggest road freight market in Europe and this has spawned the development of several large exchanges, which have then expanded into other countries across Europe.

- **International/national/local volumes**: whereas some platforms have specialized in cross-border movements, others target local freight needs such as focusing on localized movements of pallets.

- **Commodities**: some marketplaces specialize in a specific industry sector, such as steel or bulk goods, by creating a dedicated community of carriers and shippers.

## Charging models

A subscription model is often used by the marketplaces to generate revenue. For example, although some exchanges allow users the opportunity to post cargos or truck availability for free, they charge for other value-adding services, such as adding regular routes, advertising or use of their transport management system. The low rates usually charged indicate that freight exchanges need to be very competitive to acquire both loads and trucks for their platforms.

E-forwarders employ a more traditional form of revenue generation: buying and selling capacity via their platforms and retaining a margin. They can also perform many of the usual value-adding freight-forwarding tasks such as document origination. Although it may be considered that digitization would remove the necessity of human interaction, this is not necessarily the case. An attribute of some of the successful platforms involves a strong sales process and account management team. This helps to keep the rates they charge higher than the market average while ensuring long-term partnerships with the carriers at lower input costs.

## Digital marketplaces and brokerage

One of the big issues for many road freight marketplaces is that there is little to differentiate them from each other. Traditional 'freight exchanges' have undertaken load matching for some time and dominate the market in terms of scale. E-forwarders offer a different type of service, maintaining responsibility for the customer relationship, but lack the presence of the marketplaces.

Whether e-forwarder or marketplace, in order to be successful, these businesses need to maintain both an effective service and a large supply of capacity (carriers). However, as competition commoditizes the basic load-matching service they provide, shippers risk receiving low-quality service and carriers risk attaining low rates – it can become a race to the bottom based on price.

'Network effects', or demand-side economies of scale, are critical to success in these platforms. These occur when a service becomes more valuable to its users as more people adopt it, creating barriers to entry for rivals, and barriers to exit for users. Eventually, this can allow a single firm to dominate the market.

The successful companies building on the marketplace concept will integrate a range of technologies (including mobile) for their customers. Moreover, they will establish a strategic lock-in with both carriers and shippers by effectively serving the needs of both parties. While the potential advantages of a digital brokerage service are relatively clear to shippers (lower costs, flexible capacity, assets on-demand), many companies operating in this field have failed to articulate clear benefits to carriers, which has weakened their offering. (See the 'Palleter' Case Study in Chapter 2.)

In this 'chicken or egg' dilemma, other businesses have established scale by focusing on providing useful services to carriers first, before subsequently introducing brokerage operations for shippers. Notably, the US start-up Trucker Path has gained traction among owner-operators by providing them with parking, navigation and financing services. Similar methods have been applied by companies in India and China.

## Leading digital marketplace start-ups

Investment has poured into the sector over the past five years. In Europe, the market has come to be dominated by longstanding German freight exchanges as well as start-ups, such as market leader Sennder. Their dominance is a product of the country's market size. Germany possesses the largest road freight market in Europe by some distance (particularly for international freight), and as such, this overall scale makes it attractive. This is also evidenced by the market share of the top German-based road freight carriers operating in the European market (e.g. DHL, Schenker, Kuehne + Nagel, Rhenus, Dachser).

Compared with other regions such as North America and Asia, it is noticeable that there have been relatively low levels of funding for new start-ups. There are several reasons why this is the case. Firstly, the market opportunity for a road freight platform start-up company in India, China or the United States is much greater than Europe. While the overall EU market as a bloc is the largest in the world, each of the European companies are restricted as a result of variation in language, legislation and culture, as mentioned above. This is not a complete block to expansion to adjacent countries, but it does make it more difficult for development.

Moreover, the growth opportunity in Europe is nowhere near as great as it is in India and China. In these nascent markets, large-scale traditional trucking operators have not been able to develop to the same extent as in the

United States and Europe. Consequently, there are more opportunities for technology-based innovators to address weak service provision and a hyper-fragmented supply side.

In China, the two largest platforms agreed to merge in late 2017. Huochebang (also known as Truck Alliance) and Yunmanman created an enterprise, Manbang Group, valued at its IPO in 2021 at $21 billion. With an estimated 10 million truck drivers and close to 5 million customers on the combined platforms, the company is investing heavily in AI to effectively deal with data flows (Ding, 2020). As with the US platform Truckerpath (see below), load matching is just one of the services offered. They both also sell carriers toll cards, fuel, tyres as well as second-hand vehicles. Manbang Group also has plans to invest in autonomous and alternatively powered trucks, following in the footsteps of Uber.

### Competition between major European logistics companies

An important development for Europe's digital freight marketplaces has been the response of incumbent road freight companies. Specifically, three leading firms have attempted to protect themselves from the threat of disruption by buying into the space. They are:

- UPS (acquired FreightEx in January 2017)
- DHL (acquired Cillox in 2016)
- DB Schenker (invested in uShip during February 2017)

Each of the above companies has taken a slightly different approach to entering the digital road freight brokerage market.

#### UPS

UPS does not have an asset-heavy road freight business in Europe analogous to UPS Freight in North America (now disposed of). The company has scaled up its European express operations significantly over time and is also recognized throughout the continent for its contract logistics activities, but it has always lacked a trucking business.

This changed following the company's 2015 takeover of Coyote Logistics. Set up in 2006, Coyote is one of a previous generation of digital brokerage firms in the road freight space and had grown steadily over time through an approach that combined traditional brokerage with proprietary web-based software to match freight with available capacity. By 2015, the company was growing rapidly, and UPS acquired it following three years in which it had contracted the company for extra capacity during demand peaks.

With Coyote delivering strong growth within the UPS Supply Chain and Freight division, the company decided to replicate the model in Europe by acquiring a similar company, FreightEx, and establishing consistent technology and practices across both continents. The takeover of FreightEx has allowed UPS to expand into the European road freight market without committing to the development of an expensive, asset-based network of operations.

## DHL

By contrast to UPS, DHL Freight is well established as one of the largest players in the European road freight market. As such, DHL did not need to buy an established brokerage company to establish itself in the market. Instead, the company acquired an early stage start-up, Cillox, in order to gain access to its technology. Cillox was later rebranded to Saloodo! and has established a presence in Germany and the UK.

The technology behind Saloodo! was developed as a cloud-based application designed for use on various devices. The application matches shipments with capacity on-demand, manages documentation, payments and provides route information to drivers. The system is available in multiple languages.

Saloodo! differs from the integrated approach of UPS/FreightEx in that it operates solely as a software platform, with no human intermediary overseeing the carriers. Saloodo! does offer DHL Freight shipment options as an alternative service when its platform cannot provide enough capacity on-demand, but aside from this, the company offers no direct point of contact to oversee transportation operations.

## DB SCHENKER

DB Schenker is the largest road freight operator in Europe, and, as with DHL, is investing in the technology as a risk mitigation strategy, rather than in an effort to spearhead growth. Where the two companies differ is in their oversight of the respective digital brokerage operations.

DB Schenker has elected to take a more hands-off approach. In February 2017, the company announced a $25 million investment in the US freight matching platform uShip, having negotiated an exclusive licensing deal for the company's technology within Europe.

In addition to its capacity-matching function, uShip provides payments and documentation management, insurance, messaging and tracking within its application. By incorporating the company's technology into its operations, DB Schenker will have access to capacity on-demand during peak periods, complementing its core assets.

---

CASE STUDY 17.1
*Trucker Path (US)*

Trucker Path offers crowdsourced guidance to truck drivers; this includes the nearest truck stop, weigh stations, hotels, diesel fuel and freight shipments.

Freight shipments are managed through a marketplace system for regional or long-haul business, where brokers submit shipments along with deadlines, destinations and other requirements, with parking and navigation information to long-haul truckers in the United States.

The company initially launched as a free information service app, before subsequently adding the freight marketplace. As such, the business had cultivated a community of users and has built out its marketplace as an additional service within a wider eco-system.

Furthermore, Trucker Path has been successful in adding a payments service 'InstaPay'. This non-recourse factoring arrangement pays carriers immediately, issuing a one-time flat rate with no hidden fees, and addresses a major pain point amongst carriers who often wait 30–60 days before receiving payment. The company's marketplace business, 'Truckloads', is used by 1 million long-haul truckers in the United States.

---

## 'Digitalizing' the warehousing sector

It is not only the transport sector that has the potential to be disrupted by the sharing economy. New companies are entering the warehouse sector with the same aim: allowing companies to connect with customers to leverage previously underutilized space.

### Traditional warehousing market

The structure of the property market is very traditional: landlords, developers and estate agents all have vested interests in agreeing long-term deals. In addition to this there has been very little visibility of available warehousing, let alone visibility of availability of space within the warehouse.

In terms of contract logistics services, warehousing and distribution has long been characterized by a split between 'dedicated' contracts (where the customer pays for the costs of an entire warehouse operation) and 'shared'. In the latter instance, a proportion of racking is often given over to a customer inside a warehouse that caters for multiple other customers. This means that the costs are spread and are likely to be variable, depending on usage.

Although shared warehousing offers more flexibility than dedicated operations, it is still subject to a contract, with often several years duration. There will often be minimum volume levels, which provide protection to the logistics operator but reduce customer flexibility. As such it could be described as long term and static.

Many manufacturers, retailers and other warehouse users choose to retain their logistics operations in-house. This means that they will take on the responsibility for the warehouse lease, locking them into an agreement with a property company lasting much longer than the usual three- to five-year contract length with an LSP.

A lack of a transactional market and the prevalence of ad hoc fees make comparison between warehouse operations difficult and pricing structures opaque. As well as this, it is often in the interests of contract logistics providers to give as little visibility of their pricing strategy to customers as possible. 'Unbundling' of transport and warehousing services can lead to customers driving them down on price on their most profitable services.

It is this market that 'on-demand' warehouse platform providers seek to disrupt, offering increased choice, more visibility of available capacity and a dynamic pricing environment.

## 'On-demand' warehousing

The fundamental premise of on-demand warehousing is that what is already occupied can be utilized much more intensively. Much warehousing is not fully used: not only is the unutilized space not visible to other customers but, in any case, there is no traditional method of making it accessible.

On-demand companies offer:

- a search facility for suitable warehouse capacity
- scalable warehousing solutions

- efficiency of transaction
- legally backed agreements
- quality control/compliance accreditation

Unlike a room-letting service such as Airbnb, the process offered by on-demand warehousing companies is not 'real time' as it involves an electronic tendering process. However, it is much faster than traditional transactions, perhaps taking a couple of weeks rather than several months. It also involves services as well as commoditized storage, as the product still requires put away and picking, among others.

Several companies have emerged offering to provide warehousing on-demand, by leveraging cloud computing to provide quick and flexible service solutions. Specifically marketed towards fast-growing businesses and SMEs with dynamic requirements, these companies leverage empty space in existing warehouses as well as providing integration of order management and inventory management tools as a bundle.

The enabler for such solutions is software-as-a-service (SaaS), a variant of cloud computing, which enables companies to access software remotely through an internet connection rather than by locally installing the relevant systems.

This also means that it is much easier to connect together distinct software functions; for instance, to connect a cloud-based warehouse management system (WMS) to a cloud-based transport management system (TMS), the integration only needs to be achieved once, and can be done remotely. Doing so with locally installed software requires the manual integration of operations throughout a company's entire network, which is expensive and time-consuming.

The flexibility provided by software means that companies now have the option to fulfil orders from a single 'virtual warehouse', while their physical inventory is spread out over several facilities. Operations like this, once impossible, are proliferating, and the implications for industrial warehousing are a world in which space is used far more efficiently.

## Meeting e-commerce needs

A common problem for growing e-retailers is the need to expand fulfilment to accommodate demand. Not only can this process be quite difficult, but in markets with large geographic scale it can also cause considerable expense. Companies are often faced with the choice of charging customers for shipping or subsidizing shipping costs. A move towards a network of regional distribution facilities is often constrained due to the scale of initial investment and the commitment to long-term leases.

By adopting a more flexible warehousing approach, retailers can afford to test markets. Moreover, in a volatile environment, logistics providers could theoretically balance fixed and flexible warehousing capacity in the same way that they balance their transportation fleet.

This represents an alternative to the common approach applied currently, whereby many retailers adapting to the omnichannel environment contract out their expanding need for e-fulfilment to logistics providers. These logistics providers then deploy support through large-scale multi-client facilities, until such a time as the client chooses to move on; for example, when the scale of their operation necessitates a dedicated facility. It is important to state that this story of expansion is by no means set in stone; both Walmart and Target are aggressively expanding their e-commerce capabilities through intensive investment in-house.

## Dealing with volatility

The modern supply chain is designed to be agile and flexible, dealing effectively with risks such as falling/increasing demand; trade wars; natural disasters or terrorist events. While many parts of the logistics process can be flexed to meet these changing demands, warehousing is often the exception. As discussed above, shippers frequently enter into long-term warehousing contracts, often based on inevitably inaccurate forecasts.

It is inconceivable that on-demand warehousing will replace the traditional warehousing market in its entirety. However, what it does offer customers is a way in which peaks and troughs of demand can be better balanced. Instead of buying or leasing enough warehouse capacity to deal with the peak of demand, as has often been the case, customers will be able to provision for what is called a 'baseload' demand and add in capacity to meet seasonal peaks throughout the year. This means that waste in the system is minimized. For those warehouse users with too much capacity, on-demand offers the ability to market the space, providing a revenue-generating opportunity.

## Pros and cons of 'on-demand' warehousing

- On-demand warehousing turns a fixed investment into an operational cost that will improve balance sheet strength.

- Large investments become much smaller and spread over a longer time.
- It will allow customers to better meet peaks and troughs of demand.
- Warehousing capacity can be selected closer to end-user demand, making it quicker to serve customers.
- Risk is mitigated over many more locations.
- Users can hedge their warehouse needs against volatility.
- Reduction of transport carbon emissions due to distributed warehousing networks.
- Multiple warehouses can be integrated into a nationwide network while retaining a single point of contact.

One industry KPI puts warehouse utilization at around 80 per cent (Opsdog, 2018). This average figure could be viewed in two ways. Firstly, it shows that there is still considerable spare capacity, which could be potentially released onto the market. But secondly it also suggests that this capacity is not necessarily enough to deal with a peak of demand, for example in the holiday season. Consequently, a warehouse user with an average of 80 per cent utilization may require shared warehousing to deal with overspill.

On-demand warehousing could be described as a halfway house between warehouse ownership (or leasing) and outsourcing. However, the concept is not without its weaknesses. Beyond the major contract logistics providers, dedicated e-fulfilment providers (such as Ingram Micro's Shipwire) provide a compelling proposition, offering to exploit their access to global markets through freight forwarding, thus fulfilling cross-border sales that are currently unobtainable through the on-demand approach.

Another confounding factor is control. Although on-demand providers operate their own WMS, which can be integrated into client ERP systems, the actual fulfilment operations within the warehouses are controlled by the seller, not the buyer. This means that whoever owns the warehouse will be fulfilling the buyer's operations, regardless of their specific needs.

## Environmental considerations

Better utilization of warehouse space has environmental implications as well as operational. The first is obvious. Building large warehouses has an impact on the local environment in terms of:

- land use
- water run-off

- energy use
- greenhouse gas emissions
- pollution
- embodied carbon (that emitted during the manufacture of the building materials)
- local environment and communities

The better utilized a warehouse is, the fewer required to be built. It is obviously very difficult to quantify the impact that on-demand warehousing could have on utilization but the World Economic Forum estimates that shared warehouse capacity could benefit society through a reduction in emissions of 1.3 billion metric tons (WEF, 2016).

Distributing inventory at warehouse locations around a market also has an impact on the transport required to move it to the end-user and hence the carbon emissions. Centralization of inventory has been shown to provide many benefits operationally, but if full visibility of inventory can be maintained while holding stock further downstream, this could potentially have positive environmental and supply chain benefits.

---

CASE STUDY 17.2
*On-demand warehouse providers*

Profile: Flexe

Flexe acts as a marketplace for warehousing space, connecting lessees and lessors with cloud-based software, and makes money by charging commission on top of the leasing fees set by the latter. The company's SaaS offering also provides a warehouse management system, inventory management and billing services, which can be accessed and managed by customers through an internet browser.

Flexe operates in the United States and Canada, where its marketplace covers a network of over 1,500 warehouses. The average Flexe fulfilment customer operates in six to eight locations. The minimum utilization requirements for those looking to access warehousing space are a 30-day lease and at least 50 pallets of goods. However, once qualified, inventory owners have the advantage of a fast and flexible service, including software that was until relatively recently quite expensive to purchase.

The company offers a marketplace for asset owners to rent out their warehousing for short durations, thus offering an option to companies that are not prepared for the financial investment of a long-term lease. For companies looking to scale-up quickly or try out a new product line, on-demand warehousing could provide a useful solution.

Profile: Stowga

Stowga is a start-up B2B marketplace, based in the UK, which enables spare warehousing capacity to be matched with the short-terms needs of customers. It was acquired by Value Chain Lab (VCL) in 2021. The company has more than 4,000 warehouses listed on its platform.

Rather than 'on-demand', Stowga describes its services as Warehousing-as-a-Service (WaaS). This is perhaps more accurate, as on-demand conveys an immediacy that is not part of the core attributes of this sharing-economy innovation. Rather, the short term and flexible nature is of more importance.

Stowga's management describes its WaaS as allowing customers to more effectively meet the peaks and troughs of demand. It counts UK drinks manufacturer Nichols, owner of the Vimto brand, among its customers.

## Summary

Theoretically, digital platforms have the potential to dramatically disrupt many of the world's least efficient road freight/trucking markets. However, the extent of this disruption is far from clear. In Europe the opportunity may not be as big as many start-ups believe and the market has already become crowded. To succeed, platforms will need to focus relentlessly on specific market segments and build targeted communities, integrated and served by exceptional technology and a range of services. China and India would seem to hold greater opportunities. In comparison with the relatively high-quality road freight markets in Europe and North America, the industry is plagued by inefficiencies. The giant logistics platforms that have developed see themselves not so much as freight exchanges but as disruptive technology platforms that can transform the entire industry. In contrast, the role of the digital freight platform in Europe and North America will perhaps always be complementary to the dominant incumbent trucking operators.

Although the warehousing industry will never become 'on-demand' in the way that road freight transport may do, there are certainly opportunities to improve efficiencies in the sector. Of course, as with any disruptive technology or business model there will be winners and losers. As the World Economic Forum states, 'Shared warehouse agreements provide companies [customers of logistics companies] an opportunity to reduce their logistics costs by as much as 12 to 15 per cent. We estimate that companies implementing these agreements could save close to $500 billion in operating costs, but this could have a negative impact to the tune of $35 billion in operating profits for logistics companies' (WEF, 2016).

# References

BCG (2018) Why road freight needs to go digital – fast, Boston Consulting Group, 24 April, www.bcg.com/en-gb/publications/2018/why-road-freight-needs-go-digital-fast.aspx (archived at https://perma.cc/KCV2-GVSG)

Ding, L (2020) Manbang, China's Uber for truck cargo, raises $1.7 billion, SupChina, 30 November, https://supchina.com/2020/11/30/manbang-chinas-uber-for-truck-cargo-raises-1-7-billion/ (archived at https://perma.cc/9PUU-ADYC)

Opsdog (2018) Warehouse space utilization, https://opsdog.com/products/average-warehouse-capacity-used (archived at https://perma.cc/JU23-WDDT)

WEF (2016) How can digital help logistics be more sharing?, World Economic Forum, http://reports.weforum.org/digital-transformation/cutting-costs-through-sharing-logistics-assets/ (archived at https://perma.cc/ZX8L-T3PC)

# 18

# The digitalization of international freight forwarding

**This chapter will familiarize the reader with:**

- The progress towards digitization in international trade and freight forwarding
- What digitization will mean for the industry and threats for the incumbents
- The rise of digital freight platforms
- The digital offerings of the main freight forwarders
- What digital freight forwarders, such as Flexport, have to offer customers
- How forwarders will adapt and survive in the new digital environment

## The importance of digitization

The freight forwarding industry has long been regarded as a laggard in the adoption of digital technologies. Reinforcing this perception, global freight booking platform, Freightos, conducted a study in 2021 of the top 20 freight forwarders, which found that less than one-fifth of price requests were quoted for instantly (Freightos, 2021). Surveying a wider group of 60 forwarders, a 'mystery shopping' exercise resulted in only 18 per cent providing an instant digital response. Some forwarders, of significant size, are still reliant on email and telephone communications to contact carriers and establish quotations and bookings. This results in inefficiencies and lost business opportunities. Freightos found that 8 out of 10 forwarders that received manual requests failed to respond and those that did took an average of 51 hours.

This is not to say that progress has not been made. The new breed of 'pure play' digital forwarders are far more likely to offer instant quoting capabilities and most shipping lines now offer online services, including booking. An increasing number of freight forwarders are adding functionality to their digital services, such as allowing shippers to compare air and sea quotes side by side or sorting results by price, departure date or transit time.

However, it has taken a long time to reform paper-based processes. A notable example of this is the system of air waybills (AWBs): documentation that represents the contract of carriage between the shipper and the carrier for air transportation. Since 2008, the International Air Transport Association (IATA) has encouraged carriers and forwarders to adopt electronic air waybills (eAWBs) in order to speed up the process of exchanging and sorting documentation through electronic data interchange (EDI). Though certain trade routes, such as those governed by the Warsaw regime, require the submission of physical documents, some 80 per cent of global cargo volumes travel on routes compatible with eAWBs. Figures from IATA for May 2021 claim that eAWB penetration (for routes where legally feasible) rose to 75.4 per cent (IATA, 2021). Although this sounds impressive, this figure has only been achieved after 13 years of effort. Moreover, as the AWB represents only one of 30 paper documents that are required to conduct air freight transportation, there is some way to go before a complete e-freight system is in place.

The slow uptake of digital systems is at least partly derived from a lack of flexibility within the internal systems of forwarders and carriers themselves. As with many companies throughout the supply chain, carriers and freight forwarders tend to run expensive and complex, locally installed, enterprise resource planning (ERP) systems. At the upper end of the market these tend to be set up by enterprise software leaders such as SAP, Oracle and Epicor. ERP systems manage the internal data flows of an organization, integrating and automating back-office functions throughout the enterprise, including procurement, human resources and customer relationship management. These systems are effective in this function but are highly rigid and are difficult to adapt to new external requirements. They therefore limit an organization's ability to match changing customer needs. As a result of this difficulty, alterations are often also prohibitively expensive, which suppresses the incentive of organizations to change.

An example of the complexities of adapting an ERP system is DHL Global Forwarding's attempted 'New Forwarding Environment' (NFE) project. NFE was conceived as a means of enabling improved global shipment visibility and a reduction of paperwork through greater use of a document management system, amongst other upgrades. A significant driver of the project was the understanding that improved visibility throughout the organization would allow DHL to apply its enormous economies of scale more effectively. This was not to be, with increasing lead times, implementation errors and spiralling costs leading to the suspension and eventual cancellation of the project.

Given these issues, a number of software companies, providing services built upon a cloud architecture, have stepped up. By using Big Data analytics, these companies sort through data aggregated from forwarders and, in some cases, carriers, in order to automatically map industry spot rate fluctuations in real time. These companies have the advantage of being able to facilitate real-time quotation and booking services, based on the spot rate data, and have attracted attention for shining a light on a volatile market.

## The implications for freight forwarders

The overwhelming takeaway from this is the dramatic improvements brought about in booking, quoting and price visibility. As regards implementation, many of the largest freight forwarders have developed their own online systems such as Kuehne + Nagel and Agility. Many other forwarders have elected to licence this technology from the SaaS platforms. These platforms are more significant facilitators than they are competitors for freight forwarders.

The cost for companies not adopting a uniform, company-wide platform, on the other hand, is stark. Regardless of whether or not forwarders buy or licence the means to operate company-wide data platforms, there may be an industry-wide decoupling between these data-unified companies and the less profitable data-fragmented ones, in which the former exercise a significant advantage over the latter.

For companies that may see themselves as the losers in this scenario, their position will be somewhat improved by the fact that the adoption of new cloud-based services comes at a much more reasonable price than implementing on-site enterprise software. As a result, smaller companies could find that they are actually in a position to achieve data unification. Meanwhile, larger incumbents maintaining expensive legacy systems will find it more difficult to make the transition.

## Digital freight forwarding platforms

Given that 'broking' (i.e. buying and selling carrier capacity) is such a major element of freight forwarders' business it would be imagined that they should be quick to recognize the threats and opportunities stemming from the rating/spot pricing platforms. Indeed, the larger forwarders who have longstanding relationships with their clients and various carriers, do use technology extensively. But as the margins in the forwarding business are generally low across the board, levels of investment in technology have also been low. This has been a major problem.

Established forwarders invested heavily in technology 10–15 years ago and many continue to use those systems. Although they are by now embedded into the core of the organization, they are unwieldy, difficult and expensive to maintain. As a result, clients demanding more information and more agile IT solutions become dissatisfied and the forwarders are usually forced to introduce external solutions from the 'cloud' that are not integrated with their core systems. Ironically, the new entrants into the market can take advantage of the newer solutions at much lower cost, because they don't have to worry about integration with older legacy systems.

As with all these things, any solutions they introduce must add value for the customer. Just introducing a standalone rate selection engine will be pointless, unless it is combined or integrated with an order and shipment management system to seamlessly flow information directly from the client to the carrier.

In short, there are lots of solutions that solve a specific problem, but unless the forwarder can introduce them into a coherent IT solution set, they may be wasting their money. Established forwarders have to deal with the challenge of updating legacy systems while maintaining service levels and reducing cost. This is expensive and will get more expensive as time goes on and ultimately unsustainable. It is easier to do a wholesale replacement exploiting a lower-cost cloud service, but that requires skill and expertise to pull off. It is also massively difficult politically to sell internally, especially if senior management included the people responsible for the initial investment.

## Survey: the use of online platforms

Results from a Ti survey contained in the Global Freight Forwarding Report 2019 show that the adoption of online forwarding services and the use of digital forwarders is rapidly taking hold across global businesses (Ti, 2019) (see Figures 18.1–18.5). Half of the respondents have used such platforms but frequency of use varies.

FIGURE 18.1    How often do you use online freight booking platforms/marketplaces or digital forwarders?

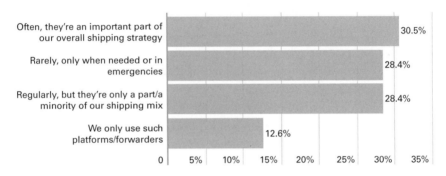

FIGURE 18.2    Which of the following services are you using on online freight booking platforms/marketplaces or digital forwarders?

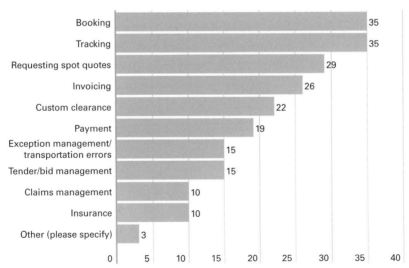

Number of respondents that use platforms/marketplaces/digital forwarders for the specific services

Of the 10 functionalities listed in Figure 18.2, booking, tracking and requesting spot quotes were the most commonly used services used across air, sea and road transport modes.

It is evident that shippers mainly turn to online freight booking platforms/marketplaces/digital forwarders for the very basic forwarding services and processes, such as booking and requesting spot quotes, but are not making great use of the more complex, value-added services, such as 'exception management/transportation errors', 'tender/bid management', 'claims management' and 'insurance'. It might be argued that shippers are mainly using the very basic forwarding services and processes on these platforms as these are the areas they were initially designed to deal with and the areas in which they promise to add value by removing the standard, repetitive tasks from the human. This is not to say that the technology will not advance in the future and provide booking platforms and marketplaces with the tools that will enable them to provide shippers with full supply chain visibility and value-added services.

The survey also identified that online freight booking platforms/marketplaces/digital forwarders appear most suitable for SMEs and ad hoc shippers (Figure 18.3). Of the logistics companies surveyed 40 per cent stated that these services are most suitable for small and medium-size companies and more than one-quarter stated that they are most suitable for ad hoc/irregular shippers.

FIGURE 18.3  What type of shippers do you think online freight booking platforms/ marketplaces or digital forwarders are most suitable for?

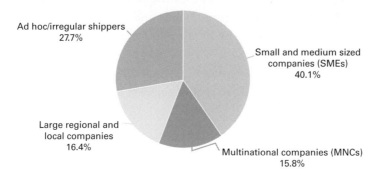

Ad hoc/irregular shippers
27.7%

Small and medium sized
companies (SMEs)
40.1%

Large regional and
local companies
16.4%

Multinational companies (MNCs)
15.8%

FIGURE 18.4  Overall, how satisfied are you with the performance of the online freight booking platforms/marketplaces or digital forwarders you are using?

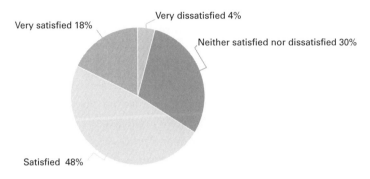

It seems that it will be some time (if ever) before platforms/marketplaces become suitable channels through which large shippers manage their global or regional shipping needs. Large shippers with complex, diverse and multi-year requirements will continue to put their logistics needs out to tender and have large forwarders bid for the opportunity with a negotiating team.

Of those using online freight booking platforms/marketplaces/digital forwarders 66 per cent reported being either 'satisfied' or 'very satisfied' with the service they receive (Figure 18.4). This is a big change from the equivalent survey undertaken by the consultancy in 2017, suggesting that the performance of online freight booking platforms/marketplaces/ digital forwarders has improved considerably over a short period of time.

For over one-third of shippers who have not used digital alternatives, satisfaction with the level of service provided by their existing suppliers plays a role in the decision to forgo online and digital forwarding services (Figure 18.5). The results of the survey also suggest that the reluctance to start using online forwarding services is not necessarily rooted in online freight booking platforms/marketplaces/digital forwarders' inefficiencies but lack of awareness – 23.3 per cent of shippers are not aware of this type of online forwarding service.

## Digital freight success: make or buy?

As investment in the global digital freight market increases, freight forwarders are faced with the choice of either developing products in-house using

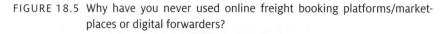

FIGURE 18.5  Why have you never used online freight booking platforms/market-places or digital forwarders?

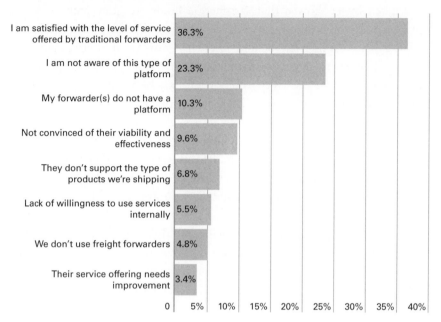

their own, sometimes significant, technology resources or buying in capabilities from the host of start-up companies that have sprung up in recent years. In fact, most have adopted the strategy of combining both approaches – building themselves if their need is highly customized or they think they can gain a competitive advantage; but not being afraid to buy off-the-shelf if they think it will be too long or costly a process to develop a capability themselves.

This pragmatic approach has replaced the natural instinct of many companies to employ large numbers of software developers themselves. In many respects, the new digital technologies have become what consultants like to call 'hygiene factors' in much the same way that transport management systems did in the 1980s and 1990s when they replaced paper and spreadsheets, i.e. they are no longer a competitive advantage.

Digital technologies have become what could be termed 'table stakes' – you need to have a responsive digital online quotation, booking and track-and-trace system just to get in the game. As Ethan Buchman, Freightos's chief marketing officer, has commented, 'For a year or two, tech was a core start-up differentiator. Today, it's the standard; tomorrow, it will be a given.'

That is not to say that the systems being deployed by the major global forwarders are perfect – but they are getting better, and fast. The survey undertaken by Ti showed that satisfaction levels are quite high, and this contrasts with the position even a year earlier.

The risk of getting left behind in such a fast-paced environment has persuaded many managers that unless the in-house option is good and 'ready to go' it is far less risky to buy what may be a generic option but is at least available straight away. There is obviously the cost implication of getting things wrong, too. Although in a slightly different context, DHL wrote off €345 million after abandoning its New Forwarding Environment (NFE) modernization programme in 2015, thus showing the huge amounts at stake. The fallout from this project (using SAP software and implemented by IBM) was still being felt operationally up until relatively recently and only a company as financially strong as DP DHL would have been able to survive. This project involved replacing multiple legacy systems with a single harmonized SAP system – a very worthy aim but one that, in retrospect, was doomed to failure. DHL's latest strategy of migrating volumes to a third-party system, CargoWise One, seems to have had much more success.

The willingness of many companies to see some technologies as commoditized is part of a broader trend for forwarders to focus on increasing value in supply chains. As Tim Scharwath, DHL's CEO of Global Forwarding, Freight, commented in an investor day, there needs to be change of mentality from a focus on buying and selling freight – the traditional function of a forwarder – to 'engineering'. That is, using data to optimize flows of volumes, buying power and freight rate leverage with the carriers. This will be a very different skill set, which will need a different type of employee. This is an industry-wide trend and not just one affecting DHL.

Moving volumes to a third-party platform or using an external company to provide the infrastructure for a transport management system, for example, is not without risks itself. When the responsibility for such a fundamental and critical part of forwarding and freight operations is given to a third party, the contracting company needs to be completely confident that:

- the functions it has outsourced will be competently carried out
- there is no risk of that company going out of business or befalling other commercial hazards (or even perhaps being taken over by a rival forwarder)

CASE STUDY 18.1

*Flexport*

Established in 2013, Flexport was one of the first of the new breed of digital freight forwarders. Since its start-up, it has raised $1.3 billion from a range of investors including SoftBank. Based in San Francisco, the company is primarily focused on the Eastbound Trans-Pacific trade lane from Asia to the US West Coast, but also has operations in the Netherlands.

Flexport's software can provide customers with pallet-level visibility. The company also runs software for compliance, a platform for asset-owners (principally road freight companies) and can facilitate the integration of shippers and carriers through its purchase order management software. While other companies can offer these services, they are often based on older technologies and come at a greater cost. Significantly, Flexport has built all of its applications from the ground up as part of a unified software platform, which avoids the integration issues that larger forwarders experience as a result of siloed business units or M&A.

This backend allows for far easier interfaces for shippers and carriers, and the company's self-service web interface is a big draw for SME customers, which represent a large portion of Flexport's customer base. According to its CEO Ryan Petersen, this is principally made up of three types of customer: small companies selling on Amazon; large, traditional businesses interested in both air and sea freight (including Bridgestone Tyres); and fast-growing e-commerce companies that have not had time to develop their logistics capabilities (including Harry's Razors).

CASE STUDY 18.2

*Freightos*

A marketplace platform for international freight movements, Freightos has established two main service platforms, one for shippers (freightos.com) and the other for freight forwarders, branded 'WebCargo'. Freightos uses pricing and routing algorithms to automate spot market quotation and booking for international freight shipments. The company's integration with a large number of freight forwarders' systems helps it to provide accurate freight rate results on-demand, while using a platform allows shippers to review the rates and services of a range of different forwarders.

According to its founder, Eytan Buchman, 'Freightos and WebCargo have put out a unified global freight booking platform, connecting carrier pricing, capacity, and e-booking with forwarders (that's WebCargo), while connecting forwarders with importers (freightos.com)' (Buchman, 2021).

The company's systems can be integrated with its customers' transportation management systems (TMSs) to maintain shipment visibility. Freightos's cloud-computing architecture has allowed the company to establish reliable APIs with the main TMS providers, easing the integration process for customers.

In total, 23 of the top 25 forwarders are customers of Freightos. This includes Hellmann, Panalpina, CEVA and Nippon Express. More than 10,000 freight forwarders and 30 airlines use the WebCargo platform for air freight booking and quotes.

---

## Why freight forwarders will adapt and survive

For many years it has been asserted that freight forwarders risk being 'disintermediated' by shippers and carriers, going the same way as many travel agents in the air passenger sector. However, in our view, this will not be the case.

In addition to aggregating shipments in order to negotiate bulk prices from carriers, many freight forwarders also handle goods in warehouses at origin and destination centres. Furthermore, they offer transportation to and from these facilities, sometimes managing the entire end-to-end process all the way to a customer's doorstep.

What is clear is that freight forwarders have much more to offer than just the facilitation of point-to-point transportation. By comparison, this is all that is provided by the current generation of SaaS platforms, as well as the carriers they serve. This means that a shipper still has to deal with getting their shipment to and from the port or airport facility, a service that freight forwarders will offer as standard.

An additional advantage for freight forwarders, especially when considering the potential threat from Amazon or Cainiao, is that their businesses function as impartial intermediaries between two partners. While the likes of Amazon represent an entire, vertically integrated operation, which many shippers may find themselves in competition with, forwarders are totally independent. They can therefore exploit this position of neutrality to act as a partner to all agents throughout the supply chain – indeed, this is the reason freight forwarding was established in the first place.

The key for success is genuine collaboration. Freight forwarders in the information age have the potential to drive network effects by sharing information more freely with their clients. By deploying cloud-based network solutions, which engage every stakeholder in a supply chain, forwarders can build upon their current position as intermediaries in the transportation process.

With such transparency comes a broadening of scope, as the forwarding process comes to integrate more deeply with other business functions. By integrating the forwarding process with that of other supply chain information systems, such as demand sensing, it appears likely that freight forwarders are moving towards becoming fourth-party logistics providers (4PLs).

Often referred to as lead logistics providers, 4PLs perform a coordination and management function, sitting above the third-party logistics providers operating as part of a client's supply chain. By contracting out a supply chain to a 4PL, a company is essentially handing over their entire operation to an external provider, who, with expert knowledge and technology, offers cost savings and efficiency improvements.

The nerve centre of a 4PL operation is often referred to as the 'control tower' (see Chapter 13). Control towers facilitate the collection and analysis of data from their agents, customers and trading partners, enabled by specialist supply chain management software, which allows interoperability between the diverse systems utilized by network partners. With the manipulation of the supply chain's entire information flow, the control tower is able to maintain security, optimize efficiency and execute interventions to ensure the process runs smoothly. By properly applying this model to their operations, freight forwarders can ensure that they remain not only relevant, but indispensable, in their function as supply chain intermediaries for the 21st century.

The fundamental potential of the 4PL model could be even greater, however. For a freight forwarder, the ultimate significance of acting as a platform in this manner is the ability to oversee an entire supply network, not just a collection of individual supply chains. While individual shippers are only concerned with their own operation, a forwarder facilitating partnerships throughout an entire supply network would have the capacity to encourage 'horizontal collaboration' (see Chapter 1) amongst nominally competing supply chain actors, in a scenario in which all benefit. The basic logic is this: if several retailers source from the same supplier, why not collaborate on transport and logistics if it can improve efficiency and save money for all involved?

## Summary

There is no doubting that the freight forwarding sector is undergoing a digital revolution. A new breed of digital forwarder, such as Flexport, is entering the market and successfully taking share from bigger and slower-moving incumbents. However, the future is certainly not bleak for the existing freight forwarders. Those that are able to adopt the technologies that are under development and build upon their position as supply chain coordinators have the opportunity to propel themselves into a much higher value business than formerly.

What is more, freight forwarders are ideally placed to coordinate and manage complex, global flows of data, finance and goods in future supply chains, ensuring that they will adapt and survive for many decades to come.

## References

Buchman, E (2021) Freight innovation and the lesson from a dead remote control tech play, Freightos, 25 May, www.freightos.com/freight-innovation-and-the-lesson-from-a-dead-remote-control-tech-play/ (archived at https://perma.cc/AYX7-GD65)

Freightos (2021) The evolving landscape of logistics technology, Freightos, www.freightos.com/wp-content/uploads/2021/04/Mystery-Shopper-2021-Evolving-Digital-Freight-v421.pdf (archived at https://perma.cc/M4PB-LFGT)

IATA (2021) e-AWB international Monthly Report, May, IATA, Geneva

Ti (2019) Global Freight Forwarding Report 2019, Ti Insight, UK

# 19

# Disrupting trade finance

*Blockchain, banks and freight forwarders*

**This chapter will familiarize the reader with:**

- The importance of trade finance to international supply chains and how it works
- Why the sector in its traditional form is failing shippers in many parts of the world
- The opportunities this has provided for innovators and new technologies
- Some of the market entrants that are developing new trade finance products and platforms
- Blockchain and the role of 'smart contracts'
- Opportunities for freight forwarders in their role as supply chain intermediaries

## Introduction

Trade finance is one of the most essential aspects of international commerce. For many centuries, letters of credit, insurance and guarantees have facilitated cross-border trade by assuring that the necessary levels of trust exist between parties within supply chains, backed in the main by banks and their correspondents. In other words, the system gives exporters the assurance that they will be paid by customers who could be located anywhere in the world. Buyers have a guarantee that goods will be delivered when and where the exporter says they will.

Despite the model seemingly working well over the years (after all, it enabled globalization), the sector is on the verge of a revolution, set to become a key competitive battleground shaken up by new technologies. There is also the hope that this disruption will provide an opportunity for freight forwarders to cash in on their role as intermediaries in the supply chain, allowing them to break out of their present low-margin business model. For although trade finance works well for multinationals (which generate the majority of global goods flows), many small and medium-sized enterprises (SMEs), especially in the developing world, are being increasingly excluded.

It is for this reason that organizations such as the World Trade Organization (WTO), World Economic Forum (WEF) and International Monetary Fund (IMF) are encouraging changes to the system. This chapter explores the reasons why and the opportunities it will create.

## What is trade finance?

Trade finance is often described as the 'lubricant' of international commerce due to its role in bridging the gap between importers' and exporters' expectations on when payment for goods should be transferred.

Trade finance typically falls into two categories:

- **Inter-company credit**: this type of relationship involves the advance of credit by either the buyer or seller who effectively takes on the risk of the transaction. If there is complete trust between the parties, then transactions could be settled on an 'open account' basis. Although figures are hard to come by, it is thought that this type of arrangement accounts for 40–50 per cent of agreements (WTO, 2016a).

- **Bank-intermediated finance**: when such levels of trust do not exist, intermediaries become involved to facilitate the transaction and typically 'letters of credit' are used to specify the terms of the contract. The 'letter of credit' sets out a commitment by the buyer's bank to pay for the purchased goods if a number of obligations are met by the seller. These can include the conditions of delivery and the relevant documentation. Banks can even go further and provide finance to the exporter, which allows it to buy goods from its suppliers and progress the order. This type of finance perhaps accounts for a similar proportion of the market as intercompany credit – around 40 per cent.

Although statistics vary, the WTO estimates that up to 80 per cent of global trade is supported by finance or credit insurance (the two categories above), the rest being comprised of 'cash-in-advance' (WTO, 2016a).

## Why does the sector need shaking up?

According to a report by the Asian Development Bank, 'where trade finance functions well, it enables firms that would otherwise be considered too risky, to link into expanding global value chains and thus contribute to employment and productivity growth' (WTO, 2016).

However, it does not seem to be working well everywhere. This is a conundrum for many in the industry as trade finance is seen as a particularly low-risk form of finance. The International Chamber of Commerce asserts that the default rate is only 0.021 per cent, of which more than half is recovered by the sale of the asset on which the bank has a call, i.e. the merchandise (ICC, 2018).

According to the WEF, problems accessing trade finance are a consequence of the 2009 financial crisis, which led to increased levels of risk assessment and enhanced due diligence. This has been compounded by diverse terrorist threats, which have led to tightened regulations (WEF, 2017), and most recently by the Covid-19 pandemic. The Organization for Economic Co-operation and Development (OECD) states that the 'risk appetite' of Western commercial banks has diminished even though their own balance sheets are very much stronger due to a decade of increased regulation. This has led to short-term liquidity problems for exporters and their supply chains (OECD, 2021).

The result of these crises and threats is that lack of trade finance has become one of the main barriers to international trade, particularly for emerging markets in Africa, the Caribbean, Central Asia and parts of Europe. The IMF believes that this is due in part to money-laundering regulations and the cost of compliance, which makes financing trade deals unattractive to many commercial banks. It says the withdrawal of these banking services, '[could] disrupt financial services and cross-border flows, including trade finance and remittances, potentially undermining financial stability, inclusion, growth and development goals' (IMF, 2016). The WTO also says, 'in the post-financial crisis era global banks are less inclined to invest in many developing countries' (2016a).

What is more, there is a perception that this squeeze on trade finance reinforces the competitive advantage of the larger shippers due to their preferential access to banks and intermediaries. Another problem is the administrative burden. Small and medium-sized companies, in developed as well as developing countries, are hampered by the levels of bureaucracy involved, or, at least, are less able to deal with it. The WTO says that half of all trade finance requests from SMEs are rejected by banks, compared with just 7 per cent of multinational companies (2016a).

This has led to what is called a 'financing gap', which has proved to be a headwind for the growth of global trade. The gap is particularly evident in Africa and other developing regions although it is very difficult to put an actual figure on its scale.

## Trade finance innovators and disruptors

The mismatch between supply and demand that these systemic problems have caused has created an opportunity in today's digital world. However, first the paper-heavy trade documentation systems have to be digitized. If the process underpinning bills of lading and letters of credit can be made more efficient and faster, then meeting the needs of regulations such as 'Know Your Customer' (KYC) and anti-money laundering can be more easily met. An electronic audit trail is fundamental to ensuring effective compliance. If the high level of shipment data that is generated can be harnessed, risk levels can be assessed and this allows companies to innovate, not least in the provision of trade finance.

Creating supply chain visibility through layers of software also has other benefits. The trust it can engender in the transaction has led to the development of derivative products in the trade finance sector, building on the concept of invoice factoring. Investors can pool their capital into an asset class, which can be provided to SMEs to help fund their exports.

In an increasingly crowded sector, here are some examples of just a few trade finance innovators:

**essDocs** provides SaaS fintech and supply chain technology solutions for the export, trade and logistics industries with a goal to enable paperless trade. Solutions are provided through its CargoDocs platform, which digitizes the creation and approval as well as exchange of electronic original documents and also enables users to apply for, sign, stamp and receive back original certificates required for global trade. CargoDocs combines title, quality, condition, location and other key data to reduce risk and improve visibility and control. Key electronic documents covered include: bills of lading, warehouse warrants, certificates of origin, commercial invoices and inspectors' certificates.

**Bolero** (which has been around since the 1990s) is another solutions provider working to digitize the sector. In conjunction with an enterprise software company, R3, it has embarked on a new electronic bill of lading (eBL) service that it says will connect multiple trade networks. Relevant parties will be able to endorse and verify an eBL's title without needing to revert to paper.

A more recent market entrant is **Interlinkages,** based in Hong Kong. It describes itself as 'a cross-border trade finance-bidding platform that endeavours to democratize the international trade finance marketplace by providing the most efficient, cost-effective and bank-neutral solutions for trade finance transactions of corporates and SMEs'. The platform matches 'buyers' (those with money to lend) with 'sellers' (those who need to borrow to finance their trade deal) using an 'eBay model' (as described by the founders). It allows lenders to reach markets in which they might not have a physical presence and allows exporters and traders to access funds that otherwise would not be available to them. The platform matches supply and demand but does not bear the risk of the transactions.

**Chained Finance** is a joint venture between a subsidiary of manufacturer Foxconn and online lending marketplace Dianrong. In its launch communication it said its aim was to 'meet the hugely underserved needs of supply chain finance in China' (Dianrong, 2017). The company went on to say that it believed the existing trade finance arrangements only served about 15 per cent of suppliers needing financial resources affecting 40 million Chinese SMEs. Its focus will be on electronics, automotive and fashion manufacturing sectors and its platform will employ the latest blockchain technology, thereby eliminating many of the trust issues faced by counter-parties and deliver automated execution.

In Europe banks are also stepping up their presence in this sector. Eleven banks, including Deutsche Bank, HSBC, Rabobank, KBC, Commerzbank and Société Générale have asked IBM to build a platform that will provide similar services to Chained Finance based on blockchain technology and aimed at European SMEs. The consortium has been named Batavia. Speaking to the *Financial Times*, Rudi Peeters, CIO of KBC, commented that blockchain was the obvious technology for trade finance as existing processes were paper-based, complex and expensive (Arnold, 2017). He said that initially the banks would target cross-border road-based trade routes although the product would subsequently be expanded to intercontinental shipping routes. The platform will be accessible to shippers and freight forwarders as well as other banks and credit agencies, allowing SMEs to track shipments and using smart contracts that trigger payment when invoices are raised or delivery completed. Other banks are establishing similar platforms.

It is interesting that IBM initially plans to focus on European cross-border trade, with plans to expand internationally at some point after that. This approach might appear unduly conservative in a sector where venture-funded start-ups are known for their ambition and desire for scale. IBM is a well-established enterprise that understands the consensus-building approach and has to be deliberate in building alliances that do not conflict with their existing commercial arrangements. But they are disadvantaged when trying to compete in the same pool with smaller companies who do not have those concerns.

As an example, it is instructive to look at the number of cross-border digital payment companies that have come from nowhere in the past five years and evolved into significant forex players before being acquired for billions of dollars by established banks. The established companies could match them in terms of technology but could not keep up with their aggressive and agile business development approach.

## Blockchain and 'smart contracts'

The concept of 'smart contracts' has been around for much longer than blockchain technology. A 'smart contract' has been defined by lawyers Allen & Overy as 'a set of promises, agreed between parties and encoded in software, which, when criteria are met, are performed automatically' (2017). They don't exclusively involve trade finance contracts, but due to many of the issues set out above (trust, complexity, time and paper-based inefficiencies) the benefits that smart contracts can deliver to the sector are substantial. As the legal company says, blockchains provide an underlying trusted network conveniently and efficiently.

By 'hardwiring' the financial transaction process into software code, certain events can be triggered at specified milestones. The most obvious of these is at the point when the goods have been delivered. When the final delivery is made and a scan or electronic proof of delivery is generated, a signal can automatically be sent back up the supply chain, authorizing, for example, the release of funds to the exporter.

This all assumes that the 'smart contract' works in the way that both the exporter and importer intended. While they may reduce human error by eliminating human intervention, this is not to say that errors cannot be made in programming the hard code in the first place. How this plays out in legal terms has really yet to be seen. According to lawyers, there is a reversal of the burden of litigation with the exporter having to pursue a claim for damages, as the shipment will have already been delivered and the importer will be in possession of the merchandise. At present it would fall to the importing party to pursue a claim for damages when delivery had *not* been made under the terms of a contract.

In addition, there are legal question marks over what happens when the 'smart contract' becomes impossible to perform or there is misrepresentation or illegality. In some cases a 'smart contract' may not be a 'contract' at all as it is not recognized by certain jurisdictions.

However, more positively, the way that blockchain works in creating a single and unalterable record means that documentation duplication and even fraudulent invoice financing will become impossible.

## The new competitive battleground for freight forwarders?

Freight forwarders are critical parties in the international supply chain process and so it would seem obvious for them to be at the forefront of the trade finance revolution. In 2009 DHL, in partnership with Standard Chartered Bank in India, provided a first step in digitizing trade documents by scanning them in specially equipped courier vans and sending them digitally to the requisite bank, reducing the time it took to courier these documents physically.

But it is new market entrant Flexport that is now capturing the headlines. Part of its investment plans include rolling out a new trade finance offering to its customers. It believes that the huge amount of supply chain data it is able to generate and analyse will allow it to assess the risk of making temporary loans to many manufacturers and other exporters. This would be a step change in the level of sophistication of services available through forwarders to SMEs, and a huge competitive advantage.

Another company, Beacon Technologies, has made an impact although more for its wealthy backers, which include Amazon's Jeff Bezos (Lyon,

2020). The well-funded UK start-up understands that most businesses using forwarding services have a problem with cash flow. Consequently, they provide supply chain finance and discounted shipping rates in an attempt to entice SMEs to move across to their operating platform. The intention is to provide a simplified and streamlined experience that is much more user friendly than conventional offerings.

If this additional product were rolled out, it would allow freight forwarders to increase their value add by leveraging their own balance sheets. Forwarding is a low-margin business and operators in the sector are always looking to increase profitability, some more successfully than others. If they are to achieve this goal, however, forwarders will have to move fast and partner with companies that have the appropriate levels of expertise. There is no reason why trade finance could not become a unique selling point for forwarders, not only generating a new revenue stream but also attracting the volumes of higher-margin SMEs. If they do not move quickly it will be left to the many other trade finance innovators to disrupt the market and gain this particular prize.

## Summary

The trade finance sector is being shaken up by new technologies such as blockchain, which will provide greater levels of trust between supply chain parties. This will have highly positive implications for exporters in many parts of the developing world, which struggle to access competitive sources of finance. Trade finance will also prove to be an important competitive battleground for freight forwarders. The new breed of digital forwarders have an advantage in that the data they can collect on shippers' behaviour will enable them to make loans to SMEs, providing an important new revenue stream.

## References

Allen & Overy. Smart contracts for finance parties [blog] Allen & Overy, 3 May 2017. www.allenovery.com/en-gb/global/blogs/digital-hub/smart-contracts-for-finance-parties (archived at https://perma.cc/2A8B-FDTX)

Arnold, M (2017) European banks to launch blockchain trade finance platform, *Financial Times*, 26 June, London

Dianrong (2017) Chained Finance: first blockchain platform for supply chain finance, Dianrong, 6 March, www.prnewswire.com/news-releases/chained-finance-first-blockchain-platform-for-supply-chain-finance-300418265.html (archived at https://perma.cc/CYB6-ML92)

ICC (2018) New ICC report confirms trade and export finance are not risky business, International Chamber of Commerce, 6 March, https://iccwbo.org/media-wall/news-speeches/new-icc-report-confirms-trade-export-finance-not-risky-business/ (archived at https://perma.cc/L3JY-VMS4)

IMF (2016) The withdrawal of correspondent banking relationships: a case for policy action, International Monetary Fund, http://www.imf.org/external/pubs/ft/sdn/2016/sdn1606.pdf (archived at https://perma.cc/69LT-B44Z)

Lyon, K (2020) Beacon: trade finance as the key to supply chain data mining, *Ti*, 4 June, www.ti-insight.com/briefs/beacon-trade-finance-as-the-key-to-supply-chain-data-mining/ (archived at https://perma.cc/E4D3-88N7)

OECD (2021) Trade finance in the Covid era: current and future challenges, 23 March, www.oecd.org/coronavirus/policy-responses/trade-finance-in-the-covid-era-current-and-future-challenges-79daca94/ (archived at https://perma.cc/NU8T-XV39)

WTO (2016a) Trade finance, World Trade Organization, www.wto.org/english/thewto_e/coher_e/tr_finance_e.htm (archived at https://perma.cc/AW3X-7EGF)

WTO (2016b) Why do trade finance gaps persist: and does it matter for trade and development? World Trade Organization, https://www.wto.org/english/res_e/reser_e/ersd201701_e.pdf (archived at https://perma.cc/6WGY-A3QL)

WEF (2017) The role of law and regulation in international trade finance: the case of correspondent banking, World Economic Forum, http://www3.weforum.org/docs/WEF_White_Paper_The_Role_of_Law_and_Regulation.pdf (archived at https://perma.cc/T75Z-KRG2)

# PART FIVE

# Innovating for sustainability

# 20

# The role of new technologies in mitigating climate change

**This chapter will familiarize the reader with:**

- How new technologies can reduce emissions through improving efficiencies
- Why new technologies do not provide the complete solution to reducing carbon emissions
- The role that governments must play in facilitating the development of new technologies
- The controversy that exists in the shipping industry over which sustainable fuel to adopt

## Using technology to drive efficiencies

Technology undoubtedly has an important role to play in reducing carbon emissions and will be fundamental in enabling companies and governments to meet their net zero targets. As well as alternative fuels (which will be discussed in more detail in Chapter 21) there are less obvious ways in which technology can benefit the environment. Many of these benefits accrue indirectly from gains in efficiency or from the ability it gives companies to 'measure and manage' their operations more effectively. Technology, in this respect, can be used to 'baseline' their current business in order to drive year on year improvements.

The development of transport management systems (TMSs) is a very good example of how technology that is designed to create operational efficiencies also benefits the environment (Manners-Bell, 2017). TMSs can:

- reduce the distance travelled by vehicles (optimized route planning)

- select the most fuel-efficient roads to use (i.e. choosing between less-congested primary routes and shorter, more congested residential streets)

- create better utilization of vehicle payloads by planning more efficient collections and deliveries

- enable an operator to schedule backhauls, thereby increasing vehicle utilization

- allocate appropriate vehicles to each route

- dynamically update driver and management on traffic congestion and suggest alternative routes

- consolidate multiple individual shipments into full loads, thereby optimizing flows of goods to individual customers or locations

- influence modal choice, with lower carbon options being used

The development of the 'Internet of Things' (IoT) also has environmental benefits. The use of sensors, technology and networking to allow buildings, infrastructures, devices and additional 'things' to share information can create efficiencies that ultimately reduce carbon emissions. Fleet and asset tracking is an example of this capability and many logistics operators have installed new tracking technology across their fleets of vans, trucks, trailers and intermodal containers. Tracking technology can deliver continuous, real-time information regarding the location and load status of each trailer and container, often using solar or cellular power. This allows companies to pinpoint the exact location of empty containers and trailers, making the planning and dispatch process more efficient, while reducing drivers' wasted time and empty miles.

The increased level of sensor use and vehicle telematics allows logistics managers to gather data daily on mechanical performance of vehicles and behavioural patterns of drivers. This includes:

- vehicle speed

- direction

- braking

- performance of engine and mechanical components

This can be used to improve driver behaviour, reducing wear on vehicle and fuel consumption (thereby reducing CO2 emissions). This results in the improved maintenance of vehicles, less downtime and fewer breakdowns.

Autonomous driving (Chapter 16) also offers huge gains in efficiency, which will result in environmental benefits (as well as a reduction in accidents, injuries and deaths to road users). These benefits include:

- reduced fuel consumption and emissions – computers drive vehicles more fuel efficiently
- 100 per cent connectivity and location services, which allow for 'perfect' route planning
- diagnostic services that ensure correct maintenance and fewer breakdowns
- less waste of energy through unnecessary braking: gaps between vehicles will be adhered to
- routes can be replanned around known areas of congestion
- more trucks can use the same road capacity, reducing road-building pressures

With vehicles being able to communicate with each other, there is also the possibility of 'platooning'. Trucks (and even eventually cars) will be able to travel in convoys along the motorway, drafting the vehicle in front. According to the US Department of Environment, this can create fuel cost savings of 8–11 per cent (Lammert et al, 2014).

## Is there an over-reliance on prospects for technology development?

As outlined above, new technologies have a direct and indirect role to play in mitigating the impact of climate change by reducing carbon emissions. However, some experts believe that companies and governments place too much reliance on their development, which could come too late to prevent catastrophic global warming.

A statement by the Intergovernmental Panel on Climate Change (IPCC) in March 2021 made it clear that efforts to create a carbon neutral economy by the mid-21st century were 'not on track'. Existing commitments indicate that by 2030 there will be only a very small reduction in total emissions – less than

1 per cent – compared to the 2010 benchmark (Hodgson, 2021). The IPCC asserted that by 2030 emissions would need to be reduced by 45 per cent compared to 2010 if temperature rises were not to exceed 1.5°C by the end of the century (SR1.5) and net-zero achieved by 2050. To limit global warming to below 2°C (SR2), CO2 emissions would need to decrease by about 25 per cent from the 2010 level by 2030 and reach net zero by around 2070.

According to the International Transport Forum (ITF), freight transport accounts for 39 per cent of global transport CO2 emissions and about 8 per cent of total emissions (ALICE, 2019). However, the sector has an almost complete dependence on fossil fuels, a situation that, in the words of Kuehne Logistics University's Professor Alan McKinnon, is 'hard to abate' (McKinnon, 2017). Following the disruption to the world's economy in 2020 due to Covid-19, freight CO2 fell by 28 per cent – but this fall is likely to be reversed in 2021 and may even accelerate due to the boom in e-retail last-mile deliveries.

If the freight industry is to reduce its carbon intensity to meet corporate and government commitments, it will have to adopt the so-called 'avoid–shift–improve' strategy as outlined in Professor McKinnon's book *Decarbonizing Logistics*:

- **Avoid**: this part of the strategy involves the reduction of underlying volumes by restructuring supply chains. This could involve reducing their dependence on international transport through steps such as near-sourcing, localization of suppliers or decentralization of inventory. It would also require industry to adopt elements of 'circularity' such as the shared economy, 3D printing and miniaturization of products.

- **Shift**: moving freight from carbon-intensive modes such as road to rail or short sea shipping. The problem with this approach is that, even if alternative modes are available or appropriate for shippers, they will need to considerably reduce their own carbon emissions through the greater adoption of clean energy. There are high levels of variation throughout the world in terms of their use of renewable sources of energy.

- **Improve**: there are three elements to this approach:
  o Improve capacity utilization through, inter alia, a reduction of empty running, increased load factors and better routing by using new digital technologies.

- o Improve energy efficiency through the use of automation, telematics, driver training, fuel economy standards, lightweighting aircraft, slow steaming, etc.
- o Reduce carbon intensity by using alternative fuels such as battery electric, hydrogen, methanol, etc.

Technology developments fall into the 'improve' category. Unfortunately, in terms of the adoption of alternative fuels in the road freight sector, none of the existing options can rival the all-round utility of diesel. On top of this, comprehensive refuelling/recharging networks do not exist and, in any case, many alternative fuels cannot yet be generated by using clean energy. Then there is the problem of adoption throughout the industry. The typical life span of a truck can be 10–15 years, which means that even if the sale of new diesel trucks is banned in, say 2035, many could still be operating in 2050.

The problem for governments is that if they are to meet their targets, the peak in carbon emissions needs to occur sooner rather than later. According to Professor McKinnon (2017), a peak in 2035 means that there would be 28 per cent more accumulated $CO_2$ emissions in the atmosphere than if that peak had occurred in 2025.

So, can the targets be achieved? It is fair to say that governments seem to be 'betting the house' on the development of new technologies, especially alternative fuels, and although industry is working at a frenetic pace to bring a range of new green technologies to market, it is still very unclear which will win out. A deadline for phasing out diesel and hybrids may even be counter-productive as manufacturers will inevitably reduce their investment in developing more efficient fossil-fuel-based engines.

It seems evident that relying on the 'shifting' and 'improving' elements of decarbonization to meet the goals will be a considerable stretch and this places more emphasis on 'avoidance', requiring action by industry, government and consumers. These issues affect not only the freight transport industry – all other sectors of the economy are wrestling with the same challenges. To meet the emissions targets, there will need to be significant behavioural change by consumers, such as critical mass take-up of electric vehicles and move to electric heating. Combining the policies of generating economic growth and employment while reducing carbon emissions will be a considerable – if not impossible – challenge.

## The role of government as facilitator

One of the key problems that transport sectors have in common is that carbon mitigation solutions have been hard to find: technological developments are expensive and are still not available at scale. For example, in order to transition heavy road freight from diesel to electric or hydrogen, there will need to be sufficiently dense charging networks in place and, until this is the case, take-up by carriers will be slow. New power networks, storage facilities or pipelines will require considerable investment but, when there is so much uncertainty over which fuel technology will eventually be adopted, investors will continue to be put off by levels of market risk.

This suggests that government intervention, guidance or facilitation will be necessary, allowing the private sector to take action with confidence. However, while speed is necessary to meet climate change targets, governments must remain 'tech neutral': policy makers must not pick winners or close the door to future technologies. This conundrum is likely to delay steps to implementation although a 'pathway' approach will help the process. This could involve:

- plotting development timescales
- assessing the fuels with the biggest decarbonization potential
- examining the economic case for each
- assessing the role of transitional fuels
- advising on how private investment can be encouraged.

Not all technology options are viable or can be funded, so the role that public policy plays in facilitating the development of the most robust will be critical.

Aviation is another case in point. Policies should be put in place to strengthen demand for advanced sustainable aviation fuels (SAFs), partly by implementing carbon taxes or establishing emission trading schemes. At the same time, research and development (R&D) should be supported that would enable production at scale while reducing the price. Realistically so-called 'drop in' fuels are the only option for fast greenhouse gas reductions for the long-haul sector as these are compatible with existing technologies and infrastructure. More advanced fuel technologies (such as battery electric) are at a much lower stage of market readiness.

In the shipping sector, alternative fuels will not be developed if there is no market for low-carbon shipping, i.e. if conventional, high-carbon options are still available to the market at a lower price. One solution would be to internalize the negative externalities of bunker fuels via carbon pricing or regulation. The allocation of monies raised through a carbon tax could help with transition costs (see below for more on the challenges faced by the shipping sector), although this is controversial.

However, it seems very unclear across all the 'hard to abate' transport sectors how carbon emission targets will be met. Fuel technologies and their necessary 'ecosystems' (such as charging networks) are at very early stages of development and will need government facilitation and public/private investment on a massive, paradigm-shifting scale. The risks of backing the 'wrong' technology are very real, costing the taxpayer many billions and delaying or even suppressing the development of options that had better carbon-reducing potential. Establishing pathway structures to aid the assessment of new technologies and guide public/private response and engagement will be crucial.

## Shipping lines split on best way to decarbonize

If global manufacturers and retailers are to reach their goals of net carbon neutrality by 2050 it will be crucial that shipping lines also decarbonize their operations. However, the industry is presently undecided on the best way to reduce its dependency on fossil fuels.

The momentum towards decarbonization in the logistics industry – not just shipping – is gathering pace as an increasing number of service providers are being prompted by their customers to demonstrate their commitment to net-zero operations. According to Maersk, around half of its 200 largest customers have set or are setting 'science-based' or zero-carbon targets for their supply chains and, to be able to meet these targets, outsourced transport operators, not least shipping lines, need to play their part (Wittels, 2021).

However, despite years of discussion, the shipping industry is undecided about how it should go about reducing the levels of carbon emissions it generates – about 2 per cent of the world's total. While there has been talk about including shipping within emissions trading systems, such as those in operation in the EU, many industry executives would prefer a carbon tax or levy approach.

In an interview with Bloomberg (Wittels, 2021), Soren Skou, chief executive of Maersk, suggested that a $150 per ton carbon tax should be levied on the shipping industry, bringing the cost of fossil fuels more into line with the cost of renewables. The purpose of the tax would be to create revenues that would subsidize and promote the use of cleaner but more expensive fuels as well as to support developing countries in their efforts to mitigate climate change. This suggestion is an extension of an earlier proposal presented to the International Maritime Organization by two Pacific islands – the Marshall Islands and Solomon Islands – for a $100 per ton tax on greenhouse gas emissions.

However, Maersk's view is certainly not representative of the entire industry. Speaking after the Maersk announcement, MSC's chief executive, Soren Toft, reiterated his support for an alternative proposal of a much smaller $2 per ton carbon tax, which would provide $5 billion for research and development into new fuels (MSC, 2021). This would be undertaken by an IMO-governed 'International Maritime Research and Development Board' (IMRB): 'Despite our huge investments into our fleet and operations, scalable long-term solutions simply do not currently exist for us to deploy on our ships. There is a gap in R&D to bring these alternative fuels and technologies to the market and the industry-wide research fund will help us achieve the UN IMO's policy targets.'

Another major difference in approach by these two shipping lines is over whether or not to introduce tried and tested lower carbon-emitting fuel technologies, such as liquefied natural gas (LNG), or take a gamble on new technologies, such as ammonia, which would require significant subsidy; the former strategy is that being adopted by MSC, and the latter by Maersk. This relates closely to their public pronouncements on the best policy to encourage the reduction of carbon emissions. One advocates using and improving the only existing fuel technology that can significantly reduce emissions at this time, already available at scale, while the other believes that by choosing a sub-optimal route to carbon reduction now would only consolidate investment in old technologies and make it harder for the industry to make the green transition. Both shipping lines have made commitments to back up their words – MSC has chartered 11 LNG-fuelled ships while Maersk has placed an order for an ammonia-powered ship, which will be delivered in 2023.

Other shipping lines seem to favour MSC's pragmatic approach. CMA CGM has already ordered six 15,000 20-foot equivalent units (TEUs) dual-fuel LNG vessels. By the end of 2022 it will have 32 LNG-powered containerships in operation, which it claims will generate 20 per cent fewer carbon emissions than existing technologies as well as providing major improvements in air quality. Hapag Lloyd, meanwhile, has ordered six 23,500 TEU dual-fuel LNG vessels in a $1 billion investment.

A carbon levy of the magnitude suggested by Skou would provide Maersk's strategy with a considerable boost, while negating the advantage of bunker fuel/LNG. If Maersk's faith in new technologies is rewarded, it would then provide it with a huge head start over rivals when costs eventually decrease, leaving competitors needing to renew their ships before they have paid back their investment.

The fundamental difference of opinion between Maersk and other shipping lines revolves around the speed of 'creation destruction' (Adner and Kapoor, 2016). It is usual for innovative technologies to exist in parallel with old technologies before they are abandoned once the necessary innovation 'eco-system' has been developed and scale achieved. In what might be called 'usual times' it is only when old technology has no more room for improvement and when the infrastructure that supports the innovation is in place that substitution can start to happen in a meaningful way.

The problem for companies making investments is that it is difficult to judge how quickly infrastructure or eco-system issues will be addressed, especially as the dynamic is continually shifting. Not only are there business investment and technological developments to take into account, but also government intervention. Subsidies for green energy initiatives, which may kickstart a technology (or skew the market, depending on your perspective), depend on public policy and can vacillate depending on the administration and thinking of the time.

The low risk strategy – in commercial terms – is that being employed by MSC, CMA CGM and Hapag Lloyd. However, it is no longer publicly acceptable just to measure outcomes solely in financial terms. 'Old' technologies such as conventional bunker fuels and LNG, with all the advantages that they have in terms of infrastructure and cost, will dominate for years to come unless there is intervention in the market along the lines suggested by Maersk. In order to meet carbon reduction targets being set by governments, many would argue that there is just not the time to adopt a wait-and-see policy. However, even this is a simplification of the difficult investment decisions that shipping lines face. Even with government support, there is no guarantee that the carbon-neutral technologies favoured by Maersk would be an appropriate substitute. Millions of dollars could be wasted backing the wrong option – whether ammonia, hydrogen or even electric – while LNG, a less carbon-emitting alternative, is ignored.

Inevitably, any additional levy will have to be borne by all the supply chain actors. Shipping lines will no doubt attempt to pass on these costs to their customers who would then take the decision as to whether to pass them on to the final consumer. Who bears the costs will only be determined by the state of the market at the time, although it has to be said that shipping lines have been very effective at passing on fuel surcharges in the past. Maersk argues that due to its huge economies of scale even such a large rise in the cost of fuel would only result in a small increase to the price of an individual item for the end consumer. A pair of training shoes, for example, may only increase in price by a few cents. Unfortunately, this argument has been used to justify tax increases of all types over the years, the problem being that this is not the only 'green tax' being suggested or levied at the moment. Governments will have to be honest with consumers that the cost of food, clothes, furniture, electronics, fuel and anything else moved globally will have to increase if climate change targets are to be met.

What is clear is that the shipping industry will have to coalesce quickly around a single carbon emissions strategy or risk one being imposed upon it. Under pressure from their electorates, governments are determined to address climate change and are unlikely to put up with a protracted discussion process as the IMO attempts to achieve consensus amongst its members. If patience runs out, an administration such as the United States is likely to impose its own regulations that the entire global industry will then have to adhere to, like it or not.

## Summary

Although many industry practitioners, energy companies and politicians are hoping for game-changing fuel technologies, there are other approaches that can have immediate effects – increasing utilization of transport assets, for instance, by improving loading and routing efficiencies; addressing volumetric issues by reducing packaging; sourcing where possible from local suppliers or using less carbon-emitting modes such as short sea shipping or intermodal. Expecting technology companies to 'pull a rabbit out of the hat' is not a viable proposition if governments, shippers and carriers really want to meet their carbon emissions reduction targets. This is especially the case in the shipping industry where it is particularly unclear which new fuel technology will be adopted.

# References

Adner, R and Kapoor, R (2016) Right tech, wrong time, *Harvard Business Review*, November, https://hbr.org/2016/11/right-tech-wrong-time?referral=00060 (archived at https://perma.cc/YP4A-XX5Z)

ALICE (2019) Roadmap towards zero emissions logistics 2050, Alliance for Logistics Innovation through Collaboration in Europe, December, www. etp-logistics.eu/wp-content/uploads/2019/12/Alice-Zero-Emissions-Logistics-2050-Roadmap-WEB.pdf (archived at https://perma.cc/YE4S-ECBL)

Hodgson, C (2021) Global warming will hit 1.5C by 2040, warns IPCC report, 9 August, *Financial Times*, London

Lammert, M, Duran, A (National Renewable Energy Laboratory), Diez, J, Burton, K (Intertek) and Nicholson, A (2014) Effect of platooning on fuel consumption of class 8 vehicles over a range of speeds, following distances, and mass, *The SAE International Journal of Commercial Vehicles*, 7 (2), doi:10.4271/2014-01-2438

Manners-Bell, J (2017) *Supply Chain Ethics*, Kogan Page, London

McKinnon, A (2017) *Decarbonizing Logistics*, Kogan Page, London

MSC (2021) MSC CEO Soren Toft calls for global approach to R&D and carbon pricing, *MSC*, www.msc.com/en/newsroom/news/2021/june/msc-ceo-soren-toft-calls-for-global-approach-to-rd-and-carbon-pricing (archived at https://perma.cc/X4FG-8G8F)

Wittels, J (2021) Maersk seeks $150-a-ton carbon tax on shipping fuel, Bloomberg, 2 June, www.bloomberg.com/news/articles/2021-06-02/shipping-giant-maersk-seeks-150-a-ton-carbon-tax-on-ship-fuel (archived at https://perma.cc/BG7S-E33Z)

# 21

# A guide to alternative propulsion systems

**This chapter will familiarize the reader with:**

- Why alternatives to diesel- and petrol-powered engines are being developed

- How adoption of alternative fuels will depend on issues such as range and payload

- The types of alternative fuels that are being developed; their benefits and disadvantages

- Which fuels are being adopted and trialled in the fleets of major operators

- How hybrids work and their effectiveness

- The choices facing fleet managers

- The development of charging networks to meet the needs of electric vehicles

It is clear from the environmental and public health policies being adopted by most administrators and regulators around the world that diesel-powered vans and trucks will make up a much smaller proportion of the commercial vehicle fleets in the years ahead. It is also clear that, despite a wide range of alternatives, not one single form of fuel or technology will be able to replace diesel across the board.

This chapter will summarize some of the main alternatives to diesel powertrains, highlighting their strengths and weaknesses. It will discuss briefly the initiatives taken by commercial vehicle manufacturers, their claims and the reality. It will also look at the role of some of the largest fleet owners and operators in providing a market for the vehicles and the input they have had in the development of alternatively powered vans and trucks.

## Different powertrains for different needs

The demands placed on commercial vehicles are very different not least due to the diverse functions that these vehicles undertake, the weight of freight they move, the number of stops they make and the range they require.

Light commercial vehicles (vans), for example, are likely to make multiple drops, work within urban areas and carry lighter loads. Heavier goods vehicles, in contrast, need greater range, will stop fewer times and obviously carry heavier loads. One of the main advantages of diesel power is its versatility; it performs well in multiple roles. This is certainly not the case for alternative powertrains – at the moment, there is no single technology able to supersede diesel-powered (or for that matter petrol) engines. As ACEA Secretary General, Erik Jonnaert, stated, 'different transport needs require different transport solutions' (ACEA, 2017). Policy must recognize and support this market-based approach.

Another issue for industry is that without government support or, indeed, environmental regulation, alternative propulsion systems are unlikely to have been developed. The overwhelming operational advantages and the scope for making diesel technology even more efficient would have provided little impetus for investment in sub-optimal technologies. This is important because it has led to the trial of a proliferation of technologies, often subsidized, many of which are highlighted in this chapter. For a fleet procurement manager, the choices used to be much simpler, based on efficiencies, power and cost with all van/truck manufacturers providing similar products. Now the landscape looks set to become much more complex with not only competing manufacturers but competing technologies against a backdrop of shifting government regulation and subsidy.

Although there is no overwhelming consensus on which technology is necessarily right for which vehicle, it seems clear that electric or electric hybrid technology is being favoured for vans, especially for intra-urban deliveries, although hydraulic hybrids are also being developed (see page 321 for an explanation of the terms).

The advent of electric-powered heavy goods vehicles (HGVs) is much further off, despite work being undertaken by manufacturers in the United States such as Tesla. Indeed, the UK's National Grid takes a very negative view of the potential for electrically powered HGVs. It says that, 'Currently the electrification of heavy goods vehicles is not considered viable and other fuel types are considered more likely for these larger vehicles' (National Grid, 2017). It believes that natural gas will be the fuel of choice and in the intervening years since the publication of this report it has not changed its opinion.

This is not a view shared by all. Pasquale Romano, president and CEO of ChargePoint, has commented: 'The drivetrain debate has ended and electrification has won out as the propulsion method of choice across transportation categories, as evidenced by the growing interest in electrifying semi-trucks, aircraft and beyond' (Behr, 2018). This would suggest he believes that advances in technology will reduce the size and weight of the batteries while still providing the power to carry large payloads over long distances.

It is useful to categorize commercial vehicles in order to assess their needs and consequently the likely most appropriate alternative powertrain. For this purpose, the International Energy Agency suggests three classifications (IEA, 2017):

- heavy freight trucks (HFTs) (those with a gross vehicle weight (GVW) of more than 15 tonnes)
- medium freight trucks (MFTs) (those with a GVW of between 3.5 and 15 tonnes)
- light commercial vehicles (LCVs) (those with a GVW of less than 3.5 tonnes)

HFTs account for the majority of road freight activity, not least due to the level of intensity of their use. The IEA (2017) estimates that they account for 70 per cent of road freight activity and 50 per cent of truck energy usage.

LCVs have seen the highest level of growth over the last decade as a result of the surge in e-commerce deliveries. Also, the more regulation of HFTs, the greater the increase in lighter vehicles.

It is also useful to examine the make-up of the global fleet of commercial vehicles (Table 21.1) to assess the market size for the most appropriate forms of propulsion.

TABLE 21.1  Structure of the global commercial vehicle fleet

| Vehicle type | Number |
| --- | --- |
| LCVs | 130 million |
| MFTs | 32 million |
| HFTs | 24 million |

SOURCE  IEA

A model developed by the IEA (see Figure 21.1) suggests that there is considerable variance in the distance travelled by the different classifications of vehicles across regions. This is due to the impact of factors such as:

- quality of roads and networks (developing countries have a larger proportion of MFT to HFT partly due to poor roads)
- urbanization (more vans)
- geography (large countries with longer distances between cities favour more HFTs)

One of the key issues affecting the adoption of alternative powertrains is their range. By using IEA figures related to the total annual travel of a vehicle and dividing them by the number of working days in a year, a simple average daily range can be calculated.

FIGURE 21.1  Daily commercial vehicle travel (kilometres)

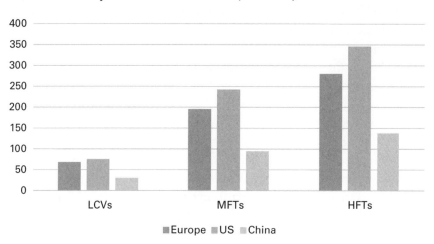

SOURCE  Authors/IEA

The stats shown in Figure 21.1 suggest:

- HFTs travel over four times further a day than LCVs and around one and a half times further than MFTs.

- Daily distance travelled by commercial vehicles in China is much lower than in Europe or the United States.

- An average daily distance travelled by an HFT in Europe is 281 kilometres and in the United States 346 kilometres. This has implications in terms of the range of the vehicles and the capabilities of the engine technology required (and potentially for charging-station infrastructure, if electric).

- For China, the distance travelled by an HFT is much lower (138 kilometres on average daily) so consequently this might not be such a problem.

- LCVs (vans) have an average daily travel of 69 kilometres in Europe, 77 kilometres in the United States and just 31 kilometres in China. This would seem to be well within the range of electric options, which can presently provide 100–150 kilometres before the need to recharge.

Obviously, this is a very simple exercise designed to demonstrate the contrast between vehicle needs against just one metric, range, across a number of geographies. It does not take into account weight of components, such as batteries, which reduces payloads, or the cost of the technology. Nor does it take into account the fact that many vans will require the capability to travel longer distances, for instance deliveries to semi-rural and rural areas. However, it provides some insight into the problems that manufacturers face when developing vehicles for a certain geography or sector. Unlike diesel technology, one size does not fit all.

Return on investment (ROI) also varies by size of company. Research undertaken in the United States (Schoettle et al, 2016) suggests that small companies with fleets of 1 to 20 will only invest in technologies with a payback of 6–36 months (average one year). Larger companies may consider a long payback period (18–48 months) averaging two years. Investment in vehicles using new propulsion systems will therefore be constrained by the levels of fragmentation in the industry. The fact that many logistics providers subcontract to owner-drivers means that levels of adoption will be further supressed or delayed, either from the more limited payback horizon or due to a lack of capital.

Consequently, some believe that the structure of the industry requires government intervention. If the 'cargo-owners' are not willing or are unable to force adoption of alternatives to diesel then a combination of regulation and subvention is needed. These include higher diesel taxes; higher vehicle duties for the most polluting and potentially increased tolls (when within a government's remit). These can be combined with scrappage schemes for older vehicles and support for the purchase of new ones through subsidy of the retail price.

## Types of alternative fuel

Governments and companies around the world have invested heavily in alternative fuel strategies with the aim of replacing some or all carbon-based fuels with sustainably produced substitutes. However, using alternative fuels in engines designed for oil-based fuel is not straightforward. For example, if bioethanol makes up more than a certain percentage of the fuel by volume, its corrosive nature means that engine components must be replaced more regularly. Costs of conversion and fuelling infrastructure can outweigh the cheaper costs of the alternative fuels (such as natural gas) within the total cost-of-ownership equation.

Presently the overwhelming demand of final energy by commercial vehicles is provided either by diesel or petrol (96.6 per cent). The alternative fuel portion of the market is comprised of the following.

### Biofuels

The development of biofuels – fuel that has been derived from organic matter or animals – is becoming increasingly important not only for

TABLE 21.2  Breakdown of alternative fuel use

| Biofuels | 2.2% | |
| --- | --- | --- |
| Of which | Biodiesel | 1.6% |
| | Bioethanol | 0.6% |
| | Biomethane | <0.01% |
| Natural gas | 1.2% | |

SOURCE IEA

commercial vehicles but as a replacement for bunker fuels for ships or aviation gas. These fuels can be used on their own or mixed with diesel (so-called 'dual fuel').

### BIODIESEL

Biodiesel is made from plant or animal oils. The main source of these oils varies from region to region depending on crops that suit local growing conditions. In North America, soy bean oil is preferred while in Asia the greatest source is palm oil. In Europe, however, rapeseed oil is most popular.

### BIOETHANOL

Bioethanol is produced from any feedstock that contains sugars such as starch. This means that crops as diverse as wheat, corn, willow and sugar-cane can be used.

There are problems with the sustainability credentials of biofuels. Firstly, studies have shown that although carbon monoxide, hydrocarbons and sulphur dioxide emissions can be reduced, other pollutants such as nitrous oxide and volatile organic compounds (VOCs) increase. Evidence on carbon dioxide emissions is ambiguous depending on the life cycle assessment (LCA) used. Obviously, there are considerable carbon emissions involved in the growing, harvesting, production and transport of biofuels.

### BIOMETHANE

Biomethane can be produced by the anaerobic digestion of organic material and can be generated by the diversion of landfill waste to biogas plants. However, there is unlikely to be enough biomethane generated from this source alone to meet the demand for alternative fuels.

## Natural gas (NG)

Natural gas is an alternative source of methane but can only be transported in the form of compressed natural gas (CNG) or liquified natural gas (LNG). This provides enough 'volumetric energy density' for it to be used in trucks.

One of the operational disadvantages of the fuel is that fuelling stations need expensive and complicated equipment (such as cryogenic storage tanks), adding to costs and availability. In addition, twice as much LNG is required as diesel to travel the same distance.

One of the major disadvantages of NG is its environmental credentials. As a fossil fuel it is considered 'unclean'. Methane (one of the most frequent gases uses) has a global warming potential of 21 times that of carbon dioxide (McKinnon et al, 2012). Part of the reasons for this is that some methane remains unburnt after the combustion process and re-enters the atmosphere.

NG does have its advantages, though. There are around 220,000 medium and heavy-duty trucks powered by NG in the world, their popularity driven by low emissions of nitrogen oxides and particulates. They are also quieter than equivalent diesel-powered engines, which makes them well suited to urban deliveries in particular.

Many analysts believe that biofuels and natural gas will eventually become the fuels of choice, especially in the MFT and HFT sectors. There is a long way to go, as presently natural gas-powered trucks account for only about 1 per cent of the world's total truck fleet.

## Hydrogen fuel cell

Hydrogen has the potential to be a completely clean form of energy in terms of tailpipe emissions. Electricity is produced from the chemical reaction between hydrogen and oxygen leaving only water vapour as the waste residue. The electricity is then used to power the vehicle and in this respect the technology competes with other energy storage options, such as batteries or hydraulic. This is very much a technology in development, although it is favoured particularly for use in urban environments due to the lack of pollutants.

However, hydrogen is not the answer to all pollution problems. The element has to be produced and, depending on the energy source used (coal or gas for example), there could be high levels of carbon emissions involved. Another issue will be the development of a hydrogen refuelling network in order to prevent 'range anxiety' dampening the technology's adoption.

### UPS TRIALS HYDROGEN PROTOTYPE

US express parcels company UPS has undertaken various trials over the past five years of fuel cell electric vehicles (FCEVs) in its rolling laboratory fleet of alternative fuel and advanced technology vehicles. UPS is working with the US Department of Energy (DOE) and other partners to design zero tailpipe emission medium and heavy-duty delivery trucks that meet the same route and range requirements of its existing conventional fuel vehicles.

The vehicles use the onboard fuel cell to generate electricity to propel the vehicle. The first FCEV prototype was deployed in Sacramento in a trial to validate its design and core performance requirements by testing it 'on the street'. All of the trucks will be deployed in California due to the ongoing investment in zero tailpipe emissions transportation and the instalment of hydrogen fuelling stations around the state.

'The challenge we face with fuel cell technology is to ensure the design can meet the unique operational demands of our delivery vehicles on a commercial scale', said Mark Wallace, UPS senior vice president (global engineering and sustainability), speaking at the launch of the initial trial. 'This project is an essential step to test the zero tailpipe emissions technology and vehicle on the road for UPS and the transportation industry' (UPS, 2017).

However, subsequent statements by company executives have struck a cautious note. 'Hydrogen is... very much part of the future', said Thomas F Jensen, senior vice president for transportation policy at UPS, during a webinar. 'But that future is yet to be defined, frankly' (Fuller, 2021).

## Electric vehicles

Electric vehicles (EVs) have attracted much of the publicity in recent years as 'zero-tailgate' emissions have become the political imperative. From an operational perspective, the main challenges facing electric van and truck manufacturers are the range (dealt with earlier in this chapter) and that the batteries required to power freight-carrying vehicles are relatively large and heavy. This means that the vehicles are only appropriate for certain sectors, such as city logistics. However, hybrid vehicles, which use a combination of diesel fuel and electric, have become more widely adopted.

The advantage of EVs is that there are virtually no emissions from the exhaust pipe and they are also very quiet. While local pollution may be eliminated, in terms of carbon emissions, the sustainability of EVs is reliant on the type of fuel used to generate the electricity that charges the batteries. If power stations supplying the grid are coal-, oil- or gas-based, vehicle emissions are in effect being transferred upstream. However, if the ultimate power source is either nuclear or from renewables, EVs become much more sustainable.

Tesla, Daimler, BMW and other truck manufacturers are investing huge sums in battery technology and it seems inevitable that in the next five years it will become feasible for even the largest trucks to be powered by electricity. Up to then, EVs will probably be restricted to urban deliveries, although given the growth of cities and megacities this is an important sector in its own right.

---

CASE STUDY 21.1
*Dachser deploys dual approach to build zero-emissions fleet*

European road freight company Dachser is investing in battery-powered trucks and company cars as well as in the requisite charging systems. Tests with hydrogen-powered trucks are also in the pipeline.

In an initial step, Dachser will introduce at least 50 additional battery electric trucks on European routes by the end of 2023. Dachser is also planning to add around 1,000 electric passenger cars to its fleet of company and service vehicles. In parallel, the company will press ahead with a range of pilot projects to develop and test hydrogen-powered trucks equipped with fuel cell technology. Dachser plans to have hydrogen-powered vehicles from a range of manufacturers operating within its network by no later than the beginning of 2023. New batteries have already been implemented by the company elsewhere.

Currently, Dachser primarily uses battery-powered vehicles for urban deliveries within its groupage network. In Europe, it has electrically assisted cargo bikes in daily operations and, above all, EVs with a gross vehicle weight rating of up to 7.5 metric tons. There are still very few all-electric production vehicles available in heavier weight classes. The only vehicle of this type Dachser has in service is a pre-production model of the 19-metric-ton Mercedes-Benz eActros in Stuttgart, as part of an innovation partnership with Daimler.

In the next two years, Dachser will introduce at least 50 additional zero-emission trucks, including heavy battery-electric motor vehicles and truck tractors from a range of manufacturers, either through direct purchase or in cooperation with transport partners. There are plans to create over 40 fast-charging stations for trucks, each with a charging power of 180 kW.

---

## Hybrid electric vehicles

Hybrid vehicles use either a petrol or diesel engine, but they are augmented by an alternative propulsion system.

PETROL OR DIESEL/ELECTRIC HYBRID

These vehicles have been around for some time and are a common choice in the passenger sector (Toyota Prius, for example). A normal engine is augmented by an electric battery that can also be charged through regenerative braking as well as by charging stations. The electric battery is typically used at low speeds and when the speed increases the petrol/diesel engine takes over. One of the advantages is that the petrol/diesel engine can be small (as it is augmented by battery power) and so has lower emissions.

One of the problems of such vehicles is the weight of the battery and the other components required. They are not necessarily as eco-friendly as perhaps might be first thought. For example, their batteries, containing toxins, need to be recycled. As well as this, at higher speeds the petrol/diesel engines emit more pollutants than some of the most advanced fuel-efficient diesel/petrol alternatives.

HYDRAULIC HYBRID VEHICLES

There is another alternative under development: hydraulic hybrid engine systems. The petrol/diesel engine is assisted by a system that works solely through regenerative braking. The kinetic energy powers a pump, which when under braking moves fluid under pressure from a reservoir to an 'accumulator' that acts as a battery (in as much as it stores potential energy). The US National Renewable Energy Laboratory (NREL) states that up to 70 per cent of kinetic energy can be captured for deployment (NREL, 2016). The accumulator also holds nitrogen and this pressurized gas can then be used to either power the transmission or wheels directly. The fact that energy is harvested and stored during braking makes these systems ideally suited for package delivery vans due to the stop–start nature of their operation. UPS has been testing such systems in the United States since 2012. There are two types of hydraulic hybrid vehicles, series-hybrids and parallel-hybrids:

- Parallel hydraulic: a parallel-hydraulic hybrid allows the battery to provide power to the vehicle through the transmission when it is accelerating but will not work independently. This means that the conventional engine can never be shut off completely. Despite this it can deliver up to 40 per cent in fuel economy.

- Series hydraulic: a series-hydraulic hybrid transmits power directly to the wheels rather than through a transmission. This means that it is more efficient (savings of up to 60–70 per cent) and can work when the internal combustion engine (ICE) has been shut down, making it zero emission.

TABLE 21.3 Fleet choice matrix

| | Range | Payload | Total cost of ownership | Tail pipe emissions | GHG emissions | Charging/fuelling infrastructure |
|---|---|---|---|---|---|---|
| Diesel | Yes | Yes | Yes | No | Yes | Existing |
| All-electric | No | No | No | Yes | Dependent on source | Limited |
| Electric hybrid | Yes | Weight of battery issue | No | Some emissions | Some emissions | Yes |
| Hydraulic hybrid | Yes | Yes | No | Some emissions | Some emissions | Yes |
| Hydrogen fuel cell | Yes | Yes | No | No | Dependent on source | Very limited |
| Natural gas | Yes | Yes | No | Yes | No | Very limited |
| Biofuels | Yes | Yes | No | Yes | No | Very limited |

*Choices for fleet managers*

From Table 21.3 it is obvious that, in terms of most metrics, diesel power is by far the obvious choice (presently) for fleet managers. However, of course, in terms of political importance, tailpipe emissions are taking priority over many other considerations. Diesel bans in cities are an inevitability that all the major manufacturers and truck/van owners are taking into account in their long-term strategies.

## Meeting the challenge of charging electric vehicles

*The charging challenge*

A fundamental question for the EV sector is whether enough electricity can be generated to cope with the vast numbers of cars and trucks that are being forecast. One piece of research undertaken for power network provider National Grid (2017) forecasts that an additional 18GW of demand would be created in the UK alone by a take-up of EVs (both cars as well as commercial vehicles) by 2050 – almost one-third more than the peak power required in 2017. Cars and EVs will be competing with industry and domestic requirements for power. However, National Grid asserts that the demand from EVs could be dramatically reduced by the use of smart technology.

Although the research relates to consumer behaviour and its effect on demand, it is relevant in terms of attitudes to business as well. It shows that power demand will be at its highest if consumers (and businesses) charge their vehicles at peak times – a real challenge to the grid in developed countries and perhaps overwhelming in many countries with less developed generation capacities. However, the best-case scenario suggests that if consumers and businesses charge at off-peak times, the peak demand will be much more manageable. To spread demand there will need to be a combination of:

- tariffs to encourage efficient charging behaviour by consumers and businesses
- smart technology that identifies the best time to charge vehicles

*Charging options*

One of the most important factors inhibiting EV uptake has been lack of confidence by drivers that they will be able to find a recharging point, especially if they are undertaking journeys outside of urban areas. As we will see, this has prompted huge investment by a large range of different players, encouraged by government subsidy. The extent to which this impacts on parcels delivery companies is not so clear. Many vans will be recharged at a depot overnight and the charge may be sufficient to last for a day, depending on routes and loads. In which case, charging 'on-the-go' may not be so important, at least for urban deliveries.

Consequently, in addition to national networks of charging points, a proportion of infrastructure investment will need to be focused on central-ized recharging hubs where the demands of charging considerable numbers of vans over a short period of time will place considerable strain on local power networks.

Of course, not all parcels companies will operate on this basis. In a sector that is increasingly dominated by the use of owner-drivers (the so-called 'gig economy') many drivers take their vehicles home at night and will therefore be charging their vans from a domestic charging point. This will spread the intensity of demand over a larger area, although it will not, of course, reduce the overall demand placed upon the power generation companies.

## Charging in the depot

As highlighted above, there are challenges related to charging large numbers of electric freight vehicles. When announcing a recent partnership with UPS related to a project undertaken in a London depot, Tanja Dalle-Muenchmeyer, programme manager (electric freight) at Cross River Partnership, said, 'Our previous work on electric freight vehicles has shown that local grid infra-structure constraints are one of the main barriers to their large-scale uptake. We need to find smarter solutions to electric vehicle charging if we want to benefit from the significant air quality and environmental benefits these vehicles offer' (Middleton, 2018).

Upgrading the external power grid to a depot is a very expensive under-taking that would put off many companies from adopting electric freight vehicles. However, the UPS smart-grid solution uses a central server that is connected to each EV charge post as well as the grid power supply and the on-site energy storage. This has allowed the company to increase the number of trucks it charges from 65 to 170 by spreading the charge throughout the night, in tandem with the other power requirements of the building, without exceeding the maximum power available from the grid.

The smart-grid solution will be rolled out in conjunction with other innovations. These include conventional power grid upgrade, smart grid, on-site energy storage with batteries and local power generation (using, for example, solar energy generated on facility roof tops).

Also in the UK, London-based delivery company 'Gnewt by Menzies Cargo', with EO Charging, installed what it believes to be the UK's largest single-site EV charge point location with a total of 40 new EO smart-chargers at its depot in Bow, London. Gnewt by Menzies has a fully electric delivery fleet at over 120 vehicles.

In the United States, Italian energy company Enel has acquired eMotorwerks, smart technology that allows charging stations to be controlled remotely for what is termed 'grid balancing' purposes. This decides the best time for connected vehicles to be charged. The stations also have a storage element that can be charged at off-peak times and can then be used to charge the vehicle once connected.

## 'On the go' charging

Away from the depot, investment is gathering pace for the development of charging stations. At present the major investments have come in Europe, the United States and China. The key difference between domestic charging and public points is the speed of charge.

### EUROPE

Many believe that a huge increase in charging points is needed in Europe if the infrastructure is to support the forecast number of EVs. The bank Morgan Stanley estimates that 1–3 million public charging points will be required in Western Europe by 2030 (Nishizawa, 2017) compared to the present number of around 225,000.

Although most parcels companies will be rolling out fleets of EVs in urban areas where 'on-the-go' charging is not so much a problem, it will mean, eventually, that with the improvement in battery technologies, national fleets may go fully electric rather than a mix of both diesel and electric.

European initiatives include:

- Shell has formed a partnership with IONITY (a group consisting of BMW, Ford, Volkswagen and other vehicle manufacturers) to develop a high-power charging network across Europe.

- BP has invested $5 million in FreeWire Technologies, a US manufacturer of charging systems for EVs. FreeWire's EV charging systems will be added to filling stations in the UK capable of fully charging an EV in 30 minutes.

- Not to be outdone in terms of diversification from its core energy business, Shell has acquired NewMotion, a company that specializes in building fast-charging public EV stations. As with BP, they have started rolling out charging points in the UK with plans to expand in other locations in Europe. This will operate alongside Shell's network of points at its forecourts. With access to more than 64,000 public charge points, NewMotion has the largest charge network in Europe covering Belgium, Germany, the UK, France and the Netherlands.

- Another collaboration between US ChargePoint and French company Engie is also planning to build a pan-European network of high-voltage fast-charging stations.

- ChargePoint is part owned by BMW, Daimler and Siemens and it has entered into a partnership with French-based TSG (previously owned by Tokheim), which provides maintenance services to filling stations in France, Germany, Ireland, the Netherlands and the UK.

## Outlook for charging networks

Investment is pouring into the EV charging-station sector. Government regulations and incentives will encourage consumers and freight operators to adopt EVs over a relatively short timeframe and the infrastructure will need to be in place to support this growth.

Despite the rush to build large numbers of charging stations, a more focused response would be to develop fewer, but faster-charging points. This would encourage consumers and companies to charge during the day rather than at peak times, such as the evening.

Smart technologies that 'grid-balance' will become important, especially in parcels depots, to decide on the best time to recharge vans.

Amongst the parties involved are:

- oil companies looking to diversify from fossil-fuel dependence

- power distribution companies seeing the market as a major opportunity

- automotive companies who need dense recharging networks in place in order to encourage consumers to buy EVs

- the technology hardware and software companies developing the charging stations
- facilities management, retailers, filling-station forecourt owners, etc, looking to leverage the location of their assets
- governments and local authorities developing public policy for climate change and public health

## Summary

Public policy is demanding that alternative propulsion systems must be developed to reduce the impact of transport on the environment and public health. Many of the world's largest manufacturers and fleet operators have willingly invested in the new technologies that will ultimately supersede diesel power. However, to date, no technology is able to match diesel in terms of its all-round utility.

Consequently, it seems probable that instead of all-out bans on diesel- and petrol-engined vehicles, more sensible targets will be set for the industry, taking into account advances in technology and encouraging investment.

As well as supporting the development of new technologies and fuels, governments will continue to facilitate the investment in charging and refuelling stations as well as ensuring that electricity supply is plentiful enough not only to charge vans and trucks but also the numerous electric cars that will appear on the roads.

As Preston Feight, president of DAF Trucks and chairman of the ACEA Commercial Vehicle Board said, 'The affordability of alternatively powered vehicles is key, as operators simply have to make money with their vehicles. Taxation policies, incentives and public procurement can be useful tools to stimulate sales of alternatively powered vehicles. But it is crucial that there is sufficient clarity, harmonization and long-term stability in this regard' (ACEA, 2017).

## References

ACEA (2017) What will power our trucks, vans and buses in the future? European Automotive Manufacturers Association, Brussels, 1 December, www.acea.be/news/article/conference-what-will-power-our-trucks-vans-and-buses-in-the-future (archived at https://perma.cc/YLQ4-Y98K)

Behr, M (2018) ChargePoint develops 2-MW charger for electric aircraft, 10 May, *Electrans*, https://electrek.co/2018/05/10/chargepoint-2-mw-charger-electric-aircraft-and-semi-trucks/ (archived at https://perma.cc/2PM2-A9R8)

Fuller, S (2021) Amazon, UPS say hydrogen is further down the road than battery-electric, Transport Dive, 6 July, https://www.transportdive.com/news/Amazon-UPS-hydrogen-battery-electric-trucks-emissions-EVs/602581/ (archived at https://perma.cc/AS7K-UXXN)

IEA (2017) The future of trucks, *International Energy Agency*, Paris

McKinnon, A C, Browne, M and Whiteing, A (2012) *Green Logistics: Improving the environmental sustainability of logistics*, Kogan Page, London

Middleton, N (2018) Switch to smart grid to enable all-electric fleet at UPS, EV Fleetworld, http://evfleetworld.co.uk/switch-to-smart-grid-to-enable-all-electric-fleet-at-ups/ (archived at https://perma.cc/M2Y3-YEJH)

National Grid (2017) *Future Energy Scenarios*, July, National Grid, London

Nishizawa, K (2017) The world must spend $2.7 trillion on charging stations for Tesla to fly, Bloomberg, 11 October, www.bloomberg.com/news/articles/2017-10-11/tesla-ev-network-shows-a-2-7-trillion-gap-morgan-stanley-says (archived at https://perma.cc/KK8T-WYEU)

NREL (2016) Hydraulic hybrid fleet vehicle evaluations, National Renewable Energy Laboratories, www.nrel.gov/transportation/fleettest-hydraulic.html (archived at https://perma.cc/4DFT-N4WY)

Schoettle, B, Sivak, M and Tunnell, M (2016) *A Survey of Fuel Economy and Fuel Usage by Heavy-Duty Truck Fleets*, University of Michigan, Ann Arbor

UPS (2017) UPS unveils first extended range fuel cell electric delivery vehicle, *UPS*, www.globenewswire.com/en/news-release/2017/05/02/975621/30428/en/UPS-Unveils-First-Extended-Range-Fuel-Cell-Electric-Delivery-Vehicle.html (archived at https://perma.cc/67PA-VFCR)

# 22

# Designing smart and circular supply chains

This chapter will familiarize the reader with:

- What is meant by a circular supply chain
- How circularity and strategic autonomy have become conflated
- The impact of circular supply chains on trade volumes
- The economic benefits of changing from linear to circular supply chains
- Specific impacts on the 'fast fashion' sector

Following the Covid-19 crisis many governments have been keen to put in place 'green recovery' programmes, combining the need for economic growth with sustainability. This has been a key part of politicians' 'messaging' – that the crisis should be used as an opportunity to create sustainable economies and that a 'rebound' must not come at the cost of the environment.

The development of a 'circular economy' is one element of these programmes. Although not new, the concept of supply chains structured around recycling, refurbishment, remanufacture, reuse and the prolongation of product life is being taken up by governments with renewed enthusiasm, for reasons that will be discussed below.

Since the crisis, many politicians have sought to highlight the inability of linear global supply chains to deliver personal protective equipment (PPE) and have promoted localization of production as a potential alternative, not just for PPE but for medicines, food and other critical supplies. In many people's minds, future resilience will only be achieved by reducing economies' reliance on extended supply chains, which have been shown to be at risk from protectionist trade measures, production bottlenecks and transport disruption. Circular supply chains form a key part of this narrative, as they reduce reliance on global sources of raw materials and promote higher levels of (re)manufacturing activity in locations within end markets.

'Circularity' also provides a potential solution for many environmental problems as well as making supply chains more resilient in the face of crises – not only that caused by the Covid-19 pandemic, but also others related to security (such as Huawei's involvement in the construction of 5G networks).

This mix of public policy goals can be bundled together as a way of achieving so-called 'strategic autonomy'. According to European Commission President Ursula von der Leyen, speaking in April 2020, 'A circular economy will make us less dependent and boost our resilience. This is not only good for our environment but it reduces dependency by shortening and diversifying supply chains' (Howie and Nolan, 2020).

Hence, circularity (see Figure 22.1) is being promoted as a way in which supply chains can be made more resilient, alongside other strategies such as re-shoring, near-sourcing and 'optionalization' or 'China +' (optionalization and China+ strategies reduce supply chain risk by increasing the number of suppliers across a region or multiple regions and in particular limiting reliance on China).

For European Union politicians, China and the United States are clearly the targets of this policy. Talking prior to the last presidential election, Greek MEP Anna-Michelle Asimakopoulou put it bluntly: 'We need policies that

FIGURE 22.1  Conflation of strategic autonomy/sustainability goals

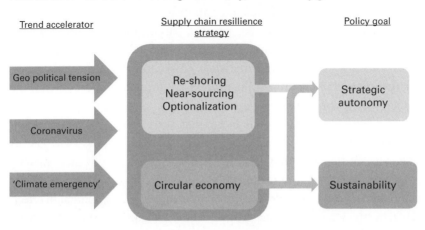

safeguard and grow our industries against Chinese unfair competition and President Trump's out-of-control tariff diplomacy.' Talking about China specifically she went on, 'It is baffling that we are only just waking up to our reliance on what the European Commission calls "a systemic rival"' (Asimakopoulou, 2020).

For some raw materials, Europe and North America are widely self-sufficient. However, for many critical raw materials (CRMs) used in the high-tech sector (e.g. antimony, beryllium, cobalt, gallium, germanium, indium, platinum group metals (PGMs), natural graphite, rare earth elements (REEs), silicon metal and tungsten) this is not the case and the regions are highly dependent on China in particular.

At product end-of-life, the vast majority of CRMs end up in landfill with only a tiny proportion recycled. One of the difficulties of recycling certain elements is their dispersed nature throughout a product. The waste results from the technical and economic challenges that have slowed progress towards circular supply chains and that will have to be overcome if the concept is to become reality.

## What does a circular economy mean?

The circular economy is seen as an alternative to existing 'linear' economies where products, materials and components are discarded when their usefulness comes to an end, also known as 'take, make, waste'. While in the latter model the value of materials reduces to zero over the lifetime of the product, in a circular economy, design at the outset ensures that these materials retain some of their value, which consequently ensures that it is economically viable to reuse them in one function or another.

In a traditional manufacturing process, 'virgin' materials are typically used and there is the assumption of cheap and easily accessible energy. External costs of disposal and the wider environmental disbenefits generated throughout the manufacturing process are borne by society and not the producer or the consumer.

The circular economy would mean that there would be fewer virgin materials used and this has a double benefit. Firstly, it means that there is less impact on the environment in terms of the extraction of these materials – a key point in terms of sustainability. Secondly, there will be less reliance on the countries that provide or control these materials, e.g. China. In effect, circularity divorces economic growth from the consumption of natural

FIGURE 22.2  Impact of circular economy on trade

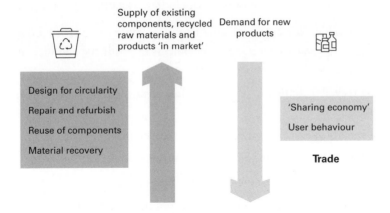

*International trade volumes reduce due to a combination of increase in supply of materials/products in circulation reduction in demand as asset use intensifies and purchase of 'second-hand' products becomes more widely acceptable.*

resources, resulting in economic and environmental benefits as well as improved supply chain resilience.

However, the shift from linear supply chains to circular will be very challenging. Marina Mattos, a post-doctoral associate at the MIT Centre for Transportation and Logistics, comments: 'A critical supply chain challenge is how to reconfigure distribution channels, forecast methods and technology to generate value across business eco-systems. To achieve this goal, companies must create new business models and improve supply chain management functions' (Mattos, 2019).

One way in which to improve levels of circularity will be to reduce product complexity and this can only be achieved at the design phase. If a product contains multiple materials, each one will have its own 'loop', which in turn will have to be closed if circularity is to be attained.

In March 2020, the European Commission set out a number of policy objectives within its Circular Economy Action Plan, part of the 'European Green Deal'. At the time, executive vice-president for the European Green Deal, Frans Timmermans, commented: 'To achieve climate neutrality by 2050, to preserve our natural environment and to strengthen our economic competitiveness requires a fully circular economy. Today, our economy is still mostly linear, with only 12 per cent of secondary materials and resources being brought back into the economy' (EC, 2020a). The objectives include:

- improving product durability, reusability, upgradability and reparability, addressing the presence of hazardous chemicals in products, and increasing their energy and resource efficiency
- increasing recycled content in products, while ensuring their performance and safety
- enabling remanufacturing and high-quality recycling
- reducing carbon and environmental footprints
- restricting single-use and countering premature obsolescence
- introducing a ban on the destruction of unsold durable goods
- incentivizing product-as-a-service or other models where producers keep the ownership of the product or the responsibility for its performance throughout its life cycle
- mobilizing the potential of digitalization of product information, including solutions such as digital passports, tagging and watermarks
- rewarding products based on their different sustainability performance, including by linking high performance levels to incentives

## Impact on trade

Given that a large proportion of the raw materials and finished goods consumed in Europe and North America are produced in Asia (especially China), a move to a circular economy could have a profound impact on global trade (see Figure 22.2). Fewer products would be shipped due to a combination of a reduction of demand (as products would have longer lives and more assets would be 'shared' thereby increasing asset utilization) and an increasing amount of goods and components remain in circulation in consumer markets. User perception and behaviour will also have an important impact on demand for new products. If consumers can be convinced that using refurbished products involves no diminution of quality, no issue with data protection (for electronics) and is more socially acceptable, then there will be less reason to buy new releases of goods.

The effect of the shift is shown in Figure 22.3. Presently, large volumes of new products and raw materials are shipped typically from Asia to the rest of

FIGURE 22.3 The shift from linear to circular supply chains

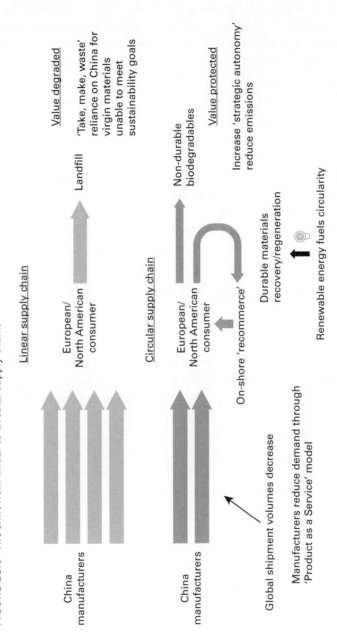

the world. They start off with high value but their value rapidly diminishes and a large proportion of the volume ends up in landfill. If refurbishment technology can be improved, if products can be designed for recovery of parts and if the concept of circularity and 'sharing' is accepted by consumers, a much greater proportion of parts and products will stay in circulation in the end-user markets.

This will mean that shipment volumes from Asia will necessarily decrease, although it is impossible to say by how much. Even if all waste was transformed into secondary raw materials, there would still be a need to import primary raw materials as demand would exceed supply.

If materials can be recovered in Europe and North America, they can be used to feed local manufacturing presently dependent on their import. They may even be exported back to other manufacturing locations in developing markets as input into intermediate components. Unless Europe and North America develop/re-shore far greater downstream manufacturing capabilities, however, it would seem unlikely that recovery of materials would have a major impact on volumes of finished goods being imported from Asia. At present, the low-cost labour available in these markets for the assembly of products is too much of a competitive advantage, although this may change with the development of 3D printing.

One sector that may benefit is the trade of second-hand goods to developing countries. However, the benefits are not unalloyed. Exporting products that have reached their end-of-life in developed markets has the effect of breaking the closed loop systems that are being set up to ensure recycling/refurbishment, etc. Once a product has been exported it is difficult to enforce 'extended producer responsibility' regulations or to ensure that the product is properly dealt with once its value has diminished to such an extent that there is no further use for it in its secondary market.

As part of its Action Plan, the European Commission (EC) has spoken about 'mainstreaming circular economy objectives in free trade agreements, in other bilateral, regional and multilateral processes and agreements, and in EU external policy funding instruments' (EC, 2020b). What this actually means for future trade arrangements remains to be seen but ensuring closed loop systems may be part of its objectives.

## The economic impact

The shift to a circular economy could have positive economic benefits. The Ellen McArthur Foundation published research which claims that the circular economy could result in a net materials cost-savings opportunity for the high-tech and automotive sector of $340–380 billion per annum, rising to $520–630 billion per annum for more radical changes. For the fast-moving consumer goods (FMCG) sector (packaged food, apparel, beverages, etc), circularity could bring savings of over $706 billion per year (WEF, 2014). According to the EU, manufacturing firms spend on average about 40 per cent on materials. It believes that 'closed loop' models can increase companies' profitability, while sheltering them from resource price fluctuations (EC, 2020b).

It is hoped that by investing in refurbishment technology more value will be retained in a product, allowing the reseller to sell at a higher price. This will generate value in the supply chain, which will allow for investment in reverse logistics and additional technologies, creating a virtuous cycle. This could be reinforced by establishing second-hand markets with more transparent pricing as well as information on condition and performance – important issues when overcoming the barriers for consumers of buying pre-used devices.

## Industry sector circularity

### High tech

This sector is of high priority given that waste levels are continuing to rise (in the EU they are growing at 2 per cent per year) and that less than 40 per cent of electronic products are recycled. An Ellen Macarthur Foundation report estimated that, in 2016, 44.7 million tonnes of e-waste were generated globally, of which 435,000 tonnes were mobile phones (Paddison, 2017). In Europe an Ecodesign Directive has been proposed that will increase products' energy efficiency, durability, reparability, upgradability, maintenance, reuse and recycling. There are also plans for a 'common charger' across brands and an EU-wide take-back scheme for old phones.

### Batteries and vehicles

Given the importance of electric vehicles (EVs) to the automotive sector, the volume of batteries that will need to be disposed of at their end-of-life will be very substantial. One estimate suggests that sales of EVs in 2017 alone produced 250,000 tonnes or 0.5 million cubic metres of unprocessed waste (Harper et al, 2019). For this reason, the EC is implementing rules on recyclable content and the recovery of valuable content in Europe. It is also promoting 'product-as-a-service models' to ensure better utilization of existing assets, which will reduce the demand for virgin materials. Lithium-ion batteries contain cobalt that is mined extensively in the Democratic Republic of Congo. The industry there has attracted criticism for child labour practices, environmental mismanagement and the sale of conflict minerals to support local warlords. Recycling this element within the end-user market would reduce this reliance, although efforts are being hampered as batteries are presently difficult and dangerous to disassemble.

---

### EV BATTERY-RECYCLING INITIATIVE ADDRESSES WASTE REDUCTION, BUT FAR MORE BESIDES

Moving to a circular supply chain for EV batteries is essential to reduce tons of toxic waste ending up in landfill. However, it also has less obvious economic, security and ethical implications for supply chains.

While reducing carbon emissions is at the forefront of everyone's minds, it is important to note that many decisions related to decarbonization can have unintended consequences. To date most concerns relate to the economic impact of migrating from fossil fuels to alternative energies, but there are wider ethical, security and even environmental risks that must be taken into account.

The manufacture of battery cells for EVs is a case in point. Little consideration has been given to how to deal with the volume of batteries at the end of their lives. This is just one of the reasons why the recent announcement by Northvolt, the European supplier of battery cells and systems, is so important. It has produced its first battery cell with 100 per cent recycled nickel, manganese and cobalt from battery waste with a performance on a par with cells produced from freshly mined metals. All recycling and production processes were completed in Sweden and a 'giga-plant' is presently under construction, due to commence production in 2023, which will also have the capability to recycle lithium from batteries.

Emma Nehrenheim, Northvolt's chief environmental officer, commented: 'What we have shown here is a clear pathway to closing the loop on batteries and that there exists a sustainable, environmentally preferable alternative to conventional mining in order to source raw materials for battery production.'

This is obviously good news in itself but it also has a number of other major supply chain implications:

- The success of European battery cell manufacturers will be important strategically to the region's automotive sector. China is the dominant manufacturer of batteries for EVs and European auto companies risk losing their market competitiveness.

- Europe and the United States find themselves in competition with China for many of the critical raw materials used in batteries. China has spent billions in establishing control of mines and transport systems in Africa, Asia and Latin America. Recycling batteries would help the West create self-sufficiency at a time of rapidly deteriorating relations.

- Ethics: little consideration is paid to the conditions in which miners in emerging and 'frontier' markets work. In places such as Congo, the industry has attracted criticism for child labour practices, environmental mismanagement and the sale of conflict minerals to support local warlords.

The ability to manufacture batteries from recycled materials is absolutely critical to the future success of the EV market. Moving from linear 'take, make waste' supply chains to circular alternatives will be essential if environmental, ethical and security considerations are to be overcome. Northvolt's initiative will go some way to lessen the West's need for virgin materials, reduce end-of-life waste as well as create strategic autonomy.

SOURCE  Ti (Manners-Bell, 2021)

## Plastics and plastic packaging

With packaging requirements reaching record levels due to a surge in home shopping during the Covid-19 crisis, the reduction of over-packaging is a priority for all administrations. The reduction of the complexity of packaging is being researched and this will help to increase recyclability. A labelling system for different types of packaging is also being assessed.

Much of regulators' focus is being directed towards the reduction of microplastics and the marine pollution by single use plastics. According to the World Economic Forum, 95 per cent of plastic packaging material value ($80–120 billion) is lost annually after a short first use (WEF, 2016). Regulations could include mandatory requirements for recycled content and other waste reduction measures. However, as the Institute for European Environmental Policy puts it, 'the current trends of a restriction in opportunities for the export of plastic waste for recycling, suggest a need to develop a more active European market for recycled plastics, alongside measures to reduce the generation of plastic waste. The challenge lies in the lack of well-defined quality standards for plastic waste and recycled plastics' (IEEP, 2020).

*Textiles and fashion*

Only an estimated 1 per cent of textiles are recycled into new clothing, resulting in an economic loss of more than $100 billion of materials per year (EMF, 2017). There are hopes that it would be possible to create a secondary market that would stimulate textile reuse and other initiatives such as providing better access to repair services. There may also be laws such as extended producer responsibility, which pushes the responsibility for recycling upstream (see below for a detailed discussion of circularity in this sector).

## Consequences for logistics

Logistics will have a key role to play if government and industry are to facilitate the transformation of supply chains from linear to circular. Geographic considerations are important as companies may have marketing distribution structures in place in multiple countries, but not the ability to handle returns, refurbishment, redistribution, recycling, maintenance or the ability to enable the other important aspect of circularity, 'sharing'. A further challenge is creating a predictable flow of returned goods, which would allow a stable structure to be put in place to handle them.

The development of distribution structures will be one way in which logistics service providers will be able to support their customers. Many of the larger companies have dense international, national and local networks of facilities. Express companies will, for instance, be able to develop returns operations using parcels shops. Logistics companies can provide testing and repair services before reintroducing the products back into the supply chain (increasing so-called 'inventory velocity'). Although these services have been provided for several decades, logistics companies will benefit from larger volumes at higher margins. In addition, they may also undertake the recovery of materials from end-of-life product as a value-adding service, either through partners or at their own facilities.

There certainly seems to be an appetite for more 'reverse logistics'. That said, many elements of a circular economy will have negative consequences for the logistics industry. The transition from linearity to circularity will ultimately result in less international transportation, as fewer finished goods and raw materials are moved out of Asia. There will be less warehousing space required to store internationally sourced goods or packaging required to protect them. On the other hand, this shift will benefit domestic and regional logistics providers – mainly road-based – as increased levels of secondary raw materials, intermediate and finished products circulate within markets.

## Circular fashion: solutions to fast-fashion waste

Fashion supply chains are on the verge of a major transformation that will have dramatic effects on the associated logistics industry. These changes are being thrust upon the manufacturers and retailers in the sector due to the growing unease about their environmental impact and, in particular, the trend towards fast fashion. In a world in which sustainability is becoming engrained in many companies' business models, the 'buy, wear once and then throw away' model that has been so successful for many retailers is becoming regarded as outdated. Waste does not just occur at the finished product stage. It is also endemic in upstream supply chains with many byproducts from the process being incinerated or dumped.

Instead, some brands are turning towards 'considered design'. According to one consultancy this term apples when 'the designer considers the materials and their impact, the production, and the consumer use stage, to minimize the negative effects on the world around them' (Zoltkowski, 2022). This involves 'cradle to cradle' design where there is either a:

• biological cycle, with products being returned harmlessly to nature or,

• industrial cycle, with non-degradable material being recycled

Closing the loop in fashion supply chains would have significant impact on the amount of clothing being sent to landfill. In the UK alone £12.5 billion worth of clothes, 300,000 tonnes, were disposed of in landfill in 2017 according to waste charity WRAP (Ellison, 2018). On a European-wide basis, another report states that 'In 2015, between a quarter and a half of the clothing bought in Europe is likely to end up in residual waste. This represents a huge quantity of clothing; given the total consumption of clothing is over 6 million tonnes' (ECAP, 2017).

Digital technologies can be employed to reduce these levels of waste and, as this chapter will go on to discuss, are being rolled out in downstream supply chains. However, they also have a role to play upstream to mitigate waste in the production phase.

## Upstream supply chains

According to a white paper published by consultancy Reverse Resources, manufacturing byproducts, also termed 'pre-consumer leftovers', represent 25 per cent of total consumption in the fashion industry. In some cases, it amounts to as much as 47 per cent of the fibres and fabrics bought by a factory (Reverse Resources, 2017).

Types of waste can include:

- sample garments
- defective yarns
- surplus fabric
- cutting scraps
- roll ends
- defective garments
- overproduction

The consultancy believes that the level of waste has been systemically underestimated by manufacturers, which has meant that the issue has not been given the level of importance it deserves. The authors of the report go on to assert that 'It will soon be technically possible to recycle at least 80 per cent of all textile leftovers of any solid or mixed fibre compositions commonly used in the fashion industry.'

Tracking of byproducts would help the global brands understand what proportion of scraps were being downcycled or dumped, and the proportion that was being fed into the proportion of new yarns. In fact, many large offcuts could be used in the production process without recycling, i.e. in sections of a garment that are unseen.

### OTHER UPSTREAM SUSTAINABILITY INITIATIVES

Another initiative, 'ForestMapper', supported by H&M, Marks & Spencer and Inditex, amongst others, identifies all the areas of forest in the world and then maps the locations of sources of raw materials being used in the fashion industry. This allows greater levels of material traceability and highlights the impact of deforestation.

The Open Apparel Registry (OAR) (supported by C&A Foundation) is a database of all garment production facilities in the world open to all organizations in the fashion industry. It assigns each facility a unique identifier number, allowing companies greater visibility of supply chains including who else their suppliers may work for. By sharing information, this database, in theory, should allow organizations to use the most ethical suppliers and standardize processes.

**Blockchain** is also being used to create visibility and ensure supply chain integrity. Start-up Bext360 has partnered with the Organic Cotton Accelerator and other not-for-profit organizations as well as tech companies and retailers such as C&A, Zalando and PVH Corp to trace bags of cotton from the farms where they were produced to the processing plants. A next stage will involve providing visibility from processor to consumer, generating 'tokens' that will provide digital 'fingerprints' to prove origin and authenticity. This will eventually play an important role in identifying the materials present within a clothing item, creating the potential for higher levels of recycling.

As will be discussed later in this chapter, recycling a larger proportion of waste in the upstream supply chain will have a significant impact on the amount of raw materials required. This will have important implications for the logistics industry.

## Downstream supply chains

### CIRCULARID/CONNECT FASHION GLOBAL INITIATIVE

One of the major problems involved in recycling second-hand clothing is identifying the materials used in its production. A barcode may describe certain product attributes such as size, style and colour, but as they were never meant for use post-sale they contain little specific information about materials. The result of this is that recycling becomes very difficult and a large proportion of goods are sent to landfill.

One solution to this is to tag products with identifiers that do contain this information. This may involve an RFID tag or QR code, for instance. The tag would link this to the product's digital identity on the internet. According to one global initiative, Connect Fashion, the digital identity makes it possible to connect a product to the Internet of Things (IoT), and exchange information about the product via the internet.

The Initiative 'CircularID' has three components (Eon, 2022):

1  A digital 'birth certificate' consisting of core data on the permanent attributes of a product and information necessary for the regenerative processing at end of life. This includes name, brand, SKU, colour, description, manufacturing location and material content.

2 A 'digital passport' showing when a physical identifier (tag) has been used to access the data held on the product. This builds up a record of product usage and durability although security is required to ensure privacy of the wearer.

3 Physical identifier – this could be a RFID tag, NFC, QR code, UPC barcode. The main issue is making sure that the identifier remains on the clothing product for its entire life cycle.

CircularID is a global standard, which in theory will enable any company anywhere to access the data stored on a tag. Whereas presently such information, where it exists, may be held in multiple databases even within a single company. In contrast it is an open system with a shared protocol that will allow any number of stakeholders to access the data, whether retailer, brand or companies active in resale, rental, recycling, reusing or disassembly processes. Retail partners include H&M, Target and PVH as well as Microsoft and chaired by EON and Closed Loop Partners.

## Online clothing rental market

A fast-growing segment of the market is that of clothing rental. One estimate put the global market size at over $1 billion in 2017 and it is expected to grow to almost double that by 2023 (PR Newswire, 2017). Services are aimed at consumers who cannot afford to buy a new outfit on a regular basis or, crucially, choose not to on the basis of thrift or sustainability. As with car sharing, this trend relies on asset ownership no longer being as important to a new generation of consumers – the so-called 'millennials'. Although rental of expensive, special occasion outfits (such as formal wear for weddings) has always been popular due to the infrequent nature of their use and the relative cost, the online clothing rental market is aimed at a much broader audience. In the UK a survey by shopping mall owner Westfield in 2017 suggested that 50 per cent of 25–34 year olds would be willing to pay more than £200 per month on clothing rental (Pinnock, 2019).

As well as supporting many retailers' sustainability credentials and providing shoppers with an ever-changing wardrobe at a lower price point, online clothing rental reduces wardrobe space required (especially important as space is more of a premium in urban areas) and provides consumers with the opportunity to try new brands.

Mobile commerce has also been a driver of demand, making the rental much more convenient and not just in Europe and North America. Consumers in Asia Pacific are adopting the model, especially as levels of disposable income increase.

Urban Outfitters is an example of a retailer entering this new market. Its service, called Nuuly, provides subscribers with a six-item box selection of clothes to rent for $88 per month. Selection can be made from the range of clothes provided by the retailer and its brand partners Reebok and Levi's. Its management believes that the opportunity could be worth $50 million a year to the company, attracting a target of 50,000 subscribers within its first year.

Another rental start-up, Haverdash, is more aggressive on price, allowing subscribers to swap three rented items as often as they like for $59 per month, providing clothes from retailers such as French Connection and Cupcakes and Cashmere. Shipping, returns and dry cleaning is free of charge. American Eagle's offering 'Style Drop' comes in at $50 a month.

Perhaps the best known in the market, Rent the Runway, has been around for a decade and has a turnover of in excess of $100 million. It allows subscribers to rent four items per month for $89 and an unlimited selection for $159 from over 550 designer partners. In 2018 it received a $200 million investment from Temasek on a valuation of $800 million.

Other smaller retailers can use specialist 'white label' clothing rental fulfilment providers, such as Caastle (CaaS standing for 'Clothing as a Service'). They can develop websites and also provide the logistics infrastructure required. Most retailers in the market have developed the business as separate to their mainstream operations and have different brands, distribution channels and returns systems.

This is not just a US trend, as already mentioned. In Europe a number of start-ups are trying to attain first mover status, such as Front Row, renting clothes from Dolce & Gabbana, Chanel, Fendi and Stella McCartney; and Girl Meets Dress or Hire Street, the latter focusing on high-street brands. In Germany, retailer Tchibo has launched Tchibo Share for children's clothes (Pinnock, 2019).

In Asia, Yeechoo has been active in Hong Kong since 2014, aimed at the designer segment of the market, and it now has 30,000 users. Pret-a-Dress is a more recent start-up, as is Wardrobista, although the latter adopts a different business model, creating a consumer-to-consumer (C2C) market for the rental of used dresses under a 'share your dress' initiative.

As with many e-retailers, there is no single model for logistics operations. Nuuly handles fulfilment, logistics and laundry in-house. To cope with demand it has built a dedicated warehouse, fulfilment and laundry/dry-cleaning centre in Philadelphia.

Rent the Runway has also decided on an in-house fulfilment and logistics process to enhance its customers' experience, and while doing so it has built the largest dry-cleaning facility in the United States. Its processes are slick to enable high inventory velocity, with returned items received, cleaned and made available within a day at its 150,000-square-foot fulfilment centre.

The following system allows the high levels of efficiency:

1 Returned items are received (via express carrier UPS) and after scanning the system decides which need to be processed fastest based on levels of demand.

2 Items are inspected and allocated for regular cleaning, stain removal or mending.

3 Dry-cleaning machines can sterilize and clean in under a minute.

4 If stain removal is required the item is sent to a specialist team to use the appropriate cleaning materials.

5 Seamstresses are employed to mend items or refix sequins.

6 Items are made available for dispatch and if necessary picked, packed and dispatched (HBS, 2017).

The scale of the operation is critical to the success of the company. Logistics inefficiency would kill the business model, not only by increasing the level of inventory required to fulfil customer needs to unsustainable levels, but by compromising customer service. The company says that by owning the logistics infrastructure it provides critical insight into customer behaviour, which allows it to remain flexible and meet the needs of the fast-growing market.

## What are the implications for the logistics industry?

The initiatives that are being proposed and, in some cases, have already gained traction, are set to have a range of impacts on the logistics industry, some negative, some positive. On the positive side, clothing rental could provide a huge opportunity for companies involved in the last-mile and returns sector.

Whereas in the traditional fashion supply chain multiple items are delivered to a single store in a single consignment, online rental requires an item to be delivered most probably to a home address. When the item of clothing has been worn, it then requires a return to a processing centre where it will be assessed for damage, wear and cleaning. Once the cleaning is complete, it can then be returned to the warehouse and listed on the WMS as available to rent. So, not only is there an additional transport element but there are several steps and value-adding processes within the returns warehouse.

Upstream, however, the trend to more recycling has negative implications for the industry. Vast amounts of textile raw materials are produced and transported each year – 72.5 million tons of cotton alone, without taking into account synthetics (Townes, 2020). China, India and the United States are the top three producing countries and others in the top 10 are similarly geographically diverse – from Pakistan to Brazil, Indonesia to Turkey. By cutting down on the waste of byproducts, less cotton will be required to be moved from places of origin to processing hubs and garment manufacturing facilities. While a considerable volume of this traffic is domestic (intra-China and intra-India), much involves the international movement of cotton to markets such as Bangladesh, Italy, Turkey and Vietnam.

There are also implications downstream. More recycling could mean that fibres designed to be renewable and sustainable could be reused in the production of new garments. The business case for recycling would be improved if the manufacturing process was re-shored and international shipping costs were eliminated. This would mean that the collection and recycling of materials would occur close to, or in, the markets of final consumption in the West, i.e. Europe and North America. Asian and, in particular, Chinese manufacturers would turn their focus to local consumers in the Asian region where demand for fashion items is already strong and growing. Hence, there would be a transformation of supply chains from global to regional, some based on recycled materials and some still based on the use of virgin materials.

If this indeed occurs, intercontinental freight forwarders, shipping lines and air freight carriers would lose out. In contrast, domestic or regional carriers (particularly trucking companies) would benefit both from the movement and storage of recycled materials to locally based garment manufacturers as well as from the storage and distribution of finished products.

## Summary

The likelihood of a transformation of economies from linear to circular is unlikely to be driven by the market alone or be achieved in a short period of time. Presently the lack of value left in products and their constituent parts once 'out of the wrapper' militates against new circular business models being established, at least in mass markets. However, this may change. Governments may be minded to intervene in markets where they believe external disbenefits are not being addressed. These disbenefits include environmental impacts as well as security or medical (e.g. PPE), from a 'strategic autonomy' perspective. This intervention could well take the form of taxes on consumption and on production as well as increasing regulations such as producer responsibility. This may provide a compelling case for companies to create circular supply chains through a series of local recovery, regeneration, repair and recycle loops.

Parts of industry prefer a different approach. According to techUK, a technology membership organization, governments should 'Encourage market pull for non-virgin products and materials: Focus on positive incentives and tackle the disjointed approach which adds complexity to the policy landscape and generates perverse incentives that discourage the right behaviours' (techUK, 2015).

As far as the logistics industry is concerned, circularity will benefit domestically focused, road freight-based or value-adding logistics companies. However, there will inevitably be negative consequences for international transport companies and freight forwarders. As Europe and North America strive for greater levels of 'strategic autonomy' and sustainability, volumes from Asia and in particular China will face a concerted headwind. The extent of this headwind is yet to be determined and to a large degree depends on the level of government intervention in the sector.

# References

Asimakopoulou, A (2020) 'Open strategic autonomy': a vision for Europe's raw materials future, Euractiv, 4 June, www.euractiv.com/section/circular-economy/opinion/open-strategic-autonomy-a-vision-for-europes-raw-materials-future/ (archived at https://perma.cc/29Q3-WJYF)

EC (2020a) New circular economy action plan shows the way to a climate-neutral, competitive economy of empowered consumers, European Commission, https://ec.europa.eu/newsroom/growth/items/671357 (archived at https://perma.cc/53LQ-FAQC)

EC (2020b) Circular economy action plan, European Commission, https://ec. europa.eu/environment/strategy/circular-economy-action-plan_en (archived at https://perma.cc/7LJ2-EVZU)

ECAP (2017) Mapping clothing impacts in Europe, European Clothing Action Plan, December, http://www.ecap.eu.com/wp-content/uploads/2018/07/ Mapping-clothing-impacts-in-Europe.pdf (archived at https://perma.cc/35AJ-C5SW)

Ellison, A (2018) Clothes worth £12.5bn are thrown in bin, *The Times*, 16 March, www.thetimes.co.uk/article/clothes-worth-12-5bn-are-thrown-in-bin-b8rqfrcg2 (archived at https://perma.cc/4NVK-5XTY)

EMF (2017) A new textiles economy, Ellen Macarthur Foundation, 1 December, https://emf.thirdlight.com/link/2axvc7eob8zx-za4ule/@/preview/1?o (archived at https://perma.cc/S5X4-U98A)

Eon (2022) The global data protocol for digital identification, Eon Group, https:// www.eongroup.co/circular-product-data-protocol (archived at https://perma.cc/ A6ZP-TZCH)

Harper G, Sommerville R, Kendrick E, Driscoll L, Slater P, Stolkin R, Walton A, Christensen P, Heidrich O, Lambert S, Abbott A, Ryder K, Gaines L, Anderson P (2019) Recycling lithium-ion batteries from electric vehicles, *Nature*, https:// pubmed.ncbi.nlm.nih.gov/31695206/ (archived at https://perma.cc/LG6Z-RTUS)

HBS (2017) Rent the Runway: a trendsetter behind the scenes too, Harvard Business School, 14 November, https://digital.hbs.edu/platform-rctom/ submission/rent-the-runway-a-trendsetter-behind-the-scenes-too/ (archived at https://perma.cc/2NJW-NLPP)

Howie, C and Nolan, L (2020) Why should countries and regions look to a circular approach? Climate-KIC, 25 November, www.climate-kic.org/opinion/why-should-countries-and-regions-look-to-a-circular-approach/ (archived at https:// perma.cc/RM7Q-CUBP)

IEEP (2020) EU circular economy and trade: improving policy coherence for sustainable development, Institute for European Environmental Policy, 24 January, www.ieep.eu/news/eu-circular-economy-and-trade-improving-policy-coherence-for-sustainable-development (archived at https://perma.cc/ 5JRT-K2A3)

Manners-Bell (2021) EV battery recycling initiative addresses waste reduction, but far more besides, Ti, 30 November, https://www.ti-insight.com/briefs/ev-battery-recycling-initiative-addresses-waste-reduction-but-far-more-besides/ (archived at https://perma.cc/2CP7-LW6J)

Mattos, M (2019) How a circular economy changes supply chain loops, 3BL Media, 8 August, https://www.3blmedia.com/news/how-circular-economy-changes-supply-chain-loops (archived at https://perma.cc/YX8Q-RXXR)

Paddison, L (2017) The world generated 4,500 Eiffel Towers' worth of electronic waste last year, *Huffington Post*, 13 December, www.huffingtonpost.co.uk/entry/electronic-waste-recycling-un-report_uk_5a311ae1e4b07ff75aff1c25#:~:text=The%20world%20produced%2044.7%20million,Bangkok%20and%20back%20%E2%80%9528%2C160km (archived at https://perma.cc/6UA6-X28Y)

Pinnock, O (2019) A hire purpose: the opportunities in rental fashion, Drapers Online, 23 January, https://www.drapersonline.com/insight/analysis/a-hire-purpose-the-opportunities-in-rental-fashion (archived at https://perma.cc/FCF5-4QML)

PR Newswire (2017) Online clothing rental market is expected to reach $1,856 million, globally, by 2023, Allied Market Research, 6 April, www.prnewswire.com/news-releases/online-clothing-rental-market-is-expected-to-reach--1856-million-globally-by-2023---allied-market-research-618522543.html (archived at https://perma.cc/4K5H-NYZM)

Reverse Resources (2017) Creating a digitally enhanced circular economy, *Reverse Resources*, August

techUK (2015) *The Circular Economy: A perspective from the technology sector*, techUK.org, London

Townes, L (2020) Top 10 largest cotton producing countries in world, Business Finance Articles, 26 February, https://businessfinancearticles.org/cotton-producing-countries (archived at https://perma.cc/Z2ZL-D3M6)

WEF (2014) Towards the circular economy: accelerating the scale-up across global supply chains, World Economic Forum, Switzerland

WEF (2016) The new plastics economy rethinking the future of plastics, World Economic Forum, Switzerland

Zoltkowski, A (2022) What on earth is a clothing supply chain? Good on You, 27 January, www.goodonyou.eco/what-is-a-clothing-supply-chain/ (archived at https://perma.cc/HT9G-SSUV)

# 23

# 'Shifting to Green' survey

**This chapter will familiarize the reader with:**

- Logistics and supply chain companies' attitudes to sustainability
- The proportion of companies measuring their carbon emissions
- Companies' commitment to net-zero carbon strategies
- How likely industry executives think that government targets will be met
- Which types of alternative fuels will dominate the industry in the future
- The impact of sustainability policies on logistics costs

In 2021, market consultancy Ti Insight undertook a perception and usage survey examining a range of issues related to the sustainability policies employed within the logistics and supply chain industry. It reveals how business models and operations are changing to take into account environmental imperatives (Ti Insight, 2021).

## Survey sample profile

Representing all major sectors of the industry, both supply- and demand-side, 143 executives from around the world took part in the study. As can be seen from Figure 23.1 just over three-quarters of the respondents worked for logistics service providers while just under one-quarter were employed by manufacturers, retailers and other types of shipper.

FIGURE 23.1  How would you best describe your company's function?

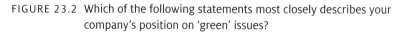

Manufacturer/Retailer
Shipper/Cargo Owner
24%

Logistics Service
Provider/Other
76%

## Attitude to sustainability

Over the past decade, there has been a significant change in the way that logistics and supply chain executives view sustainability. Although the drivers of environmental action will be reviewed below in more detail, in general terms almost half of respondents said that they believed environmental initiatives gave their company a competitive advantage; a further one-third stated that it improved their corporate image, while only a small minority suggested that regulatory compliance was the only reason behind a focus on sustainability (Figure 23.2).

FIGURE 23.2  Which of the following statements most closely describes your company's position on 'green' issues?

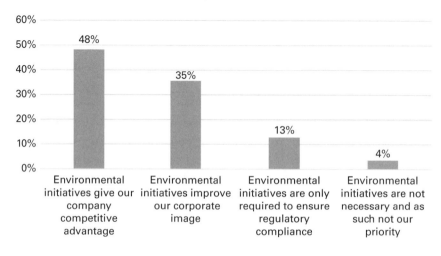

FIGURE 23.3   Does your company have a formal environmental policy as part of a corporate and social responsibility (CSR) strategy?

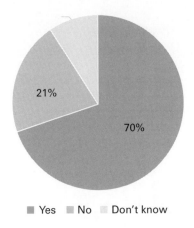

■ Yes  ■ No  ■ Don't know

As will be revealed, motivations behind engagement in environmental initiatives and the culture change that this requires are often complex. However, the responses to this question suggest that the way in which companies are perceived by their customers, suppliers and government has become overwhelmingly important.

Although many business sectors (including within logistics and supply chain) have been criticized for so-called 'greenwashing' (that is, paying 'lip service' to environmental issues), it seems from our survey that the majority take sustainability importantly enough to have put in place a formal environmental policy. However, this may not be as encouraging as it first may seem. When Ti Insight undertook its first environmental survey in 2008 the equivalent response was 64 per cent. It seems, as shown in Figure 23.3, that the proportion has only slightly increased over the intervening 13 years.

As shown in Figure 23.4, the majority of respondents stated that they believed their corporate environmental policies were 'moderately effective' with a further one-fifth saying that they were 'highly effective'. In some respects the positive view of the effectiveness of environmental policies is very encouraging. However, the results are broadly similar to Ti Insight's last survey conducted in 2016, showing that little progress has been made. In the coming years it will be important for companies' environmental and social governance departments to show that their policies have moved from being regarded as moderately to highly effective.

FIGURE 23.4 In your opinion, how effective is the environmental policy within your organization?

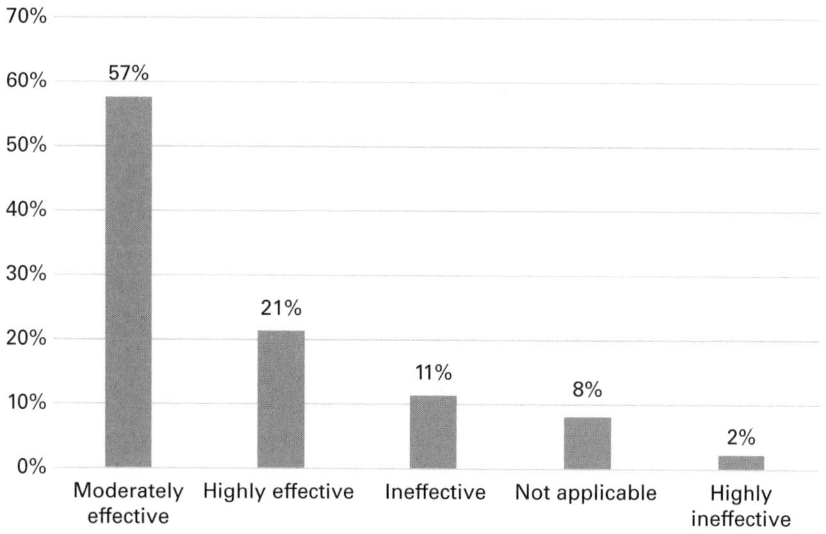

## Carbon emissions measurements and targets

One of the key areas of interest probed by the series of Ti's environmental surveys over the years has concerned carbon emissions measurements and net-zero targets. It can be seen from Figure 23.5 that initially there was considerable progress in terms of emissions' measurement. The proportion of respondents saying that their companies measured emissions almost doubled between 2008 and 2016. However, there has been far less progress over the last five years. This is quite worrying as recently it has become far easier to track emissions. Without measuring them it will be impossible to assess progress towards net-zero targets.

The proportion of respondents that stated their company had committed to achieve a net-zero target was just over half (Figure 23.6). It is not surprising (given the number of companies that have yet to start measuring emissions) that over one-third had still to commit to a target. In the coming years, it is inevitable that more companies will adopt targets, not least due to regulatory and investor pressure.

Respondents were also asked about how likely it was that government goals would be reached by 2050 (Figure 23.7). There was a fair degree of scepticism: almost two-fifths thought these goals would not be achieved. This is obviously very worrying given the importance that has been placed upon mitigating climate change.

FIGURE 23.5  Does your company attempt to measure the impact of its business on the environment (e.g. carbon footprint)?

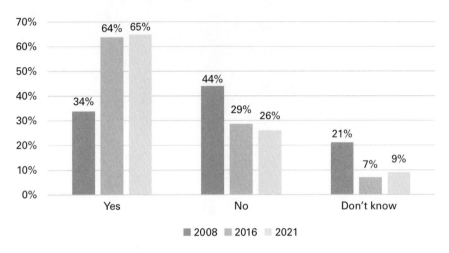

FIGURE 23.6  Has your company committed to achieving a net-zero emissions target?

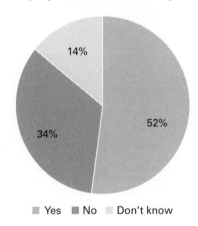

## Factors driving adoption and perceived benefits

The survey also questioned executives about the main drivers of their sustainability policies. Despite the belief that sustainability is good for competitiveness and brand equity (Figure 23.2), it seems that motivation is mainly driven by compliance with governmental and customer demands (Figure 23.8). A more altruistic desire to protect the environment is the third

FIGURE 23.7 Do you think government goals to achieve net-zero greenhouse gas emissions by 2050 are achievable?

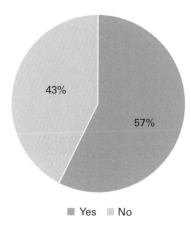

43%

57%

■ Yes  ■ No

pressure identified, followed by a desire to be a 'thought leader' in sustainability. Clearly policies are being driven by a range of different factors, some regulatory, others customer led, as well as a desire to 'do good' and market perception.

It is interesting that factors which may have been thought as important such as the need to reduce risk, and operational issues, including the reduction of transport costs, are far lower down the list. This would seem to suggest that sustainability policies are perceived as predominantly meeting exogenous needs – whether these are for compliance purposes or actually to reduce direct impact on the environment. A much smaller proportion of respondents believed that adopting sustainable practices can improve business or operational performance.

This is borne out by the answers to a further question asking respondents to identify the main benefits of implementing a sustainable supply chain and logistics strategy (Figure 23.9). Brand image is by far the most important named, although benefits such as reducing greenhouse gas emissions and local environmental impacts are considered important. We can see that respondents ranked the reduction of transportation costs and warehouse costs low down the list. This suggests there is plenty to do in demonstrating that sustainability practice is good business practice.

FIGURE 23.8 What do you believe are the main pressures driving your sustainable supply chain and logistics policies?

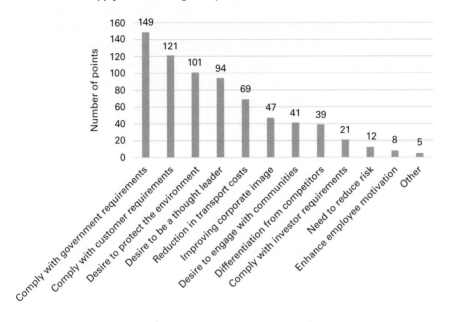

FIGURE 23.9 What do you believe are the main benefits of implementing a sustainable supply chain and logistics strategy?

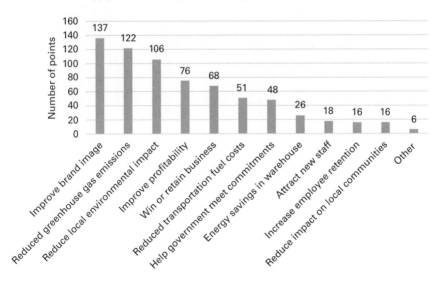

## Corporate environmental initiatives

Respondents were asked to identify the focus of environmental initiatives being undertaken by their companies (Figure 23.10). From the results, it would seem that managers have recognized that more effort needs to be expended in making progress towards measuring carbon emissions (an issue identified in Figure 23.5). Almost one-fifth of respondents stated that this was the main focus for their company.

Apart from emissions measurement, a broad range of initiatives is being supported by respondents' companies.

The survey also looked at altruistic corporate behaviour. Just over half of respondents indicated that their company had undertaken an environmental initiative that had no commercial benefit (Figure 23.11).

What impact has Covid-19 had upon environmental initiatives? The good news is that more than four-fifths of respondents said they would continue their investment despite the operational and financial impact of the global pandemic (Figure 23.12).

FIGURE 23.10  If your company is undertaking an environmental initiative, in what area does it focus?

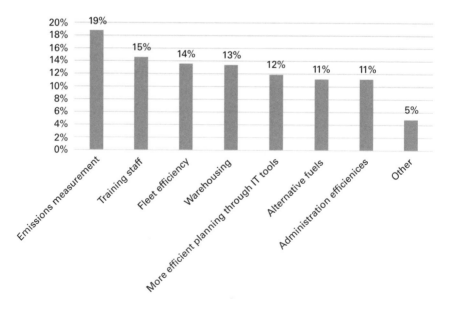

FIGURE 23.11  Has your company spent money on an environmental initiative that
has no direct commercial benefits?

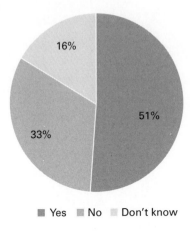

■ Yes  ■ No  ▨ Don't know

FIGURE 23.12  In light of the Covid-19 crisis, will you continue to invest in environmentally friendly services or infrastructure in the future?

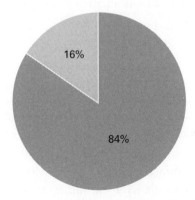

■ Yes, we will continue to invest in environmentally friendly alternatives
▨ No, cost cutting will mean we will look for the lowest-cost services or infrastructure

## Outsourcing

An important way in which a company can ensure that its outsourced
suppliers comply with a set of environmental standards is through the
tendering process. According to the survey, about half of respondents stated
that they had made environmental compliance part of the tendering procedure (Figure 23.13). Of these, only two-fifths said that they consequently

FIGURE 23.13  Is environmental compliance an important part of your tender
documents when you are contracting out or buying services?

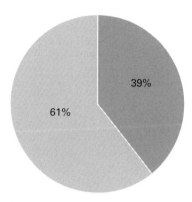

■ Yes, and we consequently make provision for extra costs
■ Yes, but we don't make provision for extra costs

made provision for extra costs, a fact that is unlikely to be appreciated by suppliers, who will regard this as an attempt by customers to push environmental costs onto them.

## Future fuels

Respondents to the survey were also asked their views on which alternative fuels would replace diesel in the road freight/trucking sector (Figure 23.14). A large majority considered that battery electric vehicles would come to dominate the lighter commercial part of the industry (77 per cent). However, there was far less consensus over the future of heavy-duty trucks. While hydrogen was considered likely to gain the widest adoption (44 per cent), followed by LNG (34 per cent), almost one-fifth believed that battery electric technologies would win out.

Obviously, there are many challenges facing the migration to alternative fuels from diesel. Of these, a lack of charging network was highlighted as the main barrier to adoption, followed by the cost of new vehicle acquisition and geographic range (Figure 23.15).

Given the all-round utility of diesel engines in a wide range of operational settings, it is likely that the only way industry will adopt future fuels will be through government regulation. Already many countries have set

FIGURE 23.14  Which alternative propulsion system is most likely to gain widest adoption for vans and heavy-duty trucks?

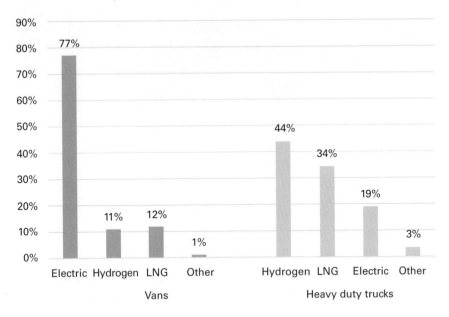

FIGURE 23.15  In your opinion, what are the biggest barriers to adoption of alternative propulsion systems?

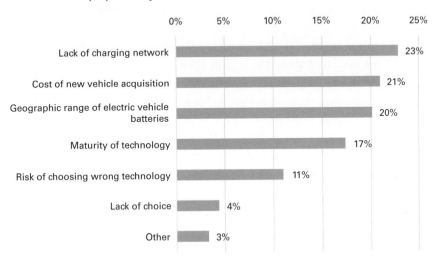

FIGURE 23.16  Do you think it is feasible to ban the sale of diesel-engined trucks from 2040?

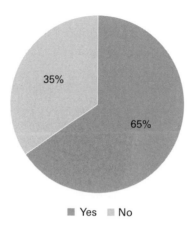

■ Yes  ■ No

deadlines for the phasing out of the sale of new internal combustion engine vehicles. The survey asked whether respondents felt that a ban from 2040 (many jurisdictions have stated they will ban them from an earlier date) was feasible. As can be seen from Figure 23.16 a sizable minority (35 per cent) was sceptical of these plans, even with a 20-year timeline. It would seem that there will need to be considerable progress in e-fuel technology if a significant proportion of the industry are to be convinced that a ban is a good idea.

Also related to present and future regulation of diesel-engined vehicles, executives were asked about the impact upon logistics costs of diesel bans in urban areas. Over 90 per cent thought that costs would go up, with two-fifths believing that they would go up 'significantly' (Figure 23.17). These costs will be driven not only by more expensive and less efficient battery electric trucks and vans (at least in the short term) but the disruption to supply chains caused by the need to tranship consignments to zero-carbon vehicles at the limit of the urban area. This will almost inevitably involve further operational costs and delays.

Finally, respondents were asked their views on modal shift given the regulatory pressure being applied to road freight. Almost half of executives believed that rail would benefit to some extent, although more than one-third indicated that they thought there would be no change, despite the extra cost road freight/trucking will have to bear (Figure 23.18).

FIGURE 23.17  In your opinion, what impact will diesel bans in urban areas have on logistics costs?

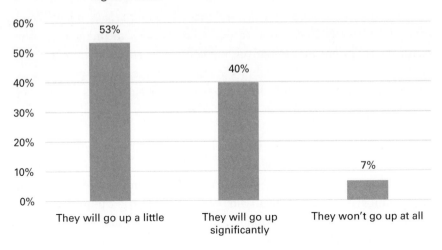

FIGURE 23.18  In your opinion, which transport mode will shipment volumes migrate to from road?

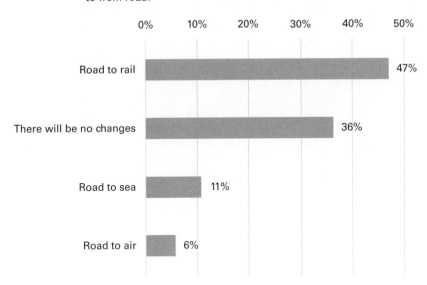

## Summary

There is no doubt that sustainability is regarded as a crucial business issue with major implications for the future of the industry. However, it is disappointing that more companies do not have formal environmental programmes in place, and progress in other key areas has also been slow. More than two-fifths of respondents are sceptical of government net-zero targets and a large proportion also feel that a ban on the sale of new diesel-engined vehicles by 2040 is not feasible. Compliance is the main motivating factor for environmental initiatives and companies generally do not recognize the importance of sustainability in improving operational performance. While many companies include environmental considerations within their tender process, the majority do not consider that they should share the cost with their suppliers.

There is consensus that battery electric power will dominate the lighter commercial vehicle sector but the industry is split on which e-fuel will be most widely adopted for heavy-duty trucks. Most think hydrogen will win out, although LNG could be an alternative and electric cannot be written off. Executives believe that urban diesel bans will result in significantly higher costs, which will have to be absorbed by the industry or passed on in the form of higher prices to customers.

In conclusion, the survey hints at a certain amount of passivity within the industry. Minor changes are being driven by governmental regulation with the major benefit perceived as being brand enhancement rather than operational efficiency. However, the industry will need root-and-branch transformation over the next 10 years if climate change targets are to be met. Unfortunately, from the survey findings, there seems little evidence to suggest that executives are ready to make this leap.

# Reference

Ti Insight (2021) Logistics and Supply Chain Sustainability Report 2021, Ti Insight, www.ti-insight.com/product/sustainability- report/?reportTitle= Logistics%20&%20Supply%20Chain%20Sustainability%20Report%202021 (archived at https://perma.cc/WJ65-X525)

# PART SIX

# Future directions for global supply chains

# 24

# The 'Great Reset'

## The post-pandemic future

**This chapter will familiarize the reader with:**

- The concept of the 'Great Reset' developed by the World Economic Forum
- The impact of the Covid-19 crisis on global structures
- Criticism of globalization and pressure for change
- China's push for self-sufficiency and its influence in Asia
- Increasing protectionist sentiment and its impact on supply chains
- Why a 'reset' started two decades ago

## Covid-19: a catalyst for change

Since 2020, the world has struggled to get to grips with the impact of the Covid-19 pandemic and its tragic consequences. The focus of many governments and business leaders has inevitably been on the short-term political, societal, health and economic implications of the crisis. However, from the outset there were others who believed the pandemic could be a catalyst for restructuring the entire functioning of the global economy and, with it, inevitably, 'globalization'. The World Economic Forum (WEF), the non-governmental lobby under the leadership of Klaus Schwab, has led the calls for change and dubbed this proposed transformation the 'Great Reset' (WEF, 2020).

According to the WEF, the pandemic offers an opportunity to 'improve' the economic system and replace it with 'responsible capitalism'. The aspiration has three main themes:

1 The encouragement of stakeholder capitalism, i.e. a system that delivers 'fairer' outcomes.

2 Underpinning economic development with sustainability.

3 Harnessing the innovations of the Fourth Industrial Revolution (4IR).

One commentator described the initiative as refocusing the world's economy on 'values' rather than 'value creation'. A number of world leaders and former politicians have embraced the concept, including Prince Charles and John Kerry. The slogan 'Build Back Better' was adopted by many, including UK Prime Minister Boris Johnson and US President Joe Biden, to communicate their political aims that directly or indirectly have been influenced by the thinking behind the 'Great Reset'.

In essence, the WEF is promoting a 'triple bottom line' approach of 'people, planet and profits', founded upon the new 4IR technologies and disruptive business models. According to Schwab, 'the pandemic represents a rare but narrow window of opportunity to reflect, reimagine, and reset our world to create a healthier, more equitable, and more prosperous future' (WEF, 2020).

Despite using the term 'reset', the WEF's plans do not call for a complete tearing down of the structures on which the global economy is based. This is unsurprising as the organization's own stakeholders include politicians, financiers and business leaders, all of whom have a vested interest in maintaining the 'old order' or at least a recognizable version of it. However, the initiative has raised some important questions over the future for the global economy and, perhaps most importantly, whether 'globalization', the defining macro-economic trend of the past 50 years, is still fit for purpose.

## Globalization under fire

The phrases 'Build Back Better' and the 'Great Reset' are underpinned by the belief that global economic, financial and trading systems need improvement or, in some cases, complete reform. In fact, many people believe that 'globalization' is no longer fit for purpose, citing a diverse range of short-term and structural failings including:

- misfiring logistics systems such as the backlog of ships at US ports and the high levels of air and sea freight rates

- the way in which many emerging markets were effectively excluded from global supply chains at the height of the Covid-19 pandemic when shipping capacity was switched to more lucrative trade lanes

- the inability to supply PPE to healthcare workers at critical periods of the pandemic

- inequitable access to Covid-19 vaccines across the world

- the difficulties that many small and medium-sized exporters in Asia, Latin America and Africa have found in accessing trade finance

- trade barriers that prevent emerging market companies tapping Western markets

- structural unemployment created by offshoring of manufacturing jobs from the West to Asia

- the use and misuse of low-cost labour including ethnic groups such as the Uighurs in China

- the role that international logistics and transport plays in the generation of carbon emissions

At times it has seemed that globalization has been in an existential crisis due to the systemic vulnerabilities exposed not only by the pressures of Covid-19 but other risks such as natural disasters, terrorism and geo-political insecurity. However, the greatest threat to global systems was the economic fallout from the worldwide recession of 2008–09. In the aftermath of the crisis, trade was seriously impacted and global flows of finance dried up, with many markets in the emerging world hit the hardest. Governments complained bitterly at their treatment at the hands of Western bankers and turned to an eager China to fill the investment void. This added impetus to China's Belt and Road Initiative, leading to a pivot of supply chains towards the East, long before there was any talk of a reset, 'Great' or otherwise.

## Pressure from all sides

Globalization has been accused of fostering a world of 'haves' and 'have nots'; of millions of people working long hours for meagre pay in dangerous conditions to supply voracious Western markets. Disasters such as the Rana Plaza factory collapse in 2013, in which over 1,000 Bangladeshi textile workers died, helped bring this issue to the attention of global media. Despite protestations from organizations such as the World Bank that globalization has helped to raise over 1 billion people out of poverty, such events have created an overwhelmingly negative public perception of the 'unfair' consequences of globalization.

Exploitation of labour has long been a charge levelled against multinational corporations (MNCs), but perhaps one of the fundamental changes of the past five years has been that the benefits of global supply chains have been increasingly called into question by the governments that had previously been their strongest proponents. For example, populists, such as Republican politician Donald Trump, have challenged the inevitability of the loss of Western manufacturing jobs to Asian or Mexican markets. While consumers in North America and Europe have benefited from the lower prices that have resulted from offshoring production, it is undoubtedly the case that many workers have lost their livelihoods, with their jobs transferred to often highly subsidized and/or state-backed competitors on the other side of the world.

Indeed, in many cases, 'global free markets' have turned out to be anything but. MNCs have often benefited from being able to tap into these subsidies, either directly from setting up their own off-shored operations, or indirectly through a lower-cost supply base. Instead of educating and training unemployed European and US workers to take advantage of a shift towards high-value manufacturing or services, Western governments have allowed parts of society, especially in previously industrialized regions, to become disaffected. In the minds of many, governments and multinationals have conspired in this decline, a situation only recently being addressed by so-called 'levelling up' policies.

## The rise of China

What's more, in terms of international relations, supporters of globalization have been accused of unwittingly facilitating the rise of China's soft power. Years of offshoring have left the West at a competitive disadvantage in terms of production facilities and know-how. Moreover, China's investment in Africa and Latin America has allowed it access, sometimes exclusively, to raw materials, many of which are critical to future manufacturing strategies such as alternative propulsion technologies. In some cases, Chinese tech companies, such as Huawei, have achieved market-leading positions in the supply of electronic components, raising security fears over the potential for hostile intelligence agencies to gain access and compromise information and communication networks.

Running counter to much of the rest of the world, China's private sector has been in retreat over the past 10 years. As Thomas Cullen says in a recent analysis for Ti Insight, 'These organizations [i.e. Chinese privately owned companies] have been characterized by a strategic marketing policy of gaining market share through undercutting the prices of competitors in the short term. This has been facilitated by access to capital resources from the state banking system and other state-controlled resources such as land and energy' (Cullen, 2022). In other words, they have become conduits for Chinese government policy.

This has resulted in the growth of Chinese-based global brands, such as ChemChina, Haier, Lenovo, Geely and, of course, Huawei. Many of these companies started off as suppliers to Western OEMs but have developed their own brands and invested heavily in their own technology. In doing so they have migrated up the value chain, from competing on cost to quality.

Their ambitious strategies have set alarm bells ringing in the West. Big acquisitions, such as ChemChina's purchase of Swiss-giant Syngenta, have fuelled fear of a transfer of intellectual property to China. Again, critics would say, globalization has been hijacked by Chinese-backed corporations working to their own strategic or even political ends.

In the long run this will be counter-productive. According to Cullen:

- Countries that perceive certain industries as 'strategic' will seek to avoid dependence on Chinese suppliers in those sectors.
- Companies will seek to construct supply chains that rely on suppliers that are politically stable and reliable.
- Investment in assembly operations for servicing markets outside China will be less likely to be located in China.
- Assembly operations in China will increasingly be dedicated to supplying the Chinese market.

It has also become Chinese policy to capture more supply chain value by undertaking the manufacture of intermediate goods. In the 'Factory Asia' model, components produced across the region have typically been transported to China for final assembly. This means that Chinese manufacturers lose out on much of the value-adding process, the final assembly being a low-cost and commoditized undertaking dependent on low-cost labour. The government recognized that for its industry to rise up the value chain it had to invest in the know-how and facilities that would obviate the need to import components from competitors throughout the region – a calculated, strategic and successful move.

On top of this, the imposition under President Trump of huge US trade tariffs on Chinese imports has resulted in an 'In China, for China' industrial strategy. Encouraged by the country's political leaders, consumers are purchasing Chinese-made rather than foreign goods in increasing volumes, a massive shift in behaviour from only a few years ago. This trend is particularly evident in the younger demographic who take pride in buying domestically produced goods.

These trends will result in China both becoming more self-sufficient in intermediate goods as well as finished products. However, it also increases the likelihood that China becomes increasingly excluded by Western manufacturers from their supply chains.

## Unfair criticism?

Besieged from all sides of the political spectrum, there is no doubt that global finance and trading systems are under pressure. This is despite the fact that most of the blame for the issues highlighted above cannot be laid at the door of globalization. For example:

- **Vaccine.** Although the Covid-19 vaccine has not been distributed to emerging markets as quickly as it could have been, this has largely been a result of individual government policy seeking to protect domestic supplies in the West. The development of the vaccine was facilitated by global flows of intellectual property between 'big pharma' companies as well as cross-border collaboration to source the medical peripheries such as vials and syringes. Its rollout was achieved by the coordination of complex temperature-controlled logistics on an international basis, undertaken by global networks developed by the express and logistics companies.

- **PPE.** Again, criticism has been levelled at the failure of globalized production strategies to ensure the supply of personal protective equipment at the outset of the crisis. Although there is certainly an argument that countries should maintain either a strategic supply of PPE or the capacity to manufacture it, many of the problems were caused by government policy, which introduced export bans in order to stockpile domestic supplies (as with the vaccine). The 'weakness' of globalization in this respect, it seems, is its vulnerability to government intervention.

- **Port crisis and shipping rates.** At various times the container shipping industry has appeared to many as dysfunctional. Ports, especially on the West Coast of the United States, have been overwhelmed due to a lack of capacity as well as a driver and equipment shortage, and this has resulted in delays and soaring freight rates. However, the chaos was largely caused by a surge in Western consumer spend driven by government stimulus packages; a lack of infrastructure investment, as well, it might be argued, by outdated working practices. It was not an organized attempt at profiteering by the carriers working as a cartel, as some have asserted.

- **Sustainability**. While globalization is undoubtedly responsible for a large proportion of hard-to-abate carbon emissions due to the international transport of goods by road, air and sea, global finance and technology sectors are fundamental to many of the initiatives to reduce carbon dioxide and could ultimately be responsible for slowing global warming.

Criticism of the way in which emerging markets have been treated both throughout the pandemic and also the Great Recession of a decade earlier carry more weight. New ways of thinking and a different attitude to countries in parts of Asia, the Middle East, Africa and Latin America need to be developed if they are not to feel excluded from the global trading system.

## Trade keeps on growing

Despite all the negativity and the criticism from all sides of the political spectrum, it must be noted that global trade is still growing. According to the World Trade Organisation (WTO), year-on-year trade volume growth is expected to come in at 10.8 per cent in 2021 to be followed by a 4.7 per cent rise in 2022. Even a change of Western policy to promote diversification of sourcing strategies away from China will only have a limited impact on globalization. The focus on Vietnam and other countries in Southeast Asia as alternative low-cost manufacturing locations to China will not result in less globalization, just a change in its structure. The creation of new pan-Asian supply networks will increase the density of upstream transport demand across the region, rather than diminish it.

That is not to say that no 'reset' is needed. The world has changed significantly since the establishment of institutions such as the International Monetary Fund (IMF) and World Bank at Bretton Woods in 1944 and General Agreement on Tariffs and Trade (GATT), the forerunner of the World Trade Organization, in 1947. These institutions have overseen the development of globalization, with all its attendant benefits and disadvantages, but now need to adjust to the perils and pitfalls of the market environment they have helped to create. For example, as highlighted above,

China is undoubtedly using the economic and political muscle it has been gifted by globalization to extend its influence throughout the world. What it does – and what it is allowed to do by global institutions – with its relatively recently acquired power will probably define the geo-political and economic environment of the next century.

Domestic policy is also increasingly dominated by issues related to the 'fairness' of globalization – although perhaps not in the way that the WEF had in mind. For many politicians and their electors, both in developed and developing markets, 'fair' outcomes can only be achieved by protection of markets and not from liberalization. This is to be regretted as the potential exists for value to be created for all stakeholders – but only if the benefits of globalization are shared across the whole of society. To a greater or lesser extent, Western economies have failed to pivot to a high-value manufacturing model focused on intellectual capital and this has created disaffection. This, combined with the unwillingness or inability to address market subsidies and rigging (most egregiously in China but also elsewhere), is the real failure, not globalization.

## A 'Great Reset' is already under way

So, what are the implications of a 'Great Reset' for the world economy? In reality, a 'reset' started many years ago entwined with the birth of the internet, e-retailing, the liberalization of financial markets and even the development of ship building. Innovative and disruptive technologies (the Fourth Industrial Revolution) are already transforming the sector on many levels – automation, electric vehicles, digital market platforms, the Internet of Things, 3D printing, to name just a few. Sustainability and carbon emissions are front and central on corporations' list of strategic imperatives, although 'fairness' of outcome, the other WEF aspiration, will always be subjective and very difficult to measure. There has already been a 'revolution' – it has just taken place over several decades.

This is not to say that in the future there will not be further changes. The world's markets will start to fragment as political, economic and security priorities unravel 75 years of liberalization. Re-shoring, near-shoring and diversified sourcing strategies will gather momentum in strategic sectors as the world bifurcates between the West and China. This trend will be reinforced by rising oil prices and the likely imposition of carbon taxes making international transport less attractive to shippers.

# Summary

In summary, a good deal of the changes called for in the World Economic Forum's 'Great Reset' have been under way for many years. Although useful to promote debate, bundling together many existing ideas, innovations and disruptive technologies, it ignores many of the real threats to the global economy. The rise of China, disaffected 'rust belt' workers in the West, the exclusion of emerging countries from global markets, emasculated global institutions and soaring international transportation costs all risk fracturing the world into competing regional or politically aligned trading blocs. The resultant destruction of economic value will have severe implications, not least in terms of the prospects for the poorest in society but also in terms of developing technologies to address climate change.

# References

Cullen, T (2022) *Short and Long-Term Supply Chain Trends*, Ti Insight, UK
WEF (2020) The Great Reset, World Economic Forum, www.weforum.org/
    great-reset/ (archived at https://perma.cc/NU3N-HM4M)

# Conclusion

*Future scenarios for the supply chain and logistics industry*

**This chapter will familiarize the reader with:**

- The profile of the supply chain and logistics industry in 10 years or more
- Which new innovations will be successful and their likelihood of industry-wide adoption
- The impact that disruption will have on jobs in transport and warehousing
- How supply chains may change in character, from global to regional or even local
- Futuristic solutions to logistics challenges presently in the early stages of development

Nowhere will the effects of the 'Fourth Industrial Revolution' be felt more than in the development of the transport, logistics and supply chain industry. However, it is far from clear whether the outcome for the industry will be positive or negative – much will depend on choices being made in the coming years.

It is also far from obvious which of the many innovations that are being researched and developed will go on to become mainstream. Figure 25.1 attempts to predict those that will be widely adopted and those that will remain niche.

We consider that warehouse automation leads the way in industry-wide adoption over the next 10 years and beyond. Not only will automation become much cheaper over the coming years but trends such as labour

FIGURE 25.1  Industry-wide adoption or niche application?

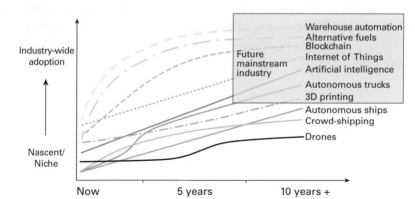

shortages will make it much more attractive for warehouse operators to invest in capital goods rather than be squeezed by rising labour costs. We see that investment will ramp up significantly in the next five years. The effects of the Covid-19 pandemic will also mean that labour-intensive sectors, such as warehousing, are seen as a major source of operational and financial risk.

Further, investment in alternative fuels will rise significantly, driven by public policy decisions to impose diesel bans in urban areas and the phasing out of new fossil-fuel-driven trucks.

The IoT and AI will be steadily integrated within the supply chain and logistics sector, but there may be unexpected consequences and problems as the technology is adopted. Likewise, blockchain, after the hype has disappeared, will become just another form of technology, efficiently facilitating trade flows and increasing trust in commerce.

Other technologies will develop but, due to a number of challenges, will not be as widely adopted. Despite becoming technically feasible, autonomous trucks will still face regulatory hurdles as well as negative public perception. 3D printing will become an increasingly important part of the manufacturing process but it will still be many years before costs fall to a level that will see it integrated into mass production. Crowd-shipping will be a niche part of the last-mile delivery process although gradually gaining traction. Autonomous ships gradually gain acceptance in the shipping industry, but the long investment horizons in the sector mean that industry change is by evolution, not revolution.

Drones, despite massive hype, only ever fulfil a niche role in the industry, at least in terms of last-mile delivery. However, in some geographies, particularly remote areas subject to existing extreme weather events or areas effected by global warming events where transport infrastructure fails, they become vital tools. In developed economies, they are more widely adopted in warehousing and other non-public spaces where they prove useful in terms of scanning items and stocktaking.

## Speed of adoption

Although, as this book has pointed out, identifying innovations that will have a material impact on the industry is hard enough, it is even harder to determine the timing of the impact. For instance, it took a further decade after the dot-com boom (and bust) at the turn of the twenty-first century before mainstream retailing was significantly affected. Likewise, it has been difficult to judge the speed of adoption of 3D printing, the IoT or road freight marketplaces.

One of the reasons for this is that these innovations are not developed in a vacuum. The challenges they are designed to meet are ever shifting and this can have a major impact on the levels of value they can generate. At a company level, the incumbent players in the market do not stand still and they are often adept at assimilating new technologies or developing competing and more effective ones.

Take alternative fuels, for example. There is no doubt that if diesel engine technologies had not advanced to the extent that they have, the adoption of hydrogen cells, electric vehicles or biofuels would have been much faster. The fact of the matter is, however, that diesel engine vehicles have become more efficient, which has consolidated the technology's market leading position in terms of cost and all-round utility. Manufacturers believe that there are many enhancements to come, and if it had not been from the public policy imperative, there would be few commercial reasons for change.

In addition to this is the concept of an innovation 'eco-system' (Adner and Kapoor, 2016). This essentially means that the required infrastructure needs to be in place before an innovative new business model can be adopted. Alternative fuels are, again, a good example. Before drivers or companies feel confident in investing in the new type of electric propulsion system, a comprehensive charging network must be built to address concerns over 'range anxiety'.

It is only when old technology has no more room for improvement and when the infrastructure that supports the innovation is in place that substitution can start to happen. It is rare that what Adner and Kapoor call 'creation destruction' occurs quickly. More often, technologies will exist side by side for a period until old technology or business models are abandoned. This description could apply to the continued use of paper documents in international trade. While everyone accepts that it can only be a matter of time before all processes are digitized, the eco-systems for this to take place are still not there. Likewise, hybrid engines are a very good example of this coexistence. The new technology works in parallel with the 'old', removing the problem of the lack of charging infrastructure.

Another example of this is printed barcodes and RFID sensors. It would seem logical that the amount of information that can be stored on a sensor and the uses to which this could be put would have led to fast adoption by the industry. However, the cost of the sensor versus low-cost printing, the ubiquitous nature of the barcode's eco-systems (from retailers to manufacturers and the logistics providers in between) and its reliability, have meant that the RFID 'revolution' has taken decades to occur.

The problem for market analysts or managers is that it is difficult to judge how quickly these infrastructure or eco-system issues will be addressed, especially as the dynamic is continually shifting. Not only are there business investment and technological developments to take into account, but also government intervention. Subsidies for green energy initiatives, which may kickstart a technology (or skew the market, depending on your perspective) depend on public policy and vacillate depending on the administration of the time. The change in attitude towards diesel over the past 10 years is a case in point. Once encouraged as a way of cutting greenhouse gas emissions it is now vilified as a source of noxious pollutants, despite no change in quantifiable evidence.

## Future profile of logistics segments

It is possible to see any number of alternative pathways for each of the main logistics segments. However, in our opinion, the key attributes of each segments will be as shown in Figure 25.2.

### Road freight

Over the next 15–20 years, diesel engines will be phased out as governments actively support alternative fuels. The demand for high-frequency small

FIGURE 25.2 Logistics market attributes 2035

| Logistics segment | Road freight transport | Warehousing | Freight forwarding/ international trade | Shipping | Express/parcel | Air cargo |
|---|---|---|---|---|---|---|
| **Alternative fuels** | Electric or hydrogen | Photovoltaic | n/a | Electric or natural gas 'Clean' sulphur-free fuel | Electric or hydrogen | Electric |
| **Digital technologies** | Platforms/exchanges Collaborative Shared | Shared Virtual Artificial intelligence | Digitized Control towers 4PL Blockchain/smart contracts Freight marketplaces | Digitized meta-documents Blockchain/smart contracts | On-demand Artificial intelligence Crowd-shipping (niche) Route planning Dynamic delivery options | Digitized meta-documents |
| **Automation** | Autonomous (semi) Platooning | Automated and robotic Augmented/virtual reality 'Tiny' fulfilment | n/a | Autonomous (semi) | Automated hubs Robotics Autonomous vans (semi) | Autonomous (semi) |
| **Physical technologies** | Predictive maintenance Asset tracking IoT tracking | Drones IoT inventory management | n/a | Larger ships IoT tracking | Drones (niche) 3D printing | IoT tracking |
| **Notes** | Higher utilization rates | 'Smart' and green Smaller units | Broking becomes less important as segment increases value add through manager role | Lower unit costs Consolidated industry South-south volumes | Optimized for city deliveries | 3D printing impacts intermediate high tech volumes Faster clearance |

package e-commerce deliveries will mean that electric vehicles become the main alternative for urban areas. Natural gas and hydrogen cells are the preferred technologies for longer distance and higher payloads.

Vehicles have a high degree of automation, and platooning will become commonplace on main trunk roads. Investment in road infrastructure means there is a continuous flow of data between vehicles and highways' control towers as well as between vehicles themselves. In most administrations, drivers are still a requirement by law but have a negligible role in driving the trucks. However, drivers' hours regulations have been loosened, which means that vehicle utilization has increased significantly, improving profitability.

Greater visibility of loads has meant an increase in vehicle utilization, and more unitization of shipments has facilitated transhipment opportunities, speeding up deliveries. Networks become more dynamic, with complex routing and delivery decisions being made by AI-driven transport management systems.

## Warehousing

Warehousing has become largely automated. Robots are responsible for most of the functions that would have been fulfilled by humans and are controlled by AI. E-commerce dominates the warehousing sector, so large numbers of single items are picked on a frequent basis.

However, rather than large, centralized distribution centres predominating, e-retailers make use of local warehouses to store most frequently ordered items, providing same-day delivery services in urban areas. These fulfilment centres are based at retail parks or even in high streets, utilizing large retail premises that increasingly became redundant in the 2020s as online sales grew in popularity. Inditex SA, the parent of Zara, has already announced that it is exploring the use of existing stores as mini-fulfilment centres or distribution centres. This strategy allows them to fulfil customer orders from the closest store, in the event the item is not available in a central facility. This will become the norm.

Distribution centres have become greener, powered by solar energy. Heating and lighting is of less consequence as human workers rarely enter the picking areas. Warehouse footprint will also decrease as autonomous trucks approach docks more efficiently and large carparks for workers are no longer required.

In addition, warehousing-as-a-service platforms mean that the market becomes much more flexible with many fewer long-term leases. Warehouse management systems have visibility of inventory wherever it is located and the distribution of stock across a wide geographical area reduces transport costs and the risks of disruption to centralized operations.

### Freight forwarding

Freight forwarding is still an essential function in the facilitation of international trade. However, parts of the traditional role have become automated such as quotation, documentation and freight booking. Instead, the forwarder will fulfil a 'control tower' role, acting as a neutral manager of shipment flows, assessing risks and rerouting as necessary. AI will play an important part of their offering.

Forwarders' unique visibility of multiple transport networks will mean, for many shippers at least, that disintermediation is pointless and the forwarder's ability to consolidate multiple shipments will remain a competitive advantage.

### Shipping

The transportation element of the shipping industry will have experienced significant change by 2035. Propulsion will be by electric engines, ammonia or liquid natural gas (LNG) and ships will be increasingly autonomous although still not entirely 'crewless'. Ships' spare parts will be 3D printed at facilities at ports and then flown to ships by drone. Sensors on board ships will provide for predictive maintenance.

Shipbuilding technology will increase the capacity of each ship but this will limit the number of ports at which they will be able to call further. Networks of smaller feeder ships will become as important, linking ports with smaller capacity, especially those in Africa, Latin America and parts of Asia. Transit time between 'hub' ports will decrease as alternative, low-carbon fuel costs will fall and there will be no need for slow steaming.

Looking further on, some larger decommissioned container ships may take on a role as floating manufacturing or distribution centres that are able to be moved to where demand is required. 3D printing and other advanced manufacturing could very well take place on board, where the requirements are access to raw materials, power and decent communications.

## Express and parcels

Electric vehicles will dominate the last-mile segment of the express and parcels industry with dense networks of recharging stations. Increasingly vehicles will be autonomous, although a 'vehicle manager' will replace the driver. Their role will be primarily to move the package from vehicle to end recipient.

The market will be characterized by a wide number of operating models. These will include drone delivery to remote locations, robot delivery in a specific urban context and crowd-shipping with increased use of public transport as well as personal vehicles. On-demand operations will become an important addition to the established hub-and-spoke networks of the express parcels carriers.

The huge volumes of e-commerce deliveries will require coordination by control towers using AI. Parcels hubs will be completely automated although faster-moving items will be stored at local centres in urban areas for on-demand delivery.

## Air cargo

The world's aircraft fleet will be powered by a mix of traditional jet fuel and hybrid electric. Reduction in jet engine noise will allow airports to operate 24/7, meaning that additional runways will be unnecessary. Eventually a step change in battery technology will allow the development of all-electric planes, reducing weight, increasing payload and eliminating emissions.

The reduction in the cost of air cargo will stimulate demand and make it economic for shorter-distance movements of freight. The development of air taxis (as proposed by Uber) could result in high-value, low-weight cargo being moved on a localized basis by air.

All air waybills and other documentation will be digital, improving efficiencies and reducing clearance times. Use of sensors will enable air cargo to be tracked in real time as well as provide comprehensive data on the status and environment of the consignments.

A headwind for the industry will be the adoption of 3D printing, which will reduce the need for the movement of air cargo around the world.

## The future for transport and warehousing jobs

Speaking in 2016, Oliver Cann of the World Economic Forum predicted that 'The Fourth Industrial Revolution, combined with other socio-economic and demographic changes, will transform labour markets in the next five years, leading to a net loss of over 5 million jobs in 15 major developed and emerging economies' (Cann, 2016). It is impossible to say whether or not his prediction was correct due to a range of conflicting trends but it is clear that, as a whole, the transport and logistics sector has not been immune from the impact of the emerging technologies. It is not just manual positions that are at risk. AI will automate many of the positions filled presently by white-collar office workers.

However, there is an alternative view of this issue. Instead of looking at the new technologies as a threat, they could turn out to provide a boost to many companies. Labour shortages in the sector are endemic and technologies that increase efficiencies, assist existing workers in their jobs or fill a labour gap will help to keep down supply chain costs.

## Warehousing automation

As has been discussed earlier, robots are already starting to play an important role in warehouses. The logical conclusion of this trend is the development of so-called 'dark warehouses'. In fact, unmanned and completely automated fulfilment centres are already beginning to come online. One such dark warehouse, built for Chinese e-retailer JD.com, occupies 40,000 square metres in Shanghai's Jaiding District. The facility has the capacity to fulfil 200,000 orders per day and is operated by a combination of robotics and other automated technologies, which can self-calculate how to avoid collisions and optimize routes. The facility has just four human employees.

Such automation, though, comes with restraints as the facility can only handle certain types of goods – uniform in size, shape and weight – as the robotic picking arms cannot lift packages heavier than 3 kilograms. However, it must be assumed that advances in technology will extend the type and weight of products that are compatible with automation.

## Truck drivers to truck managers?

The controlled nature of the warehouse environment (and for that matter cargo handling facilities and areas in ports and airports) means that the substitution of robots for labour could be viewed as an inevitability. Outside of highly regulated areas, however, it is far more difficult to replace human workers. Even if the role of the driver was completely eliminated, without considerable advances in robot technology the delivery of the package from curb to the end-user would still need a human, at least for the foreseeable future. Having said that, it is far easier to envisage a full load or even a part load being delivered by fully autonomous truck. The technology will be in place, but whether the public or politicians are ready to accept completely driverless vehicles is another matter. Therefore, it is likely that the role will change rather than be eliminated.

## The transformation of global supply chains?

From the 1980s onwards, the world's economy has become ever more integrated, allowing manufacturers to unbundle and outsource production processes to remote suppliers. Globalization, it was assumed, would be unstoppable as manufacturers and retailers looked for ever-cheaper sources of labour with which to produce goods for markets in the West, exploiting the comparative advantage that some countries have developed in certain sectors and processes. In some cases this advantage lay in the level of value-add that they could contribute; in others, to lower costs, especially those related to labour.

However, it is not necessarily the case that globalization will continue as the unrivalled supply chain dynamic in perpetuity. Although global movements of goods will continue for the foreseeable future, a rebalancing of supply chains will occur, firstly through the regionalization of downstream distribution and then to location-specific supply chains. Some of the drivers for this are highlighted below.

### 3D printing

3D printing will act as an accelerator of a trend towards localization of both upstream and downstream supply chains.

The technology has the potential to reduce the volume of intermediate goods – and consequently unravel the concept of 'Factory Asia'. Instead of components being produced in another location or country, there would be a rebundling of Tier 1+ activities. China is a major investor in 3D printing with the precise aim of recapturing value-add, which is presently 'lost' to manufacturers in other Asian countries.

From a logistics perspective, the impact of this is that fewer transport and logistics services will be required as more goods are manufactured in a single factory prior to final distribution. Given that 3D printing is already being adopted widely by many industry sectors, this scenario really is not too far off.

The impact of 3D printing on downstream supply chains is less imminent. 'Consumerization' of manufacturing, however, is definitely a possibility, in which case global and regional supply chains could be rendered redundant (in some sectors at least). Consumers may end up being able to print some objects in their home, or at least visit a local facility and have them printed there. This would eliminate the need for the movement of many products, although the types would be limited.

## Growth of emerging markets

The transformation of emerging markets from being predominantly sources of low-cost labour for Western manufacturers to consumption markets in their own right has been occurring for some time. After the recession of the late 2000s, many countries in the developing world (such as China) were forced to focus their investment on domestic infrastructure to maintain their rate of economic growth as export markets slumped. This, combined with the increase in living standards, has meant that products manufactured in a developing region are more likely to stay there. Global economic growth has consequently not resulted in the high levels of trade that were seen prior to the 2008 recession.

For many of the global consumer goods manufacturers, sales growth in emerging markets will not necessarily result in higher global flows of goods. That is because successful penetration of emerging markets relies on developing products for specific, local markets and delivering these quickly, cheaply and efficiently. This, and the development of 'megacities', will mean that emerging markets will become the focus for supply chain investment. Asia, Latin America and Africa will develop their own logistics eco-systems rather than depend on connections to Europe and North America.

## Focus of logistics on megacities

Another factor in the 'localization' of supply chains in emerging markets will be the development of 'megacities' – usually defined as a city of more than 10 million people. The top 10 fastest growing megacities in the world are all in emerging markets.

Megacities will create their own economies of scale, supplied by local/regional production facilities:

- Consumer goods will be customized to local tastes.

- Each city will develop its own unique eco-system, which takes into account the movement of people, data, finance, energy, waste, goods and services.

- Transport demands will be specific to each city's needs and capabilities: poor planning and infrastructure will result in high logistics costs.

- Fulfilment, packaging, miniaturization and reverse logistics will require increased intensity of logistics provision.

Inevitably, logistics will increasingly be focused around cities rather than countries.

## Science fiction or science fact?

Many of the technological innovations already outlined in this book would, just a few years ago, be regarded as in the realms of fantasy. Therefore, although it would be easy to regard a number of the transport-related investments of wealthy individuals or companies as vanity projects, or at least unrealistic, they may well prove their detractors wrong. Three of these are highlighted below.

### Elon Musk's Hyperloop

Hyperloop is an ambitious project that uses a sealed capsule inside a vacuum tube, propelled by magnetic levitation. The capsules could conceivably transport passengers or freight across long distances at speeds of 600–1,000 kilometres per hour.

Taking the top possible speed of 1,000 kilometres per hour, Hyperloop would allow a four-day truck journey, or 23-hour flight, to be completed in 16 hours. It is also claimed the cost is just 1.5 times more than trucking, although this does not account for the vast sums needed to build the brand-new infrastructure in the first place.

One of its uses could be for urban e-commerce deliveries. Hyperloop could give shippers the opportunity to build large distribution centres further outside population centres, thus making savings on more expensive city warehouse space. Hyperloop would be able to transport products into the city centre at rapid speeds, saving time despite the longer distances between warehouses and population centres. The system would also allow larger distribution centres to serve multiple population centres at once. One touted proposal is for a Hyperloop connecting Barcelona and Madrid in just half an hour. A distribution centre built in the middle would have the ability to serve both centres.

However, with passenger transport being the most obvious application of the technology, there is no guarantee that freight movement would gain precedence.

### Airships

There has been considerable interest in developing airships with the capability of delivering heavy cargo to regions with no airport infrastructure, especially in remote locations. Companies such as Lockheed Martin have invested considerable sums of money into these vehicles, which eventually will be able to carry more cargo than airplanes and be faster than ships. The latest designs for its Hybrid Airship deploy an air cushion landing system (ACLS) that allows the airship to land anywhere on 'hoverpads'.

A start-up company, 'Flying Whales', has attracted investment from the French Government as well as a forestry agency and China's aviation industry corporation. The airship is being designed to extract timber from remote forests. Its launch is due in 2022.

A UK rival, Airlander, is being developed to fulfil communication, cargo and surveying functions. The Airlander 50, presently in the design phase, will carry 50 tonnes of cargo in a loading bay consisting of 500 cubic metres. It is also aimed at the project/bulk cargo market.

Despite technical and economic challenges that have delayed commercial rollout, it is possible that in the next decade they will become common features in our skies.

### Amazon's flying fulfilment centre

While the previous two developments have received substantial backing from serious investors, a more fantastical idea is Amazon's patent for a 'flying fulfilment centre'. Resembling an airship with an underslung cargo compartment, this hub is designed to dispatch hundreds of delivery drones from above urban areas, with the idea that each drone would be able to glide towards its target drop zone, thus saving power and increasing range.

The patent filings assume that the drones would not have sufficient power to return to the airborne hub after conducting deliveries; instead, the vehicles would fly to the nearest ground-based facility, before being sent back up to the airborne hub in regular batches, transported by a smaller 'shuttle' airship.

This would seem to be at the very margins of what would seem either reasonable or sensible. However, it forms part of Amazon's strategy of continually pushing back the boundaries of logistics thinking. The concept of a flying fulfilment centre may not come to anything, but there is no doubt that by delivering a stream of new ideas and business models Amazon has cemented its position as the industry's premier disruptor.

## Summary

Every aspect of society and business is being transformed by a new generation of innovative solutions – and the supply chain and logistics sector is no exception. Whether societal, economic or environmental, innovators are scrutinizing the industry's greatest challenges and developing new business models and concepts with which to address them.

Many of these innovators come from outside of the industry and this has resulted in entirely new approaches to seemingly intractable problems. Using models from, amongst others, the financial services, gaming, IT and personal mobility sectors, and integrating these with advances in new technologies as well as ideas from the 'sharing' and 'circular' economies, no part of the business is immune from disruption.

Where does this leave the incumbents that have dominated the industry for so long? Or the relationships between shipper, carrier, forwarder and customer that are seemingly set in stone? Survival and success will rely on the ability for all parties in the supply chain to continually examine the value they generate and, where necessary, adapt to the new business environment.

There are many reasons for optimism. The improvements in logistics efficiency, reduced levels of environmental impact and a model that focuses on value generation rather than on labour costs will create long-term sustainability for the industry. However, there are also many unanswered questions. If the logistics sector is transformed from one of high labour intensity to one characterized by high technology and automation, what are the societal implications for the many millions of workers no longer required? This will be a major conundrum for politicians.

The next decade will see the industry-wide adoption of many innovations that are presently in the early stages of development. Amongst the most successful will be warehouse automation; alternative fuels; autonomous vehicles; the IoT, AI, 3D printing and blockchain.

The speed of adoption relies to a large extent on the improvements of existing technologies as well as the speed of adoption of the innovation 'ecosystem' on which these technologies rely. An example of this is the development of the charging network required to remove 'range anxiety', which will encourage companies or individuals to invest in electric trucks.

Every logistics sector will see major changes over the coming years. Digitized platforms will better match supply and demand; alternative fuels will reduce emissions; automation will increase efficiencies and reduce costs. Disruption will affect many incumbent players unable to keep up with the speed of change.

Supply chains are also set to change. Globalized East–West flows of goods will be augmented by more complex regional and localized networks, especially those serving megacities in the developing world. At the same time completely new technologies may (or may not) change existing logistics systems, such as Elon Musk's Hyperloop.

## References

Adner, R and Kapoor, R (2016) Right tech, wrong time, *Harvard Business Review*, November, https://hbr.org/2016/11/right-tech-wrong-time?referral=00060 (archived at https://perma.cc/RT2A-5LLJ)

Cann, O (2016) Five million jobs by 2020: the real challenge of the Fourth Industrial Revolution, *World Economic Forum*, 18 January, https://www.weforum.org/press/2016/01/five-million-jobs-by-2020-the-real-challenge-of-the-fourth-industrial-revolution/ (archived at https://perma.cc/9KDJ-HA82)

# INDEX